MASS INCARCERATION 21ST CENTURY

This reader presents a comprehensive review of the research on mass incarceration as it relates to causes, impact, and solutions. Assembling contributions from leading experts in a variety of disciplines as well as the voices of directly impacted people, the editors have created a diverse collection of chapters addressing prison, punishment, incarceration, reentry, and reintegration embedded in the context of the ever-evolving discussion around ending mass incarceration.

The effects of the exponential prison growth in the United States over more than 50 years have been catastrophic, resulting in disparities that especially plague the poor, communities of color, and women. Mass incarceration is a culmination of policies and practices that benefit the privileged praxis and consequently disproportionally disenfranchise marginalized communities. The ideology affects every stage of the criminal justice system, from policing to release, and this book meets the need to expand the examination beyond departments of corrections to explore the administration behind laws, biased practices, and an unforgiving societal stigma. It deepens comprehension and engagement with concise and accessible readings that offer nuance and provoke thought.

The book is ideal as a primary or supplementary textbook for corrections, prisons, or penology courses, as well as courses focused on law, policy, sociology, social work, and social justice. It also will serve as a valuable reference book for any individual searching for knowledge on the past, present, and future of mass incarceration.

Addrain Conyers, Ph.D., is an Associate Professor of Criminal Justice at Marist College. His scholarship focuses on public administration, social deviance, and diversity, equity, and inclusion.

Vanessa Lynn, Ph.D., is an Assistant Professor of Criminal Justice at Marist College. Her research interests include correctional rehabilitation programs, narrative criminology, and restorative justice circles.

Margaret E. Leigey, Ph.D., is a Professor of Criminology at The College of New Jersey. Her research focuses on the correctional experiences of special populations, including older people, individuals serving life sentences, women, and juveniles incarcerated in adult facilities.

MASS INCARCERATION IN THE 21ST CENTURY

Realities and Reflections

Edited by
Addrain Conyers
Vanessa Lynn
Margaret E. Leigey

Routledge
Taylor & Francis Group
NEW YORK AND LONDON

Designed cover image: © Getty Images

First published 2024
by Routledge
605 Third Avenue, New York, NY 10158

and by Routledge
4 Park Square, Milton Park, Abingdon, Oxon, OX14 4RN

Routledge is an imprint of the Taylor & Francis Group, an informa business

ISBN: 978-1-032-22813-6 (hbk)
ISBN: 978-1-032-22462-6 (pbk)
ISBN: 978-1-003-27429-2 (ebk)

DOI: 10.4324/9781003274292

Typeset in Sabon LT Pro
by codeMantra

CONTENTS

NOTES ON CONTRIBUTORS

Ronald H. Aday is a Professor Emeritus of Sociology at Middle Tennessee State University. His research on aging issues in the field of corrections has contributed significantly to the public policy debate. He has authored *Aging Prisoners: Crisis in American Corrections* and co-authored *Women Aging in Prison and Women Lifers: Lives Before. Behind, and Beyond Bars.*

Maria João Lobo Antunes, Ph.D., is an Associate Professor at Towson University. She is a Quantitative Criminologist with specializations in feminist and social justice criminology, juvenile delinquency and exposure to crime, immigrants and criminal justice, and the nexus of neighborhoods, parenting, and youth behaviors.

Ashley M. Appleby, Ph.D., is an Assistant Professor of Criminal Justice at Endicott College. Her research interests include the incarceration experience, conditions of confinement, and higher education in prison. She is a student alumnus and trained instructor with the Inside-Out Prison Exchange Program, along with a trained instructor and volunteer for the NJ-Step and Petey Greene Programs. Her dissertation utilizes a multi-method approach to understand how pedagogy, correctional and university policies, and access to technology influence teaching in prison.

Elyshia Aseltine is an Associate Professor at Towson University (TU) in Maryland. Her research focuses on racial inequalities and the criminal justice system. She is also the College of Liberal Arts Mitten Professor, the founding Director of TU's Fair Chance Higher Education initiative, and 2019 Open Society Institute-Baltimore Community Fellow.

William Ash-Houchen, Ph.D., is a Research Analyst with the Oregon Criminal Justice Commission. Previously, he worked as Assistant Professor in the College of Juvenile Justice at Prairie View A&M University. He taught coursework and conducted research relating to the intersections of behavioral health and criminal justice, particularly the relationship between trauma, mental health, and substance use across the lifespan.

Patricia Becker, Ph.D., is an Assistant Professor in the Department of Criminology at The College of New Jersey. Her primary research interests include gender and crime, victimology, desistance and reentry, and policy implications of gender and social control.

Andrea Belánová, Ph.D., is a researcher at the Institute of Sociology of the Czech Academy of Sciences. She earned her Ph.D. in Religious Studies at Masaryk University, Brno. Her research interests include the intersection of religious and secular sphere, institute of chaplaincy, religions in prisons, and religion and education.

Deirdre Caputo-Levine is an Associate Professor in the Department of Sociology, Social Work and Criminology at Idaho State University. Her research interests include reentry and reintegration following incarceration, and the role played by academics in constructing understandings of race and ethnicity.

Nicole Cook is a Lecturer in Sociology/Criminology at Tennessee Tech University. Nicole's current research focuses on pathways to prison, prison adjustment, polyvictimization, and reentry among women serving life. With previous practical experience working as a felony probation officer, her teaching interests include domestic violence, mass incarceration, and gendered justice issues.

Hannah G. Cortina, Ph.D., is a Policy Specialist at the Crime and Justice Institute where she works on projects that aim to reduce the impact of incarceration. Her research focuses on changing experiences of incarceration through programming and policy in the hopes of helping people transition back to the community.

Megan T. Demarest is an Assistant Professor of Criminal Justice at Delaware Valley University. Her research examines emotions and the law, correctional programming, and reentry.

Jeffery P. Dennis received Ph.D., in Sociology, with a concentration in criminology, from Stony Brook University in 2001. He is currently an Associate Professor in the Department of Criminal Justice at Minnesota State University, Mankato. He has published over fifty research articles and five books, including Queering Teen Culture and The Myth of the Queer Criminal.

Meredith Huey Dye is a Professor of Sociology and Associate Dean of the College of Liberal Arts at Middle Tennessee State University. Her research centers on the experiences of incarcerated women with a focus on suicide in prison and women serving life sentences. She co-authored *Women Lifers: Lives Before, Behind, and Beyond Bars.*

Paddy Farr is an independent researcher, activist, and psychotherapist in Oregon. Focusing on abolition, their most recent publications include "Crashing Bodies: Toward an Intersectional Assemblage Theory of Domestic Violence" in *Feminist Theory* and "Toward a Critical Race Analysis of the COVID-19 Pandemic in US Carceral Systems" in *Critical Social Policy.*

Yola Gómez is a first-generation queer xicanx non-binary femme activist, writer, and felon for assault on an officer. Their work has appeared in *Puro Chicanx Writers of the 21st*

Century, *Weeping Women: The Haunting Presence of La Llorona in Mexican and Chicanx Lore*, and literary journals including *Entropy*, *Nat-Brut*, *Utterance*, and *Cutthroat*.

Terrence J. Graham is one of thousands of people sentenced to die in prison for a crime that he committed as a juvenile. His Supreme Court case, *Graham v. Florida*, changed hundreds of these cruel sentences. He is still incarcerated in Florida and prays to be free in the next few years.

Kelli Grant is a doctoral candidate at Kansas State University. She has worked to facilitate policy change through her career and community activism. She is focused on system and community improvement generally and through the criminal justice system. Kelli has a track record of transformational work throughout her career.

Diamond Guitar-Judd, a system-involved wife and mother, has been instrumental in developing a support group for families in Idaho dealing with incarceration. Her involvement made her realize that advocacy required a college degree. She will be graduating with a minor in Political Science and double B.A.s in Criminology and Psychology.

Tiana M. Herring is the Data Storyteller at the Death Penalty Information Center. She was previously a Research Associate at the Prison Policy Initiative.

Ashley Kilmer, Ph.D., is an Assistant Professor at Towson University. She is a qualitative criminologist with research interests in the areas of punishment and incarceration, comparative corrections, stigma and collateral consequences of criminal convictions, impacts of sex offense policy on registrants and their families, and critical criminology.

Karen F. Lahm, Ph.D., is a Professor of Sociology at Wright State University in Dayton, OH. She is currently the Coordinator of the Crime and Justice Studies Program. She teaches both undergraduate and graduate courses. Her research interests include prison programming, women in prison, and prison misconduct and victimization.

Lin Liu, Ph.D., is an Assistant Professor in the Department of Sociology and Criminology & Law at the University of Florida. Her primary research interests include reentry, life-course criminology, and gender- and race-informed approaches of rehabilitation.

LeAnna T. Luney, Ph.D., is an Assistant Professor in the Department of African and African American Studies at Berea College. Dr. Luney earned her Ph.D. in Comparative Ethnic Studies from the University of Colorado Boulder and her M.A. in Pan-African Studies from the University of Louisville.

Maya T. Luney-Ballew, MHRL, is the Equity Success Coach at Sinclair Community College. She holds a Master's degree in Human Relations specializing in diversity, equity, and social justice from the University of Oklahoma, and earned a B.A. in Human Development and Social Relations focusing in African American Studies from Earlham College in 2017.

Briana L. McGinnis is a political theorist who specializes in inclusion and exclusion, punishment, and democratic political community. She is an Assistant Professor of Political

Science at the College of Charleston, where she teaches courses on political theory and constitutional law.

Benjamin Meade is an Associate Professor of Justice Studies at James Madison University. He received his Ph.D. in Criminology and Criminal Justice from the University of South Carolina. His research interests include institutional corrections, inmate behavior, and religion/religiosity and crime/corrections.

Nikki Michaels is a degree candidate for a Bachelor of Science in Sociology (Criminology emphasis) at Montana State University (MSU). Before returning to MSU to continue her studies, Nikki spent eight years working in Indonesia as an advocate for incarcerated human trafficking survivors.

Heather E. Mooney, Ph.D., is an Assistant Professor of Sociology at Northern Michigan University. She studied formerly delinquent youth's experiences of attending a therapeutic boarding school, one type of total institution in the troubled teen industry. She has published articles in *Critical Criminology* and *The Conversation* about her research findings.

Shantaé M. Motley, Ph.D., is an Assistant Professor of Justice Studies in the College of Juvenile Justice at Prairie A&M University. She teaches and conducts research on criminal justice and criminalistics topics such as adverse childhood experiences, substance use, racial disparities in criminal justice, death investigations, crime scene issues, and juveniles convicted of sex offenses.

Justin Murray is an Associate Professor of Law at New York Law School. He teaches criminal law, criminal procedure, constitutional law, and race, bias, and advocacy. He also co-directs NYLS's Criminal Justice Institute. Professor Murray's scholarship focuses on prosecutorial discretion and on strategies for preventing and penalizing illegal conduct on the part of prosecutors and other criminal justice actors. His academic work has been published in a number of law journals, including the *Harvard Law Review*, the *University of Pennsylvania Law Review*, and the *Fordham Law Review*.

Alia Nahra is a joint J.D./Ph.D. student in the Sociology department at Columbia University. Prior to joining Columbia, she worked in the Justice Program at the Brennan Center for Justice at NYU School of Law, conducting research and policy advocacy aimed at ending mass incarceration.

Ashley Nellis, Ph.D., is Co-Director of Research at The Sentencing Project. Her research documents the expansion of life and long-term imprisonment to its current unprecedented levels. Her studies serve as resources for academics, advocates, and policymakers. She is the coauthor (with Marc Mauer) of *The Meaning of Life: The Case for Abolishing Life Sentences* (The New Press, 2018).

Arne Kvernvik Nilsen has experiences in church ministry, prison chaplaincy in Norway and England. He has 24 years of service in The Norwegian Correctional Services, including ten years in The Ministry of Justice, Department for Correctional Services. He has been an international adviser to Georgia and other European Countries. He has served as the Governor in Bastøy prison and a Chief Probation Officer. He has also been a guest lecturer at several universities in Europe. Today, he is a practicing Gestalt therapist.

Janette Richardson is an incarcerated artist and advocate whose work ranges from comics, prison wall morals, portraits, and stand-alone pieces of art. She enjoys working in the prison law library and assisting other incarcerated people with legal advice. Janette's art and many others can be found at www.abocomix.com.

Kristan N. Russell, Ph.D., is currently a Senior Research Associate at the National Center for Juvenile Justice, Research Division of the National Council of Juvenile and Family Court Judges. Prior to this, she worked as an Assistant Professor of Justice Studies in the College of Juvenile Justice and a Research Scientist in the Texas Juvenile Crime Prevention Center at Prairie A&M University. She teaches coursework and conducts research relating to youth on topics where psychology and the legal system intersect.

Kaelyn Sanders is a Ph.D. student in the School of Criminal Justice at Michigan State University. Kaelyn's research primarily focuses on incarceration and community supervision, reentry, and intersections of gender, race, and crime. Her recent research has appeared in the *Journal of Criminal Justice* and *Feminist Criminology*.

Leslie Scott is Sentencing Resource Counsel for the Federal Defender Organization, where she represents defender interests before the U.S. Sentencing Commission. Following graduation from law school and two judicial clerkships, Ms. Scott served as an Assistant Federal Public Defender in Buffalo, NY. She has also taught courses in evidence, criminal procedure, criminal law, and race & policing.

Emily Sorenson is a Senior Director for Reentry Programs in New York State for a Rochester-based non-profit, PathStone Corporation. Emily earned her Master's degree in Criminal Justice from The University of Cincinnati in 2014 after earning her Bachelor's degree in Criminal Justice from SUNY Brockport in 2012.

April N. Terry, Ph.D., is an Associate Professor of Criminal Justice at Fort Hays State University, specializing in four lines of research: juvenile corrections, gender and crime, rural criminology, and gender-based violence. Dr. Terry has dozens of publications advocating for community and system responses regarding at-risk youth and incarcerated populations.

Jan Tomášek, Ph.D., is a Researcher at the Institute of Criminology and Social Prevention. His research interests include criminal career, desistance, probation, and restorative justice. He has participated in the evaluation of Probation and Mediation Service programs and is a member of the Ministry of Justice board for rehabilitation programs.

Tereza Trejbalová, Ph.D., is a Researcher at the Institute for Criminology and Social Prevention. She earned her Ph.D. in Criminology & Criminal Justice at the University of Nevada, Las Vegas. Her research interests include predicting recidivism and misconduct of different system-impacted populations, and the treatment and experiences of those incarcerated.

Emily I. Troshynski is an Associate Professor at the University of Nevada, Las Vegas (UNLV) where she also has affiliated appointments with UNLV's program on Gender and Sexuality Studies, School of Law, and School of Medicine. Troshynski's research interests include understanding the social causes of deviance, violence, and victimization. The goals of her research are to critically, theoretically, and empirically uncover how law and society inform justice system policies and practices. This line of research has had two main foci: (1) experiences of gendered violence and justice system responses and (2) realities of community corrections and reentry as experienced by previously incarcerated persons.

Tania N. Valdez is a lawyer and an Associate Professor of Law at The George Washington University Law School. Her academic research is focused on immigration law. Over her past decade of legal practice, she has defended migrants from deportation and engaged in broader civil rights and social justice work.

Kaitlyn Victoria is completing a Bachelor's degree in Political Science at the College of Charleston. Kaitlyn's award-winning scholarship combines her passions for politics and medicine in service of social justice. She plans to put her studies to work in a career in medicine after graduation.

Vineeth Vijayan, M.Sc., is doctoral student in the Juvenile Justice Ph.D. program at Prairie View A&M University. He has research interests in juvenile justice, cybercrime, victimology, forensic science, and police administration.

Cody Warner is an Associate Professor of Sociology in the Department of Sociology and Anthropology at Montana State University (MSU). His research and teaching interests are centered around corrections, and especially the housing and residential consequences of contact with the criminal justice system.

Carolyn Willis is a Ph.D. candidate in the School of Public Policy and Leadership at the University of Nevada, Las Vegas (UNLV). Her research interests include crime/criminal behavior, victimization, community-based corrections, restorative justice, reintegration, advocacy, public policy, and non-profit management. Having a multidisciplinary perspective has allowed Carolyn to merge her experiences and education to become an advocate in the reentry community as she works as the Program Manager at a local non-profit organization.

INTRODUCTION

Realities of Mass Incarceration

Vanessa Lynn, Margaret E. Leigey, and Addrain Conyers

Background of the Mass Incarceration Phenomenon

In "Introduction: The Meaning of Mass Imprisonment" (2001), David Garland offered the term "mass imprisonment" to define the system of social control that emerged in the U.S. and resulted in an unprecedented and unparalleled increase in incarceration. Specifically, Garland described a "rate of imprisonment and size of the prison population that is markedly above the historical and comparative norm for societies of this type [liberal democracies]" (p. 5). It means that in 2001, over two decades ago, as concluded by scholars, the U.S. had become the global leader in incarcerating its people.

Garland (2001, pp. 5–6) offered two essential features to define mass imprisonment: (1) "sheer numbers" and (2) "social concentration of imprisonment's effects." Beginning in the 1970s, the U.S. experienced an unprecedented increase in its prison population which has culminated in it becoming the world's largest jailer. The U.S. makes for 25% of the world's total prison population, whereas in comparison, it has 5% of the world's general population (Wagner & Bertram, 2020). On the second essential feature, Garland differentiates between *imprisonment* and *mass imprisonment* stating, "Imprisonment becomes *mass imprisonment* [emphasis in original] when it ceases to be the incarceration of [individuals] and becomes the systematic imprisonment of whole groups of the population" (p. 6).

While Garland advanced the understanding of "mass imprisonment," it was not until Michelle Alexander (2010), civil right lawyer and legal scholar, published *The New Jim Crow: Mass incarceration in the age of colorblindness* that *mass incarceration* as we know it entered the mainstream imagination. She specifically highlights how mass incarceration is a crisis that has created racial injustices of a magnitude that is not well understood. These injustices are based on historical and contemporary ideologies, policies, and practices that sustain this phenomenon. Grounded in a racialized history of social control that extends beyond jails and prisons, mass incarceration is a reality in the 21st century with far-reaching impacts.

DOI: 10.4324/9781003274292-1

REALITIES TO CONSIDER

1 Mass incarceration is a worldwide phenomenon.
2 In the U.S., approximately two million individuals are incarcerated in prisons and jails, with most incarcerated in state prisons and local jails (Carson, 2022; Zeng, 2022).
3 As we will explain more fully below, mass incarceration is more than prisons or prison crowding.

Reality – Mass Incarceration Has a Racialized History

Scholars argue that mass incarceration, excessive punishment, and racial disparities in incarceration are the legacy of slavery (Alexander, 2010; Wacquant, 2010). Slavery in the U.S. was a racialized institution of social control with lasting consequences (Ward, 2022). It was a caste system that subjected Black enslaved people to excessive unpaid labor, punishment, denial of education, poor diet, separation from family, sexual abuse, and other dehumanizing treatment (Brown & Webb, 2007). In 1865, slavery was abolished by the 13th Amendment of the U.S. Constitution:

> Neither slavery nor involuntary servitude, except as a punishment for a crime whereof the party shall have been duly convicted, shall exist within the United States, or any place subject to their jurisdiction.

However, as can be seen in the Amendment, an exception was made for people in prison, which allowed for their continued abuse and exploitation of labor. Courts provided little relief for imprisoned individuals challenging their confinement, and in fact, in *Ruffin v. Commonwealth* (1871, p. 1026), the Virginia Supreme Court declared that a person in prison was "a slave of the state." As such, scholars have argued that the 13th Amendment did not end racialized social control, but merely provided a way for it to be preserved in a new form – imprisonment (Alexander, 2010; Goodwin, 2019).

Following the Civil War, the number of Black and African American people who were imprisoned increased dramatically, especially in the southern states. Douglas A. Blackmon (2008) refers to the treatment of Black and African American people during this time, Civil War to World War II, as "Neoslavery." Delaney et al. (2018) provide insight into the social, economic, and political forces that shaped the treatment of Black Americans in this period:

> This was the result of state governments reacting to two powerful social forces: first, public anxiety and fear about crime stemming from newly freed Black Americans; and second, economic depression resulting from the war and the loss of a free supply of labor. State and local leaders in the South used the criminal justice system to both pacify the public's fear and bolster the depressed economy.
>
> *(p. 38)*

The government conserved racialized social control through oppressive norms, rhetoric, laws, and policies. For example, Southern states passed "Black Codes" and "Jim Crow" laws to target newly freed Black and African American people. Vagrancy and other minor offenses became criminalized behavior for only Black Americans. Once incarcerated, these individuals became a part of the convict lease system where states leased them to plantations, farms, factories, railroads, mines, and other venues for physical labor (Muller, 2018). Blackmon (2018) examines this period in his book, *Slavery by another name: The re-enslavement of Black Americans from the Civil War to World War II*. By the 1870s, 95% of individuals incarcerated in Southern states were Black (Delaney et al., 2018). Through convict leasing, states profited greatly by selling the labor of people in prison to private businesses. For example, at the turn of the 19th century, convict leasing was responsible for nearly three-quarters of Alabama's state revenue (African American Registry, n.d.). Chain gangs, another harsh and dehumanizing penal practice reminiscent of slavery, were also almost exclusively composed of Black and African American people (Delaney et al., 2018). Alabama was the last state to outlaw convict leasing, but forced labor of Black people persisted until it was abolished by the Department of Justice via Circular #3591 in 1941(National Archives and Records Administration, n.d.). While Black Codes, Jim Crow laws, and convict leasing were eventually outlawed, their purpose – racialized social control – continued in the 20th century through several laws and policies.

Several decades later, another historical period emerged that illustrates how racialized social control impacted Black and poor communities in the U.S.: the "war on drugs." In 1971, President Richard Nixon declared a "war on drugs." It was later revealed by John Ehrlichman, a top Nixon aide, that the war on drugs was racially motivated (Baum, 2016, para 2):

> You understand what I'm saying? We knew we couldn't make it illegal to be either against the war or black, but by getting the public to associate the hippies with marijuana and blacks with heroin. And then criminalizing both heavily, we could disrupt those communities. We could arrest their leaders, raid their homes, break up their meetings, and vilify them night after night on the evening news. Did we know we were lying about the drugs? Of course we did.

By 1973, President Nixon established the Drug Enforcement Administration (DEA) through the consolidation of personnel and resources and with the aim of enforcing drug laws (Drug Enforcement Administration, n.d.). Nixon resigned in 1974, and the war on drugs lay dormant until President Reagan was elected to office in 1980. During Reagan's tenure as President, the *Comprehensive Crime Control Act of 1984*, the *Anti-Drug Abuse Act 1986*, and the *Anti-Drug Abuse Act of 1988* were enacted. These acts established many laws and policies that have contributed to mass incarceration such as: the *Sentencing Reform Act of 1984* (a component of the *Comprehensive Crime Control Act of 1984*); the abolishment of parole at the federal level; the increase of the number of drug offenses; the establishment of mandatory minimums for drugs offenses; and the creation of the Office of National Drug Control Policy. While these laws appeared to be racially neutral, Reagan's racial rhetoric and the criminal justice system's biased enforcement of the laws show that race was a factor in their creation and how they were carried out (Alexander, 2010; Nunn, 2002). By 1994, President Bill Clinton was now in office and signed the *Violent Crime Control and Law Enforcement Act* that capitalized on the racialized image of "super-predators" (Boehme et al., 2022; Gilliam & Iyengar, 1998; Pizarro, 2007). The act helped to pass more tough-on-crime laws, increased aggressive policing strategies, incentivized truth-in-sentencing guidelines, denied Pell grants to incarcerated individuals, and many other policies that contributed to mass incarceration (Rosenfeld, 2020).

The impact of the *Anti-Drug Abuse Act of 1986, 1988* and *Violent Crime Control and Law Enforcement Act of 1994* is still evident in contemporary policing, sentencing, and incarceration rates. Research indicates that police are more likely to arrest and prosecutors are more likely to pursue harsher sentences for people of color (i.e., Black and African American, Latinx, and Indigenous people) than their white counterparts, culminating in stark racial disparities in the prison population (Edwards et al., 2020; Drug Policy Alliance, n.d.). Almost 80% of individuals incarcerated at the federal level and approximately 60% of individuals incarcerated at the state level for drug offenses are Black or Latinx (Drug Policy Alliance, n.d.). The increased risk of incarceration for Black men continues today as The Sentencing Project notes that their lifetime likelihood of imprisonment is 1 in 3 (Ghandnoosh, 2021). Additionally, 1 in 6 Latinx men can expect to be incarcerated in their lifetimes (Ghandnoosh, 2021). Among white men, the lifetime likelihood of imprisonment is 1 in 17. At 1 in 18 and 1 in 45, respectively, Black and Latinx women are at a much higher risk of experiencing incarceration in their lifetimes as compared to white women, 1 in 111 (Ghandnoosh, 2021).

No other western country on the planet incarcerates its people at the rate that the U.S. has historically and continues to. Not just any people, mass incarceration also means whole groups of people are systematically impacted; Garland (2001) explains it's not the imprisonment of individuals but the "mass imprisonment" of a group of people.

James Baldwin stated: "History is not the past. It is the present. We carry our history with us. We are our history" (as cited in Peck, 2016). The reality is that mass incarceration in the 21st century is a result of the U.S.' racialized history of slavery, excessive punishment, and biased laws.

Reality-Mass Incarceration throughout the Criminal Justice System

Many associate mass incarceration with imprisonment, but it is more complicated than imprisoning a person. Mass incarceration is a culmination of policies and practices

REALITIES TO CONSIDER

1 Mass Incarceration has historically and in contemporary times disproportionately impacted a variety of groups and marginalized communities.
2 People of color are overrepresented in all facets of the criminal justice system (The Sentencing Project, 2018).
3 Similar to people of color, LGBTQ+ individuals are over incarcerated (Jones, 2021; Stammen & Ghandnoosh, 2022).
4 Over the last five decades, the incarceration rate of women has been double that of men, with markedly higher rates of incarceration for Black and Latinx women than white women (The Sentencing Project, 2022).

that benefit privileged individuals and consequently disproportionally disenfranchise marginalized communities. In the 21st century, racial disparity "permeates every stage of the U.S. criminal justice system, from arrest to trial to sentencing to post-prison experiences" (The Sentencing Project, 2018, para 7). Each phase of the criminal justice system, from policing to release, contributes to this social problem; therefore, in order to have a complete understanding of mass incarceration, it is essential to examine it beyond jails and prisons.

Criminal Laws and Policies

Beginning in the 1970s, as part of its "law and order" movement, the U.S. embraced a more punitive sentencing and correctional agenda; consequently, federal and state legislatures created laws that reflected this "tough-on-crime" approach (Cullen & Jonson, 2017). As with the 13th Amendment, described above, the *Anti-Drug Abuse Acts of 1986* and *1988* and the *Violent Crime Control and Law Enforcement Act of 1994* are embedded with punishment clauses that make it easier to arrest, prosecute, and imprison anyone who violates them (Goodwin, 2019).

It is important for readers who are interested in studying mass incarceration to understand that criminal laws, policies, and practices provide the foundation that mass incarceration is built upon. These laws impact critical decisions related to arrest, prosecutorial charging, pretrial release, sentencing, and supervision. And any efforts to end mass incarceration – another reality explored in this book – would need to challenge the legal underpinnings of mass incarceration.

Law Enforcement

Much of the public attention on law enforcement these days focuses on police brutality and the deadly use of force, but this phase of the criminal justice system also has an important role in mass incarceration. Police are the gatekeepers to the criminal justice system and we need to understand policing practices as contributors of mass incarceration. In the context of the war on drugs, and the law and order rhetoric, Alexander (2010) argues law enforcement benefits from few legal rules in its use of discretion. Case in point, a federal court found that the New York City Police Department engaged in racial profiling and unconstitutional stops with the practice of stop and frisk (Floyd v. City of New York, 2013). This contributes to the over-policing of communities of color, broken-windows policing – excessive enforcement of minor offenses – and "concentrated policing in targeted areas far disproportionate to their percentage of the population and likelihood of violating the law" (Neusteter et al., 2019, p. 4). Additionally, another way in which law enforcement contributes to mass incarceration is that police are often called to resolve social problems not related to public safety such as homelessness and mental health crises (Jones & Sawyer, 2019). In the course of these encounters between police and civilians, individuals are arrested and thus enter the criminal justice system. Over-policing and misuse of law enforcement leads people right to the jail door.

At a time when jail admissions have increased while crime and arrest rates have fallen, "police enforcement has become an expressway to jail" (Neusteter et al., 2019, p. 1). Mass incarceration also includes the number of people in jail; 80% of whom are not yet convicted of a crime (Sawyer & Wagner, 2022). According to Jones and Sawyer (2019), 4.9 million people are sent to jail each year. Some are waiting to post bail, while many are too poor and remain in jail until they have a trial or, most likely, will have to accept a plea deal. Police are the gatekeepers to our justice system, but repeat arrests related to poverty, race, mental illness, and substance abuse lead people to jail who should be assisted through other services (Jones & Sawyer, 2019).

Courts

The courts and their actors also sustain mass incarceration. Early on in the judicial process, prosecutors make critical decisions that greatly impact the outcome of an individual's case. Prosecutors have much discretion in determining whether to file charges or not and, if so, what the specific charges are. They also guide plea bargaining, all of which matter in terms of the possible sentence, for example, probation, jail or prison time, or even death (Brennan Center for Justice, n.d.). Concerns about the racial impact of prosecutorial decision-making are well known (for example, see Kutateladze et al., 2014 for their study of the Manhattan, New York District Attorney's Office).

In addition to prosecutors, judges play an important role in determining case outcomes. Not only do they guide the sentencing process, but also bail and pretrial release decision-making. If a person cannot make bail, then they are held in jail until their case is resolved. This decision has serious ramifications for the individual, including their work and family responsibilities, but also on the ultimate outcome of the case. People who are denied bail are more likely to be convicted and receive a harsher punishment (Digard & Swavola, 2019). The injustices of the bail system have been criticized, and more recently, bail reform has been implemented in some states. For example, the elimination or curtailment of cash bail in New York and New Jersey (Grawert & Kim, 2022; Lyons, 2022) has emerged as a way to address race and class-based injustices in the system. Jail or prison, courts play an important role in mass incarceration.

Community Corrections

Mass incarceration has led to "mass supervision" (Bradner et al., 2020, p. 1). Similar to the dramatic increase in the number of people incarcerated in the U.S., the number of people on between probation and parole has skyrocketed. For example, in 1980, there were approximately 1.1 million people on probation (Bureau of Justice Statistics, 1995). At year-end 2020, the number had tripled to approximately three million people (Kaeble, 2021). In the same 40-year period, the number of people on parole has quadrupled from about 220,000 to about 880,000 individuals (Bureau of Justice Statistics, 1995; Kaeble, 2021). Given the disparate impact of mass incarceration and "mass supervision" policies, people of color are overrepresented in the probation and parole populations. In fact, Black and African American people were "2.6 times as likely to be on probation, and nearly 4 times as likely to be on parole, as white people in 2018" (Bradner et al., 2020, p. 6).

Probation and parole systems fuel mass incarceration because people can be incarcerated as a result of a technical violation of their community supervision agreement; for example, missing an appointment with their probation or parole officer, breaking curfew, or failing a drug test are all considered technical violations. Two former criminal justice

REALITIES TO CONSIDER

1 Every stage of the criminal justice system contributes to mass incarceration.
2 The human costs are staggering with profound negative effects on the health and well-being of individuals, groups, and communities (Robert Wood Johnson Foundation, 2021; von Hoffman, 2015).
3 Prisons can exacerbate the mental health conditions of residents who already are disproportionately involved in the criminal justice system (Quandt & Jones, 2021).
4 The fiscal costs have been exorbitant as incarceration has cost upwards of $80 billion (Wagner & Rabuy, 2017).
5 Approximately 95% of incarcerated individuals will be released from prison and return to their communities (Hopwood, 2021).

practitioners describe community supervision as "a tripwire that perpetuates incarceration based on crimeless technical violations" (Aroni Krinsky & Schiraldi, 2020, para 2). In their analysis, Bradner et al. (2020) found that twice as many people were sent to prison for violating the technical conditions of probation or parole than for being convicted of a new criminal offense.

Recidivism rates in the U.S. are alarmingly high. Based on the results of a longitudinal study, Antenangeli and Durose (2021) note that of every 10 people released from prison: 8 of 10 will be arrested, 7 of 10 will be convicted, 6 of 10 will be returned to prison within 10 years of their initial release. And, connecting this with the information presented above, we are reminded of the reciprocal relationship between mass incarceration and mass supervision. Upon release from prison, individuals confront both immediate and long-term challenges: finding a job, securing housing, accessing medical care, remaining sober, etc. They face societal stigma as a result of their prison record. According to Jones (2018, para 11), "long supervision terms, strict conditions, and intense surveillance" combine to create a situation in which people on community supervision are designed to fail.

Reality – Mass Incarceration Has a Far-Reaching Impact

Many people are negatively impacted by mass incarceration. The individuals who are incarcerated are the first to immediately come to mind. However, the ripple effects of mass incarceration extend beyond adult prisons operated by the criminal justice system. In order to truly understand the impact of mass incarceration, we must understand the influence it has exerted – and continues to exert – on individuals, groups, and systems. Below, we provide just a few examples.

Children and Families

About five million children in the U.S. have experienced the incarceration of a parent (The Annie E. Casey Foundation, 2016). Given the racialized nature of mass incarceration, as described above, Black and African American children are six times as likely to have an incarcerated parent than white children (Morsy & Rothstein, 2016). Parental incarceration can have a harmful effect on the physical and mental well-being of a child as it is associated with negative outcomes in physical health, mental health, educational attainment, future earnings, and interpersonal relationships (Lee et al., 2013; Mears & Siennick, 2016). Research also suggests that children with an incarcerated parent are more likely to end up on a trajectory that increases their lifetime likelihood of incarceration (Mears & Siennick, 2016).

Mass incarceration has separated incarcerated people from their families, and for many, for a substantial period of time. One of the greatest pains of imprisonment reported by both incarcerated men and women is missing their loved ones (Crewe et al., 2017), and family support is a crucial element of a successful return following incarceration. In their recent study of the impact of mass incarceration on families, Lee and Wildeman (2021, p. 277) described the incarceration of a relative in U.S. families as "crushingly common, shockingly unequally distributed" as they noted that almost half of all adults between the ages of 18 and 49 have an immediate family member who has been incarcerated. And, given the disparate impact of mass incarceration, Black and African American families have been especially impacted as about 60% of adults report the incarceration of an immediate family member (Lee & Wildeman, 2021). Researchers have documented the damaging impact that mass incarceration has had on families in the following specific areas:

1 Financial hardship as a result of the loss of income due to incarceration and the difficulties of finding employment that offers a liveable wage to support a family after release; consequently, there are increased risks of maternal stress and homelessness (Lee & Wildeman, 2021; van Agtmael, 2016).
2 Despite the efforts of many incarcerated people, an inability to be as present or engaged in their families because of the physical absence and barriers to communication (Lee & Wildeman, 2021).
3 Family structure and instability as incarceration is associated with increased rates of divorce/relationship dissolution and lower rates of marriage following release, and especially for children with incarcerated mothers, an increased likelihood of placement in foster care (Lee & Wildeman, 2021).

Continuing with our focus on children, the juvenile justice system has also been affected by mass incarceration, as we explore below.

Juvenile Justice System

Youth under the age of majority are usually processed in the separate juvenile justice system. Similar to the number of people incarcerated at the adult-level, the number of juveniles confined in residential facilities increased dramatically in the 1980s. In 1985, there were approximately 67,000 juveniles confined; by 2000, the population reached its apex of confined children at about 109,000 (National Juvenile Justice Network & Texas Public Policy, 2013). While in recent years, the number of juveniles confined has steadily declined to about 36,000 in 2019 (Office of Juvenile Justice and Delinquency Prevention, 2021), the U.S. continues to confine juveniles at a much higher rate than other countries (Mendel, 2022) and additional issues exist with juvenile confinement. Among them, empirical research indicates that it is ineffective in preventing juvenile delinquency (Mendel, 2022) and rife with concerns about racial disparity and victimization; about 67% of the juveniles confined in 2019 were youth of color (Hockenberry, 2022). Additionally, abuse and mistreatment is sadly an all-too-common experience for juveniles during their confinement. According to Mendel (2022, p. 5), "surveys of currently or previously incarcerated youth reveal that many have been abused physically or sexually in their facilities by staff or peers, and that most have witnessed abuses – often repeatedly." These issues are just the tip of the iceberg, other areas of concerns include: school to prison pipeline, carceral conditions, access to programs and services, transfers to adult courts, and sexual victimization (Heaton et al., 2016; Scott, 2017; Sawyer, 2019).

Immigration System

Mass incarceration also encompasses people who are detained in immigration detention centers. Just as the prison population in state and federal prisons was increasing in the 1970s, so did the population in immigration detention centers (Bosworth & Kaufman, 2011). The criminalization of immigration policies, also called "crimmigration," has led to an expansion of people trapped in the criminal justice system (Immigrant Legal Resource Center, 2022). People can be incarcerated for criminal or civil reasons, but the immigration detention system operates under civil law (Saadi et al., 2020). This distinction has important ramifications, for example, most people involved in the immigration system are not afforded the same rights, such as the right to legal representation, as they would in a criminal law proceeding. Sawyer and Wagner (2022) note that the Federal Bureau of Prisons incarcerates the majority for crossing the border without permission. In the past few years, the conditions of detentions sparked outrage across the nation (Joung, 2019). Additionally, the federal government contracts private immigration detention centers. In fact, the Federal Bureau of Prisons is the largest prison system to rely on private prisons, with the largest population being immigration detention (Buday & Nellis, 2022).

Private Prisons

The convict lease system is often viewed as the beginning of the privatization of corrections (Eisen, 2018). Today private prisons demonstrate, once again, the intersection of race, capitalism, and correctional policy across centuries. Private prisons represent the far reaching impact of the U.S.' racialized history of mass incarceration. Private prisons exist and are scattered throughout the country. Sawyer and Wagner (2022) find that less than 8% of people incarcerated are in private prisons. However, even if they represent a relatively small fraction of people incarcerated, it is important to highlight that it is a system that profits from incarcerating people, as described below:

> The emergence of private prisons in the late twentieth century does not mark the first time private industry has profited from U.S. prisoners. Indeed, whether through slavery or incarceration, the United States has a long history of using captive labor for economic purposes, separate and apart from the moral or ethical questions that these practices present. Incarcerated people, much like slaves, were first and foremost a cheap and disenfranchised form of labor.
>
> *(Eisen, 2018, p. 47)*

Private prisons are not the core or heart of mass incarceration, but a "parasite" that benefits from the phenomenon (Wagner, 2015). Their influence also extends into the political arena

REALITIES TO CONSIDER

1. Mass incarceration policies have been harmful to youth, families, and communities in a variety of capacities.
2. It is a public health issue inextricably linked to the social problems of substance abuse, homelessness, physical and mental health problems, among others (Cloud, 2014; Jones & Sawyer, 2019).
3. Disenfranchisement has compromised the fundamental right of five million citizens who are unable to vote because of a previous criminal record (Chung & Muhitch, 2021).
4. Mass incarceration also impacts correctional staff. Their rates of PTSD are higher than law enforcement and are comparable to war veterans. Their average life expectancy is just 59 years, 16 years shorter than the national average of 75 years (Delaney et al., 2018).

through their lobbying and campaign donations for candidates who support tougher crime and immigration policies (Cohen, 2015; Leary, 2016; Meyer, 2019). Additionally, many of the issues that we have discussed throughout this introduction, including victimization, conditions for both residents and staff, and access to programs and services are magnified in private prisons (Equal Justice Initiative, n.d.). As noted above, there are just a few examples of mass incarceration's impact. We invite students to consider others and explore them more deeply.

Conclusion

This introduction – intended to be a succinct primer to provide readers with a foundation of knowledge and historical context – could easily evolve into a book in its own right if we were to explore all of the present realities of mass incarceration! While a few have been explored here, and more will be explored in the pages to follow, this book is not exhaustive. A reality of mass incarceration is that it continues to change shape; this is even evident in how we refer to *incarcerated individuals.* Society should rethink terms such as juvenile delinquents, inmates, convicts, felons, prisoners, offenders, and illegal immigrants. This language is disparaging and dehumanizing; the reality is that these are human beings and deserve to be acknowledged as such (Bryant, 2021). The labels should be replaced with more appropriate descriptions such as justice-involved, justice-impacted, or noncitizens (Tran et al., 2018). Labeling individuals based on past behavior and previous criminal justice involvement perpetuates stereotypes that creates challenges as they try to regain acceptance in a society that only wants to see them in one status.

In conclusion, mass incarceration was created by people and can be abolished by people. Dorothy Roberts (2019) has identified tenets central to an abolitionist philosophy. In short, we must recognize that the racialized and capitalist history of mass incarceration continues today and our "system functions to oppress black people and other politically marginalized groups" (p. 7). As such, ending mass incarceration requires a major overhaul of our criminal justice philosophies, policies, and practices such that rehabilitation and restorative justice should be at its core (Porter, 2021). We return to Roberts' and their final tenet to transforming the criminal justice system where "We can imagine and build a more humane, free, and democratic society that no longer relies on caging people to meet human needs and solve social problems" (2019, p. 7).

REALITIES TO CONSIDER

1 Language matters and the use of humanizing language to describe those involved in the criminal justice system is an important component of change.
2 Mass incarceration is a system that was created by people, and as such, can be undone by people too. The choice is ours.

References

African American Registry. (n.d.) *The American convict leasing program, a story*. https://aaregistry.org/story/the-american-convict-leasing-program-a-story/

Alexander, M. (2010). *The New Jim Crow: Mass incarceration in the age of colorblindness*. The New Press New York.

The Annie E. Casey Foundation. (2016). *A shared sentence: The devastating toll of parental incarceration on kids, families and communities*. https://assets.aecf.org/m/resourcedoc/aecf-asharedsentence-2016.pdf

Antenangeli, L., & Durose, M.R. (2021). *Recidivism of prisoners released in 24 states in 2008: A 10-year follow up period (2008–2018)*. Bureau of Justice Statistics. https://bjs.ojp.gov/BJS_PUB/rpr24s0810yfup0818/Web%20content/508%20compliant%20PDFs

Anti-Drug Abuse Act of 1986, 21 U.S.C. § 1801 *et seq*. (1986).

Anti-Drug Abuse Act of 1988, 21 U.S.C. § 1501 *et seq*. (1988).

Aroni Krinsky, M., & Schiraldi, V. (2020, November 19). Community supervision, once intended to help offenders, contributes more to mass incarceration. *USA Today*. https://www.usatoday.com/story/opinion/policing/2020/11/19/supervision-once-intended-help-offenders-ups-mass-incarceration-column/3765824001/

Baum, D. (2016, April). Legalize it all: How to win the war on drugs. *Harper's Magazine*. https://harpers.org/archive/2016/04/legalize-it-all/

Blackmon, D.A. (2008). *Slavery by another name: The re-enslavement of Black Americans from the Civil War to World War II*. Doubleday.

Boehme, H.M., Cann, D., & Isom, D.A. (2022). Citizens' perceptions of over- and under-policing: A look at race, ethnicity, and community characteristics. *Crime and Delinquency*, *68*(1), 123–154. https://doi.org/10.1177/0011128720974309

Bosworth, M., & Kaufman, E. (2011). Foreigners in a carceral age: Immigration and imprisonment in the United States. *Stanford Law and Policy Review, 22*(1), 429–454.

Bradner, K., Schiraldi, V., Mejia, N., & Lopoo, E. (2020). *More work to do: Analysis of probation and parole in the United States, 2017–2018*. https://justicelab.columbia.edu/sites/default/files/content/More%20Work%20to%20Do.pdf

Brennan Center for Justice. (n.d.) *Prosecutorial reform*. https://www.brennancenter.org/issues/end-mass-incarceration/changing-incentives/prosecutorial-reform

Brown, D., & Webb, C. (2007). *Race in the American south: From slavery to civil rights*. Edinburgh University Press.

Bryant, E. (2021, March 21). *Words matter: Don't call people felons, convicts, or inmates*. Vera Institute of Justice. Retrieved January 10, 2023, from https://www.vera.org/news/words-matter-dont-call-people-felons-convicts-or-inmates

Buday, M., & Nellis, A. (2022). *Private prisons in the United States*. The Sentencing Project. https://www.sentencingproject.org/reports/private-prisons-in-the-united-states/

Bureau of Justice Statistics. (1995). *Correctional populations in the United States*. https://www.ojp.gov/pdffiles1/Digitization/153849NCJRS.pdf

Carson, E. A. (2022). *Prisoners in 2021–Statistical tables*. Bureau of Justice Statistics. https://bjs.ojp.gov/sites/g/files/xyckuh236/files/media/document/p21st.pdf

Chung, J., & Muhitch, K. (2021). *Voting rights in the era of mass incarceration: A primer*. The Sentencing Project. https://www.sentencingproject.org/app/uploads/2022/08/Voting-Rights-in-the-Era-of-Mass-Incarceration-A-Primer.pdf
Cloud, D. (2014). *On life support: Public health in the age of mass incarceration*. Vera Institute of Justice. https://www.vera.org/downloads/publications/on-life-support-public-health-mass-incarceration-report.pdf
Cohen, M. (2015, April 28). *How for-profit prisons have become the biggest lobby no one is talking about*. The Washington Post. Retrieved January 9, 2023, from https://www.washingtonpost.com/posteverything/wp/2015/04/28/how-for-profit-prisons-have-become-the-biggest-lobby-no-one-is-talking-about/
Comprehensive Crime Control Act of 1984, 18 U.S.C. § 3141 *et seq*. (1984).
Crewe, B., Hulley, S., & Wright, S. (2017). The gendered pains of life imprisonment. *British Journal of Criminology, 57,* 1359–1378.
Cullen, F.T., & Jonson, C.L. (2017). *Correctional theory: Contexts and consequences* (2nd ed.). Sage.
Delaney, R., Subramanian, R., Shames, A., & Turner, N. (2018). *Reimagining prison*. Vera Institute of Justice.
Digard, L. & Swavola, E. (2019). *Justice denied: The harmful and lasting effects of pretrial detention*. Vera Institute of Justice. https://www.vera.org/downloads/publications/Justice-Denied-Evidence-Brief.pdf
Drug Enforcement Administration. (n.d.) *Our history*. DEA. Retrieved January 15, 2023, from https://www.dea.gov/about/history
Drug Policy Alliance. (n.d.) *Race and the drug war*. https://drugpolicy.org/issues/race-and-drug-war
Edwards, E., Greytak, E., Madubuonwu, B., Sanchez, T., Beiers, S., Resing, C., Fernandez, P., & Galai, S. (2020). A tale of two countries: Racially targeted arrests in the era of marijuana reform. American Civil Liberties Union. https://www.aclu.org/report/tale-two-countries-racially-targeted-arrests-era-marijuana-reform
Eisen, L.B. (2018). *Inside private prisons: An American dilemma in the age of mass incarceration*. Columbia University Press.
Equal Justice Initiative. (n.d.). Prison conditions. https://eji.org/issues/prison-conditions/
Floyd v. City of New York, 959 F. Supp. 2d 540 (2013).
Garland, D. (2001). Introduction: The meaning of mass imprisonment. *Punishment & Society, 3*(1), 5–7.
Ghandnoosh, N. (2021). *Trends in US corrections*. The Sentencing Project. https://www.sentencingproject.org/app/uploads/2022/08/Trends-in-US-Corrections.pdf
Gilliam, F.D., Jr., & Iyengar, S. (1998). The superpredator script. *Nieman Reports, 52*(4), 45–46.
Goodwin, M. (2019). The Thirteenth Amendment: Modern slavery, capitalism, and mass incarceration. *Cornell Law Review, 104*(4), 899–990.
Grawert, A., & Kim, N. (2022). *The facts on bail reform and crime rates in New York state*. Brennan Center for Justice. https://www.brennancenter.org/our-work/research-reports/facts-bail-reform-and-crime-rates-new-york-state
Heaton, L., Cantor, D., Bruce, C., Ren, W., & Hartge, J. (2016). *Facility-level and individual-level correlates of sexual victimization in juvenile facilities*. Bureau of Justice Statistics. https://bjs.ojp.gov/content/pub/pdf/flilcsvjf12.pdf
Hockenberry, S. (2022). *Juveniles in residential placement, 2019*. Office of Juvenile Justice and Delinquency Prevention. https://ojjdp.ojp.gov/publications/juveniles-in-residential-placement-2019.pdf
Hopwood, S. (2021). How atrocious prison conditions make us all less safe. Brennan Center for Justice. https://www.brennancenter.org/our-work/analysis-opinion/how-atrocious-prisons-conditions-make-us-all-less-safe
Immigrant Legal Resource Center. (2022). *If you build it, ICE will fill it: The link between detention capacity and ICE arrests*. https://www.ilrc.org/sites/default/files/resources/if_they_build_it_ice_will_fill_it_report_2022.pdf
Jones, A. (2018). *Correctional control 2018: Incarceration and supervision by state*. Prison Policy Initiative. https://www.prisonpolicy.org/reports/correctionalcontrol2018.html

Jones, A. (2021). *Visualizing the unequal treatment of LGBTQ people in the criminal justice system.* Prison Policy Initiative. https://www.prisonpolicy.org/blog/2021/03/02/lgbtq

Jones, A., & Sawyer, W. (2019). *Arrest, release, repeat: How police and jails are misused to respond to social problems.* Prison Policy Initiative. https://www.prisonpolicy.org/reports/repeatarrests.html

Joung, M. (2019, July 12). *What is happening at migrant detention centers? What to know.* Time. Retrieved January 15, 2023, from https://time.com/5623148/migrant-detention-centers-conditions/

Kaeble, D. (2021). *Probation and parole in the United States, 2020.* Bureau of Justice Statistics. https://bjs.ojp.gov/content/pub/pdf/ppus20.pdf

Kutateladze, B., Tymas, W., & Crowley, M. (2014). *Race and prosecution in Manhattan.* Vera Institute of Justice. Vera Institute of Justice. https://www.vera.org/downloads/publications/race-and-prosecution-manhattan-summary.pdf

Leary, A. (2016, August 24). Behind Marco Rubio, a powerful ally: Private prison operator Geo Group. *Tampa Bay Times.* https://www.tampabay.com/behind-marco-rubio-a-powerful-ally-private-prison-operator-geo-group/2290600/

Lee, H., & Wildeman, C. (2021). Assessing mass incarceration's effects on families. *Science, 374*(6565), 277–281.

Lee, R.D., Fang, X., & Luo, F. (2013). The impact of parental incarceration on the physical and mental health of young adults. *Pediatrics, 131*(4), e1188–e1195.

Lyons, K. (2022, August 7). New Jersey mostly got rid of cash bail. Why hasn't Connecticut? *CT Monitor.* https://ctmirror.org/2022/08/07/new-jersey-cash-bail-reform-abolish-connecticut-ct-bond-jail-prison/

Mears, D.P., & Siennick, S.E. (2016). Young adult outcomes and the life-course penalties of parental incarceration. *Journal of Research in Crime and Delinquency, 53*(1), 3–35.

Mendel, R. (2022). *Why youth incarceration fails: An updated review of the evidence.* The Sentencing Project. https://www.sentencingproject.org/reports/why-youth-incarceration-fails-an-updated-review-of-the-evidence/

Meyer, T. (2019, June 21). Who lobbies for private prisons. *POLITICO.* https://www.politico.com/newsletters/politico-influence/2019/06/21/who-lobbies-for-private-prisons-449574

Morsy, L., & Rothstein, R. (2016). *Mass incarceration and children's outcomes.* Economic Policy Institute. https://www.epi.org/publication/mass-incarceration-and-childrens-outcoms/

Muller, C. (2018). Freedom and convict leasing in the Postbellum South. *The American Journal of Sociology, 124*(2), 367–405. https://doi.org/10.1086/698481

National Archives and Records Administration. (n.d.). *Classification 50: Involuntary servitude and slavery.* National Archives and Records Administration. Retrieved December 29, 2022, from https://www.archives.gov/research/investigations/fbi/classifications/050-slavery.html

National Juvenile Justice Network & Texas Public Policy. (2013). *The comeback states: Reducing youth incarceration in the United States.* https://www.njjn.org/uploads/digital-library/Comeback-States-Report_FINAL.pdf

Neusteter, S.R., Subramanian, R., Trone, J., Khogali, M., & Reed, C. (2019). *Gatekeepers: The role of police in ending mass incarceration.* Vera Institute of Justice. https://www.vera.org/downloads/publications/gatekeepers-police-and-mass-incarceration.pdf

Nunn, K. B. (2002). Race, crime and the pool of surplus criminality: Or why the "war on drugs" was a "war on blacks." *The Journal of Gender, Race, and Justice*, 6(2), 381–445.

Office of Juvenile Justice and Delinquency Prevention. (2021). *OJJDP statistical briefing book.* https://www.ojjdp.gov/ojstatbb/corrections/qa08201.asp?qaDate=2019

Peck, R. (Director). (2016). *I am not your negro* [Film]. Velvet Film.

Pizarro, J.M., Chermak, S.M., & Gruenewald, J. A. (2007). Juvenile "super-predators" in the news: A comparison of adult and juvenile homicides. *Journal of Criminal Justice and Popular Culture, 14*(1), 84–111.

Porter, N.D. (2021). Top trends in state criminal justice reform, 2020. The Sentencing Project. https://www.sentencingproject.org/policy-brief/top-trends-in-state-criminal-justice-reform-2020/

Quandt, K.R., & Jones A. (2021). *Research roundup: Incarceration can cause lasting damage to mental health.* https://www.prisonpolicy.org/blog/2021/05/13/mentalhealthimpacts/

Robert Wood Johnson Foundation. (2021). *Prison & jail reentry & health*. https://www.healthaffairs.org/do/10.1377/hpb20210928.343531/full/health-affairs-brief-prison-community-reentry-russ-1635782008603.pdf
Roberts, D.E. (2019). Foreword: Abolition constitutionalism. *Harvard Law Review*, *133*(1), 1–122.
Rosenfeld, R. (2020). The 1994 Crime Bill: Legacy and lessons – Overview and reflections. *Federal Sentencing Reporter*, *32*(3), 147–152. https://doi.org/10.1525/fsr.2020.32.3.147
Ruffin v. Commonwealth, 62, Va. 790 (1871).
Saadi, A., Young, M. E. D. T., Patler, C., Estrada, J. L., & Venters, H. (2020). Understanding US immigration detention: Reaffirming rights and addressing social-structural determinants of health. *Health and Human Rights*, *22*(1), 187.
Sawyer, W. (2019). *Youth confinement: The whole pie 2019*. Prison Policy Initiative. https://www.prisonpolicy.org/reports/youth2019.html
Sawyer, W., & Wagner, P. (2022). *Mass incarceration: The whole pie 2022*. Prison Policy Initiative. https://www.prisonpolicy.org/reports/pie2022.html
Scott, D. (2017). Developing the prison-to-school pipeline: A paradigmatic shift in educational possibilities during an age of mass incarceration. *Journal of Correctional Education*, *68*(3), 41–52.
The Sentencing Project. (2022). *Incarcerated women and girls*. https://www.sentencingproject.org/app/uploads/2022/11/Incarcerated-Women-and-Girls.pdf
The Sentencing Project. (2018). *Report to the United Nations on racial disparities in the U.S. criminal justice system*. https://www.sentencingproject.org/reports/report-to-the-united-nations-on-racial-disparities-in-the-u-s-criminal-justice-system/
The Sentencing Reform Act of 1984, 21 U.S.C. § 1501 *et seq*. (1988).
Stammen, E., & Ghandnoosh, N. (2022). *Incarcerated LGBTQ+ adults and youth*. The Sentencing Project. https://www.sentencingproject.org/app/uploads/2022/10/Incarcerated-LGBTQ-Youth-and-Adults.pdf
Tran, T.T., Baggio, S., Dawson, A., O'Moore, E., Williams, B., Bedell, P., Simon, O., Scholten, W., Getaz, L., & Wolff, H. (2018). Words matter: A call for humanizing and respectful language to describe people who experience incarceration. *BMC International Health and Human Rights, 18*. https://bmcinthealthhumrights.biomedcentral.com/articles/10.1186/s12914-018-0180-4#citeas
van Agtmael, P. (2016). *More on incarceration's impact on kids and families*. Vera Institute of Justice. http://humantollofjail.vera.org/the-family-jail-cycle/
Violent Crime Control and Law Enforcement Act of 1994, 42 U.S.C. § 13701 *et seq*. (1994).
von Hoffman, E. (2015, March 6). How incarceration infects a community. *The Atlantic*. https://www.theatlantic.com/health/archive/2015/03/how-incarceration-infects-a-community/385967/
Wacquant, L. (2010). From slavery to mass incarceration. In M. Tonry (Ed.), *Why punish? How much?: A reader on punishment* (pp. 387–402). Oxford University Press.
Wagner, P. (2015). Are private prisons driving mass incarceration? Prison Policy Initiative. https://www.prisonpolicy.org/blog/2015/10/07/private_prisons_parasite/
Wagner, P., & Bertram, W. (2020). What percent of the US is incarcerated? And other ways to measure mass incarceration. Prison Policy Initiative. https://www.prisonpolicy.org/blog/2020/01/16/percent-incarcerated/
Wagner, P., & Rabuy, B. (2017). Following the money of mass incarceration. Prison Policy Initiative. Retrieved January 15, 2023, from https://www.prisonpolicy.org/reports/money.html
Ward, M. (2022). Enduring consequences of dehumanizing institutions: Slavery and contemporary minority social control in the U.S. Northeast and South. *Social Problems*. https://doi.org/10.1093/socpro/spac021
Zeng, Z. (2022). *Jail inmates in 2021–Statistical tables*. Bureau of Justice Statistics. https://bjs.ojp.gov/sites/g/files/xyckuh236/files/media/document/ji21st.pdf

SECTION I
Laws and Policies

Mass incarceration exists because of laws and policies; the enforceable rules created by the government. These laws and policies regulate the conduct of both citizens and practitioners of the criminal justice system. A government can decide which behaviors to punish and the methods of enforcement and processing when violations of law occur. This is especially true in the phenomenon of mass incarceration as the government determines which behaviors are violations of criminal law and prescribes the specific punishment for them. Students may be familiar with certain criminal laws including mandatory minimums, three-strikes laws, and truth-in-sentencing laws—all of which are drivers of mass incarceration (Cullen, 2018). This first section of the book discusses other examples of the laws and policies that create, sustain, and maintain mass incarceration.

The authors consider the reality of laws and policies that maintain mass incarceration in the 21st century. The section begins with Justin Murray highlighting the role that criminal procedure plays in the United States addiction to mass imprisonment in his chapter, "The Procedural Architecture of Mass Incarceration." The discussion continues with Karen Lahm's chapter, "Bail, Pretrial Detention, and Mass Incarceration." The author examines how bail and pretrial detention practices fuel mass incarceration among the poor and disenfranchised. Next, Tania Valdez reviews immigration law and its impact on immigration mass incarceration in her chapter, "Immigration in an Era of Mass Incarceration." Ashley Nellis' "Life Imprisonment as a Hallmark of Mass Incarceration" examines the expansion of life imprisonment as a tactic of mass incarceration. This section concludes with a reflection from Terrence Graham, "Growing Up On the Inside," who discusses growing up as a juvenile in an adult prison system. In his eponymous Supreme Court case *Graham v. Florida* (2010), the Court determined that it is a violation of the Eighth Amendment's prohibition against cruel and unusual punishment to sentence juveniles to life without the possibility of parole for non-homicide offenses.

DOI: 10.4324/9781003274292-2

References

Cullen, J. (2018, October 5). *Sentencing laws and how they contribute to mass incarceration*. Brennan Center for Justice. https://www.brennancenter.org/our-work/analysis-opinion/sentencing-laws-and-how-they-contribute-mass-incarceration
Graham v. Florida, 560 U.S. 48 (2010).

1

THE PROCEDURAL ARCHITECTURE OF MASS INCARCERATION

Justin Murray

LEARNING OUTCOMES:

Upon successful completion of this chapter, readers will be able to:

1. Explain how the law of policing facilitates mass arrests.
2. Explain how the law of bail, plea negotiation, and defense representation enable the criminal justice system to efficiently imprison, convict, and punish vast numbers of arrested persons.
3. Identify potential reforms to these four areas of procedural law that might help advance the struggle against mass incarceration.

Introduction

There are many interrelated stories one can tell to conceptualize and, in part, explain the stunning growth of America's system of imprisonment—an expansion that has produced a population of incarcerated people far higher than this country, or *any* country, has ever seen (National Research Council, 2014). Some accounts emphasize disruptions in America's social structure such as the collapse of Jim Crow and the ensuing backlash against civil rights gains, deepening economic inequality and disinvestment in poor communities, and the emptying of institutions that once warehoused vast numbers of people with mental disabilities. Others focus on the rise in certain kinds of crime—or the exaggerated fear of crime engendered by sensationalistic media coverage and elite-driven narratives. The law, too, features prominently in many analyses of mass incarceration—especially substantive law, which is the body of law that determines what counts as a crime and which punishments are authorized upon conviction. A vast literature documents the steady growth of new criminal offenses, the broadening of old ones, the intensification of criminal penalties, and the connections between each of these developments and mass incarceration. Less appreciated, however, are the insidious yet profound ways in which procedural law has helped propel the unprecedented carceral buildup of the past half-century, forming what this chapter terms the procedural architecture of mass incarceration.

DOI: 10.4324/9781003274292-3

The chapter begins by examining procedural rules and practices related to policing, which legitimize widespread intrusions and arrests disproportionately targeting people of color and the poor and pave the way for mass prosecutions, convictions, and imprisonment in later stages of the criminal process. It then turns to the law of bail and pretrial release, which empowers prosecutors and judges to incarcerate vast numbers of people pending trial—people who stand convicted of no crime and, supposedly, are presumed innocent—on account of their poverty and race. The following two sections discuss the law that governs plea bargaining and the right to counsel, arguing that the judiciary's toleration of coercive negotiation tactics and of a cash-starved, dysfunctional indigent defense system throws America's putatively adversarial system completely off-balance and facilitates the mass production of convictions and punishment. The chapter concludes by suggesting that those engaged in the struggle for freedom should include among their core demands a program aimed at dismantling the procedural architecture of mass incarceration.

Unreasonable Arrests and Arbitrary Stops: The Law of Policing and Mass Incarceration's Front Door

If, following the suggestion of this chapter's title, one were to form a mental picture of the U.S. imprisonment system as a building and to visualize procedural law as the architectural blueprint for that building, policing might be thought of as the system's "front door" (Miller et al., 2018) and the law of policing as the design that determines the door's shape and size. A tightly drawn scheme of legal regulation for policing—in particular, one that meaningfully restricted investigative activity and arrests—would trim down the system's front door and naturally limit the number of people who could advance into the building's inner recesses, while a lax scheme would achieve the opposite. On the whole, the law of policing fits the latter description, often serving to "legitimize police activity rather than curtail it" (Ristroph, 2017, p. 1194) and funneling a steady supply of arrested persons, most of them poor and Black, into the criminal adjudicative process to be made into "prisoners."

The most direct link between policing and incarceration lies in the power of police to arrest. An arrest not only initiates a criminal prosecution, carrying with it a high likelihood of eventual conviction and, potentially, a sentence of imprisonment; it also typically results in the arrested person getting booked and incarcerated in a local jail facility while waiting for a judge or prosecutor to review the arresting officer's decision. Many arrestees languish in jail for days, weeks, or sometimes even months before anyone—judge, prosecutor, or defense counsel—meaningfully scrutinizes the legality of their arrest or the need for prolonged pretrial incarceration. Some arrestees simply give up and plead guilty to escape the nightmare of pretrial incarceration, never receiving the benefit of any criminal process beyond the arresting officer's unilateral decision (Metzger & Hoeffel, 2020).[1]

Nor does the underlying legal standard for judging the validity of an arrest—the probable cause standard—significantly constrain police authority. Statutory definitions of crime cast a net sufficiently wide to make criminals out of many people much of the time. Jaywalking, driving with a broken taillight, driving 60 mph in a 55 mph zone, playing music at a volume that troubles a neighbor, and rolling a joint—each of these commonplace behaviors and countless others may violate a criminal statute, furnishing a police officer with probable cause and, hence, the power to effect an arrest (Butler, 2016). In fact, the Supreme Court has held that the Constitution permits officers to arrest, book, and jail a person for committing fine-only traffic offenses, paradoxically empowering the police to incarcerate people who have not been convicted of a crime based on nothing more than probable cause in situations where judges would lack the power to impose incarceration as the sentence for a conviction supported by proof beyond a reasonable doubt (*Atwater v. City of Lago Vista*, 2001).

It is certainly true that police officers frequently exercise discretion not to make arrests in scenarios where the law permits them to do so—and the same goes for other key policing techniques such as stops, frisks, and vehicular searches. But this is hardly a satisfactory solution to the underlying problem, for "the power to be lenient is the power to discriminate" (Davis, 1976, p. 176). By rendering a large cross-section of the population vulnerable to police intrusion and, potentially, arrest but leaving officers almost entirely free to pick and choose their targets as they wish, procedural law enables police to inundate the criminal courts with people who bear stigma and lack power—often people of color, people living in poverty, and people with mental disabilities—while generally sparing those who conform to white middle-class standards of respectability. Both of these dynamics contribute to mass imprisonment: the first by furnishing bodies to fill prison beds, and the second by undermining the prospects for broad-based countermobilization backed by elites to resist the relentless expansion of the carceral state.

Incarceration without Conviction: The Law of Bail and Pretrial Release

Of the 1.9 million people living behind bars in the United States, around one in three are housed in a jail as opposed to a prison or other carceral facility (Sawyer & Wagner, 2022). A staggering 533,000 people—which accounts for 28% of the entire incarcerated population—are pretrial detainees who have not been convicted of any crime (Sawyer & Wagner, 2022). Most pretrial detainees are poor people who cannot afford to post bail, and a disproportionate share of them are people of color (Arnold et al., 2018). As Wiseman (2018) and others have shown, America's sprawling and discriminatory pretrial detention scheme powers mass incarceration through various mechanisms. Most directly, it relegates hundreds of thousands of people each year to jail while their criminal cases await resolution—a period that often lasts weeks or months but occasionally drags on for years. Beyond this, it also (1) pressures detained defendants to take unfavorable plea offers, (2) hampers their ability to consult with counsel and defend themselves at both the guilt/innocence and sentencing stages, and (3) stymies political mobilization against mass incarceration by sheltering those with financial resources and racial privilege from the horrors of imprisonment.

Money bail is the most common tool that American courts use in deciding who should be released pending trial and who must wait in jail during the pretrial period. In theory, when bail is set, the bail amount is supposed to be no higher than what is needed to ensure the defendant shows up for court and, in many jurisdictions, to prevent commission of new crimes on release. Yet in practice, bail-setting judges all too often fail to carefully assess whether a defendant presents a serious risk of no-showing for court or committing new crimes on release and how much bail, if any, is necessary to manage that risk. Bail hearings are rushed, informal affairs that last no longer than a few minutes on average. At this early stage, many defendants have no lawyer to assist them in making the case for low bail or release without bail, prosecutors are rarely required to disclose relevant information to the defense, and judges typically have little or no information about the alleged offense or the defendant's risk profile beyond the crumbs that can be gleaned from a police report and a rap sheet. At the risk of stating the obvious, this is not a recipe for fair and informed decision-making. To the contrary, the dearth of available information and the hurried, often uncontested nature of the bail proceeding invites prosecutors and judges to rely on racial and class biases and other cognitive shortcuts in lieu of facts when evaluating the risk posed by criminal defendants (Stevenson & Mayson, 2017).

Bail proceedings also typically fail to adequately consider each defendant's financial condition and how much cash or collateral, if any, the defendant can put forward to secure release. Many judges, in fact, do not consider these factors *at all*: in much of the country, judges simply pick a number off a bail schedule that lists predetermined bail amounts for various charges—say, $1,000 for trespass or $5,000 for a robbery—even if that amount exceeds what the defendant can scrape together and thus will lead to the defendant's pretrial incarceration (Pretrial Justice Institute, 2009). To be sure, efforts to reform the pretrial process have gained considerable ground over the past few years, especially efforts to diminish or eliminate reliance on money bail and expand alternatives to bail such as nonfinancial release conditions (common examples include supervision by a pretrial services agency and routine drug testing) or release on recognizance. But the progress we have seen so far has been geographically uneven (rural areas are lagging), vulnerable to backlash, and insufficiently ambitious (Baughman et al., 2021). As a result, the law of bail remains a cornerstone in the procedural architecture of mass incarceration, enabling the transfer of millions of bodies from the community into jail cells for pretrial detention every year (Sawyer & Wagner, 2022) and ensuring that the burdens of incarceration fall disproportionately on the shoulders of poor people and people of color.

The Charge-to-Conviction Pipeline: The Law of Plea Negotiation

The adjudicative process for criminal offenses contemplated by those who wrote the U.S. Constitution revolved around the adversarial and public trial: a trial where the defendant would have the opportunity to dispute the prosecution's allegations and where the arbitrary exercise of government power would be restrained, or so the theory went, by giving lay jurors control over the verdict and by opening the criminal process to the watchful eye of an engaged citizenry (Bibas, 2006). Criminal trials, however, have all but vanished from the American legal landscape. Instead of trials, the modern criminal justice apparatus generates convictions and incarcerative sentences without adversarial contestation or public scrutiny through guilty pleas, which now account for more than 95% of felony convictions and, in all likelihood, a far greater share of misdemeanor convictions (Kohler-Hausmann, 2014; Turner, 2017). Mass incarceration depends on this arrangement. Whereas trials consume scarce resources and yield uncertain outcomes, guilty pleas help prosecutors efficiently convert mere allegations into convictions and, often, jail or prison sentences. By lowering the price of criminal adjudication, guilty pleas increase the criminal justice system's demand for and production of punishment (Hessick, 2021), making the law of plea negotiation an integral component of mass incarceration's procedural architecture.

Until relatively recently, American law allowed defendants to plead guilty if they wished but generally did not permit prosecutors and judges to pressure them into doing so by dangling promises of leniency for incriminating themselves or by threatening harsher punishment for going to trial. To be sure, there were precursors to the modern plea agreement that cropped up during the 19th century, and negotiated dispositions had become prevalent by the 1920s and quite possibly earlier. These early plea markets, however, operated underground and were widely condemned as illegitimate by elite segments of the bar. As plea agreements continued to proliferate, the legal profession and the courts gradually came to embrace them (Ortman, 2020). In a string of cases decided between 1970 and 1978, the Supreme Court declared that plea bargaining was constitutional (*Brady v. United States*, 1970), praised it as "an essential component of the administration of justice" (*Santobello v. New York*, 1971, p. 261), and even countenanced the tactics of a prosecutor who offered a five-year plea for the crime of writing a bad check in the amount of $88.30 while threatening that, if the defendant turned down the plea, the prosecutor would seek to convict him under a "habitual offender law" carrying a mandatory life sentence (*Bordenkircher v. Hayes*, 1978). Although judges still pay lip service to the rule that a guilty plea must be voluntary and not coerced, they routinely sign off on plea agreements in which defendants trade away their constitutional rights out of fear of the stiff penalties that lie in store for people who take their cases to trial (Turner, 2017).

In the context of any particular criminal case, of course, a guilty plea will often be the best option available to a defendant and will lower the expected punishment the defendant is facing. But that is only because prosecutors, armed by legislatures with a lengthy menu of possible charges, some of which carrying exorbitant or mandatory penalties that can be relinquished for leverage, as well as judges reserve criminal law's most draconian punishments for the few defendants who have the audacity to profess their innocence and insist on having a trial. Substantive criminal law (defined above) has evolved in conjunction with the deregulation of plea negotiation such that defendants who plead guilty do not in any meaningful sense catch a break or "beat the house" (*Lafler v. Cooper*, 2012, dissenting opinion of Justice Scalia, p. 186). Instead, they tend to receive more or less the punishment that law enforcers and lawmakers consider appropriate under the circumstances. Defendants who plead not guilty, by contrast, are exposed to inflated charges and disproportionate sentences in order to make an example out of them and thereby deter future defendants from going to trial. The modern system of pleas allows criminal justice officials to have their cake and eat it too, streamlining the mass production of convictions without substantially decreasing the average penalty per conviction and drastically expanding the criminal justice system's overall capacity to punish (Alschuler, 2021).

Adversarial Imbalance: The Anemic Right to Counsel

Most people who stand accused of a crime in this country are too poor to hire a lawyer; without governmental assistance, they would have to navigate the complexities of the modern criminal process—and square off against a legally trained prosecutor—without the guiding hand of counsel. In an effort to equalize access to legal representation, the Supreme Court held in *Gideon v. Wainwright* (1963) that, at least in felony prosecutions, the state must furnish counsel to defendants who cannot afford to retain counsel on their own. Yet half a century later, the project of guaranteeing effective representation for indigent criminal defendants remains radically incomplete. Zealous defense advocacy is vital not only to safeguard individual defendants against wrongful convictions, excessive sentences, and unfair treatment, but also as a way of moderating the breakneck speed and casual indifference of criminal case processing that undergird mass incarceration. Many impoverished criminal defendants, however, do not receive a vigorous defense from a skillful, adequately resourced lawyer. Many, in fact, never receive any legal representation whatsoever.

Constitutional right to counsel doctrine is riddled with loopholes that make it possible for the state to deny or unduly delay appointment of counsel in a large subset of criminal cases. Although case law requires appointment of counsel in felony prosecutions and in misdemeanor prosecutions that result in an actual or suspended (*i.e.*, probationary) sentence of incarceration, the Supreme Court has held that *Gideon* is inapplicable in other misdemeanor cases, leaving numerous defendants charged with lower-level offenses out in the cold (King, 2013). Moreover, *Gideon* does not say how poor a defendant must be to qualify as indigent, and some jurisdictions define indigency so restrictively as to box out all but the most desperately impoverished defendants (Gershowitz, 2005). Even in cases that indisputably are covered by *Gideon*, states and localities frequently drag their feet on appointing counsel for as long as they can get away with—subjecting impoverished defendants to a heightened risk of self-incrimination, excessive bail, and pretrial incarceration while waiting for counsel to be appointed—and put pressure on defendants, especially incarcerated defendants, to waive their right to counsel and plead guilty (Harvey et al., 2018; Metzger & Hoeffel, 2020). As a result, numerous indigent defendants never get the help of a lawyer while many others receive legal representation too late to do them much good.

Ensuring that the state promptly appoints counsel for indigent defendants is just half the battle; state systems for delivering defense services must also be adequately funded and designed in a way that fosters skillful, client-centered representation. Yet "[t]here is broad agreement that indigent-defense delivery systems in this country are grossly inadequate" (Primus, 2017, p. 121). Dozens of reports distilling decades of research in a variety of court systems have documented widespread underfunding of indigent defense, appalling attorney caseloads that in some places average more than five times the American Bar Association's recommended limits, and intense pressure on appointed lawyers to tread lightly and collaborate with prosecutors and courts to close cases quickly so as to remain in the good graces of judges who control the appointment process. While right to counsel doctrine theoretically guarantees a right not only to counsel but to the *effective assistance* of counsel, the latter right is narrow in scope, legal remedies for its violation are feeble, and the reality on the ground is that indigent defense systems in many states and localities set defense counsel up to fail (Murray, 2020; Primus, 2020). Criminal defendants are thus deprived of capable advocates to protect their interests, and the adjudicative process as a whole is stripped of its putatively adversarial character, freeing prosecutors to seek convictions and harsh punishments unhindered by the restraining influence of an effective opponent.

Dismantling the Procedural Architecture of Mass Incarceration

The core claim advanced in this chapter is that procedural law has played a pivotal role in creating and sustaining mass incarceration. To substantiate this claim, I have argued that the law of policing equips officers with powerful tools to investigate, arrest, and even temporarily incarcerate people based on flimsy justifications and with little prospect of outside oversight; the law of bail and pretrial release authorizes prolonged pretrial incarceration of a vast number of presumptively innocent individuals who have not been convicted of any crime but who are too poor to pay their way out of jail while awaiting disposition of their cases; the law of plea negotiation empowers prosecutors and judges to threaten exorbitant punishments for people who take their cases to trial, coercing defendants to waive their rights through guilty pleas; and the law of defense representation leaves numerous defendants stranded without defense counsel or else represented by an ineffective, overwhelmed defense lawyer, upsetting the balance within America's ostensibly adversarial system and disabling a potential barrier to the mass production of convictions and incarceration sentences. There are surely other facets of procedural law, beyond these four, that also contribute to the swelling of America's prisons and jails. Some authors, for instance, have laid a share of the blame for mass incarceration on prosecutors' largely unregulated control over criminal charging (Pfaff, 2017), on the diminishment of parole and other so-called second look procedures (Barkow, 2019), on underinvestment in alternatives to the traditional, adversarial criminal process such as restorative justice (Sered, 2019), and on the enlargement of defendants' procedural rights at trial, which, by raising the cost and complexity of the criminal trial, may have unwittingly hastened its demise (Pizzi, 2020). Though the analysis sketched here revolves around the law of policing, bail and pretrial release, plea negotiation, and defense representation, this chapter's broader lesson is that American law fosters mass incarceration not only through the conduct it criminalizes and the punishments it authorizes (*i.e.*, through substantive criminal law), but also through the procedural mechanisms it establishes for investigating, adjudicating, and imposing punishment for crime.

Since procedural law is among the pillars propping up America's colossal system of human caging, an ambitious set of demands for criminal procedure reform needs to be part of the larger struggle against mass incarceration. Fortunately, much of the work that must be done is well underway. When it comes to policing and bail reform, in particular, activists, people directly impacted by the criminal justice system, lawyers, and policymakers have energetically challenged procedural rules and practices that disproportionately expose poor people and people of color to unjustifiable police intrusion, prosecution, and imprisonment, and this agitation has helped usher in valuable procedural reforms in states and cities across the country. But other key deficiencies in American procedural law, such as the deregulation of abusive plea bargaining and the failure to guarantee effective representation for indigent criminal defendants, continue to fly under the radar, rarely attracting attention outside the pages of academic law journals. With criminal justice reform and racial justice movements raising critical awareness and gaining momentum, the time is ripe to lay bare the procedural architecture of mass incarceration and plan for its demolition.

Discussion Questions:

1 How do criminal procedure rules and practices in the areas of policing, bail, plea negotiation, and defense representation contribute to mass incarceration? Can you think of other branches of procedural law that might also fuel America's system of imprisonment?
2 How might criminal justice advocates reform or reimagine criminal procedure so as to sever its connections to mass incarceration?

Note

1 Although constitutional doctrine entitles a defendant to a probable cause hearing within 48 hours of a warrantless arrest (*County of Riverside v. McLaughlin*, 1991), the required hearings are highly informal and nonadversarial—indeed, they can be held ex parte, outside the presence of the defendant and his or her lawyer—and they predictably lead in almost every instance to rubber-stamping the arrest. There is nothing to stop courts and legislatures from going beyond this weak constitutional rule by providing for prompt and robust review of arrest decisions, and some have done so. Many, however, choose not to (Metzger & Hoeffel, 2020).

References

Alschuler, A.W. (2021). Plea Bargaining and Mass Incarceration. *New York University Annual Survey of American Law*, 76(2), 205–234.
Arnold, D., Dobbie, W., & Yang, C.S. (2018). Racial Bias in Bail Decisions. *The Quarterly Journal of Economics*, 133(4), 1885–1932.
Atwater v. City of Lago Vista, 532 U.S. 318 (2001).
Barkow, R.E. (2019). *Prisoners of Politics: Breaking the Cycle of Mass Incarceration*. Cambridge, MA: Harvard University Press.
Baughman, S.B., Boone, L., & Jackson, N. (2021). Reforming State Bail Reform. *SMU Law Review*, 74(3), 447–474.
Bibas, S. (2006). Transparency and Participation in Criminal Procedure. *New York University Law Review*, 81(3), 911–966.
Bordenkircher v. Hayes, 434 U.S. 357 (1978).
Brady v. United States, 397 U.S. 742 (1970).
Butler, P. (2016). The System Is Working the Way It Is Supposed to: The Limits of Criminal Justice Reform. *Georgetown Law Journal*, 104(6), 1419–1478.
County of Riverside v. McLaughlin, 500 U.S. 44 (1991).
Davis, K.C. (1976). *Discretionary Justice: A Preliminary Inquiry*. Champaign: University of Illinois Press. 5th ed.
Gershowitz, A.M. (2005). The Invisible Pillar of *Gideon*. *Indiana Law Journal*, 80(3), 571–604.
Gideon v. Wainwright, 372 U.S. 335 (1963).
Harvey, T.B., Rosenfeld, J.H., & Tomascak, S. (2018). Right to Counsel in Misdemeanor Prosecutions after *Alabama v. Shelton*: No-Lawyer-Courts and Their Consequences on the Poor and Communities of Color in St. Louis. *Criminal Justice Policy Review*, 29(6–7), 688–709.
Hessick, C.B. (2021). *Punishment Without Trial: Why Plea Bargaining Is a Bad Deal*. New York: Abrams Press.
King, J.D. (2013). Beyond "Life and Liberty": The Evolving Right to Counsel. *Harvard Civil Rights-Civil Liberties Law Review*, 48(1), 1–50.
Kohler-Hausmann, I. (2014). Managerial Justice and Mass Misdemeanors. *Stanford Law Review*, 66(3), 611–694.
Lafler v. Cooper, 566 U.S. 156 (2012).
Metzger, P.R., & Hoeffel, J.C. (2020). Criminal (Dis)Appearance. *George Washington Law Review*, 88(2), 392–453.
Miller, R.J., Kern, L.J., & Williams, A. (2018). The Front End of the Carceral State: Police Stops, Court Fines, and the Racialization of Due Process. *Social Service Review*, 92(2), 290–303.
Murray, J. (2020). Prejudice-Based Rights in Criminal Procedure. *University of Pennsylvania Law Review*, 168(2), 277–329.
National Research Council. (2014). *The Growth of Incarceration in the United States: Exploring Causes and Consequences* (pp. 33–129), J. Travis, B. Western, & F.S. Redburn (Eds.). National Academies Press.
Ortman, W. (2020). When Plea Bargaining Became Normal. *Boston University Law Review*, 100(4), 1435–1500.
Pfaff, J.F. (2017). *Locked In: The True Causes of Mass Incarceration — And How to Achieve Real Reform*. New York: Basic Books.
Pizzi, W.T. (2020). *The Supreme Court's Role in Mass Incarceration*. New York: Routledge.
Pretrial Justice Institute. (2009). *Pretrial Justice in America: A Survey of County Pretrial Release Policies, Practices and Outcomes*. https://biblioteca.cejamericas.org/bitstream/handle/2015/3094/PJI_Pretrial_Justice_in_America_Survey_2010.pdf?sequence=1&isAllowed=y
Primus, E.B. (2017). Defense Counsel and Public Defense. In E. Luna (Ed.), *Reforming Criminal Justice* (Vol. 3, pp. 121–145). Phoenix, AZ: Academy for Justice.

Primus, E.B. (2020). Disaggregating Ineffective Assistance of Counsel Doctrine: Four Forms of Constitutional Ineffectiveness. *Stanford Law Review*, 72(6), 1581–1653.

Ristroph, A. (2017). The Constitution of Police Violence. *UCLA Law Review*, 64(5), 1182–1245.

Santobello v. New York, 404 U.S. 257 (1971).

Sawyer, W. & Wagner, P. 2022. *Mass Incarceration: The Whole Pie 2022*. Retrieved June 17, 2022, from https://www.prisonpolicy.org/reports/pie2022.html.

Sered, D. (2019). *Until We Reckon: Violence, Mass Incarceration, and a Road to Repair*. New York: The New Press.

Stevenson, M., & Mayson, S.G. (2017). Pretrial Detention and Bail. In E. Luna (Ed.), *Reforming Criminal Justice* (Vol. 3, pp. 21–47). Phoenix, AZ: Academy for Justice.

Turner, J. (2017). Plea Bargaining. In E. Luna (Ed.), *Reforming Criminal Justice* (Vol. 3, pp. 73–99). Phoenix, AZ: Academy for Justice.

Wiseman, S.R. (2018). Bail and Mass Incarceration. *Georgia Law Review*, 53(1), 235–280.

2

BAIL, PRETRIAL DETENTION, AND MASS INCARCERATION

Karen F. Lahm

LEARNING OUTCOMES:

Upon successful completion of this chapter, students will be able to:

1 Understand the origins of bail in the United States and the types of pretrial release.
2 Understand how changes in bail and pretrial detention have fueled mass incarceration among the poor and disenfranchised, especially in local jails.
3 Explain how a variety of bail/pretrial detention reforms could potentially decrease mass incarceration in the United States.

Brief History of Bail in the United States

Simply put, "bail is the temporary release of someone awaiting trial for a crime" (Baughman, 2017, p. 1). Bail has been a cornerstone of criminal justice systems throughout the world. It was initially created not to determine the guilt of the accused or punish them, but rather to ensure that they appeared at their trial where guilt would be decided. Borrowing from English common law, in the American Colonies, the first iteration of bail took the form of a personal surety system. In this process, the accused would have family members and/or other individuals "stand in for them" by promising to pay their fines, tariffs, or debts only if they defaulted on their payments or did not show up for trial. This system was merely a promise to pay, and not an up-front payment to have the accused released from jail (see Schnacke, 2018). The key element in the use of personal sureties was the fact that these individuals could not personally profit from or acquire any type of monetary compensation for being a surety. In fact, the surety could even have the defendant arrested and returned to jail. However, as time passed and the United States developed, there were simply not enough individuals willing to serve as a personal surety; thus, more individuals were being detained in jail.

As the use of personal sureties declined, American courts in the early 20th century began to use commercial sureties (or secured financial conditions in the form of cash or surety

DOI: 10.4324/9781003274292-4

bonds) to ensure a defendant's release from jail. This movement gave rise to the use of private bail bond companies and self-pay, leading to the more modern system of bail that we see in the United States today, where the accused has to essentially pay in the form of money or collateral for their release if a personal surety cannot be found. Defendants who used commercial bail bond companies had to pay up-front fees or provide some kind of collateral on the bail bond (VanBrunt & Bowman, 2018). Although purposeful and intentional detainment of individuals has always been prohibited by judges, this changeover to commercial sureties allowed for the pretrial detention of defendants simply because they did not have the financial wherewithal to pay for their release.

Across the world and especially in the United States, bail is often viewed as a constitutional right with its foundations in due process and the notion that a defendant is innocent until proven guilty. Although the right to bail is not specifically codified in the U.S. Constitution, the Eighth Amendment says that "excessive bail shall not be required, nor excessive fines imposed, nor cruel and unusual punishments inflicted" (U.S. Const., Amend. VIII). Based on these rights, early U.S. courts made use of bail in all cases, except capital cases per the Judiciary Act of 1789 (see Baughman, 2017). Again, bail was seen as the key mechanism to compel the accused to come back to court and stand trial. Bail was not used in determining guilt or innocence. Unfortunately, bail did not guarantee that the accused would not commit more crimes or flee before trial.

As the 20th century emerged, several reforms in bail occurred in the United States. The first of those was the Bail Reform Act of 1966. According to Wald and Freed (1966):

> It requires judicial officers, in shaping release conditions appropriate to risk, to consider the accused's family, employment, and community ties, in addition to his criminal record and history of nonappearance at trial. And it imposes severe penalties for failure to appear so that criminal prosecutions supplant bail bond forfeitures as the primary sanction against defendants who flee.
>
> *(p. 940)*

Moreover, this federal law allowed bail to be implemented in *noncapital* cases, prior to trial, if the accused could post the necessary cash bond or promise to return to court to stand trial, without bail. This ruling gave rise to the release of individuals from jail based on their own recognizance or the release from jail without paying any bail bond. The defendant had to promise to appear back in court when required to do so. Hopkins, Bains, and Doyle (2019) suggest that release on recognizance should be maximized as "very few defendants abscond pretrial" (p. 683). Moreover, they cite numerous studies indicating that the great majority of those released on recognizance successfully appear before court and do not recidivate.

Another reform to federal bail laws occurred in 1970 with the District of Columbia Court Reform and Criminal Procedure Act. Prior to this law, judges could only detain defendants based on flight risk. However, this legislation, also known as the D.C. Crime Bill, authorized pretrial detention for those who committed serious and/or violent crimes posing imminent danger to the community if released (Congress clears controversial D.C. crime control bill, 1971).

The next significant reform to bail in the United States came almost a decade later with the Bail Reform Act of 1984. This piece of legislation allowed for the use of pretrial detention of the accused based on their "dangerousness to the community" and not simply their flight risk (Baughman, 2017). Community safety became one of the lynchpins to granting bail along with the seriousness of the offense, criminal history (i.e., currently on probation, etc.), flight risk or failure to appear, and the personal history of the accused. Judges were required to hold detention hearings for defendants who fit these specific criteria. The case of *United States vs. Salerno* (1987) cemented the use of pretrial detention for those defendants who posed a perceived danger to the community upon their release (National Association on Fines, Fees & Bail Practices, 2019). As Baughman points out, "The pretrial bail decision became whether to release a person on bail rather than how to release the person on bail" (2017, p. 22). Soon after this, the early 1990s saw the emergence of pretrial service agencies whose sole job was to perform risk assessments regarding the suitability of defendants for pretrial release or detention.

In summary, it is evident that bail in the United States has shifted from a mechanism ensuring appearance at trial to one that now considers flight risk, community safety, etc., in pretrial detention hearings. Once the key pieces of federal bail reform noted above took hold, states soon followed with their own laws that allowed for the *presumption of detention* rather than a *presumption of innocence* and release on bail until trial. Over the past three decades, what has emerged is a system of bail in the United States where the wealthy can afford to pay for pretrial release and the indigent are incarcerated. This mass incarceration due to the changes to bail and pretrial detention has clogged the correctional system with poor defendants awaiting trial, especially at the local level in jails.

Types of Pretrial Release in the United States

After someone is arrested, they will usually be arraigned (i.e., a judge presents the charges and the defendant enters their plea) within 24–48 hours (Lockwood & Griffin, 2020).. At that time, the judge can either release the accused on their own recognizance where there is no fee paid, set a bail amount, or deny bail. Again, the type and amount of bail are determined by the judge. Many courts use a specific fee schedule when setting bail, and some judges are required by statute to not allow bail to specific defendants. It is important to note that "monetary bail is typically assigned without any assessment of a person's ability to pay" (Digard, 2019, p. 6). The amount of bail or whether to allow bail at all depends on several criteria, such as flight risk, severity/type of crime, future criminality, etc. If the accused is poor, it is oftentimes the family of the accused that secures a private bail bond. Unfortunately, this money is not returned after trial, even if the accused is found not guilty.

Within the United States, there are several ways that bail can be administered. As mentioned above, the surety bond is secured through a private/commercial bail bondsman and requires cash (usually 10% of the total bail cost) and some form of collateral for release. There are some states that can require 12% and up to 15% for bonds. Those who do not show up for court hearings can be returned to jail for having "skipped bail." With this type of bond, most defendants have to pay the bail bondsman back, which usually is done over time. Defendants can also pay the full cash bail amount to the court and be released from jail or post 10% of the bail amount themselves. This cash money is returned to the accused if the charges are dropped or if they are found guilty or not guilty. Next is the property bond which uses one's property, such as homes, cars, etc., as collateral instead of cash. Lastly, the accused can also be released on their own recognizance, which requires no payment but instead involves a written promise to return to court for trial. There are also bail bonds for individuals accused of federal offenses and immigration bail bonds, which are used by non-citizens of the United States who are accused of a crime. The availability of each of these types of bail bonds varies across each state in the United States

Demographic Data on Bail and the Use of Pretrial Detention in the United States

Over the past three decades or so, the U.S. jail population has skyrocketed. In 1984, there were 234,500 adults serving time in jails, with 51% of these individuals being people not convicted (i.e., awaiting court action or held for another reason) (Banuach, Sickmund & Ford, 1986). At the end of 2019, there were just under 2.1 million adults incarcerated in the United States, with roughly 734,500 confined in local jails (Kluckow & Zeng, 2022). On closer examination, in 2019, 67% of those serving time in jail were *not convicted* and 33% were convicted but awaiting a sentence (Zeng & Minton, 2021a). In urban jails, the percentage of not convicted was 68%, compared to 59% of people in jail in rural areas. Moreover, in 2019, 16 states had non-convicted jail populations at or over 70%. Illinois had the largest non-convicted jail population at 89.3% (Zeng & Minton, 2021a).

Jails are not the only pretrial detention facilities. The federal prison system also detains people awaiting trial for federal crimes. There are also immigration detention facilities, tribal jails, and juvenile facilities. Researchers suggest there could be an additional 88,000 individuals serving pretrial detention outside of county/local jails (Sawyer & Wagner, 2022). Interestingly, while the non-convicted population in jails has grown, the convicted population has remained relatively stable, with some decline. In fact, the number of convicted people serving time in jail from 2010 to 2019 dropped by 13% (Minton & Zeng, 2021). This growth in U.S. jails of the non-convicted population and the decrease in the convicted population is clearly driving mass incarceration in our jails.

Many researchers believe that it is the increased use of pretrial detention that is fueling the decades-long surge in jail populations, especially the jail population that is not convicted. More specifically, they point to the inequity in the cash bail system in the United States as the major impetus behind the proliferation of pretrial detention. Remember, bail was originally not paid before trial, but rather it was used to guarantee that someone would show up at court. Now, what we are seeing is that some kind of up-front payment—either personal bail payments or the use of a commercial bail agent—is needed to secure pretrial release. Sawyer and Wagner (2022) found that the median bail amount in the United States is roughly $10,000. A closer examination revealed that those serving pretrial detention in jail (males and females aged 23–39) reported median pre-incarceration incomes of just under $16,000 and just over $11,000, respectively. Rabuy and Kopf (2016) concluded that "most people who are unable to meet bail fall within the poorest third of society" (p. 2). These authors provide evidence that those serving time in jail are even poorer than those serving time in state/federal prisons compared to their non-incarcerated counterparts (see Rabuy & Kopf, 2016).

Reaves (2013) authored the most recent government report examining the processing of felony defendants in large urban counties. Data on state court felony filings from 40 of the nation's 75 largest counties from 1990 to 2009 were analyzed. Results from this report showed that 60% of pretrial releases in 2009 included financial conditions, with 80% of these cases using private surety bonds (Reaves, 2013). Of great importance is that 90% of the accused were unable to secure the finances to be released from jail. The report found that "those with a bail amount set under $5,000 were nearly three times as likely to secure release as defendants with a bail amount of $50,000 or more" (Reaves, 2013, p. 15). Those defendants accused of more serious person-centered crimes (e.g., rape and robbery) were the ones facing the highest bail amounts ($100,000 for rape and $1,000,000 for murder), while those accused of larceny/theft had bail amounts under the $5,000 mark. Overall, Reaves (2013) reported that the percentage of pretrial releases involving monetary conditions rose from 37% to 61% over his 30-year study period. Again, commercial surety bonds accounted for the biggest increase in these percentages. These statistics make it glaringly apparent that bail is for the wealthy, while years of indebtedness to a bail bondsman or no pretrial release at all is for the poor. Since the release of this report by Reaves, updated information on bail amounts, bail conditions, etc., has not been published. Moreover, detailed information on people in jail, especially non-convicted individuals, is quite scarce in the corrections literature.

Preceding this study, Cohen and Reaves (2007) found that 1998 was a major turning point for the use of bail and/or other financial conditions to obtain a release in advance of trial. Before 1998, non-financial releases were more prevalent for felony defendants, in particular, as compared to financial releases. This year saw not only an increase in financial releases but also saw surety bonds become the most common type of pretrial release compared to recognizance, which again was the main form of non-financial pretrial release prior to 1998 (roughly 40% of felony cases). Cohen and Reaves (2007) surmise that "the higher the bail amount set, the lower the probability of pretrial release" (p. 1).

Looking at the characteristics of people in jail in the United States reveals disparities in race, social class, etc. Unfortunately, this data does not parcel out the unique differences between convicted people and the non-convicted people. First, in 2019, there were some 10,300,000 people processed through American jails (Zeng & Minton, 2021b). That number is actually down from the 2008 numbers from a decade earlier (13,600,000 processed). Some researchers call this "jail churn." Sawyer and Wagner (2022) state that "some have just been arrested and will make bail within hours or days, while many others are too poor to make bail and remain behind bars until trial." (p. 6). This furthers the cycle of mass incarceration for the poor and disenfranchised in local jails.

Other demographic characteristics of those incarcerated in jails reveal that in 2019, the rates of jail incarceration were much higher for people of color, specifically African Americans and Native American/Pacific Islanders (600 and 420, respectively, per 100,000) versus whites (184 per 100,000). Moreover, 70% of these people in 2019 were being held on felony charges and 23% for misdemeanor offenses (Zeng & Minton, 2021b). As mentioned previously, the highest bail amounts (over $50,000) are often given to those who are accused of more serious crimes, though these same individuals may be denied bail as well (Cohen & Reaves, 2007). In 2009, median bail amounts for those detained in jail were $50,000 for violent offenses, $19,000 for property, $20,000 for drug, and $20,000 for public order (Reaves, 2013). This is the most recent information on bail amounts for detained individuals in jails. Consider these median bail amounts in light of the fact that 60% of Americans cannot afford either a $500 or $1000 emergency with the money in their savings (Bennett, 2022) and yet, we are expecting the poorest in our country to afford money bail. Even the 10% owed to a private bail bondsman is out of the reach of most Americans.

Again, these are prime examples of how money bail fuels mass incarceration among the poorest Americans.

No story better highlights the racial and class inequity in the U.S. bail system than that of Kalief Browder (see Ofer, 2017). In 2010, at the age of 16, Kalief Browder was arrested for stealing a backpack. He was charged with robbery, grand larceny, and assault. As such, his bail was set at $3,000. Unfortunately, his family could not afford to bail Kalief out of jail, so he ended up spending almost three years of pretrial detention at Rikers Island, much of which was in solitary confinement. Reports suggest that Kalief rejected several plea deals as he maintained his innocence. He was eventually released from Rikers Island when his case was dismissed. Tragically, Kalief committed suicide in 2015. This story is just one of numerous instances in the U.S. criminal justice system of how being poor results in pretrial detention for those who have not yet been found guilty of a crime. Poverty often results in jail, even if one has not been convicted.

Effects of Pretrial Detention

The long-term effects of incarceration (prison) have received a lot of attention, but researchers have just begun to explore the negative effects of short-term (jail) pretrial detention upon the accused. A study by Dobbie, Goldin and Yang (2018) of over 150,000 court records in Kentucky found that those who were detained were less likely to appear in court, with longer detentions producing greater rates of failure to appear. Detained respondents in their sample were also more likely to be found guilty, to plead guilty, and to be less successful at finding employment and securing government benefits after release.

Another recent study by Holsinger and Holsinger (2018) discovered that those who served longer time in pretrial detention were more likely to report employment disruption (e.g., job change or job loss), harm to their financial footing, residential instability, and a negative impact on their dependents. Research prior to that by Heaton, Mason, and Stevenson (2017) found similar results for pretrial detention and guilty pleas involving misdemeanor cases. Moreover, these authors also showed that pretrial detention increased future criminality in their sample. Specifically, eighteen months after detention, the authors showed a 20% increase in new misdemeanor charges and 30% increase in new felony charges (Heaton, Mason, & Stevenson, 2017). In addition, there has also been an established link between pretrial detention and sentencing outcomes. According to Digard (2019), "Research demonstrates that people who spend time in pretrial detention receive harsher sentences—sentences that are more likely to include incarceration for a longer period of time—than those who spend the pretrial period at liberty" (for a full review see Digard, 2019, p. 5). This relationship held true for people confined in pretrial detention for both low-level offenses and felonies. Lastly, Digard (2019) found that detained individuals also face higher court costs, on top of their bail fines. Thus, the cycle of debt simply continues.

Nowhere are the effects of pretrial detention due to the inability to afford bail more evident than among people of color. Again, as mentioned previously, judges sentencing defendants often do not consider the person's ability to pay bail. Rather, judges often assign fixed payments depending on the severity of the crime. Some of these dollar amounts are even set specifically by law, so judges may not be able to alter the amounts (i.e., lower them). A report by the Council of Economic Advisors (2015) reveals that high set/fixed bail amounts lead to the depletion of both the accused and their family's economic resources, thus leading to more debt. Current bail practices result in detaining the poorest defendants, who are simply at an economic disadvantage in terms of gaining release prior to trial. It is a well-established fact that people of color in the United States face higher rates of poverty and incarceration than their white counterparts. The Census Bureau reports that the highest poverty levels in the United States are for African Americans (18.8%) and Hispanics (15.7%) as compared to whites (7.3%) (Creamer, 2020). In 2019, African Americans made up 12% of the U.S. population yet comprised over 30% of the sentenced prison population (state and federal) and 34% of the U.S. jail population (Minton & Zeng, 2021). As such, it appears that race and economics compound issues of pretrial detention. To support this, Wooldredge, Frank, Goulette and Travis (2015) found that defendants in their study who were Black received higher bond amounts, were more often given pretrial detention, and were less likely to hire attorneys as compared to whites. This finding was especially true for younger Black males.

Bail and Pretrial Detention Reforms

The period from the 1990s to the present day is often identified as the third wave of bail reform. Both states and the federal criminal justice system have begun to recognize how our current commercial money bail system has led to the mass incarceration of the poor and disenfranchised. As such, several reforms have been initiated.

First, some states are getting rid of money bail altogether. California was the first state to eliminate money bail in 2018 for those who could not afford it. In place of bail, judges use a risk assessment tool and classify defendants into one of three risk levels: low, middle, and high. The risk level criteria are based on criminal history, the severity of the offense, safety concerns, and the judge's discretion. Only the highest-risk defendants have to stay in mandatory custody until arraignment (FindLaw, 2019). In addition, in February of 2021, Cook County Illinois passed the SAFE-T ACT (Safety, Accountability, Fairness, and Equity—Today), which will take effect on January 1, 2023. This act also eliminated the posting of money bail and reworded current laws using terms such as "release" and "pretrial release" rather than "bail" and "money bail" (VanBrunt & Bowman, 2018). Several other states including Kentucky, New Jersey, New Mexico, Nebraska, West Virginia, Ohio, and Indiana have also changed their cash bail systems rather than simply eliminating them.

Recently, New York state enacted sweeping changes to its bail system. They eliminated the use of cash bail and also pretrial detention. Both of these sanctions were eliminated for most all misdemeanors (except for sex offenses and certain domestic violence cases). Bail and pretrial detention were also abolished in almost all non-violent felony cases. There were some exceptions, including but not limited to sex offenses, terrorism, offenses against children, etc. Regarding violent felonies, bail and pretrial detention are still permitted, with a few exceptions (see Rempel & Rodriguez, 2019, p. 2–3). Furthermore, for those cases where bail can be granted, judges must take into consideration the accused's financial resources. Judges in New York are also encouraged to release more accused people on their own recognizance while awaiting trial and use risk assessment tools that predict the probability of returning for trial. Factors such as future dangerousness, flight risk, gender, and race are not to play key factors in determining bail and/or pretrial detention decisions. Judges are also required to set alternative forms of bail (i.e., secured and unsecured bonds), which are often the least burdensome forms of bail financially.

To alleviate jail overcrowding, many of the aforementioned states have increased the use of pretrial services departments in their states and counties. In most localities, judges can order defendants to receive pretrial supervision based on their current crime, criminal history, etc. It is the job of pretrial service workers to make sure defendants make all court appearances and follow their bond conditions, such as mental health treatment and substance abuse treatment. Typically, individuals are released from pretrial services once their case has been resolved.

Although predictive risk assessment tools have been available for decades, only now are pretrial services starting to use them to determine a defendant's eligibility for pretrial release. According to the Justice Policy Institute, "Risk assessments are tools that, when used properly, can provide a dependable prediction of whether a person will be involved in pretrial misconduct, whether by failure to appear in court or being a danger to the community" (2012, p. 31). These surveys primarily assess the level of danger that a defendant poses to the community as well as aid in determining the appropriate form of bail and/or pretrial release. Empirical research has produced a number of demographic variables that are both reliable and valid for predicting pretrial behavior. The Justice Policy Institute states, "This information can be used to increase objectivity in the pretrial decision-making process and serve as a tool to move away from financial bail in favor of appropriate pretrial supervision" (2012, p. 31). The proper assessment also provides information regarding the "conditions" that should be placed on the accused during release as well, such as employment, alcohol/drug treatment, counseling, no victim contact, etc. It is the hope that assessment plus proper conditions of release (i.e., supervision of some type) will reduce the need for pretrial detention.

Despite this, the increased use of predictive risk assessment for non-convicted people has also come under scrutiny. Some criminologists and criminal justice officials argue that bail has merely been replaced with mandatory pretrial conditions, similar to parole or probation. Yet, it is important to remember that this specific population has not been found guilty of a crime, calling into question the fairness of these actual pretrial restrictions. Do we have to ask ourselves if we are merely creating a surveillance state for those accused of a crime? In addition, scholars argue that the increased reliance on risk assessment tools for determining bail and pretrial release is unfair and discriminatory. With the dozens of risk assessments used throughout the United States, many have not proven to be reliable and/or valid in predicting what they are supposed to, whether that be what programming is needed, recidivism, sentencing, etc. In addition, some argue that these tools have also been shown to be biased against people of color (see Angwin, Larson, Mattu & Kirchner, 2016, for a full discussion). Moreover, in many states, defendants are not allowed to challenge their risk assessment score; thus, they are not aware of why they received specific outcomes scores. People entering the criminal justice system are often told their risk score, but now how it is actually calculated or what it actually is predicting. It is also important to note that many of these risk assessment tools were designed to determine programming needs, not to help set bail amounts or determine parole terms. Further research regarding the reliability and validity of these tools, in general, is needed, but the use of these same tools to determine bail and flight risk is seriously lacking.

Pretrial services are also using technology to monitor defendants while awaiting trial rather than locking them up in jail. Electronic monitoring (e.g., ankle bracelets) combined with daily reporting to probation officials is a policy that probation officials are pushing for in lieu of bail or pretrial detention. This is especially true for non-violent, first-time defendants who often cannot afford bail and who may be the most stigmatized or vulnerable when serving time in jail. Other states have started giving citations to people rather than arresting them and booking them in jails. Citations are written agreements to show up in court or pay fines in order to not be arrested. Kentucky started one such program in 2011. Using increased citations for misdemeanor offenses resulted in a significant drop in the number of cases (i.e., 17,000 fewer cases) processed compared to years prior (Justice Policy Institute, 2012). The problem with several of these alternatives to pretrial detention is that many states cannot afford them or do not have the staff resources to employ them. Moreover, there is a lack of data on those serving pretrial detention across the United States. The data that does exist uses a small sample of localities and often does not include individuals accused of both felonies and misdemeanors. According to the Justice Policy Institute (2012), "Better measures to track pretrial detention should be crafted to provide a more nuanced understanding of the United States' pretrial population and provide a platform for meaningful reform" (p. 38).

In addition, there has also been an increase in the formation and use of community and nationwide bail funds. One such example is The Bail Project, which is a national nonprofit organization that assists poor individuals with pretrial support. This organization spun off from the Bronx Freedom Fund, which was established in 2007, and expanded in 2017 to launch its nationwide revolving bail fund. With agencies across the United States, The Bail Project pays full bail without repayment required, seeks to reform current bail practices, links individuals to pretrial/social services, offers court reminders, and provides transportation to its clients ("The Bail Project: Frequently Asked Questions," n.d.).

Another example is the Community Justice Exchange, which maintains the National Bail Fund Network. Started in 2016, this group now consists of "90 community bail funds that use the regular payment of bail as well as strategic bailout actions in campaigns to end money bail and pretrial detention in both the criminal legal and immigration detention systems" (Community Justice Exchange, n.d., para 1). These community partners also educate and raise awareness regarding the link between money bail, pretrial detention, and mass incarceration.

Another suggested reform is to make legislative changes within the private bail industry itself. A 2020 report by the Marshall Project revealed that the bail bond industry and the insurance companies that underwrite it in the United States made over $2 billion dollars in profit (Lockwood & Griffin, 2020). In light of this, some states (e.g., Kentucky, Illinois, Wisconsin, and Oregon) and localities have banned private bail bondsman and their involvement in the judicial system. From the numbers above, it is obvious that the private bail bond business is quite lucrative and the industry has a keen interest in preserving its income. Scholars suggest that the courts should process financial release instead of private bail bondsmen. Moreover, they suggest that data be collected from bail bondsmen regarding who they decide to post bond for and whether their pretrial release efforts are actually successful (Justice Policy Institute, 2012). Do we really know if the use of private bail bond companies is an effective mechanism for getting defendants to show up in court and/or reducing future crime? Currently, we do not as the data is nonexistent.

Conclusion

This chapter reveals how the American criminal justice system's increased use of money bail combined with statutory changes regarding who is eligible for pretrial release has contributed to the mass incarceration of the poor in jails across the United States. Bail is a cornerstone of the law that now seems to be a privilege available only to the affluent, while those who cannot afford bail are left to languish in pretrial detention. Extensive research is needed to better understand bail amounts implemented across the country (for both felonies and misdemeanors), the characteristics of our pretrial detention population and their unique needs, and the effectiveness of proposed alternatives to money bail. Bail and pretrial detention need to be reasonable for all defendants, no matter their socioeconomic standing. Bail reform strategies must continue to focus on alleviating the mass incarceration of low-income people of color defendants in U.S. jails as well as ensuring public safety.

Discussion Questions:

1 How has the use of money bail fueled mass incarceration in American jails?
2 Besides those mentioned, what other reforms could be made to our bail system in the United States to reduce mass incarceration?
3 What types of pretrial release are used in other countries, as compared to the United States?

References

Angwin, J., Larson, J., Mattu, S., & Kirchner, L. (2016, May). Machine bias: There's software used across the country to predict future criminals. And its biased against blacks. *Pro Publica*. Retrieved from https://www.propublica.org/article/machine-bias-risk-assessments-in-criminal-sentencing

Banuach, P. J., Sickmund, M., & Ford, B. (1986). *Jail inmates, 1984*. United States Department of Justice, Bureau of Justice Statistics.

Baughman, S. (2017). *The bail book: A comprehensive look at bail in America's criminal justice system*. Cambridge University Press, New York.

Bennett, K. (2022, January 19). *Survey: Less than half of Americans have savings to cover a $1,000 surprise expense*. Retrieved from https://www.bankrate.com/banking/ savings/financial-security-january-2022

Cohen, T. H. & Reaves, B. A. (2007). *State court processing statistics, 1990–2004: Pretrial release of felony defendants in state courts*. United States Department of Justice, Bureau of Justice Statistics Special Report.

Community Justice Exchange (n.d.). *National bail fund network. Directory of community bail funds*. Retrieved April 22, 2022, from https://www.communityjusticeexchange. org/en/nbfn-directory

Congress Clears Controversial D.C. Crime Control Bill. (1971). *CQ almanac 1970* (26th ed.). http:// library.cqpress.com/cqalmanac/cqal70-1292937

Council of Economic Advisors Issue Brief (U.S.). (2015). *Fines, fees, and bail payments in the criminal justice system that disproportionately impact the poor*. Executive Office of the President, Council of Economic Advisers. https://obamawhitehouse.archives.gov/ sites/default/files/page/files/1215_cea_fine_fee_bail_issue_brief.pdf

Creamer, J. (2020, September 15). *Inequalities persist despite decline in poverty for all major race and Hispanic origin groups*. https://www.census.gov/library/stories/2020/09/ poverty-rates-for-blacks-and-hispanics-reached-historic-lows-in-2019.html

Digard, L., (2019). *Justice denied: The harmful and lasting effects of pretrial detention*. Vera Evidence Brief. Vera Institute of Justice. https://www.vera.org/downloads/ publications/Justice-Denied-Evidence-Brief.pdf

Dobbie, W., Goldin, J., & Yang, C. S. (2018). The effects of pretrial detention on conviction, future crime, and employment: Evidence from randomly assigned judges. *American Economic Review, 108*(2), 201–240. https://doi.org/10.1257/aer.20161503

FindLaw. (2019, April 16). *Bail reform and California's bail laws*. Retrieved from https://www. findlaw.com/state/california-law/bail-reform-and-california-bail-laws.html

Heaton, P., Mayson, S., & Stevenson, M. (2017). The downstream consequences of pretrial misdemeanor detention. *Stanford Law Review, 69*(3), 711–794.

Holsinger, A. M., & Holsinger, K. (2018). Analyzing bond supervision survey data: The effects of pretrial detention on self-reported outcomes. *Federal Probation, 82*(2), 39–45. https://www.uscourts.gov/sites/default/files/fedprobation-sept2018_0.pdf

Hopkins, B., Bains, C. & Doyle, C. (2019). Principles of pretrial release: Reforming bail without repeating its harms. *The Journal of Criminal Law & Criminology, 108*(4), 679–700. https://www.jstor.org/stable/48572969

Justice Policy Institute. (2012, September). *Bail fail: Why the U.S. should end the practice of using money for bail.* https://justicepolicy.org/wp-content/uploads/2022/02/bailfail.pdf

Kluckow, R., & Zeng, Z. (2022). *Correctional populations in the United States, 2020-Statistical tables.* United States Department of Justice, Bureau of Justice Statistics. https:// bjs.ojp.gov/content/pub/pdf/cpus20st.pdf

Lockwood, B., & Griffin, A. (2020). The ins and outs of bail. *The System.* https:// www.themarshallproject.org/2020/10/28/the-ins-and-outs-of-bail

Minton, T. D., & Zeng, Z. (2021). *Jail inmates in 2020-Statistical tables.* United States Department of Justice. Bureau of Justice Statistics. https://bjs.ojp.gov/ library/publications/jail-inmates-2020-statistical-tables

National Association on Fines, Fees, and Bail Practices. (2019). *Bail reform: A practical guide based on research and experience.* https://www.ncsc.org/__data/assets/pdf_file/ 0026/42587/Bail-reform-guide-3-12-19.pdf

Ofer, U. (2017, March 15). *Kalief Browder's tragic death and the criminal injustice of our bail system.* ACLU. https://www.aclu.org/blog/smart-justice/kalief-browders-tragic-death-and-criminal-injustice-our-bail-system

Rabuy, B., & Kopf, D. (2016). *Detaining the poor: How money bail perpetuates and endless cycle of poverty and jail time.* Prison Policy Initiative. https://www.prisonpolicy. org/reports/incomejails.html

Reaves, B. A. (2013). *Felony defendants in large urban counties, 2009-Statistical tables.* United States Department of Justice, Bureau of Justice Statistics.

Rempel, M., & Rodriguez, K. (2019). *Bail reform in New York: Legislative provisions and implications for New York City.* Center for Court Innovation. Retrieved from https://www.courtinnovation.org/sites/default/files/media/document/2019/Bail_Reform_NY_full_0.pdf

Sawyer, W., & Wagner, P. (2022). *Mass incarceration: The whole pie 2022.* Prison Policy Initiative. https://www.prisonpolicy.org/reports/pie2022.html

Schnacke, T. (2018). A brief history of bail. *Judges Journal, 53*(7), 4–36. https://www.supremecourt.ohio.gov/sites/PJRSummit/materials/bailHistory.pdf

The bail project: Frequently asked questions. (n.d.). The bail project. Retrieved April 22, 2022, from https://bailproject.org/faq/

U.S. Const. Amend. VIII.

U.S. v. *Salerno*, 481 U.S. 739 (1987). https://www.oyez.org/cases/1986/86-87

VanBrunt, A., & Bowman, L. E. (2018). Toward a just model of pretrial release: A history of bail reform and a prescription for what's next. *Journal of Criminal Law & Criminology, 108*(4), 701–774. https://scholarlycommons.law.northwestern.edu/jclc/vol108/iss4/3

Wald, P. M., & Freed, D. J. (1966). The Bail Reform Act of 1966: Practitioner's primer. *American Bar Association Journal, 52*(10), 940–945. https://www.jstor.org/ stable/25723775

Wooldredge, J., Frank, J., Goulette, N., & Travis, L. (2015). Is the impact of cumulative disadvantage on sentencing greater for black defendants? *Criminology & Public Policy, 14*(2), 187–223. https:// doi.org/10.1111/1745-9133.1212

Zeng, Z., & Minton, T. D. (2021a). *Census of jails, 2005–2019-Statistical tables.* United States Department of Justice, Bureau of Justice Statistics.

Zeng, Z., & Minton, T. D. (2021b). *Jail inmates in 2019.* United States Department of Justice, Bureau of Justice Statistics.

3

IMMIGRATION IN AN ERA OF MASS INCARCERATION

Tania N. Valdez

LEARNING OBJECTIVES:

Upon successful completion of this chapter, readers will be able to:

1. Recognize that the growth of immigration detention mirrors mass incarceration in the criminal context.
2. Identify aspects of immigration law that have led to the expansion of incarceration in the civil immigration context.
3. Begin to consider the human impact of immigration mass incarceration, including the impact on the people who are detained, their families and communities, and society more broadly.

Discussions of mass incarceration are incomplete without addressing a major contributing factor: the immigration enforcement system. In the United States, thousands of noncitizens are sitting in immigration detention on any given day, for a variety of reasons that are explored in this chapter. Yet, there are many people in the United States who do not know that there is such a thing as immigration prisons. Or that there are thousands of noncitizens in immigration prisons right now (U.S. Immigration and Customs Enforcement [ICE], 2022), for nothing more than civil violations of the law. It is also not common knowledge that noncitizens might have to stay in immigration prison for the whole time they are fighting their case, which may be months or years. Immigrants have been rendered close to invisible, both in terms of their status in society and also the rural locations of detention centers. Thus, this chapter begins by telling a typical story of one such person who has been swept up in the immigration enforcement system.

Esteban is a lawful permanent resident (also referred to as having a "green card") who has been in the United States for 25 years. He is married to a U.S. citizen and has two U.S. citizen kids. He is pulled over one day for speeding while driving home from work. The police officer suspects that Esteban may not be in the United States legally and calls U.S. Immigration and Customs Enforcement (ICE). ICE officers arrive and take Esteban into custody. When he appears in immigration court a few days later, he is told by the judge that

DOI: 10.4324/9781003274292-5

he cannot be released from detention and must fight his case while in custody because he has two decades-old convictions for stealing food from a grocery store.

Esteban was the main financial provider for his family. His wife and 18-year-old daughter get jobs to pay the household expenses, but it isn't enough, and Esteban's family is evicted from their housing three months after his arrest. His daughter drops out of college to work full time. Detained during the COVID-19 pandemic, Esteban is told by detention center officials that he must follow social distancing and hygiene practices to protect his health. He is held in a small cell with three other men. None of them have been provided masks. The detention center has run out of soap. Esteban has diabetes and high blood pressure and worries when he starts developing COVID symptoms, but there is only one doctor and a nurse serving 200 men so they cannot see him for several days.

Esteban's story is representative of multiple themes to be discussed in this chapter: (1) the proliferation of immigration detention, including the concept of "mandatory detention," which means that there are people who must stay in detention for months or years during their removal proceedings, and (2) the human impact of immigration prisons on noncitizens and their families.

A note on terminology: this chapter uses the word "noncitizens" to describe this group of people who have not yet become, or cannot become, U.S. citizens. Using "noncitizens" is not intended to draw a value-based line between citizens and those who are not, but rather is a broad phrase that incorporates people who migrate to the United States for many reasons, including those in temporary and permanent statuses, those who may never obtain legal status, and those seeking humanitarian protection such as refugees and asylees.

Growth of Immigration Detention

Immigration detention has not always been a central feature of the immigration enforcement system in the United States. Rather, incarceration of noncitizens for civil violations grew slowly over time and then has grown exponentially since the 1990s (Center for Migration Studies, 2018).

One might ask: where does this power to detain noncitizens for civil violations come from? The Supreme Court of the United States has declared that the federal government has the power to exclusively control immigration (*Chae Chan Ping v. United States*, 1889), which includes the power to exclude or expel people, as part of the country's authority as a sovereign nation. This broad power to regulate rules around citizenship and who is permitted to enter U.S. territory also provides the basis for the U.S. Government's power to detain noncitizens who may not be permitted to enter or remain in the United States. (García Hernández, 2014). Congress authorized detention of noncitizens seeking entry into the United States by statute, and Ellis Island was created and became such a site in 1892 (García Hernández, 2019).

In many ways, immigration detention is identical to criminal incarceration. People in immigration custody may be held in private immigration detention centers that are jail-like, or they may be held alongside people who are criminally incarcerated in county jails and federal prisons. Detainees live in cells, are watched by guards, are issued jumpsuits, and have their property confiscated. In some jurisdictions, they are brought to court in shackles. Some immigration courts are located inside detention facilities. To be released from detention, detainees generally must pay a bond. However, sometimes the bond payments are not feasible. Data shows that 40% of bonds in 2018 were $10,000 or more (Kight & Salmon, 2019).

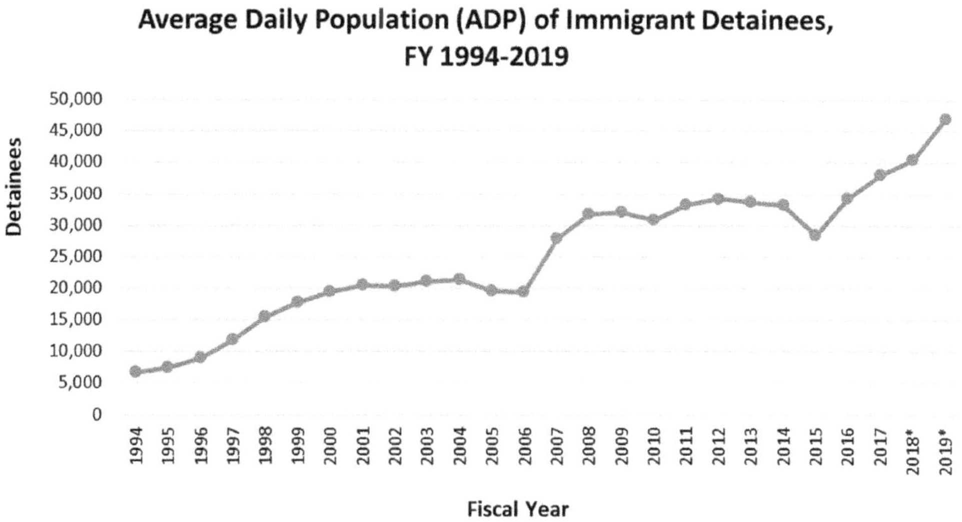

FIGURE 3.1 Average Daily Population (ADP) of Immigrant Detainees, FY 1994-2019.
Source: Center for Migration Studies (2018).

The similarities between immigration detention and criminal incarceration do not stop there. Like the mass incarceration we see in the criminal context, immigration detention is a booming business. In fact, ICE sought $4.1 billion for detention-related expenses for fiscal year 2021 (American Civil Liberties Union [ACLU], 2020). However, detention has not always been the big business it is today. As the following Figure 3.1 shows, as recent as 1994, there were just over 5,000 people detained on any given day. That number grew to more than 50,000 people detained daily during the Trump Administration. And as of September 2022, approximately 24,000 people are in immigration detention around the country (ICE, 2022).

This growth has not only paralleled mass incarceration within the prison industry as a whole, but in fact has some of the same sources. Privatization of prisons incentivizes the proliferation of detention. It's estimated that about 65% of immigrant detainees are held in for-profit prisons (García Hernández, 2019). And like other jails and prisons, ICE facilities are often built in rural areas where the local population can benefit from creation of jobs in the prison industry. Thus, such facilities have wider community support. And beds have to be filled in order for prisons to keep making money.

Moreover, as political campaigns such as the so-called "War on Drugs" have contributed to rising prison populations, increasing rates of prosecution and conviction, plus harsher criminal punishments, have led to more severe immigration consequences. For one, certain categories of crimes render noncitizens deportable. As the Supreme Court of the United States recognized in a case called Padilla v. Kentucky (2010), even though criminal convictions have not always been tied to immigration consequences,

> immigration reforms over time have expanded the class of deportable offenses and limited the authority of judges to alleviate the harsh consequences of deportation. The

> 'drastic measure' of deportation or removal is now virtually inevitable for a vast number of noncitizens convicted of crimes.
>
> *(p. 360)*

The parallels between treatment of people in criminal and immigration proceedings do not stop there. The companies that own private prisons, as for-profit operations, fuel mass incarceration by lobbying for harsher penalties and in favor of politicians that support such penalties (Margulies, 2016). A reduction in private prisons would mean less bedspace, and therefore that judges would have to consider more carefully whether a person needs to be detained.

There have been movements around the country to close private immigration centers, as about 80% of noncitizens are held in private detention facilities (Tolan, 2021). One of President Biden's campaign promises was to close private detention centers, including those detaining noncitizens. However, Biden's executive order banning new private prison contracts did not apply to the immigration context (Tolan, 2021). The ACLU has criticized the move, as the federal government is "allowing private prison companies to fill beds that were emptied out under the executive order with immigrant detainees" (2020, para. 6). Under the Biden Administration, the companies running private detention facilities (including CoreCivic and the GEO Group) are receiving about $3 million per day—more than the daily amount received under either the Trump or Obama Administrations ($2.9 million and $2.2 million per day, respectively) (ACLU, 2020).

In terms of who is detained, thousands of the people in immigration detention are asylum-seekers who have either turned themselves in or been apprehended near a border or other port of entry to the United States, which include airports and coasts. During the Obama Administration, thousands of women and children asylum-seekers were held in makeshift detention centers in border states. Other detainees are people waiting to see if they will be permitted to be released from detention, or some are those whom immigration judges have decided pose a flight risk or danger to the community. Another subset of detainees are those who have committed certain crimes that are deemed to subject them to "mandatory detention."

Mandatory Detention

Immigration law states that people who have been convicted of certain crimes are subject to "mandatory detention" (8 U.S.C. § 1226(c), 2018). Mandatory detention is just as it sounds—there is a class of people who must remain in immigration detention if they wish to fight their case in order to try to stay in the United States. They are not entitled to release on bond. Thus, even if an immigration judge believed the person did not pose any danger to the community and believed the person would show up to future court dates, the judge still could not give them an opportunity to pay a bond and be released from custody.

The concept of mandatory detention expanded exponentially in 1996 with the passage of two laws: the Antiterrorism and Effective Death Penalty Act and the Illegal Immigration and Immigrant Responsibility Act. Together, those laws expanded the definitions of "crimes and moral turpitude" and "aggravated felonies," two definitions that trigger mandatory detention under immigration laws. According to Detention Watch Network, about 190,000 people were detained in 2021 due to the "mandatory detention" provision (n.d.).

The convictions mandating detention are not limited to the crimes one might expect, such as homicide, drug trafficking, and domestic violence. Rather, a person may be subject to detention without the possibility of release for crimes as minor as "shoplifting, petty theft, drunk driving, and even low-level drug violations" (Solis, 2019, p. 371).

As an example of such a low-level violation, consider the case of Moones Mellouli, who came to the United States on a student visa and earned a college degree and master's degrees in mathematics and economics. He became a lawful permanent resident and was engaged to a U.S. citizen. Mr. Mellouli was arrested and charged with a crime for carrying four tablets of Adderall, a medication used to treat attention deficit disorder for which he did not have a prescription, in his sock. On those grounds, he pled guilty to misdemeanor possession of drug paraphernalia (the "drug paraphernalia" being the sock). The U.S. Department of Justice argued that the paraphernalia conviction subjected Mr. Mellouli to mandatory detention and deportation. Fortunately, the U.S. Supreme Court ultimately disagreed and reversed the lower court's ruling—but not before Mr. Mellouli was detained and then deported to Tunisia (*Mellouli v. Lynch*, 2015).

Remaining detained throughout a case has several impacts: the person is separated from their family and community for potentially months or years, cannot be employed, may not be able to hire or communicate effectively with a lawyer, and in some jurisdictions, will be appearing for court hearings in a prison uniform and shackles, which may affect a judge's perceptions of their trustworthiness and character.

Limited Constitutional Rights in Removal Proceedings

More than 100 years ago, the Supreme Court of the United States held that immigration proceedings are civil—rather than criminal—in nature because "deportation is not a punishment for crime" (*Fong Yue Ting v. United States*, 1893, p. 730). Although the Supreme Court more recently has recognized that "deportation is nevertheless intimately related to the criminal process" and that criminal convictions and deportations are "enmeshed," this rationalization still stands (*Padilla v. Kentucky*, 2010, pp. 365–366).

Because of the categorization of immigration proceedings as civil, as opposed to criminal, courts have declared that noncitizens are not entitled to certain constitutional rights that would apply in the criminal context. Namely, noncitizens enjoy less rights with respect to the Fourth, Fifth, Sixth, and Fourteenth Amendments of the U.S. Constitution (Valdez, 2021).

There is no right to a jury trial. Noncitizens accused of crimes do not have the right to remain silent if questioned on the stand as they would in criminal proceedings. Additionally, the Fourth Amendment prohibits unreasonable searches and seizures for people accused of crimes and allows for the exclusion of evidence obtained as a result of constitutional violations. Yet, for noncitizens in deportation proceedings, evidence illegally obtained by law enforcement can still be introduced in court (Valdez, 2021).

Moreover, unlike criminal proceedings, noncitizens are not entitled under the Sixth Amendment to be provided a lawyer to represent them in immigration proceedings. Studies have found that noncitizens were nearly five times more likely to win their cases if they had a lawyer (Eagly & Shafer, 2016). However, most noncitizens do not obtain lawyers for their removal proceedings, often due to an inability to pay for representation, which often costs thousands of dollars.

Regardless of these limits to noncitizens' constitutional rights, they certainly are entitled to due process, which means having proceedings that are *fundamentally fair*. This means they are entitled to have their cases heard and that they have the ability to fully present evidence in support of their case (Eagly & Shafer, 2016). Many lawsuits raise potential due process violations. Additionally, noncitizens have a constitutional right to be free from conditions of confinement that amount to punishment, as will be discussed in the next section.

Conditions of Detention

As discussed in the previous section, United States laws limit legal protections for noncitizens in fundamental ways. In addition to limiting other constitutional rights, oversight of conditions of confinement in immigration detention is also lacking. Noncitizens' arrest and detention, as well as opportunities for release, are largely carried out by the Department of Homeland Security and the Department of Justice, which are both agencies in the executive branch of the U.S. Government. The structure of immigration law makes it rare for there to be neutral oversight of detention by the federal courts (García Hernández, 2014). This means that the state has broad power to determine who is confined—and what the conditions of confinement are—with limited accountability.

One remedy that is available is the writ of *habeas corpus*. Habeas petitions are filed in the federal courts for the purpose of seeking release from immigration detention. Noncitizens can challenge various aspects of detention through habeas petitions, including how long they have been detained, that they were improperly found to be subject to mandatory detention, and other legal and constitutional challenges. However, depending on existing laws where a noncitizen is detained, they may or may not be able to challenge conditions of confinement in federal court.

General Conditions

Put simply, immigration detention looks exactly like criminal incarceration. Thus, the problems frequently complained of by people who are incarcerated are also echoed by noncitizens in immigration custody. Among those concerns are poor living conditions, conditions that cause trauma or aggravate existing trauma including the dehumanizing qualities of detention, excessive use of solitary confinement, abusive treatment by guards including sexual assault, and seriously inadequate medical care (Valdez, 2022). One particularly horrifying story of abuse that came to light in recent years occurred after a whistleblowing nurse reported that Black and Latina detainees were being given unnecessary gynecological surgeries that affected fertility, including hysterectomies, without their consent (Evelyn, 2020). Such blatant abuses reflect the forced sterilization of women of color during the mid-twentieth century and expose the darker underbelly of what happens to people who are treated as less-than-human.

Outright abuse aside, the quest for profits has much to do with the deplorable conditions of immigration facilities. In private detention centers, money is saved by understaffing, postponing repairs, and providing cheap food, insufficient medical care and insufficient supplies. Another manner of increasing profit is putting ICE detainees to work. Just as people who are incarcerated in criminal custody receive abysmal pay for work done while detained, people in immigration detention are also conscripted to work in the kitchens, as cleaners, as landscapers, by assisting disabled detainees, or many other positions within the facilities. Detainees have reported being forced to work, as they are threatened with disciplinary action like losing recreation time, or being put in solitary confinement, if they refuse. However, detainees are often not compensated or paid $1 a day, as explained in lawsuits in recent years. In 2021, a jury awarded ICE detainees $17 million backpay for their work done in the detention centers (Dailey, 2021). Nonetheless, new lawsuits continue to be filed alleging similar unfair labor practices.

Failure to provide adequate medical care is a widespread problem in immigration detention. Studies have found unreasonable delays for serious medical conditions, failure to provide necessary medications, poor levels of care, and botched responses to medical emergencies due to understaffing or the lack of appropriate equipment. All of these problems have been exacerbated by the COVID-19 pandemic. Lawsuits filed reflect that detainees were not given soap or masks, shared such close quarters with other detainees that it was impossible to distance, widespread failure to test staff and detainees alike for COVID, and failure to separate people who tested positive from the rest of the population.

Alternatives to Detention & the Growing Surveillance State

Another important aspect to mass incarceration of noncitizens, like mass incarceration in the criminal context, is the expansion of surveillance. People who are not detained in jails, prisons, or ICE detention centers may still be subject to another form of restriction on liberty—GPS monitoring via ankle bracelets. From the U.S. Government's perspective, the monitors reduce the possibility that noncitizens released from custody will commit crimes and also enhance the likelihood that noncitizens will appear for future court hearings. GPS monitors presented advocates and their clients with the hope that people who would otherwise be detained would be released to their families and communities.

However, the data does not show an overall decrease in immigration detention. As the American Immigration Council has noted, "Rather than serve as alternatives to *detention*, these programs have at times served as alternatives to *release without conditions*" (American Immigration Council, 2022, p. 3). Thus, people who otherwise would not have been subject to surveillance are now under these programs. There are currently more than 100,000 people being monitored by a smartphone app and about 28,000 being monitored by ankle monitors (p. 4). Others are required to have periodic check-ins, including home visits. Each of these alternatives pose practical problems, such as limiting housing and employment options. Moreover, as electronic surveillance in general raises concerns regarding privacy, there are also questions about what the data gathered is used for. And all of these problems are exacerbated for asylees who have experienced trauma, particularly when they are seeking asylum from countries where they previously faced surveillance by government actors.

Conclusion

Immigration comprises a significant piece of the mass incarceration picture. Like other mass incarceration contexts, immigration enforcement is a system where the privatization of prisons and the imposition of harsher penalties on criminal behavior have led to the imprisonment of increasing numbers of people.

A justification given for the need to detain noncitizens who are awaiting their hearings in immigration court is that immigration detention ensures that noncitizens will appear for their immigration court hearings. However, studies and experimental programs over the years have shown that noncitizens have a high rate of compliance with immigration orders when they believe that the system is fair, and when they have adequate support, including having legal representation (Ryo, 2013, 2017). Moreover, immigration detention facilities are notorious for violations of individuals' constitutional and human rights, particularly because the immigration enforcement system affects people who lack citizenship status (and therefore the ability to vote) and often have other intersecting identities by which they are oppressed, such as race and class. Noncitizens are also often used as pawns in political battles, which leads to further dehumanization in the media. Thousands of people are detained in immigration prisons on any given day—now is the time to rethink the goals of the immigration enforcement system and envision alternative approaches that recognize and protect the inherent dignity of human beings.

Discussion Questions

1 Recall that immigration detention is a civil—as opposed to criminal—system. Do you believe that civil immigration detention should exist? If so, under what circumstances do you believe that detaining a person is necessary or permissible? Is it appropriate to detain asylum-seekers who turn themselves in at the border in compliance with U.S. and international law, for example? How about someone who has been convicted of a crime but has already served their criminal sentence?
2 What do you think about the fact that constitutional rights are limited for people in civil immigration proceedings?

References

8 U.S.C. § 1226(c). (2018).

American Civil Liberties Union. (2020, April). *Justice-Free Zones U.S. Immigration Detention Under the Trump Administration*. ACLU. https://www.aclu.org/report/justice-free-zones-us-immigration-detention-under-trump-administration

American Immigration Council. (2022, March 17). *Alternatives to Immigration Detention: An Overview*. American Immigration Council. https://www.americanimmigrationcouncil.org/research/alternatives-immigration-detention-overview

Center for Migration Studies (2018, March 26). *Immigration Detention: Recent Trends and Scholarship*. Center for Migration Scholarship. https://cmsny.org/publications/virtualbrief-detention

Chae Chan Ping v. United States, 130 U.S. 581 (1889).

Dailey, K. (2021, November 1). *ICE Detainees Awarded $17 Million by Jury in $1-a-Day Pay Case*. Bloomberg Law. https://news.bloomberglaw.com/litigation/ice-detainees-awarded-17-million-by-jury-in-1-a-day-pay-case

Detention Watch Network. (n.d.). *Mandatory Detention*. Detention Watch Network. https://www.detentionwatchnetwork.org/issues/mandatory-detention

Detention Watch Network. (n.d.). *Mandatory Detention Fact Sheet*. Detention Watch Network. https://www.detentionwatchnetwork.org/sites/default/files/DWN_Mandatory%20Detention_Fact%20Sheet.pdf

Eagly, I., & Shafer, S. (2016). *Access to Counsel in Immigration Court*. American Immigration Council.

Evelyn, K. (2020, October 23). *At Least 19 Women Allege Medical Abuse at Ice Detention Center in Georgia*. The Guardian. https://www.theguardian.com/us-news/2020/oct/23/georgia-ice-detention-center-women-allege-abuse

Fong Yue Ting v. United States, 149 U.S. 698 (1893).

García Hernández, C. C. (2014). Invisible spaces and invisible lives in immigration detention. *Howard Law Journal, 57*(3), pp. 869–898.

García Hernández, C. C. (2019). *Migrating to Prison: America's Obsession with Locking Up Immigrants*. New York: The New Press.

Kight, S. W., & Salmon, F. (2019, July 21). *The Cost of Bail for Immigrants Is Surging*. AXIOS. https://www.axios.com/2019/07/21/immigrant-bail-bonds-costs-rising-ice-judges

Margulies, J. (2016, August 24). *This Is the Real Reason Private Prisons Should Be Outlawed*. TIME. https://time.com/4461791/private-prisons-department-of-justice/

Mellouli v. Lynch, 575 U.S. 798 (2015).

Padilla v. Kentucky, 559 U.S. 356 (2010).

Ryo, E. (2013, July 31). Deciding to cross: The norms and economics of unauthorized migration. *American Sociological Review, 78*, 574.

Ryo, E. (2017). Legal attitudes of immigrant detainees. *Law & Society Review, 51*(1), pp. 99–131.

Solis, J. A. (2019). Detained without relief. *Alabama Civil Rights & Civil Liberties Law Review, 10*, pp. 357–392.

Tolan, C. (2021, November 12). *Biden Vowed to Close Federal Private Prisons, but Prison Companies Are Finding Loopholes to Keep Them Open*. CNN Politics. https://www.cnn.com/2021/11/12/politics/biden-private-prisons-immigration-detention-centers-invs/index.html

U.S. Immigration and Customs Enforcement. (2022, October 18). *Detention Management*. U.S. Immigration and Customs Enforcement. https://www.ice.gov/detain/detention-management

Valdez, T. N. (2021). Pleading the fifth in immigration court: A regulatory proposal. *Washington University Law Review, 98*, pp. 1343–1402.

Valdez, T. N. (2022). Eliminating the fugitive disentitlement doctrine in immigration matters. *Notre Dame Law Review, 97*, pp. 963–1028.

4

LIFE IMPRISONMENT AS A HALLMARK OF MASS INCARCERATION

Ashley Nellis

LEARNING OUTCOMES:

Upon successful completion of this chapter, students will be able to:

1 Gain a stronger understanding of a primary mechanism in mass incarceration, as states admitted more people to prison for longer terms and placed limits on parole.
2 Acquire a deeper understanding of the characteristics of those serving life imprisonment.
3 Acquire a deeper understanding of the shift in narrative around acceptable responses to crime and those who commit it; and a bold way forward that will produce declines in lengthy imprisonment while protecting public safety.

Fifty years ago, the United States began its unprecedented experiment with mass incarceration. As such, it is an especially appropriate time to reflect on where this experiment has brought us.

Before the prison buildup that commenced in 1973, 200,000 people were incarcerated in our prisons. Today, that number of people *alone* are serving life sentences, with a total of nearly two million imprisoned overall (Carson, 2020; Nellis, 2021). One in seven imprisoned U.S. residents is serving a life sentence with parole, without parole, or a virtual life sentence of at least 50 years (Nellis, 2021). The U.S. is unique in this regard, holding 83% of the worldwide population of people serving life (van Zyl Smit & Appleton, 2019).

This chapter presents the view that the expansion of life imprisonment was a tactic of mass incarceration and an integral part of the mentality that governed the era. Despite the key role, those serving the longest sentences have been excluded from recent legislative reforms because the corresponding crimes usually involve violence. Sentencing and corrections reform proposals have become "bifurcated" such that they are underway for some aspects of mass incarceration but ignored or further entrenched in others (Seeds, 2016). Aggressive steps will need to be taken to recalibrate the system to one that responds to the most serious and violent crimes using principles of accountability combined with fairness,

DOI: 10.4324/9781003274292-6

equity, and mercy. With these principles as the guiding light in reform, it is reasonable to foresee the era of mass incarceration fading into history.

As a basic starting point, imprisonment levels are a function of how many people go to prison and how long they stay there (Clear & Austin, 2009). Mass incarceration's evolution, regarding life sentences, was dominated by the expansion of its allowable uses, inclusion of additional crimes that did not previously qualify, and a greater reliance on life imprisonment when other, lesser sentences were available. Finally, as mass incarceration took hold, individuals serving parole-eligible life sentences who would have been granted parole in earlier eras were rejected or had their freedom delayed as the politics of parole shifted to align with the "tough on crime" narrative. As a result, time served increased (Ghandnoosh, 2017; Seeds, 2022).

In the first section, I provide data on the number of people serving life imprisonment and show how these figures have increased over the period of mass incarceration. In the second section, I discuss the punitive shift in American political responses that have forged the belief that a relatively large swath of people deserves punishments previously reserved for the "worst of the worst." The third section offers steps that could be taken to curb extraordinarily long punishments and reorient the American penal system toward one that is proportional, equitable, and compassionate.

Life Sentences in the U.S.

Life sentences are allowable and used in all states[1] and the federal government. Most recently, available estimates find a total of 203,865 people who were serving life sentences around the U.S., with the highest concentrations in California, Florida, Louisiana, Michigan, and Pennsylvania (Nellis, 2021). This latest figure represents a 12% growth in the use of parole-eligible life sentences, and a 66% growth in parole-*ineligible* life sentences over the past 20 years (Mauer, King, & Young, 2004; Nellis, 2021) (Figure 4.1).

As prison populations began to grow during the era of mass incarceration, the proliferation of life sentences became an integral part. Consider the case of Louisiana, which currently leads the nation and the world in its rate of incarceration. In today's heavily carceral environment, it is difficult to believe that this state historically considered ten years to be a typical duration for an indeterminate life sentence (Gottschalk, 2015). In many states, including Louisiana, life sentences were not only discretionary but presumed to be complete in about 10 years (Gottschalk, 2015; Seeds, 2022). The state relied on a "10/6" law until the 1970s, which meant that life-sentenced individuals were typically released after serving ten years and six months if they presented a good record of conduct and had the warden's support (Seeds, 2022). Louisiana abolished parole in 1979 and life with no parole is now mandatory for convictions of first- or second-degree murder. One of five Black men in Louisiana prisons is serving life. Vulnerable populations including juveniles, the elderly, and those who are medically frail and terminally ill are included among them.

Louisiana is not alone. Just 30 years ago, the typical length of time served in California for someone convicted of first-degree murder was 12 years (Irwin, 2009). In the early 1900s, the federal system officially defined a life sentence as 15 years (Gottschalk, 2012). The average time served among lifers in Pennsylvania and Michigan was between 15 and 20 years up until the 1970s.

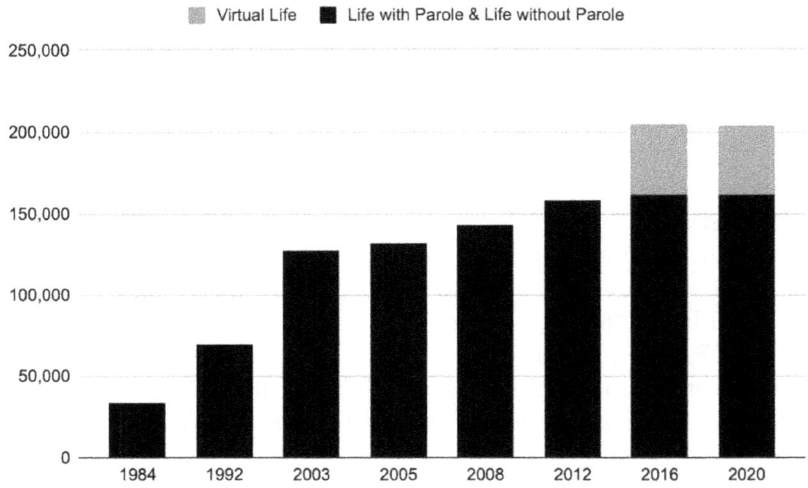

FIGURE 4.1 Expansion of Life Imprisonment in America, 1984–2020.

Sources: Mauer, M., King, R., and Young, M. (2004). *The meaning of life: Long prison sentences in context.* The Sentencing Project;, A. (2021). *No end in sight: America's enduring reliance on life imprisonment.* The Sentencing Project

Note: Data for "virtual life" sentences were obtained beginning in 2016

While eliminating parole for certain offenses and expanding life without parole (LWOP) for new offenses, states have also extended the minimum term of years for parole-*eligible* sentences considerably in recent decades (Ghandnoosh, 2017). An example lies in Tennessee. Before 1975, a life sentence was a minimum of twenty-five years, and with sentence credits ("good time"), one could expect the possibility of parole after 13.7 years (Tennessee Department of Corrections, 2014). The Sentencing Reform Act of 1982 extended the minimum time served on a life sentence to 30 years and, with sentence credits, one could reasonably expect parole review and potential for release after 19.6 years. The statute changed again just seven years later under the 1989 Sentencing Reform Act, requiring a mandatory minimum of 36 years in prison on a parole-eligible life sentence. The possibility for parole was available after 25 years with sentence credits. As part of the Truth in Sentencing Act of 2022 is the most recent change to the state's law; lifers are now required to serve one hundred percent of their 60-year minimum term before appearing before the parole board, with no exceptions.

Of the 200,000 people serving life, one-third have no opportunity for parole. Another 40,000 have sentences that are not statutorily defined as life but are so long that they are not survivable. These are commonly referred to as virtual life sentences and have been defined by a *maximum* sentence that amounts to at least 50 years in prison.[2] Survivability of such a sentence is dependent on the age of the individual at sentencing. A thirty-year sentence imposed on a 65-year-old is likely to result in death in prison, but the same sentence imposed on a 30-year-old means there is a good chance of survival to the release date. In an era that favors mandatory minimum sentencing, however, important differences like these were not considered (Table 4.1).

Women comprise a growing segment of the life-sentenced population: one of every 15 women in prison—amounting to more than 6,600 women—is serving a life sentence and nearly 2,000 of them have no chance for parole. Among imprisoned African American women, one in nine is serving life.

TABLE 4.1 Summary Statistics of Life-Sentenced Population, 2020

	Life with Parole	*Percent of LWP Population*	*Life without Parole*	*Percent of LWOP Population*	*Virtual Life*	*Percent of Vlife Population*	*Row Total*
Sex							
Women	3,673	4	1,908	4	1,060	3	6,641
Men	100,613	96	51,359	96	39,967	97	191,939
Race and Ethnicity							
White	33,533	32	17,433	32	14,549	36	65,515
Black	43,891	42	29,816	55	19,928	48	93,635
Latinx	22,112	21	5,616	10	5,654	14	33,382
Other	4,749	5	1,402	3	896	2	7,047
Juvenile Status at Time of Offense							
Juvenile	6,916	7	1,465	3	1,716	4	10,097
Adult	98,651	93	54,480	97	40,637	96	193,768
Current Age							
55 years or older	34,412	33	15,183	27	11,822	28	61,417
Crime of Conviction							
First-degree murder	37,302	36	34,875	62	10,963	26	83,140
Second-degree murder	18,817	18	4,821	9	2,216	5	25,854
Other, nonnegligent murder	3,161	3	1,695	3	2,232	5	7,088
Sex crime	21,046	20	5,177	9	12,188	28	38,411
Aggravated assault	4,914	5	686	1	2,901	7	8,501
Robbery	8,731	8	3,050	5	5,007	12	16,788
Kidnapping	2,456	2	1,224	2	1,374	3	5,054
Drug crime	903	1	1,668	3	1,404	3	3,975
Property crime	2,660	3	672	1	1,588	4	4,920
Not reported	5,577	5	2,077	4	2,480	6	10,134
Total	105,567		55,945		42,353		203,865

Source: Nellis, A. (2021). *No end in sight: America's enduring reliance on life imprisonment.* The Sentencing Project.

People of color are overrepresented among the lifer population in nearly every state and one in five Black men in prison is serving a life sentence. In Georgia, Illinois, Louisiana, and Maryland, more than two-thirds of the life-sentenced population are African American. Nationally, two-thirds of people serving life are people of color, and among people serving LWOP, 55% are Black.

More than half of people serving life (57%) have been convicted of murder and another 19% have been convicted of a sex offense. Fifteen percent of people serving life have been convicted of robbery, assault, drug, or property crime. An estimated 1,500 people have life sentences for a drug offense, 38% of whom are in the federal system.

Juveniles—typically defined as those who were under 18 at the time of the offense—make up 10,000 of those serving life sentences. The imposition of LWOP on youth has dropped substantially after recent U.S. Supreme Court cases sharply limited their constitutional use. In 2010, the Supreme Court invalidated the application of LWOP for youth convicted of nonhomicide crimes (*Graham v. Florida* 130 S. Ct. 2011 [2010]). At the time, there were just over 100 people serving these sentences nationwide, the majority of whom were sentenced in Florida (Annino, Rasmussen, & Boehme, 2009). In 2012, the Court further narrowed the allowable use of LWOP for juveniles, limiting it to instances where it had not been imposed under a mandatory minimum statute (*Miller v. Alabama* 567 U.S. 460 [2012]). In 2016, the Court clarified the *Miller* ruling to note that it applied retroactively to all individuals currently serving LWOP sentences under mandatory sentencing schemes (*Montgomery v. Louisiana* 136 S. Ct. 718 [2016]). Despite these substantial victories for youth, there remain 8,600 individuals with *parole-eligible* life or virtual life sentences for crimes committed as juveniles around the U.S. To date, lower courts have mostly ruled that these youth are not specified directly in any of the existing rulings.

American Politics

Social scientists widely agree that the decline in crime from the early 1990s through 2019 cannot be explained by the rise of imprisonment during these years. Explanations for crime's rise and fall are extremely complicated to disentangle, but common factors have included shifts in employment rates and economic opportunity, changes in social and environmental factors, an aging population, and changes in police tactics (Roeder, Eisen, & Bowling, 2015). States that reduced their prison populations over these years experienced crime drops just as states that did not (Mauer & Ghandnoosh, 2015). There are more people serving life sentences today than the entire prison population in 1970. This expansion was the result of policies such as "three strikes," mandatory life imprisonment, and the abolition of parole lengthened prison terms and sent more people to prison (Tonry, 2013).

As violent crime spiked upward in the late 1980s and early 1990s—driven largely by the crack epidemic and the wide availability of handguns—Republican and Democratic lawmakers seized the opportunity to implement policies that would gain public favor by promising to "lock 'em up and throw away the key" (Murakawa, 2014). As he signed California's notorious California Three Strikes legislation into law, Governor Pete Wilson justified the law in this way: "it sends a clear message to repeat criminals. Find a new line of work, because we're going to start turning career criminals into career inmates" (Weintraub, 1994). Such misguided policies were supported by a racialized philosophy that certain groups must be permanently removed to achieve public safety.

The imposition of life sentences on juveniles, some as young as 12 years old, was a particularly heinous component of the "tough on crime" era and serves as a reminder of the extent to which the rhetoric of the time broke with reality. Support for the practice of juvenile transfer to adult criminal court was the vehicle through which life imprisonment for youth was allowed, fueled by false claims that a new breed of "superpredator" was on the horizon that was especially violent and remorseless (DiIulio, 1995). Young, Black boys typified the superpredator profile. By arguing that only the adult criminal courts and prisons could handle such violent individuals, tens of thousands of youth at the federal and state levels were prosecuted in criminal courtrooms designed for adult defendants. Between 1992 and 1999, all but one state expanded its process for juveniles to be prosecuted in adult criminal courts (Hansen, 2001).

Transfer to adult court practice exposed youth to life sentences which are only permissible in the criminal court system and by the peak year of 2012, more than 2,600 youth were serving LWOP sentences, with another estimated 10,000 young people were serving life with parole (LWP) (Nellis, 2013, 2015). The acceptability of life sentences applied to juveniles was largely a product of the era in which these young people were aging through their crime-prone years, adolescence through mid-twenties (Neil and Sampson, 2018; Sampson & Laub, 1993). While this example pertains to juveniles specifically, it is used only to show the lengths lawmakers were willing to go to meet the demands of the era.

The impact that mass imprisonment has had on crime is negligible, but its effect on American society, particularly for a generation of Black Americans, is profound. Participation in civic, social, and economic components of society have been heavily influenced by mass incarceration (Wakefield & Wildeman, 2014). Black people are overrepresented throughout the criminal legal system, and this disparity is especially apparent in long-term imprisonment (Nellis, 2021).

Criminologists have conducted dozens of studies that examine the impact of various imprisonment levels on crime. Marc Mauer and others have written about the diminishing returns for public safety that lengthy prison terms have because most persons "age out" of criminal conduct after about ten years (Mauer & Nellis, 2018). If the goal of incarceration is to reduce crime by incapacitating known individuals, on average there will be less of an impact derived from the imprisonment of a 50-year-old than a 20-year-old.

Well-known criminologist and deterrence expert Daniel Nagin (2022, p. 2) writes, "Increases in already long prison sentences have no material deterrent effect on crime" for a few reasons. First, most people contemplating crime do not anticipate being caught, and in many instances, they are correct: the Federal Bureau of Investigation's Uniform Crime Report shows that less than half (46%) of violent crimes are cleared by arrest (Federal Bureau of Investigation, 2020). Second, even if persons contemplating crime *did* think they would be caught, it would be unrealistic to assume they know the sentence length if convicted. And third, as many as two-thirds of people who are imprisoned for a crime report having been under the influence of alcohol or drugs at the time, which reduces one's ability to make reasonable estimates or risk (National Institute of Drug Abuse, 2020).

Had policymakers relied on science rather than fear mongering to pass the draconian laws that flourished during mass incarceration, America's crime responses would have been shaped quite differently. But, as legal scholar Michael Tonry notes, "Countries have different criminal justice policies and practices for reasons of political culture and history, not because of crime levels, crime trends, or global social and economic forces." (2013, 5).

Responses to crime have enabled and reaffirmed a justice system that separates people, offenses, and sentences unnecessarily into groups considered worthy and unworthy of reform, and this separation has stalled progress in dismantling mass incarceration. Specifically, while legal reforms have produced modest reductions in imprisonment for groups convicted of nonviolent, first-time offenses, progress has been made largely by pitting those who meet these criteria against those convicted of violent offense. This process all but ensures that the latter group does not benefit from reforms (O'Leary, 2021; Seeds, 2016).

Since half of all incarcerated people have been convicted of a violent offense, it is not reasonable to exclude those with violent convictions from reform proposals and expect an end to mass incarceration (Carson, 2021; Gottschalk, 2015; O'Leary, 2021).

Contrary to concerns about public safety, research suggests that people convicted of homicide and other crimes of violence rarely commit new crimes of violence after release from long-term imprisonment (Durose, Cooper, & Snyder, 2014; Prescott, Pyle, & Starr, 2020). Though life sentences have always been part of the punishment range in the U.S., they were rarely served in full before the era of mass incarceration took hold. Instead, life sentences were imposed as an incentive to earnestly encourage rehabilitation and reform. Release through commutation was a reasonable, expected outcome of a life sentence (Seeds, 2022). But for decades of the mass incarceration era, the U.S. has justified extraordinary sentences, particularly for people convicted of violent crimes, by claiming such punishments are necessary to ensure public safety. Studies of those released find that people who commit violence evolve their thinking and conduct as they age past their twenties and, in some cases, a bit later (Laub & Sampson, 2003). To insist on imprisonment until their death is not supported on either empirical or humanitarian grounds. In other democratic nations such as Germany and Norway, accountability is paired with dignity to create a system of punishment and rehabilitation that meets human rights expectations (van Zyl Smit & Appleton, 2016, 2019). The International Criminal Court, which hears arguments on the most severe crimes, including war crimes, crimes against humanity, and genocide, allows review of life sentences after 25 years (Gottschalk, 2012). A human rights approach is centered on the notion that all individuals, even those who have committed acts of violence, merit dignity. The protection of this human right ensures proportionality and prioritizes the humanitarian value of rehabilitation. This approach is associated with lower recidivism rates in other nations.

A range of state-level studies show that people who are released from life sentences are imprisoned for new offenses at a rate of less than 5% (Neuilly, Zgoba, Tita, & Lee, 2011; Prescott, Pyle, & Starr, 2018; The Crime Report, 2011). People paroled in Michigan between 2007 and 2010 with convictions for second-degree murder, manslaughter, or a sex offense were about two-thirds less likely to be reimprisoned for a new crime within three years as the total paroled population. Louisiana State University researchers tracked arrest, conviction, and reimprisonment of 205 released lifers who had been convicted of murder or armed robbery. Both three and five-year reimprisonment rates were examined revealing a 5% and 8% reimprisonment rate, respectively (Shihadeh, Nordyke, and Reed, 2014). And New York safely reduced its reliance on life imprisonment by 5,000 people between 2004 and 2020 and maintained a declining violent crime rate over the same period (Nellis, 2021).

Moving Forward

Mass imprisonment has caused grievous harm to American society and its scale is unprecedented among liberal democracies. Criminal sentences that foreclose a meaningful likelihood of release, those at the far end of the punishment spectrum, are cruel and merciless. Drastically shrinking the prison population requires both bold legislative and judicial action as well as a cultural shift that places human dignity back into the system of corrections.

At a practical level, policies that caused mass incarceration will need to be reversed. Such reforms include ending all sentences of LWOP, capping sentences at maximum terms that are substantially shorter than current practice and eliminating mandatory minimum prison terms altogether. In 2019, The Sentencing Project launched a campaign to end life imprisonment in all its forms with a maximum term of imprisonment that does not exceed 20 years except in rare circumstances where present danger to society remains (Mauer and Nellis, 2018). The organization has refined its position to add the recommendation that all sentences be reviewed with a rebuttable presumption of release within ten years, building on criminological evidence that recidivism drops precipitously within these years (Ghandnoosh and Nellis, 2022). In recent years, other national groups have publicly acknowledged the profound harms caused by extreme sentences, including the American Civil Liberties Union, the American Bar Association, the Brennan Center, the American Law Institute, and Fair and Just Prosecution.

Shortening sentences at the front end must be paired with expanding release mechanisms at the back end for those already imprisoned. Such "second-look" policies allow a reconsideration of the original sentence imposed under the light of current circumstances—both those of the individual and of society. Though researchers warned against lengthening prison terms as a crime control tactic, today there is ample empirical evidence of their profound failure. Sentencing review units, such as one in Baltimore, Maryland, allow prosecutors to view sentences and propose post-conviction downward adjustments (Office of State's Attorney for Baltimore City, 2020). Second-look mechanisms allow course correction for the incarcerated individual as well as for society.

Finally, the American parole system is broken. The parole review process is embedded in a highly risk-averse political system in which fairness and mercy have been forsaken. A just parole system would operate independently of the politics of the executive branch both in the ultimate decision to release the individual and in the board's composition. Crime of conviction, which currently dominates most the decision whether to release, and thus places lifers at a distinct disadvantage, should not be the determining factor in the decision. The focus of the parole board hearing should be on the person's development while incarcerated, current public safety considerations, and identifying what supports are needed to ensure success after release (Nellis, 2021).

Conclusion

This chapter argued that the expansion of life imprisonment played an important role in the mass incarceration era. There are now more people serving life sentences than the entire prison population in 1970, amounting to one of every seven imprisoned persons. The racial disparity among people serving life is even more severe than at any earlier point in the criminal legal system. These uniquely American sentencing policies have allowed teenagers and young adults as well as the elderly to suffer from death-in-prison sentences.

The recommendations provided in this chapter could have the effect of shrinking the life-sentenced population, which will go far to end mass incarceration. But the broad-scale adoption of these and similar proposals also demands a shift in the well-grooved perspective among Americans that permanent exclusion is humane, equitable, or compassionate response. This view, undergirded by racialized fears, accepts as normal that some individuals do not deserve to earn their freedom.

A reformed carceral system will widen its myopic focus from merely incapacitation to one that undertakes rehabilitation and successful reintegration as its primary responsibility. Shifting to a system that prioritizes meeting the extensive needs of existing incarcerated people need not bewilder policymakers and practitioners, as such systems already exist in other nations and were once a priority in the U.S. as well. To move from an incapacitation-focused system to one that supports successful release will require a cultural shift that emphasizes second chances, even for those who caused violent harm.

Discussion Questions:

1. Can you identify two innovative methods that can produce declines in lengthy imprisonment while protecting public safety?
2. Under what circumstances do you feel a life sentence is necessary? What are the benefits of doing so for the government and society? What are the potential consequences of doing so for the government, society, and incarcerated individual?

Notes

1. Alaska does not allow a formal life sentence but does allow virtual life sentences and some crimes require a mandatory minimum of 99 years in prison.
2. Life sentences are considered to be "virtual" or "de facto" if they are 50-year terms or multiple terms that amount to at least 50 years.

References

Annino, P., Rasmussen, D. W. & Boehme, C. (2009). *Juvenile life without parole for non-homicide offenses: Florida compared to nation.* Florida State University College of Law Tallahassee.

Baltimore City State's Attorney (2020). *State's Attorney announces creation of Sentencing Review Unit.* Author.

Carson, E. A. (2021). *Prisoners in 2020 – Statistical tables.* Bureau of Justice Statistics.

Clear, T. & Austin, J. (2009). Reducing mass incarceration: Implications of the iron law of prison populations. *Harvard Law Review, 3,* 307–324.

DiIulio, J. (1995, November 27). The coming of the superpredator. *The Weekly Standard.*

Durose, M. R., Cooper, A. D. & Snyder, H. N. (2014). *Recidivism of prisoners released in 30 states in 2005: Patterns from 2005 to 2010.* Bureau of Justice Statistics.

Federal Bureau of Investigation (2020). *2019 Crime in the United States.* https://ucr.fbi.gov/crime-in-the-u.s/2019/crime-in-the-u.s.-2019.

Ghandnoosh, N. (2017). *Delaying a second chance: The declining prospects for parole on a life sentence.* The Sentencing Project.

Ghandnoosh, N. & Nellis, A. (2022). *How many people are spending over a decade in prison?* The Sentencing Project.

Gottschalk, M. (2012). No way out? Life sentences and the politics of penal reform. In Charles Ogletree and Austin Sarat, Eds. *Life without parole: America's new death penalty* (pp. 227–281). New York University Press.

Gottschalk, M (2015). *Caught: The prison state and the lockdown of American politics.* Princeton University Press

Hansen, B. (2001). Kids in prison. *The CQ Researcher 27,* 345–376.

Irwin, J. (2009). *Lifers: Seeking redemption in prison.* Routledge.

Laub, J. & Sampson, R. (2003). *Shared beginnings, divergent lives: Delinquent boys to age 70.* Harvard University Press.

Mauer, M. & Ghandnoosh, N. (2015). *Fewer prisoners, less crime: A tale of three states.* The Sentencing Project.

Mauer, M. & Nellis, A. (2018). *The meaning of life: The case for abolishing life sentences.* The New Press.
Mauer, M., King, R. & Young, M. (2004). *The meaning of 'life': Long prison sentences in context.* The Sentencing Project.
Murakawa, N. (2014). *The first civil right: How liberals built prison America.* Oxford University.
Nagin, D. (2022). Unraveling mass incarceration: Criminology's role in the policy process. *Criminology, 60,* 401–405.
National Institute of Drug Abuse (2020). *Criminal justice drug facts.* NIDA.
Neil, R. & Sampson, R. (2018). The birth lottery of history: Arrest over the life course of multiple cohorts coming of age, 1995–2018. *American Journal of Sociology, 126*(5), 1127–1178.
Nellis, A. (2013). *Life goes on: The historic rise in life sentences in America.* The Sentencing Project.
Nellis, A. (2015). *A return to justice: Rethinking our approach to juveniles in the system.* Rowman and Littlefield.
Nellis, A. (2021). *No end in sight: America's enduring reliance on life imprisonment.* The Sentencing Project.
Nellis, A. (2022). *Nothing but time: Elderly Americans serving life without parole.* The Sentencing Project.
Neuilly, M., Zgoba, K. M., Tita, G. E. & Lee, S. S. (2011). Predicting recidivism in homicide offenders using classification tree analysis. *Homicide Studies, 15*(2), 154–176.
O'Leary, R. (2022). *Compassionate release and decarceration in the states.* University of Wisconsin Law School Legal Studies, Research Paper Series, Paper 1736.
Prescott, J. J., Pyle, B. & Starr, S. B. (2020). Understanding violent-crime recidivism. *Notre Dame Law Review, 95*(4), 1643–1698.
Roeder, O., Eisen, L. & Bowling, J. (2015). *What caused the crime decline?* The Brennan Center.
Seeds, C. (2016). Bifurcation nation: American penal policy in late mass incarceration. *Punishment and Society, 1*(1), 1–20.
Seeds, C. (2022). *Death by prison: The emergence of life without parole and perpetual confinement.* University of California Press.
Shihadeh, E. S., Nordyke, K., & Reed, A. (2014). *Recidivism in the State of Louisiana: An analysis of 3- and 5-year recidivism rates among long–serving inmates.* Louisiana State University Crime and Policy Evaluation Research Group.
Tennessee Department of Corrections (2014). Administrative Policies and Procedures 2014 Index 505.1.
The Crime Report (2011, January 7). *Low recidivism rate reported for paroled NY murderers.*
Tonry, M. (2013). Remodeling American sentencing: A ten-step blueprint for moving past mass incarceration. *Criminology and Public Policy, 13*(4), 503–533.
van Zyl Smit, D. & Appleton, C. (2016). *Life imprisonment and human rights.* Hart Publishing.
van Zyl Smit, D. & Appleton, C. (2019). *Life imprisonment: A global human rights analysis.* Harvard University Press.
Wakefield, S. & Wildeman, C. (2014). *Children of the prison boom: Mass incarceration and the future of American inequality.* Oxford University Press.
Weintraub, D. (1994, March 8). '3 Strikes' Law Goes into Effect. *Los Angeles Times.*

5

REFLECTION

GROWING UP ON THE INSIDE[1]

Terrence J. Graham

My first time entering the courtroom is an experience that I will never forget. It was 2003. I was sixteen and dressed in an orange jumpsuit that had three big black letters printed on the back, "DDC," which stood for Duval Detention Center. DDC informed other people around me that I was in the custody of the law. And to make matters worse, I was handcuffed in the front with a chain around my waist connected to shackles around my feet. I was wearing a pair of orange Bob Barker shoes, and my jumpsuit was a size large, which made my 5′ 3″ frame look even smaller than it was. There were six other kids in court with me. We were told to walk in a straight line, to sit in the front row, and to wait for our name to be called. I was cold, scared, and curious about what would happen next.

I kept looking around the courtroom to see if my mom or dad or any other family member would show up to support me. After the courtroom door had closed and all the seats were filled, I knew that none of my family was coming. So I just sat still with my head down, fighting back the tears that were trying to escape. Then I heard a loud knock, and the officer announced "All rise for the Honorable Judge ____. Court is now in session." I didn't know what that meant, but I saw everyone stand up, so I did so as well. I saw kids get up when their name was called, walk to the front of the courtroom, and stand next to their mom or dad alongside another man whom I later found out was the kid's lawyer/public defender. When my name was called, I walked to the front of the courtroom with my head down and stood next to my public defender who I'd never met before. I listened as the lawyer and the judge said a few words to each other. Then I was told "go back, have a seat, your court date has been set." As I was loaded up inside the transport van, I was hurt, mad, and confused. None of my family had shown up, and I didn't know what was going on! I listened to the other kids on the van talking about being released on probation or sentenced to 21 days. I asked one of those kids if they knew what was going on with me, and he asked about my case. I told him that I was arrested for robbery, and that this was my first time ever being arrested. He explained to me that I should be allowed to go home if my parents come to get me because I did not have enough points to be held in the detention center. I was excited to get back, but things did not go like the kid said they would. I was

DOI: 10.4324/9781003274292-7

escorted back to my cell and told I would not be allowed to go home until I went before the judge again.

Forty days later I was back in the same courtroom. At first, when they called my name, I was a little more at ease because this time my mom was there, but quickly I sensed that something was wrong. After the judge and my public defender finished talking, I was escorted away from the other kids to a holding cell in the back. I was stripped of my clothes and shackles and told that I had been "direct filed." I didn't know then that the term meant I was being charged as an adult. When I asked the guard what was going on, he said I was going to the "big house," the county jail with adults. I started crying. I didn't understand why I was being treated differently from the other kids, and why I had to go to the "big house." Later that day, my best friend and co-defendant entered the county jail with me. We kept looking around, taking in our surroundings, and wondering what would happen next. At least they placed us in the same room, and we were happy about that. But soon we were approached by the sergeant who told us:

> Look here, this ain't no daycare, and y'all are not in the detention center any more. When y'all get into y'all dorm y'all better behave and bet not give me or any of my staff any trouble or I'll break y'all neck and if someone approach you for a sexual favor or for your food, either give it up or fight because ain't no checking in!

He meant we were not going to be protected. The sergeant asked if we understood. We looked at each other and said "yes, sir." To our surprise and relief, we were placed into a dorm with other kids our age that had been direct filed, as well. The dorm housed about twenty-four people at one time. And we never really saw the adults like I feared.

As I was going through the court proceedings, my parents and I got a quick education about the difference between juvenile and adult court. Instead of kids getting sentenced to a juvenile program for a few weeks or a few months, kids were being sentenced to years, decades, and even life imprisonment! My public defender never came to visit with me and never updated me on the status of my case. My first offer from the state was to plead guilty in exchange for 15 years imprisonment. I was devastated. Once my parents realized how serious this matter was, they searched for a private attorney, but this was way outside their budget. Finally, they found a lawyer who took my case for a flat fee of $1,500. But there really was no difference. That lawyer never visited me, never helped me understand what was going on, and never asked me to look over any papers.

I was released for a short period on probation. But then, one night, I stayed out past my curfew with the wrong crowd, and I was arrested again on a different charge. The judge revoked my probation and sentenced me to life in prison without the possibility of parole (LWOP). Right up until sentencing I kept telling the judge that I didn't understand what was going on, and he kept trying to explain things to me. But eventually he got frustrated and told me that he couldn't make me understand. I was told that I could file an appeal, but I didn't know what that was, and my parents couldn't afford that anyway. They finished my court proceeding and sent me on my way.

Because I was sentenced on a Friday, I had to wait a few days for the transport bus to take me to prison. I pretended to be strong, but on the inside, I was scared to death. I had only seen prisons in movies and once as a child when we went to visit an uncle. I asked the other guys around me what was prison like, and they said "nothing nice." They warned me to make an example out of the first guy that tried to rape me or take my food by either stabbing him or hitting him in the head with a lock. After hearing that, I couldn't sleep.

A few days later, on the bus ride, I sat silently and looked out of the window wondering when and if I would ever see the free world again. My heart was beating 100 mph because I wanted to cry for many reasons but couldn't. As we pulled up to the Reception Center, I saw barbed wire fences everywhere, officers with guns in towers, and buses filled with other inmates. A guard came on to our bus and started yelling,

> Shut up! I don't want to hear no talking from this point on, and if I catch you talking, I will punch your teeth out of your mouth! This is prison, and y'all belong to me now! Get off the bus, go into that building, and do as you are told.

We entered what looked like a warehouse, and we were all told to strip. I was very scared because I had never been nude in front of this many people before, and I didn't know what they were about to do to us. Naked, we walked through a metal detector into another room where staff counted us – 110 new arrivals. They made us run our hands and fingers through our hair and mouth. They had us bend over at the waist and spread our butt cheeks while male officers made sexual comments and flashed a flash light on our butts. We were told to shave our face and head bald, to shower and put on some prison blues. After this processing, they called my name and told me that I was being placed in "the box," which is another name for solitary confinement. I was confused and didn't know what I had done wrong to be placed in confinement. Later on, I found out that the Florida Department of Corrections ("FDOC") put me in the box because they didn't know how to house me. They said my sentence was too long for me to be around other kids of my age, but I was too young and too small to be around the adults.

Eventually, I was placed with the adults, but I was never given any help or advice on how to survive in prison. I walked around with a lock in my pocket just like the guys at the jail had told me to do in case I needed to fight off an attacker. And then I'd get moved to another prison for some administrative reason, and every time, it was the same thing: guards would just put me in a dorm, in a room with total strangers, and expect me to find a way to survive.

It's hard to imagine, but after about five years, things actually got worse. FDOC was hit with a budget cut. Our food portions were reduced; our canteen prices were increased; and prisons became even more dangerous. Prisoners started robbing and stealing from each other just to separate the strong from the weak; sexual assaults increased, as well. Most prisoners joined a gang in order to survive this new environment. FDOC tried to implement some programs to prevent all of this violence, but it was too late and unsuccessful. The prison population was at an all-time high of about 1,000–1,500 inmates at every major prison with only 30 officers per shift; the staff could barely keep themselves safe, let alone us prisoners safe from each other. As I came of age inside Florida's prisons, I realized I needed to learn two sets of rules: the FDOC rules and the rules of my fellow inmates. If I broke the FDOC rules, I was placed in the box and subject to more prison time. But if I broke the rules of my fellow inmates, I risked a beating with a lock in a sock or a stabbing with a homemade knife. I've managed these two sets of rules for years, wondering which will come first – going home or dying inside.

In conclusion, though my sentence of LWOP was ultimately overturned by the United States Supreme Court, no child should ever be sentenced to LWOP. Are kids not different? If so, why do our laws allow kids and adults to be sentenced the same? I wish that no child should ever have to endure this kind of punishment and the mental stress of wondering when and if they will die in prison.

Note

1 I am one of thousands of people once sentenced to die in prison for a crime that I committed as a juvenile. My Supreme Court case changed hundreds of these cruel sentences. I am still incarcerated in Florida and pray to be free in the next few years.

SECTION II
Life Inside

What does it mean to be incarcerated? Michel Foucault (1977, p. 11) summarizes it well:

> The body, according to this penality, is caught up in a system of constraints and privations, obligations and prohibitions. Physical pain, the pain of the body itself, is no longer the constituent element of the penalty. From being an art of unbearable sensations punishment has become an economy of suspended rights.

Incarceration deprives individuals of privacy, services, freedom of movement, and autonomy. The conditions of life inside prison are invisible to the public. This section is designed to highlight the realities of life inside by focusing on solitary confinement, aging individuals, carceral food, and the obstacles faced by lesbian, gay, bisexual, transgender, and queer persons (LGBTQ).

The realities of the Life Inside section begin with Demarest and Cortina's "Solitary Confinement: Controversies and Reforms in Restrictive Housing." They provide a critical overview of ongoing debates and controversies regarding the use of restrictive housing, while also introducing current policy interventions aimed at reforming this method of confinement. The section continues with Aday et al.'s chapter that describes how mass incarceration has contributed to the growing number of deaths behind bars. Next, Terry and Grant discuss the impact of carceral food environments on the overall well-being of incarcerated women. Following their chapter, Jeffrey Dennis examines the problems and obstacles that incarcerated LGBTQ persons face in "The Mass Incarceration of LGBTQ Persons." The Life Inside section concludes with a reflection chapter by Janette Richardson, who describes a typical day as a trans woman of color working in the prison library during the Covid-19 pandemic.

Reference

Foucault, M. (1977). *Discipline and punish: The birth of the prison.* London: Allen Lane.

DOI: 10.4324/9781003274292-8

6

SOLITARY CONFINEMENT

Controversies and Reforms in Restrictive Housing

Megan T. Demarest and Hannah G. Cortina

LEARNING OUTCOMES:

Upon successful completion of this chapter, students will be able to:

1. Define and describe restrictive housing practices within the United States.
2. Compare and contrast differing viewpoints regarding the use of solitary confinement inside prisons.
3. Identify empirical gaps and continued challenges to the study of restrictive housing.
4. Synthesize and assess new developments and reforms to the practice of solitary confinement.

Introduction

Restrictive housing, an umbrella term often used interchangeably with practices such as solitary confinement, special housing units, supermax incarceration, administrative segregation, disciplinary segregation, and protective custody, serves as a widely used, though controversial, correctional approach to managing prison populations across the United States (Astor, Fagan, & Shapiro, 2018; Digard, Vanko, & Sullivan, 2018; Donson & Reiter, 2018; Mears, Hughes, Pesta, Bales, Brown, Cochran, & Woolredge, 2019). In fact, a recent report estimated that between 55,000 and 62,500 justice-involved persons were held in restrictive housing in 2019 alone (CLA-Liman, 2019). This marks a decrease in the population size housed within these units from previous years, and especially during the height of the prison expansion as a result of mass incarceration-related policies and practices (Beck, 2015; CLA-Liman, 2019). Restricted housing continues to come under the scrutiny of advocacy groups, federal legislators, government agencies, scholars, media outlets, and the general public due to documented psychological and behavioral harms associated with this practice (Digard et al., 2018; Donson & Reiter, 2018; Haney, 2018a; Kapoor & Trestman, 2016) and the overrepresentation of Black and African American people held in solitary confinement (The Federal Anti-Solitary Taskforce, 2021). While there are calls to reform solitary confinement

DOI: 10.4324/9781003274292-9

policies and procedures to reduce the psychological trauma and racial injustice, a growing number of organizations maintain that long-term solitary confinement is a form of state-sponsored torture and any stays in solitary confinement that exceed 15 days should be abolished in accordance with the United Nation's Mandela Rules for the Treatment of Prisoners (Unlock the Box, 2021).

In broad terms, restrictive housing involves separating an incarcerated person from the general prison population through the use of confined isolation practices, in which human interaction, activities, and movements are limited and/or severely restricted for a period of 22 hours or more (Beck, 2015; Clark & Duwe, 2019; Cochran, Toman, Mears, & Bales, 2018; Digard et al., 2018; Mears & Bales, 2010). In 2016, the United States Department of Justice conducted an intensive review of restrictive housing which resulted in a set of guidelines outlining that such practices should be used rarely, applied fairly, and subjected to reasonable constraints (U.S. Department of Justice, 2016). The Department of Justice (DOJ) established three key elements to define restrictive housing:

1 Removal of the individual from the general population of the correctional institution;
2 Placement of the individual in a locked cell or room; and
3 The inability of the individual to leave for the majority of the day, which the DOJ specified is 22 hours or more in a cell.

However, despite these clear definitions provided by the DOJ, the use and implementation of restrictive housing across prisons within the United States varies widely (Mears et al., 2019) which makes it increasingly difficult to define, or using methodological terms, operationalize. Specifically, varying policies, procedures, and conditions within these specialized housing units across facilities poses increased challenges to the study and systematic evaluation of restrictive housing (Frost & Monteiro, 2016; Kapoor & Trestman, 2016; Mears et al., 2019). Accordingly, scholars largely caution against generalizing about the application and effects of restrictive housing (Mears et al., 2019).

Despite such ambiguity in restrictive housing practices and its consequences, tensions surrounding the practice have existed since the introduction of solitary confinement in earlyU.S. prisons to contemporary times. Proponents of restrictive housing argue that this method of confinement aids in maintaining institutional security, safety, and order (Labrecque & Mears, 2019; Stubblefield, 2002). On the other hand, critics challenge restrictive housing on moral, ethical, financial, and legal grounds (Labrecque & Mears, 2019), frequently citing the psychological harms experienced by individuals housed within these conditions as evidence of its inhumaneness and violation of human rights (Digard et al., 2018). In response to concerns regarding the long-term consequences of restrictive housing, demands for reform have fueled the introduction of policy changes and interventions within correctional realms (Digard et al., 2018; Donson & Reiter, 2018). The effectiveness and impact of such reforms remains unclear, adding further complexity to our understanding of restrictive housing, its potential advantages, its consequences, and its future within corrections. On the latter, abolitionists assert that as there are no reforms that could make solitary confinement in excess of 15 days a lawful punishment, the practice of long-term solitary confinement must end (Unlock the Box, 2021).

Therefore, within this chapter, we begin by introducing historical controversies in order to situate ongoing debates surrounding the continued use of restrictive housing practices within correctional environments. In doing so, we highlight empirical gaps in our understanding of this practice and consider how solitary confinement relates to mass incarceration. Next, this chapter takes stock of current policy changes and interventions aimed at reforming or abolishing restrictive housing. Finally, we conclude by considering how these initiatives may alter the correctional landscape in the future.

Historical Controversies and Ongoing Debates

The use of isolation has been a staple of American correctional punishment, with early traces of solitary confinement practices dating back to one of the earliest penitentiaries in the United States—Pennsylvania's Eastern State Penitentiary (Dolan, 2007; Reiter, 2016). Under the "Pennsylvania model," solitary confinement was observed as a method to encourage inner reflection, genuine repentance, and rehabilitation (Reiter, 2016); however, it fell out of favor for a period of time due to documented psychological harms associated with the practice (Dolan, 2007; Reiter, 2016). As the United States' correctional population skyrocketed in the 1980s, solitary confinement experienced a resurgence and escalation, coinciding with the "tough on crime" era, growing prison and jail populations, and the proliferation of "supermax" incarceration (Clark & Duwe, 2019; Digard et al., 2018; Frost & Monteiro, 2016; Mears, 2013; Shalev, 2009). In fact, following this point, scholars argue that isolation and segregation have been primary objectives in the construction and design of correctional facilities throughout the United States during the era of mass incarceration (Frost & Monteiro, 2016), and as a means of obtaining social control, the purpose of mass incarceration *itself*. Describing the intersection of mass incarceration and solitary confinement as "mass solitary," Lobel (2020, p. 159) explains:

> The dramatic expansion of the use of solitary confinement and the construction of new super-maximum (supermax) prisons [was] an attempt by prison officials and politicians to maintain control of prisons in the face of increasingly radicalized, rebellious prisoners—often, but not exclusively, African-American—who had organized protests and disobedient conduct in American prisons from the 1960s to the 1980s.

Lobel (2020, p. 165) goes on to highlight how the increased use of solitary confinement against Black and African American people "ran parallel to the political use of mass imprisonment as a form of social control in reaction to the political movements and disturbances of that era." Robert King's experience in solitary confinement in Louisiana State Prison, commonly known as Angola, provides support for Lobel's thesis (2010, para 2):

> In 1969, I was locked up for a robbery I didn't do and, while inside, I joined the Black Panthers. Three years later, an inmate was stabbed to death on my prison block and, because of my politics, the authorities saw a chance to pin it on me. In 2001, I was cleared of this killing but, by then, I had spent 29 years alone in a [restricted housing] cell.

Advocates of isolation housing contend that the use of segregation bolsters institutional security and, in turn, the safety of justice-involved populations and correctional staff (Frost & Monteiro, 2016; Labrecque & Smith, 2019). However, the goals of restrictive housing may vary, which in turn, may influence the conditions of confinement (Mears et al., 2019). Research has shown that isolation and segregation can be utilized for administrative reasons, for disciplinary and/or punitive purposes, for protection, as well as for the management of individuals who are violent (Cochran et al., 2018; Kapoor & Trestman, 2016; Mears et al., 2019; Shalev, 2009). It remains debated whether the use of such housing enhances order and security within institutions (Mears et al., 2019). Increasing testimonials and qualitative accounts of the psychological and physical damages experienced by those confined within these restrictive realms has generated increased attention to the potential negative effects of solitary confinement during the era of mass incarceration (Haney, 2018a). Robert King, the individual mentioned above, described his time in solitary confinement as tortorous (2010, paras 4–5, 8):

> Some days I would pace up and down and from left to right for hours, counting to myself. I learned to know every inch of the cell. Maybe I looked crazy walking back and forth like some trapped animal, but I had no choice – I needed to feel in control of my space.
>
> At times I felt an anguish that is hard to put into words. To live 24/7 in a box, year after year, without the possibility of parole, probation or the suspension of sentence is a terrible thing to endure....
>
> The worst punishment was the "cold box", our name for the cell within Camp J. It was down a long hallway through three sets of secure doors, and when they pushed me inside, the isolation was total. They would keep me there for a month, in blocks of 10 days, shoving food through a slot in the door. I went for days without speaking to anyone. That kind of sensory deprivation was torture for me – to survive I knew I had to keep my mind active.

Accordingly, critics contend that such housing practices may actually increase antisocial behavior rather than discourage it (Haney, 2012) and, in turn, perpetuate the United States' reliance on and use of mass imprisonment.

Over time, extant research has provided increasing evidence of the negative psychological effects associated with restrictive housing (Haney, 2018a). While these effects have been shown to be moderate to small (Morgan, Gendreau, Smith, Gray, Labrecque, MacLean,... & Mills, 2016), investigations continue to call attention to the psychological harms experienced by incarcerated populations housed within these units (Arrigo & Bullock, 2008; Grassian, 2006; Haney, 2003, 2018b). In fact, research has demonstrated that psychological distress (Arrigo & Bullock, 2008; Grassian, 2006; Haney, 2003, 2018b; Wynn & Szatrowski, 2004), self-harm behaviors, and suicide are associated with being housed in solitary confinement conditions (Reeves & Tamburello, 2014; Way, Sawyer, Barboza, & Nash, 2007). The negative effects of solitary confinement can continue long after the individual's time in solitary confinement ends (Smith, 2018). As a result of the risk of detrimental impact, experts within the field question its continued use within correctional environments (Digard et al., 2018; Haney, 2018a). Moreover, research has shown that restrictive housing disproportionately impacts specific criminal-justice-involved populations. As mass incarceration has disproportionately impacted BIPOC people, Black and Latinx men are overrepresented in solitary confinement as compared to their white male counterparts (Lantigua-Williams, 2016). For example, in a recent study of Pennsylvania's use of solitary confinement, Pullen-Blasnik, Simes, and Western (2021) found that "the cumulative risk of solitary confinement for Black men is three times higher than for Latino men and more than eight times higher than for white men" (para 19). While there are overall fewer women housed in solitary confinement as compared to men, the overrepresentation of Black and Latina women also exists in Pennsylvania. In addition to racial/ethnic disparities, individuals with mental illnesses, those who identify as lesbian, gay, or bisexual, younger persons, as well as individuals who have less education have been found to be more likely to be placed within these specialized housing units (Beck, 2015; Digard et al., 2018; Kapoor & Trestman, 2016). Furthermore, disparities not only exist in the placement in solitary confinement but also the length of stays. In the same study of Pennsylvania noted above, the length of time Black men were held in solitary confinement was greater than all other racial/ethnic groups (Pullen-Blasnik et al., 2021).

Recent investigations and meta-analyses, however, have raised concern over strong negative effects documented within existing scholarship, citing methodological shortcomings, cross-sectional designs, inconsistent operationalizations, varying lengths of confinement periods, and small sample sizes as noteworthy limitations to the generalizability of such findings (Frost & Monteiro, 2016; Mears et al., 2019; Morgan et al., 2016). As a result, our understanding of restrictive housing practices and its effects remains fragmented and incomplete. Accordingly, scholars continue to demand greater empirical attention to the study of diverse forms of restrictive housing, varying policies related to the placement of justice-involved persons in these housing units, and in turn, the effects of such heterogeneous housing practices on outcomes of interest (e.g., institutional safety, prison misconduct, psychological damages, and recidivism) (Garcia, 2016; Mears et al., 2019). Such developments will be paramount in policymakers and prison administrators' continued efforts to reform restrictive housing practices within correctional settings.

Current Developments in Corrections

In response to calls for reform through advocacy groups, legislatures, and justice-involved persons, restrictive housing practices have been rapidly changing in recent years. In particular, legislation has widely passed restrictions on the use of solitary confinement for special populations, including juveniles, pregnant or postpartum women, and those suffering from severe mental illness. These restrictions follow recommendations from the United States Department of Justice (2016) and research entities such as the Vera Institute (Digard et al., 2018).

While some seek to reform solitary confinement, others seek to seriously curtail or abolish the practice of long-term solitary confinement. For example, the Federal Anti-Solitary Taskforce (2021, pp. 4–10) offers the following recommendations to severely limit solitary confinement, both its overall use and duration, and to fundamentally alter the experience describing it as "the opposite of solitary confinement" (p. 6).

- End solitary confinement in all federal custody, other than (a) in emergency situations involving imminent serious physical injury, measured in hours rather than days, and with repeated engagement during that time, or (b) for medical quarantine in units overseen by medical staff, with comparable to general population services, phone calls, emails, programming with appropriate physical distance, telecommunication, and meaningful human engagement with appropriate physical distance.

- Involuntary lock-ins should only occur in an emergency situation as a last resort to de-escalate immediate conflict that has resulted in serious physical injury or makes imminent injury likely, and for as short a time as necessary to de-escalate such conflict and not to exceed four hours total immediately following such conflict, with staff rounding at least every 15 minutes and staff engagement at least every hour. No one should be held in such confinement for more than four hours total in any 24-hour period, not more than 12 hours total in any seven-day period. Even involuntary lock-ins measured in hours should be prohibited for protected special populations because of the particular harm they can face in isolation, including people 25 or younger, 55 or older, with mental health needs, with medical conditions, with disabilities, who are LGBTI, and who are pregnant or new mothers.
- Ensure that all separation from the general population or alternatives to solitary, regardless of what they are called and including any and all forms of restrictive housing, are the opposite of solitary, with full days of out-of-cell congregate time (at least 14 hours) and opportunities for congregate programming and activities (at least seven hours) aimed at addressing the reasons for separation from the general population, without restraints and with at least several other people in group spaces conducive to meaningful human engagement.
- Enhance due process protections, using neutral decision-makers and a right to representation at hearings to ensure meaningful review of allegations that can result in separation or alternatives, restricting conduct that can result in separation or alternatives to the most egregious conduct in need of an intensive intervention, and imposing strict time limits on separation or alternatives to ensure that people are not warehoused in abusive environments.

While focused at the national level, the Task Force asserts that these recommendations can be implemented at the state and local levels, and there has been some movement on these fronts. For example, the 2022 Washington D.C. Bill, Eliminating Restrictive Housing and Segregated Enclosures ("ERASE"), which would prohibit all solitary confinement, limit the use of safe cells, and require proper care for people experiencing mental health emergencies in D.C. jails. Connecticut and Maine attempted to pass similar bills in 2021 to ban restrictive housing altogether; however, neither bills have yet progressed to enactment. Although the complete elimination of restrictive housing may seem like a positive solution to avoid the mistreatment of incarcerated persons, it is unlikely to occur for many reasons. As there needs to be an internal system to address violent behavior and a way to relocate persons in a violent state from the rest of the population, legislation introducing the entire removal of restrictive housing rarely makes it far in the legal process. Instead, many states ultimately revise such "elimination" bills and pass legislation that make it difficult to utilize restrictive housing unless absolutely necessary or under certain conditions, similar to the Federal Anti-Solitary Taskforce's policy recommendations described above. For example, a 2022 Colorado Bill prohibits jails with a bed capacity of over 400 from placing individuals into restrictive housing involuntarily. Additionally, a 2021 New York Bill redefines solitary confinement to 17 hours a day except during facility-wide emergencies, limits who can be placed in solitary confinement, and creates mandatory out-of-cell programming for at least four hours a day.

Overall, restrictive housing populations have been declining as many corrections agencies have developed new strategies and programs for managing challenging populations (CLA-Liman, 2019). Although the decline in population seems promising, it should be noted that changes in terms or definitions may misrepresent significant changes. For example, if an institution defines solitary confinement as constraining a person in-cell for more than 22 hours a day, does keeping this individual locked in a single cell for 20 hours a day constitute his/her/their exclusion from the restrictive housing population count? Compared to an institution that actively works with the incarcerated person on their behavioral issues through increased programming and out-of-cell time, it would seem unfair to include both groups in the same "non-restrictive" category. It is this extreme diversity in operationalization of restrictive housing practices that cultivates inconsistent population numbers and difficulty in cross-national research (Mears et al., 2019).

With that said, there are correctional institutions around the country who have changed their practices and developed new policies to divert people away from traditional restrictive housing. Because research has found that persons suffering from mental illness can deteriorate rapidly in restrictive housing settings (Reeves & Tamburello, 2014; Way et. al., 2007), many institutions have implemented diversion programs that reroute qualifying persons to therapeutic housing units (THUs). Compared to traditional solitary confinement, THUs are often run by a team of mental health professionals who deliver treatment at an increased intensity while continuously monitoring progress or regression. The highly structured THU system provides increased security for the incarcerated person while maintaining focus on their mental health needs. Ideally, THUs are not a permanent placement but instead provide a temporary environment with increased security levels and treatment intensity while a person suffering from mental illness can recover enough to return to the general population. As such, an important component of THUs are scheduled reviews of their population to ensure appropriate and individualized steps are being made to help the person progress toward reintegration into the general population.

For those who do not meet diversion criteria for THUs, there are still many options for innovative restrictive housing policies that align with evidence-based practices. Tiered and reward systems are growing in popularity for their structured and tangible benefits associated with improved behavior within restrictive housing units (ASCA-Liman, 2018). A 2018 report on restrictive housing found that 27 states instituted stepdown or transition programs in their restrictive housing units, including Alabama, Delaware, New Jersey, and Utah (ASCA-Liman, 2018). There are many versions of tiered and stepdown systems, but generally a person will enter the housing unit at one level or "step" based on the institutional offense that brought them to restrictive housing with opportunities to move up or down the privilege and reward system based on behavior. The reward system can offer items difficult to obtain in prison which may seem mundane to the non-incarcerated but are highly sought after by those within the prison walls (e.g., different flavors of noodles, soda, and different brand of socks). Increased out-of-cell time, longer phone calls, and less rigid schedules are other forms of privileges that can be earned in exchange for improved behavior within a tiered restrictive housing system.

By incentivizing prosocial behavior, the tiered systems teach the incarcerated person the value of following institutional and/or societal rules. These systems also outline clear steps to getting out of restrictive housing and back into the general population which benefits both the correctional staff and the incarcerated person; the removal of subjectivity in the decision to reintegrate into the general population relieves correctional staff of accountability and reinstates power to the individual. The main takeaway of tiered or reward systems is that they can be very low cost yet extremely effective in motivating behavior change in people (ASCA-Liman,

2018). Although it may take some experimenting to find out what rewards or incentives the population will work hardest for, pairing these systems with increased yet reasonable security has proven successful across the country in reforming existing restrictive housing units.

The Future of Solitary Confinement: Policy Recommendations

A persistent challenge to instituting change in restrictive housing practices is internal push-back from correctional staff. Namely, it can be difficult for correctional staff to provide increased services to people they view as "the problem" in their institution. To combat this, institutional leadership needs to implement a clear plan that outlines the policy changes and, more importantly, *why* those changes are necessary. Improving restrictive housing practices can lead to a reduction in overall length of stay, decreased likelihood of readmission to restrictive housing, and a substantial reduction in use of force (Bertsch, 2019). By clearly and consistently conveying the benefits of changes in restrictive housing to staff members, leadership can increase the likelihood of lasting change.

As we collectively move away from antiquated restrictive housing practices, and some jurisdictions proposing the abolition or severe curtailment of solitary confinement, new policies will require innovation with resources and existing spaces. Reworking current buildings or areas can save an institution the financial and timely burden of building new wings to accommodate the treatment needs of those in restrictive housing (Bertsch, 2019). Progressive jurisdictions have remodeled unused closets, pantries, and even leadership offices to allocate specialized spaces for treatment of their restrictive housing populations. Within these spaces, security concerns are balanced with treatment needs by envisioning creative solutions such as modified desks that restrain the person enough for the safety of others but still allow enough movement to work with partners during class. Comparatively, free movement around the unit may raise security concerns for correctional staff which can be mitigated when such movement is earned based on clearly defined behavioral expectations. Understandably, safety concerns are likely to be the priority for all correctional staff (Labrecque & Mears, 2019), but the future of restrictive housing requires a balance of addressing those concerns while implementing targeted, individualized treatment to address underlying issues and needs.

Because building structure, policies, and laws can vary greatly state-to-state and even between jurisdictions, it is not possible to formulate a blanket solution for restrictive housing. Instead, the reformation of solitary confinement and ultimately its future lies in the hands of criminologists, practitioners, and policymakers to work together in a concerted and collaborative effort to systematically evaluate, eliminate, and transform existing solitary confinement conditions across our country (Digard et al., 2018; Mears et al., 2019).

Discussion Questions:

1 The controversial use of solitary confinement in the United States has created polarized viewpoints. How can institutional security and safety be maximized without sacrificing the human rights of those confined within these restrictive housing units? Can these goals coexist within carceral systems?

2 In acknowledgment of varied terminology, methodological shortcomings, and empirical gaps related to the study of restrictive housing, how can the criminal justice field continue to advance our understanding of solitary confinement practices?

References

Arrigo, B. A., & Bullock, J. L. (2008). The psychological effects of solitary confinement on prisoners in supermax units: Reviewing what we know and recommending what should change. *International Journal of Offender Therapy and Comparative Criminology*, *52*(6), 622–640.

Association of State Correctional Administrators (ASCA) & The Liman Center for Public Interest Law at Yale Law School. (2018). Reforming Restrictive Housing: The 2018 ASCA-Liman Nationwide Survey of Time-in-Cell.

Astor, J., Fagan, T., & Shapiro, D. (2018). The effects of restrictive housing on the psychological functioning of inmates. *Journal of Correctional Health Care*, *24*, 8–20.

Beck, A. J. (2015). *Use of restrictive housing in U.S. prisons and jails, 2011–12*. Washington, DC: Bureau of Justice Statistics, U.S. Department of Justice.

Bertsch, L. K. (2019). Reflections on North Dakota's sustained solitary confinement reform. In J. Lobel & P.S. Smith (Eds.), *Solitary confinement: Effects, practices, and pathways toward reform* (pp. 325–334). New York: Oxford University Press.

Clark, V. A., & Duwe, G. (2019). From solitary to the streets: The effect of restrictive housing on recidivism. *Corrections*, *4*(4), 302–318. https://doi.org/10.1080/23774657.2017.1416318

Cochran, J. C., Toman, E. L., Mears, D. P., & Bales, W. D. (2018). Solitary confinement as punishment: Examining in-prison sanctioning disparities. *Justice Quarterly*, *35*, 381–411.

Correctional Leaders Association (CLA) & Liman Center for Public Interest Law at Yale Law School. (2019). Time-In-Cell 2019: A Snapshot of Restrictive Housing Based on a Nationwide Survey of US Prison Systems. https://law.yale.edu/sites/default/files/area/center/liman/document/time-in-cell_2019.pdf

Digard, L., Vanko, E., & Sullivan, S. (2018). *Rethinking restrictive housing: Lessons from five U.S. jail and prison systems*. New York: Vera Institute of Justice, pp. 20–26. https://perma.cc/XHZ3- P4KM.

Dolan, F. X. (2007). *Eastern state penitentiary*. Charleston, SC: Arcadia Publishing.

Donson, J. T., & Reiter, K. (2018). Understanding federal "restrictive housing unit" environments. *Federal Sentencing Reporter*, *31*(2), 126–132,

The Federal Anti-Solitary Taskforce. (2021). *A blueprint for ending solitary confinement by the federal government*. Author. https://www.aclu.org/report/blueprint-ending-solitary-confinement-federal-government

Frost, N. A., & Monteiro, C. E. (2016). *Administrative segregation in U.S. prisons executive summary*. U.S. Department of Justice, Office of Justice Programs, National Institute of Justice. https://www.ojp.gov/pdffiles1/nij/249750.pdf

Garcia, M. (Ed.). (2016). *Restrictive housing in the U.S.* Washington, DC: National Institute of Justice.

Grassian, S. (2006). Psychiatric effects of solitary confinement. *Washington University Journal of Law and Policy*, *22*(1), 325–383.

Haney, C. (2003). Mental health issues in long-term solitary and "supermax" confinement. *Crime and Delinquency*, *49*(1), 124–156.

Haney, C. (2012). Prison effects in the era of mass incarceration. *The Prison Journal*, *0*(0), 1–24.

Haney, C. (2018a). Restricting the use of solitary confinement. *Annual Review of Criminology*, *1*, 285–310.

Haney, C. (2018b). The psychological effects of solitary confinement: A systematic critique. *Crime and Justice*, *47*(1), 365–416.

Kapoor, R. & Trestman, R. (2016). Mental health effects of restrictive housing. NCJ 250321. In L.E. Lynch, K.V. Mason, & N. Rodriguez (Eds.), *Restrictive housing in the U.S.: Issues, challenges,*

and future directions (pp. 199–232). Washington, DC: U.S. Department of Justice, National Institute of Justice.
King, R. (2010, Aug. 26). Experience: I spent 29 years in solitary confinement. *The Guardian*. https://www.theguardian.com/lifeandstyle/2010/aug/28/29-years-solitary-confinement-robert-king
Labrecque, R. M., & Mears, D. P. (2019). Prison system versus critics' views on the use of restrictive housing: Objective risk classification or ascriptive assignment? *The Prison Journal*, *99*(2), 194–218. https://doi.org/10.1177/0032885519825492
Labrecque, R. M., & Smith, P. (2019). Assessing the impact of time spent in restrictive housing confinement on subsequent measures of institutional adjustment among men in prison. *Criminal Justice and Behavior*, *46*(10), 1445–1455.
Lantigua-Williams, J. (2016, Dec. 5). The link between race and solitary confinement. *The Atlantic*. https://www.theatlantic.com/politics/archive/2016/12/race-solitary-confinement/509456/
Lobel, J. (2020). Mass solitary and mass incarceration: Explaining the dramatic rise in prolonged solitary in America's prisons. *Northwestern University Law Review, 115*(1), 159–210.
Mears, D. P. (2013). Supermax prisons: The policy and the evidence. *Criminology and Public Policy*, *12*, 681–719.
Mears, D. P., & Bales, W. D. (2010). Supermax housing: Placement, duration, and time to reentry. *Journal of Criminal Justice*, *38*, 545–554.
Mears, D. P., Hughes, V., Pesta, G. B., Bales, W. D., Brown, J. M., Cochran, J. C., & Wooldredge, J. (2019). The new solitary confinement? A conceptual framework for guiding and assessing research and policy on "restrictive housing". *Criminal Justice and Behavior*, *46*(10), 1427–1444. https://doi.org/10.1177/0093854819852770
Morgan, R. D., Gendreau, P., Smith, P., Gray, A. L., Labrecque, R. M., MacLean, N., ... & Mills, J. F. (2016). Quantitative syntheses of the effects of administrative segregation on inmates' well-being. *Psychology, Public Policy, and Law*, *22*(4), 439–461.
Pullen-Blasnik, H., Simes, J. T., & Western, B. (2021, Nov. 26). The population prevalence of solitary confinement. *Science Advances*. https://www.science.org/doi/10.1126/sciadv.abj1928#
Reeves, R., & Tamburello, A. (2014). Single cells, segregated housing, and suicide in the New Jersey Department of Corrections. *Journal of the American Academy of Psychiatry and the Law*, *42*, 484–488.
Reiter, K. A. (2016). *23/7: Pelican bay prison and the rise of long-term solitary confinement*. New Haven, CT: Yale University Press.
Shalev, S. (2009). *Supermax: Controlling risk through solitary confinement*. Abingdon: Willan.
Smith, D. G. (2018, Nov. 9). Neuroscientists make a case against solitary confinement. *Scientific American*. https://www.scientificamerican.com/article/neuroscientists-make-a-case-against-solitary-confinement/
Stubblefield, R. (2002). Prisons should not coddle inmates. In Espejo, R. (Ed.), *America's prisons: Opposing viewpoints* (pp. 100–104). San Diego, CA: Greenhaven Press.
Unlock the Box (2021). About us. Author. https://unlocktheboxcampaign.org/about/
U.S. Department of Justice. (2016). *Report and recommendations concerning the use of restrictive housing*. https://www.justice.gov/archives/dag/file/815551/download
Way, B. B., Sawyer, D. A., Barboza, S., & Nash, R. (2007). Inmate suicide and time spent in special disciplinary housing in New York State prison. *Psychiatric Services*, *58*(4), 558–560.
Wynn, J. R., & Szatrowski, A. (2004). Hidden prisons: Twenty-three-hour lockdown units in the New York state correctional facilities. *Pace Law Review*, 24(2), 497–525.

7

DEATH AND DYING EXPERIENCES OF LONG-SERVING INDIVIDUALS

Ronald H. Aday, Meredith Huey Dye, and Nicole Cook

LEARNING OUTCOMES:

Upon successful completion of this chapter, students will be able to:

1. Explain the specific ways that mass incarceration has contributed to the growing number of prison deaths.
2. Identify the factors that contribute to an increased level of death anxiety behind bars.
3. Understand the strategies women serving life often rely on to cope with their fears of dying in prison.
4. Describe the policies and practices prisons used when someone dies in prison.
5. Describe the currently available options which might assist individuals to maintain some level of control and dignity when dying in prison.

Introduction

Over the last 20 years, deaths in state and federal prisons have more than doubled from 1,630 in 1991 to 4,234 in 2019 (Carson, 2021). Of those deaths reported in 2019, 77% were considered natural deaths with roughly 60% (22,441) recorded for those age 55 and over. Chronic illnesses continue to be the leading cause of death with cancer, heart disease, respiratory diseases, and liver failure the most prevalent (Widra & Bertram, 2020). For those serving extreme sentences, or what some refer to as death by imprisonment, a variety of trepidations often surface: the feeling that dying in prison will be viewed as an indication of ultimate failure, the fears of dying alone or suffering from a painful death, and the fears of family abandonment resulting in the stigma of an unclaimed body at life's end (Aday & Wahidin, 2016; Petreca, 2021). The anticipation of such a horrible death experience behind bars can especially haunt those individuals serving life sentences or those who suffer from unforgiving medical conditions while trapped in an uncaring and vastly inadequate healthcare system (Sharp, 2022; Wang and Sawyer, 2021).

DOI: 10.4324/9781003274292-10

The Fruits of Mass Incarceration

When it comes to incarceration, the United States is viewed as the most punitive nation in the world (Clear & Frost, 2014). While the pre-COVID incarceration rate has fallen from ts high of 756 incarcerated people per 100,000 residents in 2013 to 419 per 100,000 in 2019, this country still houses 22% of the world's prison population (Sawyer & Wagner, 2022). After decades of a mass incarceration policy, about 15% (203,865) of the 1.38 million housed in state and federal jurisdictions are serving court-ordered life sentences (Nellis, 2021b). Of those serving life sentences, 55,000 persons are serving life without the possibility of parole and another 44,000 are serving virtual life with sentences of 50 years or more. Thousands of others are also sentenced to "death by incarceration" when considering probable years remaining to live at the time of sentencing. Some life sentences are solely symbolic and retributive, and equate to death sentences, as they reach upward of 600 or 999 years of stacked charges, convictions, and sentences (Dye & Aday, 2019). Over 6,600, (one of every 15) are women serving life sentences – an increase of 20% over the past two decades (Nellis, 2021a).

With tougher sentencing laws including mandatory minimums, truth in sentencing policies, and for some states, abolishing parole altogether, older incarcerated individuals make up the fastest growing demographic in the U.S. prison system. Over the past 20 years, the number of people 55 years of age and older incarcerated in state and federal prisons more than doubled from 75,300 to 180,836 (Carson, 2020). Under the current sentencing guidelines, by 2030, the 55+ prison population is predicted to make up one-third of the overall prison population. With high denial rates for release, parole boards serving as gatekeepers practically ensure that older incarcerated people will have difficulty getting their healthcare needs sufficiently met (Bedard et al., 2022). As a result, the graying prison population is generating an increasing number of challenging end-of-life issues for correctional officials as they scramble to provide adequate health services for those older and geriatric individuals who by de facto may die while awaiting release (Ethridge & White, 2015).

Due to the increasing number of incarcerated older adults, prisons are now providing special housing arrangements such as nursing homes, hospice wards, dementia units, and other additional end-of-life services for the sickest and most frail incarcerated individuals. As these trends are expected to intensify in the future, there is a need for more research that explores the coping strategies that incarcerated persons use as they come to grips with the possibility of having to spend their final years in prison. Relying on a group of women sentenced to life in prison, we examine key variables that contribute to their death anxiety. We also explore the diverse experiences of women lifers as they contemplate, not only the dire consequences of a life sentence, but also their thoughts/fears associated with the possibility of being left behind to die in prison. We were particularly interested in identifying recurring strategies the women used to cope with the distaste for dying in prison, grief reactions to the losses of family and friends, and available options for a more dignified death experience.

WHEN SOMEONE DIES IN PRISON

Dying in prison is a complicated matter as the state and the prison in which the death occurs typically play a crucial role in determining the order of events following a death (Oliveto, 2022). Ultimately, incarcerated people can decide how their bodies will be handled after they die by using advanced directives to make their wishes known. In most cases, individuals who die while incarcerated have a funeral and burial much like any other person who passes away. An immediate family member, spouse, or otherwise authorized person can claim the body after an autopsy is performed. Normally, families are given 48 hours to claim the body from the mortuary (Thompson, 2018). On occasion, remains may go unclaimed if a person has outlived his/her close kin, or if the family is estranged from the prisoner or unable or unwilling to take financial responsibility for funeral expenses. If the body goes unclaimed or burial rights are signed over to the department of corrections, the prison will then make arrangements for interment in the prison graveyard or turn the body over to the county for burial or cremation. In some cases, the prisoner or the state may donate the body for medical research.

Case Study: Women Serving Life

Research Procedures and Sample

Data for this study were collected using a convenience sample from three women prisons in Georgia. We obtained permission from the university's Institutional Review Board and the State Department of Corrections. Questionnaires consisted of close- and open-ended questions on demographics, physical and mental health conditions, prison adjustment, abuse indicators, death anxiety, and measures of religiosity. Of the 303 women serving life sentences, 214 participated in the survey. The average age of the participants was 41.4 years ranging from 19 to 78 years. Most women (92.7%) were convicted of murder charges. The majority of participants were white (46.9) or Black (46.9%). About a quarter of the sample (25.5%) reported less than a high school education, whereas 37% had finished high school and 37% had at least some college or a college degree. A little more than half (56.1%) were or had been married. Eighty-four percent of the women reported some type of abuse – physical, sexual, and/or emotional. For 95% of the women, this was their first time being incarcerated; the average time served at the time of the survey was approximately 12 years with persons serving from 1 to 35 years. On average, these women entered prison at 29 years of age, with the youngest coming to prison at age 15 and the oldest at age 70.

Measures

We used Templer's (1970) 15-item Death Anxiety Scale (TDAS) that utilized short yes/no items aimed at determining the extent to which individuals are preoccupied with death and dying issues. To capture the experiences of death and dying in prison, open-ended questions included: (1) Have you observed or been aware of other people who have died in prison? If so, please describe your general views/experiences? (2) Can you describe any concerns you might have with the possibility of your own dying in prison such as: fears, anxieties, stigma, impact on your family, lack of healthcare? (3) As a person who is serving a life sentence, what role do your religious beliefs play (if any) in helping you cope with end-of-life issues. (4) If you have suffered losses of family or friends on the outside or friends on the inside during your incarceration, how were you able to cope with that grief?

A slightly modified version of Zamble and Porporino's (1988) prison adjustment (21-item Likert-type) scale was used to rate certain aspects of imprisonment that bothered the incarcerated women (e.g., family separation, loss of freedoms, not feeling physically safe, parole status, and relationships with other incarcerated people). Mental health measures for anxiety, depression, and interpersonal sensitivity were included from the Hopkins Brief Symptom Inventory – 25 (Derogatis, 1993). Self-reported health (excellent, good, fair, poor) and number of chronic illnesses assessed participant's health status. A checklist providing a listing of possible injuries was used to assess abuse outcomes from intimate partner violence. The survey also contained six religious engagement items ranging from the importance of religion as a coping tool for imprisonment to religious activities such as prayer, bible study, and chapel participation.

Indicators of Death Anxiety

With a range from 1 to 15, the female lifers in this sample reported a mean score of 6.7 on the TDAS (see Table 7.1). Similar to other research (Deaton et al., 2009), older adults and those with more education reported lower levels of death anxiety compared to younger or less educated individuals. The women reporting lower levels of death anxiety tended to score significantly better on measures of prison adjustment. For example, those women who did not feel physically safe in prison or avoided places because they were frightened, felt trapped, hopeless, and were uncertain about their parole status demonstrated greater death anxiety. Self-reported mental and physical health, and number of chronic illnesses, had no bearing on death anxiety. However, those individuals who experienced higher levels of depression, anxiety, interpersonal sensitivity or had previously received mental health treatment scored significantly higher on the TDAS. Interestingly, death fears were also significantly advanced for those reporting a greater number of injuries instigated by intimate partner violence, indicating that such fears continue to linger decades later.

TABLE 7.1 Percentage of Agreement with Templer's Death Anxiety Measures

Scale Items	
Does the thought of death ever enter your mind?	77%
Does it make you nervous when people talk about death?	23%
Do you dread to think about having an operation?	56%
Are you afraid of getting deathly sick?	79%
Are you afraid of getting cancer?	63%
Does the thought of death ever bother you?	43%
Are you distressed by the way time flies by so rapidly	22%
Do you ever fear dying a painful death in here?	54%
Does the subject of life after death trouble you?	15%
Are you scared of having a heart attack?	58%
Do you often think about how short life really is?	82%
Do you become anxious when other people talk about death?	18%
Is the sight of a dead body horrifying to you?	44%
Do you feel the future holds something for you to fear?	26%
Are you afraid to die?	20%

Reflections about Death

How and where we die is one of the most discerning issues for people everywhere (Sanders & Stensland, 2018). As Table 7.1 shows, most women indicated that they were not afraid to die; however, three–fourths of the women reported frequent death thoughts with about one-half (43%) categorizing their death thoughts as disturbing. When asked about their initial thoughts and feelings upon receiving their life sentence, the subject of dying was frequently mentioned. Numerous women felt at that point in time they would never leave prison alive. For instance, Paulette responded, "Give me the lethal injection please. Just end my life now. Don't wait and let me die in prison." As the years passed, thoughts about an eventual death continued, especially for older adults. As Bobbie, now in her early 70s remarked, "I think about death more often than I did at 24 when I entered prison. I don't dwell on death, but at night I often think will I face another day or will I go quietly in my sleep?"

Over half of the women (54%) expressed concerns about the possibility of dying a painful death. For example, Sandra questioned, "Will I die suddenly or will I die a painful death at the end of a long struggle from some illness?" Other women who have witnessed prison deaths have expressed fears after observing how a dying person is treated (Aday & Krabill, 2011). As Barbara recalled, "I've seen a few people die here and there is little respect for the dying...This idea of handcuffing the corpse when they die in their cell is extremely painful to watch." Others mentioned the thought of leaving prison in a "body bag" or with a "toe tag" which illustrates the concern about the impersonal nature of death behind bars. As Glenda said, "It's very emotional for most of us in here. It bothers me a lot because it's one of the things I pray not to happen to me. It's a terrible feeling. I don't want to die in prison."

Given the stigma associated with being a "lifer," the view of dying in prison is often considered the final act of a failed life (Aday et al., 2014). This sentiment is illustrated by Joyce, "I don't want to die in captivity. If I dropped dead a second after stepping on free ground, at least I went [died] outside the gate." Secluded from the outside world for decades, the possibility of dying alone without being surrounded by family and friends in such desolate institutions is dreadful, devastating, and sad (Handtke & Wangmo, 2014). For example, as Julie shares, "It is contrary to my faith and to not make it out before death is an embarrassment to me and my family. As a Christian, this stigma comes to my mind often." We found that women, especially those who leave children behind, often carry guilt and shame throughout their sentence for letting their family down. Brenda, who prays daily, emphasized, "Please let me go home so I won't die in prison. I want to spend the last days with my family." Judy also shared, "Were I to die alone in here, it would have a negative impact on my family who seek to bring me home still walking, talking and singing Just a Closer Walk with Thee." Lucy, one long-serving individual who has been separated from her family for over 45 years stated, "To me death is the beginning of a new journey and I want to share that with my family and friends on the outside. I want to leave them in peace and this can't happen for me in here." Similar negative sentiments were shared by other women who expressed grief and prayers for families when a loved one died in prison.

Health Access and Death Fears

Suffering from multiple chronic illnesses and declining health, there tends to be a greater uncertainty and fear of what the future holds, especially for older women who are more cognizant of their own mortality (Aday & Krabill, 2016). Most (79%) of the women agreed that getting sick in prison was a major fear for them. In particular, having to rely on prison healthcare in emergency situations was most disturbing. The women shared their worries about being housed in prisons located in remote rural areas without easy access to medical facilities should a heart attack or other sudden life-threatening symptom arise. With a mistrust of the prison healthcare system, many of the women talked about healthcare access being continually hindered by rules, custodial priorities, poor healthcare management, incompetence, and indifference (Sanders et al., 2018). Brenda, with worsening health, disclosed, "Medical is entirely too quick to disregard symptoms and tell you it's a figment of your imagination. You must be on your death bed to receive assistance." In a similar fashion, Susan shared her anxious feelings, "I'm afraid of the healthcare here. When someone dies here it makes me think what happened to make them die. It worries me that I might not make it to my next birthday."

Prison healthcare providers have been successful in discouraging residents from using available health services by introducing co-pay fees (Aday & Krabill, 2011). We found that to be the case in the current sample as well, with almost half (46%) of the women hardly ever going to medical and citing co-pays as the primary reason. As Linda, who receives no outside financial support, indicated, "Many of us are indigent and don't have the money to go to sick call. They charge $5 for each visit and another $5 for each medication." The women also shared that medical care is often inconsistent with medications suddenly changed and/or only provided on an as-needed basis. Given the barriers to sufficient medical access such as lapses in prescription refills and long medical waits for specialists in cardiology and pulmonology, health-related fears associated with health deterioration are understandable (Widra, 2020). Rather, some of the women tried to access health information from the outside or use the commissary to supplement insufficient diets (Novisky, 2018). Our quantitative results did reveal that death anxiety tended to increase the more dissatisfied an individual was with prison health services. These impediments to healthcare access combined with the fear of deterioration in their physical heath are constant reminders of their lack of human agency.

Denial Versus Acceptance

Although death is an inevitable life event, it is typically an uncomfortable topic for incarcerated women to discuss. This can generate a variety of emotions, including fear, anxiety, anger, and frustration mixed with a glimmer of hope (Aday & Krabill, 2011). The social denial of death reduces the capacity to cope with our own death as well as the death of others. For those serving long sentences, the likelihood of avoiding the loss of loved ones is small, especially for those individuals who are now in late adulthood. Clearly, some women used similar denial practices when confronted with the reflections associated with dying in prison. For example, "I try to avoid that thought" "I pass over them and talk about something else" and "I try to read a book or get my mind to occupy something else" were frequent techniques the women shared when avoiding death thoughts.

Although the social denial of death is common, Rocke and Cherry (2002) contend that acknowledging one's own death is an important final task in old age. However, accepting one's fate when death occurs in prison, which is viewed as a tragic event, can be difficult for some. As many women indicated, the notion of dying in prison reflects immeasurably on one's personal identity. Embracing one's mortality can be especially difficult when the dying process is likely to occur in solitude (Cottrell & Duggleby, 2016) and when bereavement is not socially endorsed (Smith et al., 2020). However, Aday and Wahidin (2016) have suggested that those serving long sentences have ample time to process their eventual mortality allowing them to address any death fears and become more accepting of what comes after death. In fact, some women lifers accepted and welcomed death over an emotionally painful prison existence. Phyllis, suggesting some degree of acceptance, remarked, "We all got to die somewhere. We cannot stop it when our time comes." Judy, now in her 70s stated, "I know that death is mandatory and the old of age must die. I'm ready."

Religious engagement also seems to play an important supportive role in women's views of death anxiety including death acceptance (Dye et al., 2014). Although prayer did not play a significant role in curbing death anxiety, engaging in religious and spiritual activities such as bible study and watching religious programs tended to reduce death fears. When we inquired about the importance of religion in alleviating death anxieties, participants shared comments about the importance of faith. Ruth, a highly religious woman, revealed "My faith in God has given me spiritual discipline, courage, and hope to face possible death in prison. He has my life in his hands." Carolyn also shared, "My faith plays the main role in my end-of-life concern. Of course, I don't want to suffer in my body as the end nears. But I believe the Lord will give me the grace to bear whatever I may face."

For some, an afterlife may be the singular occasion to be reunited with loved ones lost during incarceration (Harner et al., 2011). For example, to soften the thought of dying in prison, Barbara shared her confidence in a life after death: "I believe in the afterlife and because of who my faith is in, upon my last breath, I know where I'm going. A celebration will take place, not because of me, but because of who is waiting for me." The view of death as an escape, which appeared in previous research with older incarcerated males and females (Aday, 2006; Deaton et al., 2009), was articulated by this sample as well. Jennifer shares this sentiment, "My religious beliefs are that to be absent from the body is to be present with the Lord, and it's better to be present with the Lord than be in prison." The religious theme supports the commonly held view that religious beliefs provide an important buffer against the fear of dying in prison (Dye, et al., 2014). As Aday (2003) suggested, religion helps people deal with the lonely, soul-searching experience of prison and can offer hope and optimism for those who may fear having to spend their remaining years in prison.

Grieving Losses

Managing the death of a loved one is an event that nearly half of all women in prison encounter while incarcerated (Harner et al., 2011). Losing important interactions with the outside world, the death of loved one can result in a reduction of customary phone calls, letters, and cards sent on special occasions which serve to normalize one's existence behind bars. Such losses are especially difficult for older adults who may have outlived family and friends on the outside and now must turn to others or simply go on alone. As Janice, shared, "Since my incarceration, I have been notified of the deaths of a half-sister, a grandmother, two uncles, one aunt, a cousin, one brother-in-law, one sister-in-law, a nephew, a daughter, and a son." Others mentioned the lack of opportunity to grieve with other family members which led to a feeling of disbelief because the loss in their world did not seem real. We found others grieving from the loss of losing all contact with family members, as is frequently the case for those serving life. The loss of contact with those whom they once shared a close relationship was uniquely painful for the incarcerated women. As Susan revealed, "Every day is just heartbreaking knowing that my children are out there and I can't be there for them." Others were grieving not only about the absence of family in their lives, but also the unknown whereabouts of some family members who had broken off all communications.

Similar to experiencing the death of someone in the outside world, the death of a close prison friend can generate feelings of vulnerability and heighten death anxiety for those incarcerated. For example, the death of close friends may heighten older women's awareness about aging and, in turn, one's own mortality behind bars. Losing close friends in prison is considered more significant for some than losing family on the outside, who may be viewed as strangers (Aday & Krabill, 2011). We discovered that long-serving lifers, who have shared the better part of their adult lives together, had formed close friendships. As Stephanie mentioned, "At one time it looked like all my friends would die in prison and it made me feel sad and all alone." Such losses inevitably shrink one's social world and as Brenda stated: "I miss the times we were able to spend chatting and sharing special times together." Some women recalled reaching out to other women to console them during such vulnerable times. The women also discussed the negative aspects of current prison policy that requires an immediate return to a normal prison routine without the opportunity to properly mourn the loss.

Seeking Death with Dignity

The circumstances surrounding dying in prison can vary significantly depending on the individual's health circumstances and/or medical services available within the prison milieu (McParland & Johnston, 2019). Some individuals may prefer to die in their prison home in close approximation to their friends. However, the terminal individual may be moved to the infirmary where they will be more closely monitored, but will likely die a lonely death without support from prison friends (Sharp, 2022). Since many states contract with outside health providers, sick and terminally ill patients may be transferred to a local hospital where they will likely die shackled to their bed (Hurley, 2020). Irrespective of where a person dies, research has found that recognition of a shared humanity (Cloyes et al., 2017) and fostering relationships with people inside and outside of prison are important to those nearing the end of life (Handtke & Wangmo, 2014).

During the past 20 years, hospice programs have emerged as an effective and humane practice for responding to end-of-life illnesses in the prison setting. The emphasis on palliative care has made important strides into the prison's naturally harsh environment of rigid discipline and custody (Sharp, 2022). Although some states have model programs with trained prison volunteers serving as compassionate caregivers, the hospice philosophy introduced into the prison environment is not without contradictions and pitfalls (Widra, 2020). The barriers to palliative and end-of-life care center around both physical and ideological issues (McPharland & Johnston, 2019). Prisons with their overcrowded, noisy living spaces are not an ideal environment for an equitable death experience. The conflicting priorities of compassion and comfort with custody concerns can have a negative impact on the delivery of palliative care. However, with less than 4% of the nations' prisons having operable hospice programs (Widra, 2020), more palliative resources will be needed in the future to adequately care for the growing number of terminally ill patients (Sanders et al, 2018).

With the dramatic rise in the number of aging and terminally ill, many incarcerated individuals have expressed a strong yearning to be released prior to their death. Unfortunately, medical or geriatric parole options offering compassionate release have been largely ineffective due to widespread underutilization. Some are calling for compassionate release reforms that would replace the punitive punishment philosophy, which seeks to inflict emotional and physical pain until the very end (O'leary, 2022). For example, there are rigid rules for filing for compassionate release which has been designed as a slow and deliberate process (Widra & Bertram, 2020). According to Nelson (2021), a person's medical condition, criminal record, age, and time served are important determinants of eligibility. Typically, individuals serving life sentences who have committed the most serious violent crimes are not eligible for medical release. Those released must follow a post-release supervision plan and, in some states, if the person fails to die within the medically approved time, medical release may be revoked (Nelson, 2021). States vary considerably when it comes to the approval process, but most decision-making rests with the same parole boards that typically have high rates of parole denials. Most states permit stakeholders such as district attorneys, judges, and victims the opportunity to discourage compassionate release (Bedard et al., 2022).

Conclusion

With the emphasis on the warehousing of the masses, the increasing numbers of older individuals serving life sentences will place an even greater future strain on the capability of prisons to provide adequate end-of-life services. With the enormous costs associated with caring for chronically ill geriatric persons, perhaps a more viable pathway forward is a more aggressive policy toward decarceration (O'Leary, 2022). This approach has the potential to expand the chances for early release allowing aging individuals (who are no longer a security threat) to realize their desired wish of dying among family and friends. Second-look sentencing measures would provide for automatic eligibility by a sentencing court after serving a determinant sentence in the proposed timeframe of 20–30 years (Cooper & Bernard, 2021). Geriatric release, similar to second-look sentencing measures, could be made more available to the masses. Currently, this option is reserved for those of advanced age (60+ years of age most commonly) and determined by time served for a particular crime. No medical requirements would have to be met – only age and risk factors (O'Leary, 2022). It must be acknowledged that when someone is serving a life sentence for more serious violent crimes, overcoming risk factors and other arguments against early release will prove challenging. Despite these obstacles, long-serving individuals remain hopeful for the opportunity to die a dignified death, preferably in the free world surrounded by loved ones.

Discussion Questions:

---

1. How has mass incarceration contributed to the growing number of deaths behind bars? What are the major obstacles for experiencing a dignified death in prison, especially among long-serving individuals?
2. Consider your own experiences with death, dying, and bereavement. How do such experiences compare with what incarcerated individuals and their families must endure when it comes to dying and grieving in prison?

References

Aday, R. H. (2003). *Aging prisoners: Crisis in American corrections.* Westport, CT: Prager.

Aday, R. H. (2006). Aging prisoners' concerns toward dying in prison. *Omega: Journal of Death & Dying,* 52(3), 199–216. https://doi.org/10.2190/CHTD-YL7T-R1RR-LHMN

Aday, R. H., & Krabill, J. J. (2011). *Women aging in prison: A neglected population in the correctional system.* Boulder, CO: Rienner.

Aday, R. H., & Krabill, J. J. (2016). The silenced emotion: Older women and grief in prison. In D. L. Harris & T. C. Bordere (eds.). *Handbook of social justice in loss and grief* (pp. 87–105). New York: Routledge.

Aday, R. H., & Wahidin, A. (2016). Older prisoners' experiences of death, dying and grief behind bars. *The Howard Journal,* 55(3), 317–327. https://doi.org/10.1111/hojo.12172

Aday, R. H., Krabill, J. J., & Deaton-Owens, D. (2014). Religion in the lives of older women serving life in prison. *Journal of Women and Aging,* 26, 238–256. https://doi.org/10.1080/08952841.2014.888880

Bedard, R., Vaughn, J., & Murolo, A. S. (2022). Elderly, detained and justice-involved: The mass incarcerated generation. *CUNY Law Review,* 25, 161. http://academicworks.cuny.edu/clr/vol25/ss/15

Carson, E. A. (2020). Prisoners in 2019. NCJ 255115. *Bureau of Justice Statistics.* Prisoners in 2019 (ojp.gov).

Carson, E. A. (2021). Mortality in state and federal prisons, 2001–2019 – statistical tables. *Bureau of Justice Statistics. Mortality in State and Federal Prisons, 2001–2019 – Statistical Tables* (ojp.gov).

Clear, T. R., & Frost, N. A. (2014). *The punishment imperative.* New York: NYU Press.

Cloyes, K. G., Kosenkranz, S. J., Supiano, K. P., Berry, P. H., Routt, M., Llanque, S. M., & Shannon-Dorcy, K. (2017). Caring to learn and learning to care: Inmate hospice volunteers and the delivery of prison end-of-life care. *Journal of Correctional Health Care,* 23(1), 43–55. https://doi.org/10.1177/107834581664833

Cooper, S. L., & Bernard, C. (2021). Medical parole-related petitions in U.S. courts: Support for reforming compassionate release. *Creighton Law Review,* 54, 173–202.

Cottrell, L., & Duggleby, W. (2016). The "good death": An integrative literature review. *Palliative & Supportive Care,* 14(6), 686–712. https://doi.org/10.1017/S1478951515001285

Deaton, D., Aday, R. H., & Wahidin, A. (2009). The effects of health and penal harm on aging female prisoners' views of dying in prison. *Omega: Journal of Death and Dying,* 60, 51–70. https://doi.org/10.2190/OM.60.1.c

Derogatis, L. R. (1993). *Brief symptom inventor (BSI). Administration, scoring, and procedures manual* (3rd ed.). Minneapolis, MN: National Computer Systems.

Dye, M. H., & Aday, R. H. (2019). *Women lifers: Lives before, behind and beyond bars.* Lanham, MD: Rowman & Littlefield.

Dye, M. H., Aday, R. H. Farney, L., & Raley, J. (2014). "The rock I cling to": Religious engagement in the lives of life-sentenced women. *The Prison Journal,* 94(3), 388–408. https://doi.org/10.1177/0032885514537605

Ethridge, P. A., & White, T. G. (2015). The use of medically recommended intensive supervision (medical parole) in Texas. *Journal of Correctional Health Care,* 21(4), 375–389. https://doi.org/10.1177/1078345815600158

Handtke, V., & Wangmo, T. (2014). Ageing prisoners' views on death and dying: Contemplating end-of-life in prison. *Bioeth Inquiry,* 11, 373–386. https://doi.org/10.1007/s11673-014-9548-xx

Harner, H. M., Hentz, P. M., & Evangelista, C. (2011). Grief interrupted: The experience of loss among incarcerated women. *Qualitative Health Research,* 21(4), 454–464. https://doi.org/10.1177/1049732310373257

Hurley, M. (2020). Here's how inmates face the end of their lives if they fall ill. https://nationalinterest.org/blog/reboot/heres-how-inmates-face-end-their-lives-if-they-fall-ill-157846

McParland, C., & Johnston, B. M. (2019). Palliative and end of life care in prisons: A mixed- methods rapid review of the literature form 2014–2018. *BMJ,* 9, 3033905.

Nellis, A. (2021a). In the extreme: Women serving life without parole and death sentences in the United States. The Sentencing Project. https://www.sentencingproject.org/reports/in-the-extreme-women-serving-life-without-parole-and-death-sentences-in-the-united-states/.

Nellis, A. (2021b). No end in sight: America's enduring reliance on life imprisonment. The Sentencing Project. https://www.sentencingproject.org/reports/noo-end-in-sight-americas-enduring-reliance-on-life-sentences/

Nelson, A. (2021). How compassionate is it? Suggestions for improving the compassionate release statutes in Kansas. *Kansas Journal of Law & Public Policy*, 31(1), 131–159.

Novisky, M. A. (2018). Avoiding the run around: The link between cultural health capital and health management among older prisoners. *Criminology*, 56, 643–678. https://doi.org/10.1111/1745-9125.12188

O'Leary, R. (2022). Compassionate release and decarceration in the states. *Iowa Law Review,* 107(621), 1–18.

Oliveto, J. (2022). What happens when someone dies in prison? https://www.joincake.com/blog/what-happens-when-someone-dies-in-prison.

Petreca, V. G. (2021). Death and dying in prison: An integrative review of the literature. *Journal of Forensic Nursing,* 17(2), 115–125. https://doi.org/10.1097/JFN.0000000000000318

Rocke, C., & Cherry, K. E. (2002). Death at the end of the 20th Century: Individual processes and developmental tasks in old age. *International Aging and Human Development,* 54, 315–333. https://doi.org/10.2190/L9FW-GD24-GC5H-DXHW

Sanders, S., & Stensland, M. (2018). Preparing to die behind bars: The journey of male inmates with terminal health conditions. *Journal of Correctional Health Care*, 24(3), 232–242. https://doi.org/10.1177/1078345818780686

Sanders, S., Stensland, M., & Juraco, K. (2018). Agency behind bars: Advance care planning with aging and dying offenders. *Death Studies*, 42, 45–51. https://doi.org/10.1080/07481187.2017.1303552

Sawyer, W., & Wagner, P. (2022). Mass incarceration: The whole pie 2022. Prison Policy Initiative. https://www.prisonpolicy.org/reports/pie2022.html.

Sharp, L. A. (2022). Death and dying in carceral America: The prison hospice as an inverted space of exception. *Medical Anthropology Quarterly*, 36, 177–197. https://doi.org/10.1111/maq.12688

Smith, K. V., Wild, J., & Ehlers, A. (2020). The masking of mourning: Social disconnection after bereavement and its role in psychological distress. *Clinical Psychological Science: A Journal of the Association for Psychological Science*, 8(3), 464–476. https://doi.org/10.1177/2167702620

Templer, D. (1970). The construction and validation of a death anxiety scale. *Journal of General Psychology,* 82(2), 165–177. https://doi.org/10.1080/00221309.1970.9920634

Thompson, C. (2018). Your loved one dies. The prison leaves a voice mail. The Marshall Project. https://www.themarshallproject.org/2018/06/21/your-loved-one-dies-the-prison-leaves-a-voicemail.

Wang, L., & Sawyer, W. (2021). New data: State prisons are increasingly deadly places. Prison Policy Initiative. https://www.prisonpolicy.org/blog/2021/06.08/prison_mortality.

Widra, E., & Bertram, W. (2020). Compassionate release was never designed to release large numbers of people. Prison Policy Initiative. https://www.prisonpolicy.org/blog/2020/05/29/compassionate-release/#:~:text=Compassionate%20release%20programs.

Widra, E. (2020). Deaths in state prisons are on the rise, new data shows. What can be done? Prison Policy Initiative. https://www.prisonpolicy.org/blog/2020/02/13/prisondeaths/.

Zamble, E., & Porporino, F. (1988). *Coping, behavior, and adaption in prison inmates*. New York: Springer.

8

WOMEN'S IMPRISONED BODIES

Perceptions of Carceral Food Quality and Impact on Health for Self and Children

April N. Terry and Kelli Grant

LEARNING OUTCOMES:

Upon successful completion of this chapter, students will be able to:

1. Understand how mass incarceration has disproportionality impacted women, and more specifically, mothers.
2. Explain incarcerated women's concerns regarding food quality and nutrition for themselves and their children, both before and during their incarceration.
3. Identify the short- and long-term consequences of food quality and accessibility due to women's experiences with mass incarceration.

Introduction

The United States incarcerates more people than any other country with many incarcerated persons representing vulnerable and marginalized groups (Bucerius et al., 2021). One common explanation for the rise in incarceration was due to the War on Drugs movement resulting in many non-violent offenses and mandatory prison time. Some have identified the War on Drugs as a war on women (Belknap, 2001; Bloom & Chesney-Lind, 2000) as drug laws led to "vengeful equity" where the prison population rose quickly for women (Bloom & Chesney-Lind, 2000). Rates of incarcerated women are on an upward incline with more than 60% being single mothers (Hagan & Foster 2012) and over one-third having multiple children (Glaze & Maruschak, 2010). "Imprisoned women struggle with the impact that their criminal lives and their subsequent incarceration have on their mothering ability" (Sandberg et al., 2020, p. 2). These struggles include addressing basic life necessities such as parent feeding and child eating. Women lose basic autonomy surrounding their own food ritual practices while incarcerated including even managing the quality of food or depending on food consistency (Godderis, 2006). Being unable to control one's food intake means one is unable to control the needs of their bodies (Godderis, 2006) and even less control over the food their children receive. Mass incarcerated has continued to allow

DOI: 10.4324/9781003274292-11

for the exercise of power over incarcerated people through control and access to food. Food management serves as an "institutional paradigm of punishment" (Chatterjee & Chatterjee, 2018, p. 41).

Previous research has found women struggle with identity issues, self-image, stress, and health concerns regarding poor quality food and imposed food routines in the carceral environment (de Graff & Kilty, 2016; Firth et al., 2015; Smoyer, 2015). "Inside a prison a person is an inmate, not an individual" (Godderis, 2006, p. 61). Women are not allowed to make individual choices about their food consumption as correctional facilities have rigid institutional rules and regulations that restrict this autonomy (Godderis, 2006). In this environment, food serves as another means of disrupting one's sense of identity (Ugelvik, 2011) and the food one receives may be one of the first encounters during imprisonment (Moran, 2015). According to Godderis (2006), humans have a symbolic relationship to food so dynamics surrounding food while incarcerated is a means through which expressions of power can be made. One aspect of mass incarceration has been the suppression of individual and collective identities, extending into basic choices such as food consumption, due to the authority held by correctional facility administration (Godderis, 2006). With a spike in incarceration rates for women, it is crucial to understand the impact food quality and accessibility have on incarcerated (grand)mother's perceptions regarding carceral food options and parent feeding during incarceration. As such, the current study administered a survey to 42 incarcerated mothers and grandmothers at one state's only women's correctional facility to further understand the perceptions regarding both food environments (correctional facility for self, and community for children).

Literature Review

Food in prison is notoriously poor in quality and only occasionally addressed within mainstream news (Whitman, 2019). According to news in Arizona (United States), women in the Perryville correctional facility reported "not for human consumption" stamped on boxes of meat. These incarcerated women struggled to eat the food due to a reported rancid smell (Whitman, 2019). In a 2001 state prison expenditure report, it was found that only 4% of prison operating costs are allocated to food (Stephan, 2004). The United States Supreme Court has upheld legislation related to food quality in correctional facilities by stating the use of nutraloaf, a bland and unappealing loaf of mashed ingredients, is an acceptable punishment for incarcerated populations (Zoukis, 2016). This legislation does not include the day-to-day feeding throughout the correctional system nationwide, as states are left to determine the quality and types of foods to serve. The Eighth Amendment does provide protection against cruel and unusual punishment and can be used as a legal protection for incarcerated persons regarding food issues (Naim, 2005). Kent (2005) argued that food is intentionally produced to not be gratifying as this would counter the very idea of punishment and support for mass incarceration. Therefore, facilities only need to find the balance of "adequate" and "minimal" (Kent, 2005).

Even with some legal protections, correctional staff have covert control over incarcerated persons' food. As one example, Godderis (2006) found that incarcerated women reported issues such as hair in their food. Correctional staff suggested they, "pick it out with your teeth" (p. 65). Studies consistently find many women are incarcerated for non-violent offenses and enter facilities with health risks such as addiction, trauma, homelessness, and complex diseases (Harner & Riley, 2013a). Their health-related vulnerabilities interact with negative prison conditions such as poor food and sub-par health services, leading to continued chronic health conditions (Harner & Riley, 2013b). Nonetheless, prison food quality remains a point of struggle for incarcerated populations, and especially women (de Graaf & Kilty, 2016; Smith, 2002; Smoyer, 2015; Vanhouche, 2015). Since food socialization is pervasive in many women's lives, it is important to examine how the entry into correctional facilities places women in a highly controlled and prescribed eating environment (also known as a coercive foodway) and subsequent consequences.

Women in carceral spaces report feeling lonely, isolated, and separated from loved ones as a result of the food environment (de Graaf & Kilty, 2016). Once removed from society, incarcerated people are subject to a ready-made social environment where structured food routines and menus exist. In the carceral environment, women's roles and identities surrounding food experiences are stripped away as they enter a foodway that is highly regulated. Women become part of an established coercive feeding system where food is provided, the time allotted to eat it is predetermined, and food choices are limited. Mass incarceration serves to remind women that they are deprived of the basic freedom to make decisions about their daily lives, including food consumption, resulting in feelings of helplessness (Godderis, 2006). Despite constraints, women may demonstrate small acts of resistance such as smuggling food to their cells to recreate food for themselves. Their identities are then reworked at both the person and group level (Smoyer, 2015).

This coercive environment can potentially cause long-term issues related to food (Batsell et al., 2002; Ellis et al., 2016; Galloway et al., 2006; Tan et al., 2016; Williams et al., 2017) and mental and physical health (Alves et al., 2016). Alves et al. (2016) studied differences in mental and physical health for those with pre-existing conditions and those without, upon a stint of incarceration. Food was noted by many participants as having a negative effect on their overall health. As one example, a participant stated, "The problem here is the food. The food kills me" (Alves et al., 2016, pp. 787–788). Even while behind bars, incarcerated people are forced into a capitalist society where money can buy basic condiments such as sugar and salt. Through policy enforcement, standards are set for availability of food and acceptable behavior surrounding food activities and consumption.

The food-related issues forced upon oppressed women impacted by the war on women extends beyond their stent of incarceration. These women release into difficult to navigate labor markets with felony records and low social and human capital leading to struggles associated with adequate food and shelter. Felony convictions, in many states, warrant refusal to provide government aid such as food stamps (Gamblin, 2018; Harding et al., 2014). Gamblin (2018), and others, have found that mass incarceration increases hunger. The National Institute of Health (2013) found 91% of released persons are food insecure. Additionally, 75% of released persons report "extremely difficult" or "impossible" means to securing post-release employment. One in four households headed by a released person lives in deep poverty as their overall earning potential is nearly $180,000 lower than those who have not served time (The Pew Charitable Trusts, 2010).

Issues surrounding food practices, culture, food insecurity, and punishment are all highlighted in this study. Women who are primary caregivers and preparers of food, have an important role in their respective families. Although food conditions may not be ideal prior to incarceration, there is still a significant role being filled for both the mother and her child(ren). As women enter a correctional facility, their roles are notably altered, and pieces of the mothering identity are impacted. In correctional settings, women sometimes engage in mothering roles for other incarcerated women. Specifically, they may provide guidance related to food consumption as they view this practice as meaningful for them as caregivers and as women (Smoyer & Lopes, 2017). This study aims to situate the transition into a correctional facility for mothers and grandmothers within their own identity and role association with food, and how women perceive the change in food interactions with their children.

Methods

The current study was part of a larger project seeking to facilitate (grand)mother/(grand) child bonds through a read aloud program. The current findings center on selected closed- and open-ended survey questions with a cohort of 42 incarcerated (grand)mothers at a midwestern state's only women's correctional facility. All participating mothers and grandmothers were identified as women at, or below, a basic reading level. Per the facility request, all women must have successfully completed a parenting program, had at least six months or more left to serve, and have legal rights to remaining in contact with their (grand)children. The facility posted flyers of the criteria and a description of the study and women were able to sign-up/volunteer if interested. Of the 42 participants, 31 participated as mothers and 11 as grandmothers. Racial composition of the incarcerated (grand)mothers was consistent with broader state demographics with 82.5% reporting as white and 17.5% as Black. The larger project included pre and post-participation [read aloud program] surveys regarding the participants' motivation to read and self-efficacy in parenting. Included in the survey questionnaire were self-constructed questions based on previous carceral food literature. Closed-ended questions were scored on a five-point Likert Scale from Strongly Disagree (score of 1) to Strongly Agree (score of 5). Examples of Likert Scale questions included, "*Before incarceration, I often thought about nutrition/quality food for myself*" and "*Before incarceration, I often thought about nutrition/quality food for my child/grandchild.*" Surveys also included open-ended questions such as, "*What three words describe how you felt about your food environment prior to incarceration?*" and "*What three words describe how you feel about your food environment during incarceration?*" Self-constructed questions were utilized to better understand the incarcerated (grand)mothers' perceptions about food prior to, and during, incarceration for both self and (grand)child(ren).

Findings

Findings demonstrate that most (97.6%) incarcerated (grand)mothers received government aid, such as food stamps and Temporary Assistance for Needy Families benefits prior to their incarceration. This self-identification is likely a product of the (grand)mothers' financial status prior to incarceration, suggesting they may have struggled to provide food for their children. Consistent with demographics of incarcerated individuals, those with lower socioeconomic status are more likely to be incarcerated than their middle- and upper-class counterparts. In this sample, most mothers were single parents as only seven mothers, or 16.6%, reported having a partner to co-parent prior to incarceration with an average of two children (M = 2.3, SD = 1.2) per mother. Since their incarceration, mothers reported grandparents being the most common caregiver; incarcerated grandmothers reported their grandchildren always resided with their own son/daughter.

TABLE 8.1 Survey Descriptive Statistics

	Mean	*SD*
Before incarceration, I often thought about nutrition/quality food for myself.	3.2	1.57
Before incarceration, I often thought about nutrition/quality food for my child/grandchild.	4.2	1.25
I often think about nutrition/quality of food for myself while incarcerated.	3.6	1.44
I often think about nutrition/quality of food for my child/grandchild while incarcerated.	4.3	1.12
Nutrition/food quality is important to me now.	4.0	1.31
I believe food impacts health.	4.5	0.87
Being incarcerated has negatively impacted my physical health.	3.3	1.52
I was often hungry due to lack of access to food prior to incarceration.	2.1	1.24
My child/grandchild was often hungry due to lack of access to food prior to my incarceration.	1.3	0.43
I am often hungry due to lack of food during incarceration.	1.8	1.08
I believe my child/grandchild is often hungry.	1.3	0.62
Prior to incarceration, I often talked about hunger with my child/grandchild.	1.5	0.77
Since being incarcerated, I have often talked about hunger to my child/grandchild.	1.7	1.00

Strongly Disagree = 1; Disagree = 2; Unsure = 3; Agree = 4; Strongly Agree = 5.

To understand the responses to the closed-ended questions, Table 8.1 provides the average Likert Scale response (1 = Strongly Disagree and 5 = Strongly Agree). While (grand) mothers relied on social welfare services prior to incarceration, they reported thinking slightly more often about their ability to provide nutritious/quality food for their (grand) child during incarceration than *prior* to incarceration. Mothers and grandmothers were aware of the significance of food impacting health (M = 4.5, SD = .87), including their (grand)children's, and thought more often during incarceration about the nutrition and quality of food for their (grand)children (M = 4.3, SD = 1.12) more than themselves (M = 3.6, SD = 1.44). Mothers and grandmothers indicated that they did not frequently think about food accessibility and quality prior to their incarceration (M =3.2, SD = 1.57), suggesting minimal worrying. While grandparents were the current primary caregivers for the incarcerated mothers' children, (grand)mothers reported increasing thoughts about food environments for their (grand)children in the present than prior to incarceration (M = 4.3, SD = 1.12). These findings suggest that one consequence of mass incarceration of women, especially mothers, is slightly increased thinking about their children's sustenance than before, when they required governmental assistance. They also reported that their own personal health had declined since their incarceration (M = 3.3, SD = 1.52), possibly due to the quality and accessibility of food. While correctional facilities are required to provide an appropriate caloric intake each day, the incarcerated women were generally dissatisfied with the food available to them.

The incarcerated women reported incarceration has negatively impacted their health, possibly because of the current food quality (M = 3.3, SD = 1.52) which they did not identify as a concern prior to imprisonment. This finding suggests incarcerated women have better access to nutritional options while living as low-income single mothers in the community, than when federal and state guidelines mandate an appropriate diet for them. Women's responses to describing food prior to and during incarceration further confirm this point. When asked to report three words that described how they felt about their food environment prior to incarceration, the following lists of common words shared by the (grand)mothers: "*wholesome; healthy; accessible; fulfilling; plentiful.*" They were then asked to provide three words describing their current food environment. As can be seen here, common responses were quite different: "*malnourished; gross; nasty; inaccessible; FAKE; unhealthy.*" Again, these findings suggest women were satisfied with their food prior to incarceration and their current food environments were viewed negatively.

In sum, most incarcerated mothers and grandmothers had minor concerns about food quality and accessibility prior to their incarceration, for self and children. Once incarcerated, most of these mothers and grandmothers became more concerned about the children's available food options while recognizing their imprisonment resulted in poor quality and inaccessible food and declining physical health. Incarcerated mothers already report feelings of abandonment, guilt, and shame, over their separation from their children and compensate by trying to be "good mothers" despite their incarceration and criminal pasts (Hoskins & Cobinna, 2019; Stearns, 2019). Yet, as this finding suggests, the mass incarceration of mothers creates additional negative outcomes.

Discussion and Implications

The current study was part of a larger project working with incarcerated mothers and grandmothers at one state's only women's correctional facility. In the current chapter, a cohort of 42 (grand)mothers were asked to discuss their food experiences for self and (grand)child(ren), prior to, and during, their incarceration. By use of both closed- and open-ended survey questions, the current (grand)mothers reported on their perceptions regarding food experiences and environments. Current findings demonstrate one negative outcome of the mass incarceration of single mothers—a declining report of healthy and obtainable food options for self and their children. The negative impacts of mass incarceration are far reaching and extend well beyond carceral food environments and into the lives of one's (grand)children.

While most mothers and grandmothers received prior governmental assistance, they found these services to be sufficient in terms of providing food while being incarcerated decreased their accessibility to healthy foods. Both mothers and grandmothers are concerned about their declining physical health due to their current food environment while remaining bothered by food options for their youth during their incarceration. These results are troubling, they demonstrate how even poor, single mothers, receiving welfare services, feel more secure in food quality and consumption than while under the supervision of a state body responsible for their well-being and oversight of their dependents.

Women represent one of the fastest and steepest growing demographics of those incarcerated, with most women being the primary caregivers to multiple children (Glaze & Maruschak, 2010; Hagan & Foster 2012). Women report that doing time results in many negative aspects, including losing their connections with their children and struggling to fulfill their role as mother while incarcerated (Easterling, 2012; Smith et al., 2004). Additionally, incarcerated women have shared concerns over poor food quality within the carceral environment (de Graff & Kilty, 2016). The current findings are problematic and demand changes on behalf of all incarcerated populations and their children.

There are two main approaches to addressing the current findings. The first approach requires a prevention-focused ideological shift away from incarcerating non-violent mothers and grandmothers. Women remain one of the fastest growing demographics of the incarcerated population; and many times, they are incarcerated for non-violent offenses (The Sentencing Project, 2020). Punitive policies that support mass incarceration pitch a narrative that correctional facilities serve to rehabilitate (Vuk et al., 2020). However, most research has shown this is factually incorrect. Instead, this practice of catch-and-release serves merely as a public display of punishment in the form of warehousing individuals. Local and broader narratives suggest imprisonment is rehabilitative; however, separating mothers and grandmothers from their (grand)children is damaging in the short term and long term for all involved (Bradshaw et al., 2021; Thomson et al., 2020).

Restorative practices have been shown to be effective in diverting individuals away from incarceration to allow them to remain in their communities (Rees & Hobson, 2021). Such practices would help mothers and grandmothers remain connected to their (grand)children in the community where (grand)mothers feel secure in their abilities to provide nutritional food to their (grand)children. This movement would also result in healthier (grand)mothers and (grand)children as correctional facilities are mentally and physically damaging for incarcerated populations (Bradshaw et al., 2021; Thomson et al., 2020). Research also shows the short- and long-term negative consequences bestowed upon the (grand)children of incarcerated loved ones. While this paradigm shift would not happen over time, a commitment to such efforts could produce far greater benefits in the decades to come, but the movement needs to begin now.

The second approach is more reactive and can focus on addressing uncovered food issues once women find themselves behind bars. Implications of this research suggest that carceral food environments are detrimental to overall well-being of incarcerated women and possibly their children. Food policy changes could significantly improve outcomes for women who are fully dependent on carceral food and could positively impact long-term health post-release.

Discussion Questions:

1. How does one's parenting role change upon incarceration?
2. What policy suggestions may be appropriate for addressing food quality and accessibility concerns by incarcerated mothers?

References

Alves, J., Maia, Â., & Teixeira, F. (2016). Health conditions prior to imprisonment and the impact of prison on health: Views of detained women. *Qualitative Health Research*, *26*(6), 782–792.

Batsell, W. R., Jr., Brown, A. S., Ansfield, M. E., & Pascall, G. Y. (2002). "You will eat all of that!": A retrospective analysis of forced consumption episodes. *Appetite, 38*(3), 211–219.

Belknap, J. (2001). *The invisible woman: Gender, crime and justice*. Belmont, CA: Wadsworth.

Bloom, B., & Chesney-Lind, M. (2000). Women in prison: Vengeful equity. In R. Muraskin (Ed.), *It's a crime: Women and criminal justice* (2nd ed., pp 183–204). Upper Saddle River, NJ: Prentice Hall.

Bradshaw, D., Creaven, A. M., & Muldoon, O. T. (2021). Parental incarceration affects children's emotional and behavioral outcomes: A longitudinal cohort study of children aged 9 to 13 years. *International Journal of Behavioral Development*, *45*(4), 310–316.

Bucerius, S., Haggerty, K. D., & Dunford, D. T. (2021). Prison as temporary refuge: Amplifying the voices of women detained in prison. *The British Journal of Criminology*, *61*(2), 519–537.

Chatterjee, D., & Chatterjee, S. C. (2018). Food in captivity: Experiences of women in Indian prisons. *The Prison Journal, 98*(1), 40–59.

de Graaf, K., & Kilty, J. M. (2016). You are what you eat: Exploring the relationship between women, food, and incarceration. *Punishment & Society, 18*(1), 27–46.

Easterling, B. A. (2012). *Parenting behind bars: A qualitative study of incarcerated mothers* Doctoral dissertation, University of Tennessee, Knoxville. Tennessee Research and Creative Exchange.

Ellis, J. M., Galloway, A. T., Webb, R. M., Martz, D. M., & Farrow, C.V. (2016). Recollections of pressure to eat during childhood, but not picky eating, predict young adult eating behavior. *Appetite, 97,* 58–63.

Firth, C. L., Sazie, E., Hedberg, K., Drach, L., & Maher, J. (2015). Female inmates with diabetes: Results from changes in a prison food environment. *Women's Health Issues, 25*(6), 732–738.

Galloway, A. T., Fiorito, L. M., Francis, L. A., & Birch, L. L. (2006). 'Finish your soup': Counterproductive effects of pressuring children to eat on intake and affect. *Appetite, 46*(3), 18–323.

Gamblin, M. D. (2018). *Mass incarceration: A major cause of hunger.* Briefing Paper. Washington, DC: Bread for the World Institute. February. https://www. bread.org/sites/default/files/downloads/briefing-paper-mass-incarceration-february-2018. pdf

Glaze, L. E., & Maruschak, L. M. (2010). *Parents in prison and their minor children (NCJ 222984).* Washington, DC: U.S. Department of Justice, Bureau of Justice Statistics. Retrieved from https://www.bjs.gov/content/pub/pdf/pptmc.pdf

Godderis, R. (2006). Food for thought: An analysis of power and identity in prison food narratives. *Berkeley Journal of Sociology, 50,* 61–75.

Hagan, J., & Foster, H. (2012). Intergenerational educational effects of mass imprisonment in America. *Sociology of Education, 85*(3), 259–286.

Harding, D. J., Wyse, J. J., Dobson, C., & Morenoff, J. D. (2014). Making ends meet after prison. *Journal of Policy Analysis and Management, 33*(2), 440–470.

Harner, H. M., & Riley, S. (2013a). Factors contributing to poor physical health in incarcerated women. *Journal of Health Care for the Poor and Underserved, 24,* 788–801. doi:10.1353/hpu.2013.0059

Harner, H. M., & Riley, S. (2013b). The impact of incarceration on women's mental health: Responses from women in a maximum-security prison. *Qualitative Health Research, 23,* 26–42. doi:10.1177/1049732312461452

Hoskins K. M., & Cobbina, J. E. (2019). It depends on the situation: Women's identity transformation in prison, jail, and substance abuse treatment settings. *Feminist Criminology, 15*(3), 340–358. https://doi.org/10.1177/1557085119878268

Kent, G. (2005). *Freedom from want: The human right to adequate food.* Washington, DC: Georgetown University Press.

Moran, D. (2015). *Carceral geography: Spaces and practices of incarceration.* Farnham: Ashgate.

Naim, C. (2005, Spring). *Prison food law.* LEDA at Harvard Law School. Retrieved from https://dash.harvard.edu/bitstream/handle/1/8848245/Naim05.html?sequence=2

National Institute of Health. (2013, April). *A pilot study examining food insecurity and HIV risk behaviors among individuals recently released from prison.* Retrieved from www.ncbi.nlm.nih.gov/pmc/articles/PMC3733343/pdf/nihms469405.pdf

Rees, E., & Hobson, J. (2021). Restorative practice in the criminal justice system: Examining a restorative reasoning programme in a women's prison. *Laws, 10*(4), 95–107.

Sandberg, S., Agoff, C., & Fondevila, G. (2020). Doing marginalized motherhood: Identities and practices among incarcerated women in Mexico. *International Journal for Crime, Justice and Social Democracy, 9*(2), 15–29. doi:10.5204/ijcjsd.v10i1.1538

Smith, C. (2002). Punishment and pleasure: Women, food and the imprisoned body. *Sociological Review, 50*(2), 197–214.

Smith, A., Krisman, K., Strozier, A. L., & Marley, M. A. (2004). Breaking through the bars: Exploring the experiences of addicted incarcerated parents whose children are cared for by relatives. *Families in Society, 85*(2), 187–195. https://doi.org/10.1606/1044-3894.329

Smoyer, A. B. (2015). Feeding relationships: Foodways and social networks in a women's prison. *Journal of Women and Social Work, 30*(1), 26–39.

Smoyer, A. B. & Lopes, G. (2017). Hungry on the inside: Prison food as concrete and symbolic punishment in a women's prison. *Punishment and Society, 19*(2), 249–255.

Stearns, A. (2019). Baking bittersweet: Mothers' dessert-making behind bars. *Feminist Criminology, 14*(5), 612–632. https://doi.org/10.1177/1557085118769748

Stephan, J. (2004). *Bureau of Justice Statistics special report: State prison expenditures, 2001.* Washington, DC: United States Department of Justice.

Tan, C. C., Ruhl, H., Chow, C. M., & Ellis, L. (2016). Retrospective reports of parental feeding practices and emotional eating in adulthood: The role of food preoccupation. *Appetite, 105*, 410–415.

The Pew Charitable Trusts. (2010). *Collateral costs: Incarceration's effect on economic mobility.* Retrieved from https://repositories.lib.utexas.edu/bitstream/handle/2152/15161/PEW_Collateral-Costs.pdf?sequence=2

The Sentencing Project. (2020, November). *Fact sheet: Incarcerated girls and women.* Retrieved from https://www.sentencingproject.org/publications/incarcerated-women-and-girls/

Thomson, N. D., Moeller, F. G., Amstadter, A. B., Svikis, D., Perera, R. A., & Bjork, J. M. (2020). The impact of parental incarceration on psychopathy, crime, and prison violence in women. *International Journal of Offender Therapy and Comparative Criminology, 64*(10–11), 1178–1194.

Vanhouche, A. (2015). Acceptance or refusal of convenience food in present-day prison. *Appetite, 94*, 47–53.

Vuk, M., Applegate, B. K., Ouellette, H. M., Bolin, R. M., & Aizpurua, E. (2020). The pragmatic public? The impact of practical concerns on support for punitive and rehabilitative prison policies. *American Journal of Criminal Justice, 45*(2), 273–292.

Whitman, E. (2019, September 25). Arizona prison food was labeled 'not for human consumption,' ex-inmates say. *Phoenix New Times.* Retrieved from https://www.phoenixnewtimes.com/news/ex-inmates-arizona-prison-food-was-not-for-human-consumption-11362468

Williams, N. A., Dev, D. A., Hankey, M., & Biltch, K. (2017). Role of food preoccupation and current dieting in the associations of parental feeding practices to emotional eating in young adults: A moderated mediation study. *Appetite, 111*, 195–202.

Ugelvik, T. (2011). The hidden food: Mealtime resistance and identity work in a Norwegian prison. *Punishment & Society, 13*, 47–63.

Zoukis, C. (2016, March 31). Use of nutraloaf on the decline in U.S. prisons. *Prison Legal News.* Retrieved from https://www.prisonlegalnews.org/news/2016/mar/31/use-nutraloaf-decline-us-prisons/

9

THE MASS INCARCERATION OF LGBTQ PERSONS

Jeffery P. Dennis

LEARNING OUTCOMES:

Upon successful completion of this chapter, students will be able to:

1 Explain how LGBTQ persons are criminalized at each stage of the criminal justice process.
2 Identify five problems and obstacles that incarcerated LGBTQ persons face.
3 Identify five current issues in accommodating incarcerated transgender persons.

Gender and Sexual Identities

In order to discuss the mass incarceration of LGBTQ persons, we must start with some basic definitions. One's *sexual orientation* or *sexual identity* refers to the gender of one's erotic interest (a desire for physical closeness), romantic interest (a desire for emotional intimacy), or both. There are four main sexual identities: heterosexual (primary or exclusive interest in another sex), gay/lesbian (same-sex), bisexual/pansexual (both or multiple sexes), and asexual (no or minimal interest). The term "homosexual" is outdated and widely considered offensive and therefore should be avoided (Peters, 2014). LGBT, LGBTQ, and Queer are often used as umbrella terms (GLAAD Media Reference Guide, 2022).

Trying to determine the number of people with each sexual identity is problematic: some people with non-heterosexual erotic or romantic interests, fearing discrimination and harassment, conceal their identities on surveys. Others grew up in an environment where everyone was assumed heterosexual and therefore identified as heterosexual in spite of their primary erotic interest. Some acknowledge same-sex interest but do not believe that it is adequate to warrant a bisexual or gay/lesbian identity. However, a recent survey of young adults in Britain gives us a rough idea: about 72% of respondents identified as heterosexual, 16% as bisexual or pansexual, and 8% as gay or lesbian. The remaining 4% chose "other" or refused to answer (Dahlgren & Shakespeare, 2015).

It is important to remember that one's sexual activity does not always correspond to one's sexual identity. In a survey of incarcerated people in New York, over 50% of incarcerated

DOI: 10.4324/9781003274292-12

men who identified as heterosexual stated that they had engaged in consensual same-sex activity, and 30% had engaged in same-sex romantic relationships (Rowell-Cunsolo, Szeto, Sampong, & Larson, 2016).

Gender can refer to one's biological sex, gender presentation, or gender identity. Most people have primary sexual characteristics that can be classified as male or female, but up to 3% of the population is intersex, varying in chromosomes, hormones, or sex organs. Previously intersex individuals were forced into surgery and hormone therapy to make their bodies correspond as closely as possible to "male" or "female" models, but today they are likely to assert that they are fine the way they are. Intersex Pride is often added to the LGBT Pride Flag as a purple circle on a yellow background (Intersex Advocates).

Gender presentation refers to how closely one's physical traits, voice, hair style, dress, mannerisms, and even leisure pursuits reflect conventional masculine or feminine roles. For instance, men are expected to have deep voices and facial hair, wear pants instead of dresses, have an assertive, aggressive personality, and display an interest in cars and sports. Failure to meet gender expectations results in bullying, harassment, hate crime victimization, and many more subtle forms of discrimination. Some people, however, prefer a non-binary presentation: their dress and mannerisms do not closely align with either masculine or feminine expectations. They may prefer *they/them* pronouns to avoid identifying as *he/him* or *she/her*.

Gender identity, one's sense of their own gender, can be divided into cisgender (their identity matches the gender they were assigned at birth) and transgender (it does not). In the U.S., 1.4% of juveniles aged 13–17 and .05% of adults identify as transgender. The significantly higher percentage of juveniles is probably due to the increased visibility of transgender people during the last ten years; previously many people were not even aware that transgender identities exist (Herman, Flores, & O'Neill, 2022).

Once transgender people recognize that their gender identity does not correspond to their assigned gender, that they are actually a girl raised as a boy, or a boy raised as a girl, they begin a transitioning process, acquiring a gender-appropriate name and wardrobe, and updated names and genders on legal documents such as their driver's license and passport. Hormone therapy will provide them with the appropriate secondary sexual characteristics. Finally, they may get gender affirmation surgeries to make their bodies closely correspond to the appropriate gender. These surgeries are invasive and expensive, and usually not covered by insurance plans, so many trans people cannot afford them. In the U.S., only about 25% of transgender people have had "top surgery," and 13% have had "bottom surgery" (National Center for Transgender Equality, 2016).

The Number of Incarcerated LGBTQ Persons

Estimates of the number of incarcerated adults who identify as LGBTQ vary, depending on how sexual and gender identities are defined and how likely respondents are to respond accurately. Kaeble and Glaze (2016) estimates that 2–3% of incarcerated persons identify as lesbian, gay, or bisexual, but Dennis (2014) estimates about 30%, and Meyer et al. (2017) about 20% of incarcerated men and 30% of incarcerated women. The Bureau of Justice (2012) further estimates that about 5% of incarcerated adults identify as transgender. According to the National Transgender Discrimination Survey (Grant et al., 2011), 12% of white, 13% of Asian, 30% of Native American, and 47% of Black transgender persons have been incarcerated during their lifetime.

Estimates of the number of incarcerated youth who identify as LGBTQ vary from 15% (Hunt & Moodie-Mills, 2012) to 40% (Wilson & Bouton, 2022). Among juveniles who were placed in transitional housing for the homeless as an alternative to secure facilities (similar to adult prisons), nearly 30% of boys and 40% of girls identified as gay, lesbian, bisexual, or another sexual minority and nearly 10% of boys and 5% of girls identified as transgender (Cunningham et al., 2014).

Injustice in the Criminal Justice System

There is extensive anecdotal and statistical evidence suggesting that many police officers use LGBTQ identities as valid criteria for stops, interrogation, and arrests. A study in the city of New Orleans found that 33% of white LGBTQ youth and 87% of LGBTQ youth of color were stopped and questioned by the police every year (BreakOut, 2014). LGBTQ people have been arrested for holding hands, kissing, sitting on the same side of a restaurant booth, discussing sex, and using public restrooms. The usual charges are disorderly conduct or lewd behavior, although sodomy laws, invalidated by the U.S. Supreme Court in 2003, are sometimes invoked as well (Smith, 2005, 2012; Gregory, 2013; Closson & Wong, 2022).

Although it is impossible to determine someone's sexual orientation or gender identity by looking at them, targeting occurs through hot-spot policing of gay neighborhoods and looking for visual cues such as lambdas and pride flags. The police and general public also use failure to meet conventional gender expectations, men "who look like women," women "who look like men," as a criterion for complaints, stops, and interrogation. According to the National Transgender Discrimination Survey, 18% of white, 29% of Asian, 34% of Native American, and 38% of Black transgender persons report having police ask if they are men or women, being grabbed in intimate regions to determine if they have breasts or a penis, or told that it is illegal to wear the clothing of "the opposite sex," even though crossdressing is no longer illegal in any American jurisdiction.

Public displays of affection between same-sex couples, however minor, are likely to receive police interrogation or arrests. Dwyer (2011), interviewing youth who identified as queer, found that the police expected public space to be exclusively heterosexual and interpreted any evidence of same-sex romantic or erotic desire as criminal. A bisexual girl stated that she could engage in intensive sexual exploration with a boyfriend and be ignored, but when she held hands with a girlfriend, they were arrested for "lewd behavior" (Griffin, 2019).

At their trials, LGBTQ persons are likely to face homophobic harassment from judges, lawyers, juries, and other players in the court. 70% of gay/lesbian/bisexual defendants report hearing homophobic slurs or jokes in the courtroom, 58% were asked their sexual orientation when it was irrelevant to the case, and 39% had their sexual orientation used as evidence of guilt (Lambda Legal, 2013). In a 2014 survey of 1,084 gay/lesbian, bisexual, queer, transgender, two-spirit, and nonbinary persons incarcerated in state prisons across the U.S. (Lydon, 2015), 70% of sexual minorities and 78% of gender minorities hid their sexual/gender identities during their trials in an attempt to avoid homophobic or transphobic discrimination.

Discrimination is particularly common with transgender defendants. While even the most homophobic person will admit to the existence of gay men and lesbians, many transphobic persons do not believe that transgender identity exists at all. They believe that transgender persons are faking their gender identity in order to gain access to the restrooms and locker rooms of "the opposite sex" for the purpose of sexual assault. The result is an increase in guilty verdicts and sentences of incarceration for offenses such as disorderly conduct.

Daily Struggles of Incarcerated LGBTQ Persons

The stress of being incarcerated combined with the stress of living in a homophobic environment has a negative effect on the incarcerated person's health: LGBTQ people in prison are significantly more likely than cisgender heterosexuals to suffer from heart problems, kidney problems, asthma, and HIV (U.S. Department of Justice, 2021). Gay and bisexual men in prison are significantly more likely than heterosexuals to suffer from almost all of the indicators of a negative emotional response to incarceration, such as feeling numb or empty inside (52.7% gay/bisexual, 36.4% heterosexual) and feeling that no one cares (54.1% gay/bisexual, 37.4% heterosexual). They also are more likely to report losing their temper easily, getting angry more often, thinking about revenge, giving up hope, and considering or attempting suicide. When all of the questions were combined into an emotional health index, the mean score was 3.97 for heterosexual men and 5.34 for gay/bisexual men (Dennis, 2014, 2018).

Compounding the physical and psychological problems, LGBTQ resources are often forbidden. For instance, clergy from the gay-specific Metropolitan Community Church required court injunctions to be permitted to conduct services in California and Michigan (Perry & Swicegood, 1990, p. 238), and individual wardens still sometimes ban them on the grounds that they will be "promoting homosexuality." This is especially problematic for gay men, who are more likely than heterosexual men to attend services regularly, and more likely to find religious commitment useful in forestalling depression, anxiety, and other psychological maladies (Boppana & Gross, 2019).

Books on LGBTQ history and culture, and even news magazines, such as *The Advocate*, are often forbidden on the grounds that anything mentioning LGBTQ people is pornographic. A 2016 decision by the Kentucky Supreme Court stated that convicted LGBTQ individuals must be permitted access to LGBTQ history and culture (Duke, 2016), but there are no protocols in any other state. According to the Black and Pink Survey (Lydon, 2015), only 22% of incarcerated LGBTQ persons have access to LGBTQ-affirming books.

An analysis of the daily activities of incarcerated LGBTQ persons reveals some significant differences from the cisgender heterosexual population. LGBTQ persons tend to sleep less, exercise less, watch TV less, but read more (U.S. Department of Justice, 2021). This suggests less engagement with the general prison population, perhaps due to a fear of harassment. Reading may be evidence of isolation, or it may suggest a desire for self-improvement. Although, according to the Black & Pink Survey (Lydon, 2015), 15% of LGBTQ persons in prison have been denied access to rehabilitation programs due to their gender or sexual orientation, they are more likely than cisgender heterosexuals to participate in educational activities, employment counseling, vocational training, and religious activities (U.S. Department of Justice, 2021). This suggests an increased interest in re-integrating into civilian society in spite of the constraints of a homophobic prison administration.

Prison staff are generally more likely than other criminal justice professionals, and significantly more likely than the general population, to believe that one "turns" gay or lesbian due to "moral turpitude" (Center for American Progress, 2018). They are therefore more likely to engage in harassing behavior, such as name-calling and lectures on the Book of Leviticus, as well as denying access to programs and activities. In prison, work assignments are often based upon merit: the best, most interesting, highest-paying jobs go to people whom the staff happens to like. LGBTQ persons in prison are 12% more likely than cisgender heterosexuals to be denied a job altogether, and 11% more likely to have low-status, low-paying jobs (Dennis, 2012).

Gay/bisexual men are more likely than heterosexual men to be written up for many violations, such as having an unauthorized item, verbal assault on another incarcerated individual, being out of place, and disobeying orders. They are twice as likely as heterosexuals to be disciplined for the verbal harassment and failure to obey a staff member. These infractions are both highly subjective, dependent on a staff member's interpretation of the events, so the increase in disciplinary action may be the result of the belief in innate criminality: the acts of an LGBTQ person are perceived as more disrespectful or threatening than the same acts by a cisgender heterosexual. Since LGBTQ persons are assumed to initiate sexual activity constantly, they are frequently punished, whether or not they have engaged in any activity, while incarcerated persons identified as heterosexuals go unnoticed (Mogul, Ritchie, & Whitlock, 2011, p. 97).

Staff members often engage in more violent forms of discrimination. Incarcerated LGBTQ persons are 2.4 times more likely than cisgender heterosexuals to be sexually assaulted by staff, and 5.8 times more likely to be sexually assaulted by other incarcerated persons. When they don't engage in sexual assault themselves, staff members often deliberately place LGBTQ individuals in situations where assault is likely (Lydon, 2015).

LGBTQ and gender-nonconforming juveniles are at particular risk for harassment in youth facilities, where the heteronormative mandate to require stereotypic gender roles, including expressing heterosexual desire, is intensified (Kruse et al., 2020). For example, incarcerated LGBTQ youth are twelve times more likely to be victimized by sexual assault as heterosexual cisgender youth (Gilbert & Hussey, 2015). In Louisiana, a trans girl in a male facility was raped and physically assaulted by other juveniles repeatedly in view of the staff, who either joined in or egged them on, reasoning that it is "good for the kid—gotta teach him and have it beat out of him" (Redman, 2010).

Segregation of LGBTQ persons into separate cell blocks, often suggested as a means of ameliorating harassment from staff and other prison residents, actually has the opposite effect, showing everyone in the prison where they can go to commit physical and sexual assault (Brown & Jenness, 2020). However, random cell assignments often also lead to abuse. In a Michigan prison, Rodriguez Burks, incarcerated for fleeing the police, received a new homophobic roommate who repeatedly threatened to kill him. He asked to be transferred, but three staff members refused, saying "You're not here for your convenience" and "this isn't the Holiday Inn." On the second day with his new cellmate, he was murdered (Ikonomova, 2017).

Accommodations for Transgender Individuals

One of the reasons for the increased risk of physical and sexual assault of transgender persons in prison is the common state and federal policy that unless they have gender affirmation surgery (specifically "bottom surgery"), they must be housed in the prisons for their sex assigned at birth. According to the National Transgender Inmate Survey (James et al., 2015), 20% of transgender persons in prison were housed with people corresponding to their gender identity, and 60% were not (the others were in solitary confinement or mixed housing). Most transgender persons cannot afford "bottom surgery," and only the state of Delaware provides it in prison. No states provide "top surgery" (Oberholtzer, 2019). Therefore, transgender women, who have been living as women for a decade or more, who look and act like cisgender women in every respect except their genitals, are thrust into a prison with 1,000 men. In such an environment, physical and sexual assault is practically guaranteed (Sexton, Jenness, & Sumner, 2009). Thirty-seven percent of transgender women but only 3% of cisgender women report sexual assault in prison (Wilson & Bouton, 2022).

Incarcerated transgender persons face many other accommodation issues. According to the Inter-American Court of Human Rights (Human Rights Clinic, 2020), expecting the use of one's correct name and the ability to modify that name on personal information on records and documents is a basic human right. Fifty-six percent of incarcerated transgender persons stated that most other prison residents used their correct name and pronouns, but only 20% stated that staff members usually gave them the same accommodation. Instead, they report frequent use of "deadnames," incorrect pronouns, disparaging remarks concerning transgender identity. One transgender women reported being told by an officer that "until you get your dick cut off you still a man" and "this is not a women['s] prison. You don't get special treatment cause you want to be a 'fake woman.'" Nearly all incarcerated transgender persons report invasive strip searches to determine "if they are a man or a woman" (Lydon, 2015).

Incarcerated transgender persons are legally entitled to the same level of hormone therapy that they received on the outside: testosterone or estrogen, usually injected once a month (ACLU, 2014). However, prison staff often ignores this protocol, offering hormones in ineffective pill form, or none at all; according to the Black & Pink Survey (Lydon, 2015), 44% of transgender respondents report being denied access to all hormone therapy in prison. Since biologically produced testosterone or estrogen "turns off," transgender persons need hormone therapy for much more than maintaining secondary sexual characteristics: it helps maintain their metabolic rate, muscle mass, bone density, and other bodily systems. Failure to provide adequate hormone therapy therefore results in many physical problems, as well as psychological problems such as depression, anxiety, sleeplessness, and general malaise (Cavanaugh et al., 2015).

Gender-appropriate underwear, hair, and cosmetic items are essential to the transgender person's transitioning process. Some prison wardens consider these items medical necessities, and provide them to transgender individuals through the prison clinic; others allow them to be purchased by anyone in the commissary (some cisgender men enjoy crossdressing as a hobby). Others do not permit them at all, believing that dressing in the clothing of "the opposite sex" is illegal, or instills criminal activity. According to the Black & Pink Survey (Lydon, 2015), only 21% of transgender individuals are allowed access to gender-appropriate clothing and cosmetics, even when their absence causes physical discomfort (a person with breasts denied a bra, for instance).

Transgender persons are legally entitled to be searched by someone of the appropriate gender, but again, this protocol is often ignored. There are no protocols regarding the use of showers and toilets. Some prison wardens force incarcerated transgender persons to use the facilities at the same time as everyone else, and others specify certain times for their use. Only a few allow transgender persons to specify their preferences.

Conclusion

The criminalization of LGBTQ persons begins with over a century of demonization, with social institutions such as government, medicine, mass media, and criminal justice promoting the belief that sexual and gender minorities are innately evil (Dennis, 2017). It extends through disproportions in arrests, as the police make "probable cause" decisions based partially or entirely on same-sex or gender-atypical behavior, and into the court room, with harassment from lawyers, witnesses, jurors, and judges and an increased likelihood of guilty verdicts. They are more likely to go to prison, and spend more time in prison, than cisgender heterosexuals convicted of the same crimes. While incarcerated, they face only harassment and physical and sexual assault, but denial of necessary services and resources, which often hinders their successful re-integration into the community upon release.

There is evidence that conditions are changing, at least in some prisons. In the aftermath of numerous lawsuits, several states have adopted mandatory diversity training for prison staff (Redman, 2010). In 2022, the Federal Bureau of Prisons issued a revised Transgender Offender Manual which specifies that staff must use correct names and pronouns. It further states that housing may be determined "on a case-by-case basis," rejecting the former "sex assigned at birth" policy (Bureau of Prisons, 2022). A number of activist groups, including the ACLU and Lambda Legal, are working to secure human rights for incarcerated LGBTQ persons, while others are combating the homophobic and transphobic attitudes that lead to the acts of harassment and abuse.

Discussion Questions:

1. What recommendations do you have to decrease the discrimination and harassment suffered by incarcerated LGBTQ persons?
2. You are in charge of a men's prison with 1,000 residents. About 60 are transgender women. What accommodations will you institute regarding hormone therapy, access to clothing and cosmetics, shower and toilet use, and cell assignment?

References

ACLU. (2014). *Know Your Rights: Laws, Court Decisions, and Advocacy Tips to Protect Transgender Prisoners.* https://www.aclu.org/sites/default/files/assets/121414-aclu-prea-kyrs-1_copy.pdf

Beck, A., Harrison, P., & Guerino, P. (2010). *Sexual Victimization in Juvenile Facilities Reported by Youth, 2008–09.* http://www.bjs.gov/content/pub/pdf/svjfry09.pdf

Beck. A., Berzofsky, M., & Krebs, P. (2012). *Sexual Victimization Reported by Inmates of Prisons and Jails, 2011–2012.* https://bjs.ojp.gov/content/pub/pdf/svpjri1112.pdf

Boppana, S., & Gross, A.M. (2019). The impact of religiosity on the psychological well-being of LGBT Christians. *Journal of Gay & Lesbian Mental Health*, 23(4), 412–426.

BreakOUT and the National Council on Crime and Delinquency. (2014). *We Deserve Better: A Report on Policing in New Orleans by and for Queer and Trans Youth of Color.* https://issuu.com/youthbreakout/docs/we_deserve_better_report/1

Brown, J.A., & Jenness, V. (2020). LGBT people in prison: management strategies, human rights violations, and political mobilization. *Oxford Research Encyclopedia of Criminology and Criminal Justice.* https://doi.org/10.1093/acrefore /9780190264079.013.647

Bureau of Prisons. (2022). *Transgender Offender Manual.* https://www.bop.gov/ policy/progstat/5200-08-cn-1.pdf

Cavanaugh, T, et al. (2015). *The Medical Care of Transgender Persons*. Fenway Health, Boston, MA.
Center for American Progress. (2018). *Unjust: How the Broken Criminal Justice System Fails LGBT People of Color*. https://www.lgbtmap.org/file/lgbt-criminal-justice-poc.pdf
Closson, T., & Wong, A. (2022). Port authority settlement will end undercover bathroom patrols. *New York Times*. https://www.nytimes.com/2022/06/01/nyregion/port-authority-bathroom-patrols.html
Cunningham, M., et al. (2014). Homeless LGBTQ Youth. Washington, DC: Urban Institute. https://www.urban.org/sites/default/files/publication/22876/413209-Homeless-LGBTQ-Youth.PDF
Dahlgren, W., & Shakespeare, A. (2015). One in two young people say they are not 100% heterosexual. *Yougov for Business*. https://yougov.co.uk/topics/lifestyle/articles-reports/2015/08/16/half-young-not-heterosexual
Dennis, J.P. (2014). The LGBT offender. In: Peterson, D., Panfil, V. (eds). *Handbook of LGBT Communities, Crime, and Justice*. Springer, New York.
Dennis, J.P. (2017). *The Myth of the Queer Criminal*. Routledge, New York.
Dennis, J.P. (2018). Nothing out there: Community awareness and delinquency among gay and lesbian youth. *Journal of LGBT Youth*, 16, 1–17.
Duke, A. (2016). Victory! Prison's anti-LGBT literature ban lifted. *ACLU Kentucky*. https://www.aclu-ky.org/en/news/victory-prisons-anti-lgbt-literature-ban-lifted
Dwyer, A. (2011). "It's not like we're going to jump them": How transgressing heteronormativity shapes police interactions with LGBT young people. *Youth Justice*, 11(3), 203–220.
Gilbert, C., & Hussey, H. (2015). *Young, Queer, and Locked Up: LGBT Youth in the Adult Criminal Justice System*. Campaign for Youth Justice. http:// campaignforyouthjustice.org/voices/item/young-queer-and-locked-up-lgbt-youth-in-the-adult-criminal-justice-system
GLAAD Media Reference Guide (2022). https://www.glaad.org/reference/terms
Grant, J.M. et al. (2011). *Injustice at Every Turn: A Report of the National Transgender Discrimination Survey*. National Center for Transgender Equality and National Gay and Lesbian Task Force, Washington, DC. http://www.thetaskforce.org/static_html/ downloads/reports/reports/ntds_full.pdf
Gregory, S. (2013). Louisiana sodomy sting: How invalidated sex laws still lead to arrests. *Time Magazine*. http://nation.time.com/2013/07/31
Griffith, D. (2019). LGBT youth are at a greater risk of homelessness and incarceration. *Prison Policy Initiative*. http://prisonpolicy.org/blog/2019/01/22/lgbtq_youth/
Herman, J.L., Flores, A., & O'Neill, K. (2022). *How Many Adults and Youth Identify as Transgender in the United States?* UCLA School of Law Williams Institute. https://williamsinstitute.law.ucla.edu/publications/trans-adults-united-states/
Human Rights Clinic, Austin Community Law Center, & Trans Pride Initiative. (2020). *Naming and Shaming: Violation of the Human Rights of Transgender Persons in Texas*. https://law.utexas.edu/wp-content/uploads/sites/11/2020/11/2020-HRC-Naming-and-Shaming.pdf
Hunt, J., & Moodie-Mills. A.C. (2012). *The Unfair Criminalization of Gay and Transgender Youth: An Overview of the Experiences of LGBT Youth in the Juvenile Justice System*. Center for American Progress, Washington DC.
Ikonomova, V. (2017). Michigan prisoner killed for being gay. *Detroit Metro Times*. https://www.metrotimes.com/news/inmates-michigan-prisoner-killed-by-cellmate-for-being-gay-guards-ignored-repeated-pleas-for-help-4708017
Kaeble, D. & Glaze, L. (2016). Correctional Populations in the United States, 2015. Washington, DC: Bureau of Justice Statistics
Kruse, M., et al. (2020). LGBT youth confront inconsistent, unreliable patterns of incarceration. *News 21*. https://kidsimprisoned.news21.com/lgbtq-kids-discrimination-justice-system/
James, S. E., et al. (2015). The Report of the 2015 U.S. Transgender Survey. (pp. 184–190). Washington, DC: National Center for Transgender Equality. http:// www.ustranssurvey.org/report
Lambda Legal. (2013). *Protected and Served*. https://www.lambdalegal.org/sites/default/files/ publications/downloads/ps_executive-summary.pdf

Lydon, J. (2015). *Coming Out of Concrete Closets: A Report on Black & Pink's National LGBTQ Prisoner Survey.* https://www.blackandpink.org/wp-content/uploads/2020/03/Coming-Out-of-Concrete-Closets-incorcporated-Executive-summary102115.pdf

Meyer, I., et al. (2017). Incarceration rates and trends of sexual minorities in the United States: National Inmate Survey, 2011–2012. *American Journal of Public Health,* 107(2), 267–273.

Mogul, J., Ritchie, A., & Whitlock, K. (2011). *Queer (In)Justice: The Criminalization of LGBT People in the United States.* Beacon Press, Boston, MA.

National Center for Transgender Equality. (2016). *Frequently Asked Questions about Transgender People.* https://transequality.org/issues/resources/understanding-transgender-people-faq

Oberholtzer, E. (2019). The dismal state of transgender incarceration policies. *Prison Policy Initiative.* https://www.prisonpolicy.org/blog/2017/11/08/transgender/

Perry, T., & T. Swicegood. (1990). *Don't Be Afraid Anymore: The Story of Troy Perry and the Metropolitan Community Church.* St. Martin's Press, New York.

Peters, J.W. (2014). The decline and fall of the 'H' Word: [Style Desk]. *New York Times.* https://www-proquest-com.ezproxy.mnsu.edu/newspapers/decline-fall-h-word/docview/1509258293

Redman, D. (2010). "I Was Scared to Sleep": LGBT youth face violence behind bars. *The Nation.* https://www.thenation.com/article/archive/i-was-scared-sleep-lgbt-youth-face-violence-behind-bars/

Rowell-Cunsolo, T.L., Szeto, B., Sampong, S.A., & Larson, E.L. (2016). Predictors of sexual behaviour among men and women in New York City area prisons. *Culture, Health & Sexuality,* 18(12), 1393–1406.

Sexton, L., Jenness, V., & Sumner, J. (2013). *A Demographic Assessment of Transgender Inmates in Men's Prisons.* http://ucicorrections.seweb.uci.edu/files/2013/06/A-Demographic-Assessment-of-Transgender-Inmates-in-Mens-Prisons.pdf

Smith, A. (2005). Homophobia in the halls of justice: Sexual orientation bias and its implications within the legal system. *Journal of Gender, Social Policy, and the Law,* 20, 18–34.

Smith, M. (2012). Plaintiffs in gay kiss case against city of El Paso Chico's Tacos announce settlement." *KVIA.* http://www.kvia.com/news

U.S. Department of Justice. (2021). *Survey of Inmates in State and Federal Correctional Facilities, 2016* [Computer file.] Ann Arbor, MI: Inter-University Consortium for Political and Social Research.

Wilson, B., & Bouton, L. (2022). *System Involvement among LBQ Girls and Women.* Williams Institute. https://williamsinstitute.law.ucla.edu/publications/system-involved-lbq-girls-women/

10

REFLECTION

WORKING IN THE PRISON LIBRARY DURING COVID-19

Janette Richardson

It's almost 9'o clock on a Wednesday morning and I'm still in my cell, ugh! Will they run it? On a good day, yes. Right now I should already be chit-chatting with Ms. Heffington or maybe doing my makeup because the officers rushed me out on time. I reach into my bra for my ID which has my Inmate Job Assignment taped to the back of it. It says 8:30 and it said 8:30 yesterday.

A Yard Library Assistant
8:30 to 11:30
12:30 to 15:30

I hear The Steve Wilkos Show coming on behind me as it's got to be a little after 9. I like the show and I should stay and watch it since 'they try'na make a sistah late' but that's my program. All the sudden the door opens, I'm free! All is forgiven as I scurry out of the cell and into the day room where I am sure to give the tower guard the evil eye.

Before I can make it out of the yard I am stopped by some guy who knows my name somehow. He asked if I could bring him a power of attorney form after I get off of work. Sure, I guess…But who are you? I really can't give him any attitude because he obviously needs it for something important plus I'm sure he'd get in on his own if he could. Today like yesterday is "short of staff." No program.

Before I can make it to the patio I am stopped two more times for different requests. Again, this is the Lord's work. They're just trying to get home and I'm only annoyed that I was released to go to work so late. At last! I reach the education department door guarded by the very conservative officer to whom I greet with a decorated, "Hello-"He nods and I'm through the door and I make a right. Achievement unlocked. I am instantly transported into my personal refuge. That's probably saying a lot but to me it's true. In a Cheers-like fashion I am welcomed by legal beagles and geriatrics as I make it behind the counter. I give Ms. Heffington a cheesy grin and an ultra-high-pitched "Good morning" and I get settled for my daily tasks… while I put my face on.

DOI: 10.4324/9781003274292-13

Today I have a profound understanding of how the library is run and how the law works. I've had this job for about a year. During my time as a library clerk, I got a crash course intro into the courts expectations on filing timely motions to keep your case going. I've also needed to learn a bit about legal procedures because I was the only clerk approved for work during Covid-19's lockdown.

It's crazy because I don't remember the exact date but I was approached by one of the old clerks who wanted me to be the first transgender library clerk. It sounds niche that I ironically conformed to their orders without having any knowledge of the job. A week later the prison was shut down due to the pandemic.

It was so surreal when the pandemic hit! Everyone was told to social distance or we'll get written up. Our groups, visits, and program were compromised while most inmate assignments were put on hold. Fortunately for me, the prison's law library was just as important as working in the kitchen and faculty maintenance so during this time the LTA kept calling me out to work.

This was super exciting and very scary. I even felt a lil overwhelmed. The LTA was very kind and patient every time I would screw something up. I tried to keep my questions to a minimum but I wanted to learn the job in one day. I didn't want to be in the cell all day like everyone else. I need to learn fast or else she'll change her mind, I told myself every time I mess up on copies or when I had a hard time finding a certain form or whatever. I learned later that I was preferred over the other clerks because I was a good worker. One in a million....

After building a good rapport with the LTA, I asked if I could take home some of the soft cover legal research books back to my cell, "to study," she laughed and gave me permission. Back in the building people were going crazy with minimal program. I was so appreciative of the still silence of the day. I read those awesome NOLO books and the library's legal manuals on super down days. I took advantage of access to forms to assist me on my personal civil case, one in which I taught myself how to file a civil complaint against a doctor. Around that time I was working on my appeal as well. I felt like a trans Matlock. Ego aside, I really took the time to educate myself to distract me from the horrors of the lock down. A lot of good people went back to old habits, I'm so thankful I had something to do during this time. It didn't take long to come up with the idea to help people out.

With great power comes great responsibility. I allowed myself to be approachable for delivering and accepting copy requests. My primary task was making various legal packets. It was very difficult at first, I quickly learned what forms make up a writ of certiorari and what makes a state tort. People are serious even if it comes out picky. Sometimes it was hard not to take offense. And just like that I saw a change in me, I opened up to serve to about the point where I learned from criticism. I didn't get upset at all, I realized I took time to listen more closely to a request instead of blowing up in my defense. Something I've always had trouble with prior to incarceration. I was growing socially too, which was something I needed for my own journey and my transition as I developed certain social cues and body language I didn't care for before. This helped me feel confident as a trans woman in prison and in communicating in the legal multiverse.

A couple of months into the job I started to get the hang of remembering the names and numbers of the most popular forms. I even started to bring extra forms to my cell "for just in case." Now that I look back I am amazed at how dedicated I was with the responsibility of the "extra," the stuff I didn't get paid for. To this day I never charged a soul for legal work, taking only donations on the off-hand request.

My good deeds paid in full as I enjoy the sacred ground I tread today. The pandemic behind us all and program running at full capacity my job consists of handing out petitions for resentencing (1170.95) or IRS 1040 forms. Also the previous LTA was replaced with a career librarian, Ms. Heffington. I can only describe her as a cross between Dumbledore and Mrs. Claus with a blonde streak of hair on her bangs like Rouge from X-Men. She has been my Obi-Wan since the day she was hired. Really, she's nothing short of awesome!

This job has been a positive experience in all aspects of my rehabilitation. Labels suck but I'm an incarcerated black trans woman and I totally know that there are very few places where I can say I've truly let my guard down. Even fewer places where I am respected for who I am. Prison sucks in general but I was granted a safe place to "do me" while I serve the incarcerated community.

Since working with Mrs. Huffington and the other education staff and officer, I've seen improvement in my socialization skills. I used to be really socially awkward and shy. The person who has helped me realize my inner strength is the same person who told me to leave these boys alone and just do my time. I'm fortunate to have a mentor who supports me and it's something the prison staff needs to work on together with inmates. Maybe not. But as I reach for my eyeliner pencil I am hit with another request at the library window, another 1040. The person on the other side of the window asks why do I need to wear makeup. I look at Mrs. Huffington and smile, "Cause I'ma sista with a job."

SECTION III

Prison Education

The Violent Crime Control and Law Enforcement Act of 1994 contributed to the phenomenon of mass incarceration by creating tougher criminal sentences, providing funding for prison construction, and developing the Violent Offender Incarceration and Truth-in-Sentencing program. An often overlooked section of the 1994 Crime Bill is Sec. 20411, which prohibited incarcerated individuals in federal and state prisons from receiving financial aid for higher education, including Pell grants. In the early 1990s, there were 772 college prison programs operating in 1,287 correctional facilities (Robinson & Smith, 2017; Sawyer, 2019). By 1997, this number had been reduced to eight (Robinson & Smith, 2017; Sawyer, 2019). Postsecondary education can disrupt the vicious cycle of mass incarceration by helping individuals return to their communities with education and skills that will help them be productive citizens. There has been a resurgence of interest in prison education programs since the signing of the *FAFSA Simplification Act* that restores Pell grant eligibility to incarcerated persons (Dholakia, 2022). This section of the reader reviews the realities and reflections of higher education programs in prison.

This part of the reader begins with Ashley M. Appleby's article, "The History and Operation of Prison Education Programs Today." Appleby provides a thorough review of policy decisions that have impacted postsecondary prison education programs. Next, Victoria's "Prison Education, Democracy, and Solidarity" continues the discussion by asserting that postsecondary education in college is an expression of democratic solidarity. The section concludes with two reflection chapters, Meade's "Reflections on the Design, Administration, and Value of a Prison-College Course" and Sanders' "Inside-Out: A Transformative Experience." Benjamin Meade reflects on his experience as an instructor in a prison college course, while Kaelyn Sanders describes her role in a prison-based college course that brought together campus-based students with incarcerated students.

DOI: 10.4324/9781003274292-14

References

Dholakia, N. (2022, November 1). *Filling out the FAFSA behind bars*. Vera Institute of Justice. Retrieved December 22, 2022, from https://www.vera.org/news/filling-out-the-fafsa-behind-bars

Robinson, G., & Smith, E. E. (2017). The Second Chance Pell Pilot Program: A historical overview. American Enterprise Institute. Available from https://www.aei.org/research-products/report/the-second-chance-pell-pilot-program-a-historical-overview/

Sawyer, W. (2019, August 22). *Since you asked: How did the 1994 crime bill affect prison college programs?* Prison Policy Initiative. Retrieved December 22, 2022, from https://www.prisonpolicy.org/blog/2019/08/22/college-in-prison/

11

THE HISTORY AND OPERATION OF PRISON EDUCATION PROGRAMS TODAY

Ashley M. Appleby

LEARNING OUTCOMES:

Upon successful completion of this chapter, students will be able to:

1 Explain how policy decisions have impacted postsecondary prison education programs historically.
2 Detail the benefits associated with providing access to postsecondary prison education programs for those incarcerated.

Introduction

With nearly 2.3 million individuals incarcerated across the nation, the United States makes up just 5% of the global population but incarcerates more than 20% of the world's prison population (Sawyer & Wagner, 2020).

Research consistently documents that individuals who experience contact with the justice system are largely undereducated compared to the general public. Specifically, approximately 44% of those incarcerated do not hold a high school diploma, in comparison to 18% of the general public (Bender, 2019). Therefore, offering prison education programs becomes one avenue toward upward mobility and overall success (Chesnut, Taber, & Quintana, 2022).

While prison education has made recent headlines in the policy, education, and correctional spheres due to the 2022–2023 Pell Grant Expansion made possible by the FAFSA Simplification Act signed into law on December 27, 2020, offering such programs to those incarcerated is not a new phenomenon. As early as the 1920s, students received access to education inside of prisons – by 1976, 237 programs were introduced nationwide, 350 by 1982, 772 by 1990, and over 20,000 have accessed prison education programs to date (Chesnut & Wachendorfer, 2021). Unsurprisingly, the fluctuation in access has varied as a result of the very policies and practices that influenced mass incarceration.

DOI: 10.4324/9781003274292-15

This chapter details a brief history and description of postsecondary prison education programs in the United States. The first section provides an overview of the different types of programs offered in prisons and outlines a working definition of higher education in prison for the purpose of this book chapter. The following section presents a brief overview of the history of postsecondary prison education programs and details the policies that have impacted the fluctuation of offering such programs. Additionally, this section highlights how the fluctuation in programming correlates with the same policies that led to the skyrocketing reliance on incarceration as punishment across the United States. The subsequent section presents research on prison education programs and outlines the benefits associated with offering prison education programs to those incarcerated. Finally, the last section discusses the benefits and drawbacks of technology associated with these programs.

Prison Education Programs

Individuals who experience contact with the justice system are largely undereducated compared to their nonincarcerated counterparts. Approximately 30% of individuals incarcerated across state and federal prisons lack a high school diploma or G.E.D. and are overall less likely to have a G.E.D. or high school diploma than the general public (Pompoco et al., 2017; Rampey et al., 2016). To address this reality, several programs exist inside of prisons that aim to enhance literacy skills and prepare individuals for their eventual reintegration into the community upon release. This includes, amongst others, offering G.E.D. courses toward the receipt of a formal degree, adult basic education courses, vocational training, apprenticeships, and college classes.

Programs offered inside of prisons vary widely. This means that which programs are offered, who has access to the programs, and who provides the program is up to the discretion of each individual correctional facility and is influenced by both large-scale political decisions along with the administration of each facility. For example, some correctional facilities may only offer career and technical training, while others may offer access to college courses and credit (Castro & Gould, 2018). Additionally, when large-scale political decisions, such as the reallocation of public funds, may lead to most programs becoming obsolete – it is up to the leadership and administration, such as the warden or education coordinator of the facility itself, to decide whether they find it appropriate to allow volunteers to continue providing programming inside of the facility in the absence of compensation and budget allocations.

While programming may fluctuate across academic years and semesters, the goal of such programs includes providing opportunities for rehabilitation while also preparing individuals for release. In the United States today, there are a wide variety of programs available for individuals with various levels of education and learning experiences. This includes high-school-level, college-level, and other enrichment opportunities such as workshops, job fairs, and writing groups. Although there are many different types of educational and vocational programs offered nationwide, this chapter focuses on the history and operation of college-level higher education programs across the United States. Higher education in prison is defined in this chapter as teaching and learning experiences that include (1) courses provided to students who have earned a high school diploma, G.E.D., or equivalent secondary credential, (2) courses and programs provided by or in close partnership with an accredited post-secondary institution, (3) instruction provided by two-year and four-year colleges and universities with public, private, or non-profit status, (4) credit or not-for-credit coursework, and (5) degree or non-degree granting pathways (Castro & Gould, 2018).

Brief History of Higher Education in Prison

At the onset of prison education programs, their purpose was purely rehabilitative. Political stakeholders and correctional administration believed that providing individuals with access to these programs would assist with their return to society through reforming their behavior to become law-abiding citizens.

Although prison education programs have recently become a prominent discussion amongst universities, politicians, and the public, the existence of these programs is not new. Prison education programs have been offered in correctional facilities across the United States since 1920. In the first study of prison education, Seashore et al. (1976) provided a detailed look at Project NewGate, which was the first prison education project funded by the Office of Economic Opportunity. In line with the "rehabilitative ideal" at the time, the goal of early prison education programs was to provide individuals with the necessary tools to enroll in college upon their eventual release from prison (Phelps, 2012). Along with academic and therapeutic counseling, programs such as Project NewGate were one way to improve the prison environment by providing support to those incarcerated to prepare them for reentry into the community.

While early programs began offering education in the form of tutors, correspondence courses became popular throughout the 1950s (Gehring, 1997; Seashore et al., 1976). Course materials were transferred via the mail between universities and prison facilities, and in line with the political and legal infrastructure during that time, the widespread support for these programs was motivated by the belief in expanding access to education across the nation (Seashore et al., 1976). At this time, the right to an education became a widespread movement in the United States – correctional, political, and educational leaders continued to support the implementation of prison education programs throughout the 1950s and 1960s.

The Higher Education Act of 1965 further expanded access to and support for offering higher education in prisons across the United States (Pub. L. No. 89-329). By the mid-1960s, at least one higher education in prison program was offered in almost 50% of states across the country (Oakford et al., 2019; Seashore et al., 1976). This included correspondence courses via the mail, television courses offered to students through pre-taped video cassette recordings, and in-person programs inside of the facility.

Following the 1965 expansion, the Federal Pell Grant Program of 1972 further increased the availability of financial assistance and support for students enrolled in higher education, which helped to maintain funding for prison education across the United States. The U.S. Department of Federal Student Aid (2022) defines its Federal Pell Grant Program as the largest federal grant program offered to undergraduate students, and Pell Grants are designed to assist students from low-income housing by providing them with funds to pay for college to promote access to education. This expansion led to a simultaneous expansion of prison education programs – by 1976, it is estimated that over 200 prison education programs existed nationwide (Chesnut & Wachendorfer, 2021). Correctional leadership, in collaboration with policymakers, university administration, and political constituents, continued to support the existence of these programs throughout the 1970s.

Although 350 programs were available nationwide by 1982, the steady support and expansion of prison education programs came to a drastic halt due to the political climate of the 1980s (Chesnut & Wachendorfer, 2021; Gehring, 1997). During this time, the 'get tough on crime' attitude, which was influenced by politicians nationwide, initiated the unprecedented growth of incarceration in the United States (Mauer, 2001). The incarceration rate skyrocketed while the support and funding for prison education simultaneously shrank. Moreover, the belief in rehabilitation was replaced by punitive policies and practices that emphasized deterrence and incapacitation, thus access to and enrollment in prison education programs continued to decline throughout the 1990s (Phelps, 2012). The number of available certificate programs declined by 25%, associate degree programs by 30%, and graduate offerings by over 50% (Tewksbury & Taylor, 1996). Some estimates suggest that only eight of the over 700 programs previously available to incarcerated students remained in existence as a result of such policies (Delaney, Subramanian, & Patrick, 2016). Punishment scholars have referred to this widespread growth of punitiveness and disappearance of rehabilitative programs and support as the new punitiveness, the culture of control, and the new penology (Phelps, 2012). No matter which way this time period is classified – the skyrocketing of incarceration rates and the simultaneous disappearance of rehabilitation and programming are both directly correlated to the era of mass incarceration, as corrections officials shifted their focus from providing opportunities in the prison to maintaining control of those inside the prison.

From 1994 to 2016, the Violent Crime Control and Law Enforcement Act of 1994 continued to make things worse and prohibited access to Pell Grant funding for those incarcerated, amongst other provisions (Pub. L. No. 103-322). During this time, programs lacked government funding to support the enrollment of incarcerated students and corrections officials held beliefs in line with the widespread culture of control, punitiveness, and incapacitation as hallmarks of punishment (Phelps, 2012). Throughout the 1990s and early 2000s, the culture of control and mass incarceration continued to prevail. While prison populations continued to grow at a rapid pace, access to programming and the belief in rehabilitation continued to be placed on the back burner. Support for these programs was at a halt for over 20 years – and it wasn't until 2016 that the Second Chance Pell Experimental Sites Initiative sparked interest in supporting programming for those incarcerated once again. The Second Chance Pell Experimental Sites Initiative of 2016 introduced support for programming by allowing those in state and federal prisons to access funding for participation in postsecondary prison education programs (U.S. Department of Education, 2022).

The Second Chance Pell Experimental Sites Initiative resulted in offering financial assistance to approximately 11,000 students enrolled in 67 different college and university programs across the United States (U.S. Department of Education, 2016). Furthermore, over 7,000 credentials have been awarded to more than 20,000 incarcerated students nationwide as a result of Pell Grant Funding to date (Chesnut & Wachendorfer, 2021). This number will only continue to increase as a result of the FAFSA Simplification Act signed into law on December 27, 2020. Once it takes effect on July 1, 2023, all incarcerated individuals confined in federal and state prisons will be eligible to apply for Pell Grants regardless of their sentence length and type of offense (Chesnut et al., 2022).

Research on Higher Education in Prison

Research consistently documents the benefits associated with providing students access to education while incarcerated. Amongst other promising outcomes, providing those incarcerated with opportunities for education reduces their risk of returning to prison upon release (Davis et al., 2014).

One main critique of this line of research includes the consistent issue of selection. Selection is defined as the likelihood that those who enroll in prison education programs may have certain characteristics that make them more likely to enroll and succeed in prison education programs than those who are either ineligible for enrollment or who choose not to enroll. Although addressing this issue remains a pervasive challenge, research has provided valuable insights for the continued support of prison education programs.

A host of research considers whether student participation in a prison education program while incarcerated influences the likelihood of recidivism, which is defined as the likelihood of being rearrested after release from incarceration due to a technical violation or a new crime (*see, for example,* Davis et al., 2014; Kim & Clark, 2013; Pompoco et al., 2017). The most commonly cited work in this line of research emphasizes that individuals who participate in any type of prison education program are 48% less likely to recidivate than those who do not (Bozick et al., 2018). This meta-analysis included over twenty years of aggregated research on prison education programs and has strong implications for the continued support of such programs. In line with these findings, a recent study on the Bard Prison Initiative, which is the largest study of a postsecondary prison education program to date, established that program participation substantially reduces recidivism (Denney & Tynes, 2021).

Relatedly, participation in prison education programs also has the potential to increase the likelihood of employment success and earnings upon release (Cho & Tyler, 2013; Duwe & Clarke, 2014; Pompoco et al., 2017). A recent projection estimates that by 2027, approximately 70% of all jobs will require the attainment of a degree beyond high school (Blumenstyk, 2020). Similarly, the U.S. Bureau of Labor Statistics (2017) projects that there will be nearly five million entry-level job openings annually through 2026, most of which will require the completion of a bachelor's degree. Thus, a college education is becoming more important to secure employment, and offering access to prison education programs remains a crucial component of the incarceration experience in order to promote upward mobility and success upon release (Chesnut et al., 2022; Davis, 2019).

Although a wide variety of programs and consistent promising findings exist, research estimates that there are substantial restrictions on who is able to access higher education in prison (Ositelu, 2019). While program numbers continue to rise, there remains natural attrition due to enrollment restrictions that may be in place. For example, some programmatic and university guidelines prohibit those convicted of violent or sexual offenses from enrollment, which naturally minimizes the percentage of those eligible to enroll across facilities (Walsh & Delaney, 2020).

The racial disparities pervasive across the United States are also evident inside our prisons. White students are overrepresented in the most recent enrollment cycle of the Second Chance Pell Experiment (Chesnut et al., 2022). Moreover, while Hispanic/Latinx individuals make up approximately 23% of the total U.S. prison population, and Black individuals approximately 33%, the most recent cohort of Second Chance Pell students was comprised of approximately 8% Hispanic/Latinx students and approximately 29% Black students (Chesnut et al., 2022).

Providing access to higher education programs in prison serves as not only a path toward reducing recidivism but also serves as a motivating factor in enhancing one's self-worth and connectedness with their families and communities (Baranger et al., 2018; Evans, Pelletier, & Szkola, 2018). Research on student experiences with prison education programs highlights participation as a positive opportunity for self-reflection. Specifically, findings indicate that participation has the potential to be a transformative experience for students – one that can enhance their self-perceptions and lead to a sense of empowerment, amongst other things (Evans et al., 2018; Runell, 2017).

Overall, research in this line of work emphasizes the positive impacts of prison education for those who participate in such programs while incarcerated. In turn, this reality also has implications for the safety of the facility, the safety of the public, along with an overall increase in economic savings. First, if individuals are provided with access to these programs and are less likely to recidivate upon release, this enhances overall community safety (Chesnut et al., 2022). When individuals are given the skills to succeed and find gainful employment, they are thus law-abiding citizens who positively contribute to their community. Moreover, individuals who participate in these programs are not only likely to lend a hand to enhanced community safety upon release, but research details that prisons that offer prison education programs have a lower rate of violence than prisons that do not offer such programs, which creates a better environment for both staff and those incarcerated across facilities (Pompoco et al., 2017).

Providing prison education programs to those incarcerated also leads to taxpayer savings and serves as a cost-effective way to reduce incarceration (Davis et al., 2014). Specifically, one dollar spent on prison education programs yields approximately five dollars in savings due to the reality that individuals are less likely to recidivate upon enrollment in a prison education program. Taken together, research on prison education consistently documents numerous benefits of offering prison education programs, thus calling to mind the need to consider how to best strengthen program offerings to assist students with a successful transition to the community upon release.

Technology and Prison Education

With approximately 90% of individuals eventually being released from prison, it is pivotal to consider how to best prepare students for their eventual release. Research has outlined a "digital divide" between incarcerated individuals and the general society while simultaneously acknowledging the necessity of technological competency for employment success. Those who experience incarceration lack the training to effectively use the technological methods, devices, and applications that are commonplace in society today (Jewkes & Johnston, 2009). This reality, coupled with the influence of COVID-19 modifications and the FAFSA Simplification Act, has brought technology in the prison classroom to the forefront of the discussion surrounding prison education.

As noted above, offering technology in the prison classroom has primarily been motivated by two recent factors. First, the global pandemic forced institutions across the nation to reconsider how to continue operating in the midst of COVID-19. For the field of higher education, this meant figuring out how to deliver courses and offer continued support and interactions to their students in order to continue offering access to education globally – and institutions had to come up with emergency plans virtually overnight.

For those teaching in prisons, these shutdowns required immediate and continued collaboration between their home institution and the Department of Corrections. This included arranging modifications in order to send and receive student work, adjustments to course grading options, and modifications to course objectives and outcomes due to the unique and unprecedented consequences associated with COVID-19 global shutdowns (Johnson, 2021). During this time, students were forced to work much more independently than in the past. For incarcerated students, feelings of loneliness, anxiety, and depression were only exacerbated when in-person programming, visitations, and meaningful interactions came to a halt (Burton, Morris, & Hirschtritt, 2021).

Second, the reinstatement of access to Pell Grants through the FAFSA Simplification Act has initiated conversations about how to increase access to higher education programs and best deliver high-quality programs that prepare individuals for their eventual release. While many correctional administrators, policymakers, and university actors adopted the use of technology to continue offering courses throughout COVID-19, there is now a large tension in the field about whether technology should be a primary or supplementary tool in the prison classroom (Swaak, 2022).

On the one hand, offering access to technology can provide an incentive for good behavior inside and outside of the classroom. For example, aside from technology as an educational tool for course materials and assignments, tablets can be used to order commissary, place a sick call request, listen to music, or access the library (Collica-Cox, 2022; Stewart, 2017). Additionally, those who argue for the use of technology in prison emphasize the utility of preparing those incarcerated for reentering into society, even if this just means learning to turn on a computer or tablet on and off (Swaak, 2022).

On the other hand, several correctional institutions remain hesitant when considering whether to allow their incarcerated students access to technology (Jewkes & Johnson, 2009; Tolbert et al., 2015). While the use of technology has been on the rise, particularly as a result of distance learning during COVID-19, some correctional administrators are concerned that allowing access to technology for educational purposes may lead to an abuse of the privilege itself, rather than increasing digital literacy as intended (Mufarreh, Waitkus, & Booker, 2021; Tolbert et al., 2015).

Although some hesitancy remains, programs have been increasingly supportive of providing students with access to technology nationwide (Chesnut & Wachendorfer, 2021). Prison education advocates and stakeholders across the country have been encouraging policymakers to include access to technology in the legislation for Pell Grant Reinstatement on July 1, 2023 in order to continue increasing access to technology in the prison classroom. This provision currently appears in the guidelines and recommendations for funding allocations, and it is predicted that funding for incarcerated student access to technology may be part of the 2022–2023 Pell Grant Expansion (U.S. Department of Education, 2021).

Conclusion

The FAFSA Simplification Act signed into legislation on December 27, 2020 strengthens the argument that most individuals see higher education as a meaningful investment. This is evident through not only the research on post-release outcomes but also through the research documenting positive student experiences that have the potential to lead to increased feelings of self-worth and connectedness with loved ones. After the fluctuation in the support of programming throughout the era of mass incarceration, the punitive approach of the past is now shifting, as the 2022–2023 Pell Grant Expansion is a promising piece of legislation aimed at increasing widespread financial support. As detailed throughout this chapter, the evidence for continuing to support prison education programs remains strong, and recent legislation has continued to bring this discussion to the forefront of the field to enhance access and participation nationwide.

Discussion Questions:

1 How are postsecondary prison education programs related to the causes and consequences of mass incarceration?
2 What are the benefits of providing postsecondary prison education programs?

References

Baranger, J., Rousseau, D., Mastrorilli, M. E., & Matesanz, J. (2018). Doing time wisely: The social and personal benefits of higher education in prison. *The Prison Journal*, *98*(4), 490–513.
Bender, K. (2019). *Education opportunities in prison are key to reducing crime.* Retrieved from: https://www.americanprogress.org/article/education-opportunities-prison-key-reducing-crime/
Blumenstyk, G. (2020). *By 2020, they said 2 out of 3 jobs would need more than a high-school diploma. Were they right?* Retrieved from: https://www.chronicle.com/newsletter/the-edge/2020-01-22?cid2=gen_login_refresh&cid=gen_sign_in
Bozick, R., Steele, J., Davis, L., & Turner, S. (2018). Does providing inmates with education improve postrelease outcomes? A meta-analysis of correctional education programs in the United States. *Journal of Experimental Criminology*, *14*(3), 389–428.
Burton, P. R., Morris, N. P., & Hirschtritt, M. E. (2021). Mental health services in a US prison during the COVID-19 pandemic. *Psychiatric Services*, *72*(4), 458–460.
Castro, E. L., & Gould, M. R. (2018). What is higher education in prison? Introduction to radical departures: Ruminations on the purposes of higher education in prison. *Critical Education*, *9*(1–14).
Chesnut, K., & Wachendorfer, A. (2021). *Second Chance Pell: Four years of expanding access to education in prison.* Vera Institute of Justice. Retrieved from: https://www.vera.org/downloads/publications/second-chance-pell-four-years-of-expanding-access-to-education-in-prison.pdf
Chesnut, K., Taber, N. & Quintana, J. (2022). *Second Chance Pell: Five years of expanding higher education in prison programs, 2016–2021.* Vera Institute of Justice. Retrieved from: https://www.vera.org/downloads/publications/second-chance-pell-five-years-of-expanding-access-to-education-in-prison-2016-2021.pdf
Cho, R. M., & Tyler, J. H. (2013). Does prison-based adult basic education improve postrelease outcomes for male prisoners in Florida? *Crime & Delinquency*, *59*(7), 975–1005.
Collica-Cox, K. (2022). Bringing inside-out online: Coming together in a virtual environment. *Journal of Offender Rehabilitation*, *61*(2), 61–87.
Davis, L. (2019). *Higher education programs in prison: What we know now and what we should focus on going forward.* RAND Corporation. Retrieved from: https://www.rand.org/pubs/perspectives/PE342.html
Davis, L. M., Steele, J. L., Bozick, R., Williams, M. V., Turner, S., Miles, J. N., ... & Steinberg, P. S. (2014). *How effective is correctional education, and where do we go from here? The results of*

a comprehensive evaluation. RAND Corporation. https://www.rand.org/content/dam/rand/pubs/research_reports/RR500/RR564/RAND_RR564.pdf

Delaney, R., Subramanian, R., & Patrick, F. (2016). *Making the grade: Developing quality postsecondary education programs in prison*. Vera Institute of Justice. Retrieved from: https://www.vera.org/downloads/publications/making-the-grade-postsecondary-education-programs-in-prison.pdf

Denney, M. G., & Tynes, R. (2021). The effects of college in prison and policy implications. *Justice Quarterly*, *38*(7), 1–25.

Duwe, G., & Clark, V. (2014). The effects of prison-based educational programming on recidivism and employment. *The Prison Journal*, *94*(4), 454-478.

Evans, D. N., Pelletier, E., & Szkola, J. (2018). Education in prison and the self-stigma: Empowerment continuum. *Crime & Delinquency*, *64*(2), 255–280.

Gehring, T. (1997). Post-secondary education for inmates: A historical inquiry. *Journal of Correctional Education*, *48*(2), 46–55.

Jewkes, Y., & Johnston, H. (2009). 'Cavemen in an Era of Speed-of-Light Technology': Historical and Contemporary Perspectives on Communication within Prisons. *The Howard Journal of Criminal Justice*, *48*(2), 132–143.

Johnson, C. (2021). Lessons Learned from Prison Education Interruption during Pandemic. Fact Sheet. Center for Law and Social Policy, Inc.(CLASP). https://www.clasp.org/sites/default/files/publications/2021/04/CLASP%20Coronavirus%20Prison%20Education%20Disruption%20Mar2021.pdf

Kim, R. H., & Clark, D. (2013). The effect of prison-based college education programs on recidivism: Propensity score matching approach. *Journal of Criminal Justice*, *41*(3), 196–204.

Mauer, M. (2001). The causes and consequences of prison growth in the United States. *Punishment & Society*, *3*(1), 9–20.

Oakford, P., Brumfield, C., Goldvale, C., diZerega, M., & Patrick, F. (2019). *Investing in futures: Economic and fiscal benefits of postsecondary education in prison*. Vera Institute of Justice. Retrieved from: https://www.vera.org/downloads/publications/investing-in-futures.pdf

Ositelu, M. (2019). *Equipping individuals for life beyond bars: The promise of higher education & job training in closing the gap in skills for incarcerated adults*. New America. Retrieved from: https://files.eric.ed.gov/fulltext/ED604977.pdf

Phelps, M. S. (2012). The place of punishment: Variation in the provision of inmate services staff across the punitive turn. *Journal of Criminal Justice*, *40*(5), 348–357.

Pompoco, A., Wooldredge, J., Lugo, M., Sullivan, C., & Latessa, E. J. (2017). Reducing inmate misconduct and prison returns with facility education programs. *Criminology & Public Policy*, *16*(2), 515–547.

Rampey, B. D., Finnegan, R., Goodman, M., Mohadjer, L., Krenzke, T., Hogan, J., & Provasnik, S. (2016). Skills of US Unemployed, Young, and Older Adults in Sharper Focus: Results from the Program for the International Assessment of Adult Competencies (PIAAC) 2012/2014. First Look. NCES 2016-039. National Center for Education Statistics.

Runell, L. L. (2017). Identifying desistance pathways in a higher education program for formerly incarcerated individuals. *International Journal of Offender Therapy and Comparative Criminology*, *61*(8), 894–918.

Sawyer, W., & Wagner, P. (2020). Mass incarceration: The whole pie 2020. *Prison Policy Initiative*. https://www.prisonpolicy.org/reports/pie2020.html

Seashore, M. J., Haberfeld, S., Irwin, J., & Baker, K. (1976). *Prisoner education: Project NewGate and other college programs*. New York: Praeger.

Stewart, S. (2017). *How tablets are helping clean up one Arizona prison*. Retrieved from: https://www.corrections1.com/products/corrections/articles/how-tablets-are-helping-clean-up-one-ariz-prison-pcpVlpSvZVVGHICO/

Swaak, T. (2022). *A turning point for prison education: With reinstatement of Pell Grants imminent, the programs weigh technology's long-term role*. Retrieved from: https://www.chronicle.com/article/a-turning-point-for-prison-education?cid2=gen_login_refresh&cid=gen_sign_in

Tewksbury, R., & Taylor, J. M. (1996). The consequences of eliminating Pell Grant eligibility for students in post-secondary correctional education, programs. *Federal Probation*, *60*, 60.

Tolbert, M., Hudson, J., & Erwin, H. C. (2015). Educational technology in corrections 2015. *US Department of Education. Office of Career, Technical, and Adult Education.* https://www2.ed.gov/about/offices/list/ovae/pi/AdultEd/policybriefedtech.pdf

U.S. Bureau of Labor Statistics. (2017). *Employment projections – 2016–2026.* https://www.bls.gov/news.release/archives/ecopro_10242017.pdf

U.S. Department of Education. (2016). *Answering your questions about Second Chance Pell.* Retrieved from: https://www.ed.gov/content/answering-your-frequently-asked-questions-about-second-chance-pell

U.S. Department of Education. (2021). *U.S. Department of Education announces it will expand the Second Chance Pell Experiment for the 2022–2021 award year.* Retrieved from: https://www.ed.gov/news/press-releases/us-department-education-announces-it-will-expand-second-chance-pell-experiment-2022-2023-award-year

U.S. Department of Education. (2022). *Pell Grants for incarceration students* [Webinar]. Office of Federal Student Aid, May 25.

Walsh, B., & Delaney, R. (2020). *First class: Starting a postsecondary education program in prison.* Retrieved from: https://www.vera.org/downloads/publications/first-class-post-secondary-education-in-prison.pdf

12

PRISON EDUCATION, DEMOCRACY, AND SOLIDARITY

Briana L. McGinnis and Kaitlyn Victoria

LEARNING OBJECTIVES:

Upon successful completion of this chapter, students will be able to:

1 Explain why expanding access to higher education for incarcerated people is consistent with commitments to democracy.
2 Define expressive retributivism.
3 Critique "hostile solidarity."

Introduction: Bridging a Dangerous Divide

In this chapter, we argue for public support of liberal arts college education in prisons (hereafter abbreviated LACEP). By this, we mean credit-granting classes taught by university faculty inside prisons. We are far from the first to promote this kind of program (Castro et al., 2015; Heppard, 2019; Miller, 2015; Miller & Levine, 2015). This chapter adds to existing arguments for supporting such programs, contributing another justification to the rhetorical arsenal: supporting these initiatives offers an opportunity for building solidarity between groups of citizens who have long been pitted against each other in "law-and-order" political rhetoric. This solidarity is good in itself, but it also has the potential to improve the conditions of individuals and communities impacted by mass incarceration.

Despite increasing public attention to mass incarceration and injustices in the American criminal legal system, the impulse to treat incarcerated people and people who have previously been involved in the system as second-class citizens remains built into the nation's political culture and into many state, federal, and municipal laws (McGinnis, 2018; Starr Sered, 2021). Aside from Vermont and Maine, states still limit the voting rights of incarcerated people, and in many, those restrictions remain in place post-release. Collateral consequences of conviction continue to limit the privacy rights of many formerly incarcerated people, in addition to imposing civic and economic disabilities on them (McGinnis, 2018). While public attitudes toward mass incarceration and criminalization are changing, there is still much work to be done.

DOI: 10.4324/9781003274292-16

Too often, the division between unincarcerated people, constructed as "citizens," and incarcerated people, constructed as "criminals" is presented as natural and unbridgeable (Dilts, 2014; McGinnis, 2018). Given the staggering numbers of Americans who are living with criminal records, allowing this imaginary division to persist – or worse, grow – threatens to undermine the equality that defines a democratic society. In this chapter, we propose a modest but timely countermeasure in the form of expanding support for liberal arts education programs in prisons. While this cannot solve all of the problems stemming from mass incarceration, it can materially improve the lives and prospects of incarcerated people, and it can help to reshape public conceptions of "criminality" and punishment.

We will proceed from the following premises:

1 Incarcerated people are citizens. Authorities are obligated to justify punitive measures with regard to (a) proportionality and (b) rational relationship to the purposes of punishing. Being punished by the state is not a revocation of democratic membership, even if it is a suspension of *some rights* associated with citizenship (Marshall, 2018).
2 Democratic political communities must treat members as moral and political equals, even when they have committed offenses. Penalties should address actions, not people.
3 Established relations of reciprocity and interdependence, like the ones built into everyday interactions in a democratic society, generate commitments (Marin, 2017) that bind not only individual citizens but also political institutions and communities. Committing a criminal offense does not sever these bonds. As such, political communities cannot simply dispose of offending members without undermining their own democratic legitimacy. National and state authorities that claim to speak for the people via the law when inflicting punishment are also bound by these commitments.

The Current Landscape

Programs like the Inside Out Prison Exchange Program, Georgetown University's Prisons and Justice Initiative, and the Bard Prison Initiative are all examples of programs offering credit-bearing, liberal arts courses to incarcerated students. In this chapter, we focus on liberal arts programs rather than on programs oriented toward job training. This is not intended to disparage such programs. When offered as one option among many, these programs are valuable. However, when they are the only options, they hold the potential for treating incarcerated people not like valued community members but as resources to be cultivated or exploited for the benefit of the state, private firms, or unincarcerated people (McCorkel & Defina, 2019). A related concern is expressed by Castro et al. (2015, p. 16): "when the overwhelming majority of postsecondary education programs in prisons are vocational in nature, the ideological undercurrent of discipline is revealed." Education for adults should not be exploitative, and it should not be paternalistic. The key difference lies in respecting incarcerated peoples' autonomy in choosing their own life projects for their own reasons.

For similar reasons, we will not focus on instrumental benefits of higher education programs such as reductions in recidivism or costs. The reasons for resisting this framing have been stated elsewhere, so we build on the foundation already established (Miller, 2015; Simpson II, 2019). Further, our promotion of LACEP programs includes offering access to people serving very long sentences who are unlikely to re-enter the workforce or their communities. Extending eligibility to this group expresses concern and respect for long-term incarcerated people as individuals whose value is not dependent on what they can contribute to the world outside of the prison.

Instrumental, even neoliberal, justifications for offering higher education in prisons remain common (McCorkel & Defina, 2019). We follow the common usage of the term "neoliberalism" in critical education discourse, meaning a worldview that applies cost-benefit reasoning to all questions, including moral and political ones. The popularity of this reasoning is not surprising, given that access to higher education remains out of reach for many Americans. Indeed, empirical studies of framing for surveys measuring support for higher education in prison show that conservatives and people who score highly on racial resentment inventories are likely to take the position that (1) education is a limited resource (2) incarcerated Americans are less deserving of this resource than others. They are, however, receptive to changing their position when presented with evidence that these programs benefit the society outside of the prison (Johnston & Wozniak, 2021). We reject this reasoning; education costs are a public policy problem but denying incarcerated people a high-quality education is not the answer.

It is understandable why lawmakers might be wary of supporting higher education in prisons – and especially higher education programs that are not directly related to employment training. However, one of the conclusions drawn from the same study is that Americans on both sides of the partisan divide are open to persuasion on the subject of higher education in prisons (Johnston & Wozniak, 2021). Further, additional empirical research suggests that progressives and liberals who express high degrees of distress at the oppression of Black people are motivated to support policies benefiting racial minorities (Chudy, 2021; Johnston & Wozniak, 2021). Given the widespread awareness that mass incarceration disproportionately affects communities of color, this new research suggests that there is untapped potential for motivating voters to support higher education programs that primarily benefit incarcerated individuals.

Given this possibility, we propose a justification for supporting LACEP initiatives based in concern for incarcerated Americans: framing support for these programs as an opportunity for unincarcerated Americans to express solidarity with their neighbors in prison.

Why the Liberal Arts?

Liberal arts programs are oriented not toward preparation for employment – though they certainly do that as well – but toward cultivating skills like critical thinking, careful argumentation, and close reading. An education in the liberal arts also instills habits of reflection and an openness to criticism. In sum, the liberal arts are intended to equip students with tools they can use to better understand themselves, the world, and their place in it. Georgetown University, a liberal arts institution that is also home to the Prisons and Justice Initiative, adopts the Jesuit motto "cura personalis" as its guiding principle. "Cura personalis" translates to "care for the whole person," which encapsulates one of the defining principles of the liberal arts.

For incarcerated students, the liberal arts classroom can provide a unique space. In an institution designed to dehumanize, the liberal arts classroom recasts incarcerated individuals as students engaged in a shared, open-ended process of inquiry. It also offers a protected space in which they can build (or re-build) identities as democratic citizens. Joshua Miller, political philosopher and Director of Education for the Prisons and Justice Initiative at Georgetown University, observes that prison classrooms enable incarcerated students to "...participate in the politics of their own institutions," reclaiming political agency in a context in which they are allowed very little (Miller, 2015, p. 718). In the words of one of Miller's students, "We are not Inmates. We are not Convicts. We are not Prisoners. We are Incarcerated Americans" (Miller, 2015, p. 714).

For many incarcerated Americans, taking part in LACEP programs offers an opportunity to revise both the image that society has ascribed to them and their own self-image. Johnny Page, a student involved with the Education Justice Program in Danville Correctional Center, in Illinois, said of the experience that, "[t]he classes for me were difficult, not because the work was necessarily difficult, but because they required me to look at the world through a different set of lenses" (Castro et al., 2015, p. 18). An education that focuses on the individual's interests treats the students as valued, respected individuals.

A liberal arts education is tremendously valuable. It represents a significant investment in the person and their potential. Providing this kind of education sends a potent message of respect, confidence, and acceptance to an audience that is largely neglected in philosophical discourse about the expressive powers of penal policy: the person punished. If taken up by the unincarcerated public, it also expresses solidarity – something seldom seen in American discourse surrounding prisons.

Solidarity

Linking punishment and social solidarity is hardly a new idea. Émile Durkheim gives punishment a central place in his theory of how ties of social solidarity are generated and how the expressive features of penal practices maintain them (Durkheim, 1933, p. 102; Garland, 2013, p. 33). Recent scholarship echoes Durkheim, identifying "hostile solidarity," or social bonds generated by uniting non-criminalized citizens against criminalized ones, (Carvalho & Chamberlen, 2018). However, the dynamics of hostile solidarity mirror those of some expressivist theories of punishment, separating the actor communicating ("society" in the form of law and penal institutions) from the audience (non-criminalized citizens), and more or less leaving the person punished out of the equation. It seems that traditional theories about punishment and solidarity offer little guidance for those seeking to express solidarity with incarcerated people.

This section explores possibilities for generating ties of solidarity between incarcerated and unincarcerated citizens, beginning from the premise that people who are subject to punishment do not exist outside of "society" or "the community," even if decades of scholarship, political rhetoric, and law have treated them as though they do.

Perhaps this rhetorical separation is unsurprising when compared to similar, well-documented spatial and economic separations in American communities (Kurgan & Cadora, 2006; Wacquant, 2010). Tommie Shelby argues that, for many communities ravaged by mass incarceration, most members were *never* fully integrated into the broader society (Shelby, 2007); similarly, prison educators Joshua Miller and Daniel Levine note that many Black people, "other racial minorities, and the poor, have never been adequately integrated into the political and social community in the first place" (Miller & Levine, 2015). This disjuncture between how belonging in America is conceptualized and its troubled reality parallels one of the barriers to policies supporting incarcerated people: too often, constructions of "criminality" are created in contrast to "citizenship." It is essential to reject this construction and reaffirm that incarcerated people *are* citizens.

This problem is not one of psychology, but of politics. Inclusion and exclusion are issues with which every democratic political community must reckon because any effort to define "the people" will inevitably produce exclusions. In the case of mass incarceration, those exclusions are internal – mass incarceration creates a group of formally recognized citizens who nominally belong, but who are relegated to a durable second-class status in comparison to their non-criminalized neighbors. Such a state of affairs poses serious problems for a democratic society's legitimacy. Because equality is the foundational democratic value, we approach this problem from the framework of solidarity. Solidarity is a specifically political concept that is well suited to examining social relations between members of groups linked by conflict or contestation (Dufort, 2022; Kolers, 2016). In this case, the contested issue is the treatment and perception of justice-involved citizens.

Theorists of solidarity differ in how they define it. Accounts vary regarding what kinds of obligations it generates, whether and what kinds of actions or sentiments it requires, and what its purposes are (Dufort, 2022; Guenther, 2017; Kolers, 2016; Scholz, 2008; Taylor, 2015). Avery Kolers (2016) offers a formulation of solidarity that entails collective action in pursuit of justice.

Solidarity, at its base, describes a set of relations. Democratic solidarity should be egalitarian, meaning that everyone involved should be recognized as morally and politically equal members of the solidary group – in this case, the set of people acting collectively to mitigate the injustices of mass incarceration via support for LACEP initiatives. While the possibilities for coordinating between the two groups under consideration here are constrained, unincarcerated people can nonetheless cooperate with incarcerated people by adopting Kolers' additional requirement: deference.

To maintain equality between the two parts of the group, it is vital that unincarcerated people defer to the judgments of incarcerated people regarding which ends to pursue and how to pursue them. While deference may not immediately appear to be compatible with equality, in this situation it is integral to (a) recognizing the epistemic advantages that incarcerated people hold in this arena and (b) preventing the replication of paternalistic or exploitative relations that threaten to taint educational initiatives in prisons.

How can people outside of prison learn about the judgments of people inside? Prisons tend to be located far from population centers and modes of communication are limited, factors that preserve both literal and figurative distance between the people inside and those outside. Fortunately, there are several avenues by which to look to incarcerated people for direction. First, people outside of the prison can coordinate their advocacy with LACEP programs, as their personnel have direct access to incarcerated citizens. Additionally, advocacy organizations have similar potential. More directly, they can seek outlets that allow incarcerated people to speak for themselves; for example, prison writing platforms offer direct access to incarcerated peoples' own words. Finally, several LACEP students and graduates have published their thoughts about these programs, either individually or in conjunction with instructors (Allen & Armas, 2019; Castro et al., 2015; Evans, 2018; Malakki, 2019; X, 2019).

Solidarity between unincarcerated and incarcerated people will appear largely expressive in nature, in addition to seeming what Sally Scholz terms "unidirectional" insofar as traditionally reciprocal relations between the groups involved are not possible (Scholz, 2008).

That said, the picture changes considerably when you reframe the shared purpose of the solidary group not solely as an effort to establish LACEP programs, but more broadly as a shared effort to mitigate some of the harm caused by mass incarceration.

Rooting support for LACEP initiatives in solidarity is consistent with democratic commitments to equality and respect for individuals. Unincarcerated citizens who take up this cause in solidarity with incarcerated people have a valuable opportunity to not only align their political actions with their consciences but also to express a genuine desire to repair inequalities in access and opportunity that contribute to mass incarceration.

Expressivism

Expressive retributivism is a common philosophical justification for punishment. As a philosophy, retributivism holds that

> (1) It is intrinsically valuable that offenders suffer in proportion to the gravity of the offence they have committed because that is what they deserve; and (2) it is permissible for the state to ensure that offenders get what they deserve by punishing them.
>
> *(Tadros, 2011, p. 26)*

This view takes different forms, including a widely accepted version known as "expressive retributivism," which posits that much of the moral value of punishment lies in its ability to convey moral and political messages.

Expressive retributivists often justify harsh treatment – which, in the U.S. generally takes the form of imprisonment – through the argument that penal institutions serve socially important expressive functions. Joel Feinberg popularized the idea in his much-cited 1965 article, "The Expressive Function of Punishment." In the intervening years, it has been taken up by a number of influential thinkers (Bennett, 2008; Duff, 2001; Hampton, 1984; Wringe, 2016). They posit that a society expresses concern for those who are harmed by inflicting pain or hard treatment on the people who have harmed them.

According to this theory, authorities intentionally harm people who have committed offenses, reasoning that punishments "not only are unwelcome but are intended to be, and would lose their point if they were not" (Lucas, 1969, p. 207). A key element, however, defining this treatment as legitimate punishment is that these measures convey criticism. While some argue that society could criticize wrongs without hard treatment (H. L. A. Hart, 1963, pp. 65–66; Matravers, 2000, p. 78), expressive retributivists believe that "punishment is a particularly emphatic way of expressing criticism, and some wrongs call for a degree of criticism that can only be expressed by punishment" (Hanna, 2007, p. 128). Legal scholar R.A. Duff argues that this hard treatment is necessary to express sincere denunciation of criminal behavior, stating, "to remain silent, to let the action pass without criticism, necessarily casts doubt on the sincerity of my declaration that such conduct is seriously wrong" (Duff, 2001, p. 28).

Who Speaks? Who Hears?

Expressive retributivist accounts usually offer some variation on the claim that society expresses concern and respect for people who have been harmed by inflicting pain or hard treatment on the people who have harmed them (Feinberg, 1965). Such formulations have broad intuitive appeal, but they also introduce some troubling assumptions. These theories vary in how they conceptualize the audiences for this expression, but often presume a self-evident agent expressing the message, described sometimes as "the state" (Nozick, 1981), "the community," (Hampton, 1984), or "society" (Feinberg, 1965; Wringe, 2016). This same set of actors is also identified as the audience for the message in what Bill Wringe describes as "denunciatory" accounts of expressive punishment (2016: 42–65). Oddly, the person harmed is seldom singled out as the recipient initially, despite often being marshaled to defend these theories against criticism. But if the communication is taking place between some version of the people and their representative institutions, where does this leave the person punished?

The "moral education" view of punishment, first advanced by Jean Hampton, does identify the person punished as the recipient of the message of disapproval, as does the "censure" version of expressive retributivism advanced by R.A. Duff, though Hampton is inconsistent on this point (Duff, 2001; Hampton, 1984).

There are (at least) two major problems with expressive retributivist theories when considering American penal practices. First, the theory too often reduces the person punished to the medium onto which messages are projected for the benefit of the broader society. In fact, in a particularly appalling passage, one theorist explicitly compares the person punished to a "billboard" (Primoratz, 1989). This is obviously dehumanizing. This is only the most obvious way in which they are marginalized in expressivist accounts, however. These formulations also fail to recognize that the person punished is a member of the community that is depicted as the audience. This conception reifies the division between "society" and the "criminal" so common in American discourse around mass incarceration.

Perhaps it is the high level of abstraction that makes it so easy for expressive retributivists to reify the division between (innocent) citizens and (guilty) "offenders" (Dilts, 2014). In reality, both people who are harmed and who do harm are citizens of the same political communities – communities that both suffer from and reproduce the conditions that drive mass incarceration. The same problem can be identified in the message: while philosophers of punishment generalize about "hard treatment," real, living people are relegated to prisons for lengths of time that are unimaginable to people who have not experienced prolonged physical confinement.

A full analysis of the incoherence that inevitably results from treating an institution as complex and multifaceted as a prison as the method for conveying any precise moral message is beyond the scope of this chapter, but we do want to emphasize that the messaging of the prison is overwhelmingly condemnatory (Kerr, 2019). This is hardly necessary, however. Punitive, tough-on-crime messaging is built into American entertainment, politics, news media, and law. There is no shortage of messages of disapprobation conveyed to people who commit criminal offenses. However, we do not yet want to wholly abandon the notion of law and social institutions holding expressive power.

Democratic Expressivism

In their article "Making Offenders Vote: Democratic Expressivism and Compulsory Criminal Voting," Andrei Poama and Tom Theuns introduce the concept of democratic expressivism to the prison setting. Democratic expressivism holds that, "no matter how you might otherwise justify them, some social and political institutions are warranted because they function as expressions of our commitment to democratic (or democratically relevant) values" (Poama & Theuns, 2019, p. 797). This stands in stark contrast to the commitments of expressive retributivism. Democratic expressivism emphasizes the underlying values expressed by our institutions, evaluating whether or not they are consistent with democratic values. Notably, this form of expressivism acknowledges that these institutions also convey important messages to those who are incarcerated.

Expressive retributivism has been criticized for stressing individual wrongdoing and responsibility at the expense of reckoning with systemic problems. We take the basic principles of expressive theories of punishment seriously. However, we do wish to challenge common formulations of expressivism that assume that people who have caused harm should receive only messages of condemnation, or even a message "...of the community's hatred, fear, or contempt" (Feinberg, 1965; H. M. Hart, 1958).

Expressivist positions should consider how unstated assumptions about who expresses a message, who receives it, and who is simply the subject of the expression (or worse – the medium by which it is sent) shape attitudes toward equality. Not only do victims and the non-criminalized public receive messages expressed by the criminal legal system, but the people who have committed offenses receive them as well. People who are punished should not be presented as the subject of communication or the medium by which it takes place; they are also citizens, and the treatment they receive sends multiple messages – messages about their place in the political community, about their value as citizens, and about their potential. Instead, Americans should embrace the ethos of democratic expressivism, recognizing that our institutions can also express commitments to democratic values like the moral and political equality of every citizen. If the harshest and most punitive aspects of prisons can be used to express condemnation, then the establishment of LACEP programs can be used to express acceptance, confidence in every person's capacity to change, and solidarity.

Conclusion

This chapter re-frames the practice of teaching college courses in prisons not simply as an instrumental method of reducing recidivism or promoting economic interests, but as an expression of democratic solidarity that is more important at this moment in American history than the messages of condemnation traditionally associated with punitive expressivism.

From the standpoint of democratic equality, there is value in a public demonstration of solidarity with and respect for incarcerated people. As we have argued, expressive theories of punishment tend to situate people who do harm in either objectionable or incoherent ways, neglecting them altogether, infantilizing them, or making them an object lesson for their fellow citizens and/or the people they have harmed. By repurposing the expressive features of law and the criminal legal system via the expansion of liberal arts college programs in prisons, Americans have an opportunity to make a small but significant change. Making these valuable educations available to incarcerated citizens offers a chance to erode the rhetorical division between "citizen" and "criminal" and to mitigate some of the intangible, but nonetheless significant, harms inflicted by mass incarceration.

This is an uncertain moment in American history, with high levels of polarization and intense partisan framing surrounding virtually every public issue. Scholars have documented the gradual shift in public opinion away from "tough on crime" politics, starting in the first decade of the 21st century. At the same time, studies indicate that the framing of a reform initiative can have substantial effects on what degree of public support it receives (Chudy, 2021; Johnston & Wozniak, 2021). Currently, the country is reckoning with racism and its role in driving mass incarceration, placing these issues firmly in the public eye. With the identification of a substantial segment of the population eager to address the wrongs of racist criminal justice practices and mass incarceration, it is our hope that the argument we have outlined here might be put to work mobilizing people.

Discussion Questions:

1. What specific message is sent by imprisoning someone? Does the length of the sentence modify it?
2. Have you encountered examples of the assumption that people in prison are no longer counted as citizens?

References

Allen, J., & Armas, O. (2019). Learning Inside-Out: The Perspectives of Two Individuals Who Had the Opportunity to Partake in the Soul Journey of Healing Arts and Social Change. In R. Ginsburg (Ed.), *Critical Perspectives on Teaching in Prison: Students and Instructors on Pedagogy Behind the Wall* (pp. 166–174). New York: Routledge.

Bennett, C. (2008). *The Apology Ritual: A Philosophical Theory of Punishment*. New York: Cambridge University Press.

Carvalho, H., & Chamberlen, A. (2018). Why Punishment Pleases: Punitive Feelings in a World of Hostile Solidarity. *Punishment & Society*, *20*(2), 217–234.

Castro, E. L., Brawn, M., Graves, D. E., Mayorga, O., Page, J., & Slater, A. (2015). Higher Education in an Era of Mass Incarceration: Possibility Under Constraint. *Journal of Critical Scholarship on Higher Education and Student Affairs*, *1*(1), 1–7.

Chudy, J. (2021). Racial Sympathy and Its Political Consequences. *Journal of Politics*, *83*(1), 122–136.

Dilts, A. (2014). *Punishment and Inclusion: Membership and the Limits of American Liberalism*. New York: Fordham University Press.

Duff, R. A. (2001). *Punishment, Communication, and Community*. Oxford: Oxford University Press.

DuFort, R. (2022). *Solidarity in Conflict: A Democratic Theory*. Stanford: Stanford University Press.

Durkheim, É. (1933). *The Division of Labor in Society* (G. Simpson, Trans.). London: Macmillan.

Evans, D. (2018). The Elevating Connection of Higher Education in Prison: An Incarcerated Student's Perspective. *Critical Education*, *9*(11), 1–14.

Feinberg, J. (1965). The Expressive Function of Punishment. *The Monist*, *49*(3), 397–423.

Garland, D. (2013). Punishment and Social Solidarity: The Work of Émile Durkheim. In J. Simon & R. Sparks (Eds.), *The SAGE Handbook of Punishment and Society* (pp. 23–39). New York: SAGE Publications.

Guenther, L. (2017). A Critical Phenomenology of Solidarity and Resistance in the 2013 California Prison Hunger Strikes. In L. Dolezal (Ed.), *Body/Self/Other: The Phenomenology of Social Encounters*. Albany: SUNY Press, 47–74.

Hampton, J. (1984). The Moral Education Theory of Punishment. *Philosophy & Public Affairs*, *13*(3), 208–238.

Hanna, N. (2007). Say What? A Critique of Expressive Retributivism. *Law and Philosophy*, *27*(2), 123–150.

Hart, H. L. A. (1963). *Law, Liberty, and Morality*. Stanford: Stanford University Press.
Hart, H. M. (1958). The Aims of the Criminal Law. *Law and Contemporary Problems*, *23*, II A 4.
Heppard, B. (2019). The Art of Liberating Humanity. *Critical Education*, *10*(3), 1–10.
Johnston, T. M., & Wozniak, K. H. (2021). Framing Effects and Group Differences in Public Opinion about Prison Pell Grants. *PS: Political Science & Politics*, *54*(3), 411–415.
Kerr, L. C. (2019). How the Prison is a Black Box in Punishment Theory. *University of Toronto Law Journal*, *69*(1), 85–116.
Kolers, A. (2016). *A Moral Theory of Solidarity*. Oxford: Oxford University Press.
Kurgan, L., & Cadora, E. (2006). *Spatial Information Design Lab Million Dollar Blocks: A Project and Map for Visual Communication* (SAGE Publications 5.2; pp. 241–244). SAGE Publications.
Lucas, J. R. (1969). XII – Or Else. *Proceedings of the Aristotelian Society*, *69*, 207–222.
Malakki, R. B. (2019). An Open Letter to Prison Educators. In R. Ginsburg (Ed.), *Critical Perspectives on Teaching in Prison: Students and Instructors on Pedagogy Behind the Wall* (pp. 17–18). New York: Routledge.
Marin, M. (2017). *Connected by Commitment: Oppression and Our Responsibility to Undermine It*. Oxford: Oxford University Press.
Marshall, P. (2018). Voting from Prison: Against the Democratic Case for Disenfranchisement. *Ethics & Global Politics*, *11*(3), 1498696. https://doi.org/10.1080/16544951.2018.1498696
Matravers, M. (2000). *Justice and Punishment*. Oxford: Oxford University Press.
McCorkel, J., & Defina, R. (2019). Beyond Recidivism: Identifying the Liberatory Possibilities of Prison Higher Education. *Critical Education*, *10*(7), 1–19.
McGinnis, B. L. (2018). Beyond Disenfranchisement: Collateral Consequences and Equal Citizenship. *Politics, Groups, and Identities*, 6(1), 59–76.
Miller, J. A. (2015). Democracy and Education Behind Bars. *Perspectives on Politics*, *12*(3), 714–721.
Miller, J. A., & Levine, D. H. (2015). Reprobation as Shared Inquiry: Teaching the Liberal Arts in Prison. *Radical Philosophy Review*, *18*(2), 287–308.
Nozick, R. (1981). *Philosophical Explanations*. Cambridge, MA: Harvard University Press.
Poama, A., & Theuns, T. (2019). Making Offenders Vote: Democratic Expressivism and Criminal Voting. *American Political Science Review*, *113*(3), 796–809.
Primoratz, I. (1989). Punishment as Language. *Philosophy*, *64*(248), 187–205.
Scholz, S. J. (2008). *Political Solidarity*. University Park, PA: The Pennsylvania State University Press.
Shelby, T. (2007). Justice, Deviance, and the Dark Ghetto. *Philosophy & Public Affairs*, *3*(2), 126–161.
Simpson II, D. R. (2019). Pedagogy of the Offender. In R. Ginsburg (Ed.), *Critical Perspectives on Teaching in Prison: Students and Instructors on Pedagogy Behind the Wall* (pp. 33–37). New York: Routledge.
Starr Sered, S. (2021). Diminished Citizenship in the era of Mass Incarceration. *Punishment & Society*, *23*(2), 218–240.
Tadros, V. (2011). *The Ends of Harm: The Moral Foundations of Criminal Law*. Oxford: Oxford University Press.
Taylor, A. E. (2015). Solidarity: Obligations and Expressions. *The Journal of Political Philosophy*, *23*(2), 128–145.
Wacquant, L. (2010). Class, Race & Hyperincarceration in Revanchist America. *Daedalus*, *139*(3), 74–90.
Wringe, W. (2016). *An Expressive Theory of Punishment*. New York: Palgrave Macmillan. https://doi.org/10.1057/9781137357120
X, R. (2019). Hope for Leaving a Legacy. In R. Ginsburg (Ed.), *Critical Perspectives on Teaching in Prison: Students and Instructors on Pedagogy Behind the Wall* (pp. 19–21). New York: Routledge.

13

REFLECTION

REFLECTIONS ON THE DESIGN, ADMINISTRATION, AND VALUE OF A PRISON-COLLEGE COURSE

Benjamin Meade

In fall 2019, I taught a college course at a nearby state prison. The class was comprised of individuals incarcerated at the facility and students of the university where I teach.[1] Topically, the course functioned as an introduction to crime and criminal justice. In this chapter, I will reflect on the success and failures of the course and the ways that the context of mass incarceration influenced the class.

In designing the course, I referenced literature on college courses inside correctional facilities and obtained teaching guides and materials from colleagues at other institutions. One of my primary goals in designing the course was to accommodate the incarcerated students (hereafter referred to as inside students) particularly as it related to: (1) lower average educational achievement and literacy among incarcerated populations and (2) technological limitations of incarceration. I did not want the course expectations and class materials to be intimidating to inside students. Thus, I designed a less rigorous course than an average class. Secondly, I had to abandon using the internet, learning management systems, and electronic course content for this class. I used only a textbook, I did not assign additional readings, I did not utilize exams, and I required only reflection and citation of the textbook in weekly and final papers. Finally, as this was a pilot course, I offered it as a special topics section and did not pursue the option of college course credit for the inside students.

I was excited and optimistic about the beginning of class meetings; however, the first week of class was a far greater challenge than I anticipated. Although I sincerely made a conscious effort to recognize and mitigate my privilege as a free person, my efforts in actuality insulted the inside students and magnified the distinctions between inside and outside students. For example, a source I read on alleviating the anxiety of inside students about taking a college course recommended offering the option of not being graded on a college level. Unbeknownst to me, a large number of students had already taken college courses through other universities. The inside students were appalled that I would not have the same expectations of them as I did the outside students and were eager to be intellectually challenged and stimulated. Ultimately, the inside students academically excelled as much or more than the outside students, and two of the inside students tied with an outside student for the highest grade in the class (98.6%).

DOI: 10.4324/9781003274292-17

In addition, because the inside students had taken other college courses and received credit for it, they were frustrated that they were not receiving college credits through my class/institution. One student articulated that they felt used and manipulated for our (outside) purposes, and that their academic work deserved the same credit as the other students in the course. I assumed that the opportunity to have contact with outside students and engage in intellectual discussions in a classroom setting would be a sufficiently enticing and exciting opportunity for incarcerated persons. I intended to eventually create a credit option for the inside students after this pilot course and once my class/the program became more established. However, after the critical feedback and response I received, I worked to retroactively confer college credits to the inside students. I realized that I had misjudged the inside students by both underestimating and almost infantilizing their ability to scholarly perform in a college course and overestimating their willingness to work and participate in the course without official recognition.

Both sources of frustration on the part of the inside students stemmed from the facet of mass incarceration referred to as warehousing. John Irwin (2005) coined the term warehouse prison to describe how individuals sent to prison are classified, housed, and then shipped out when they are ready for release. In contrast to rehabilitation, the warehouse prison abandons the notion of doing anything to or for incarcerated persons and focuses on the efficient, orderly, and safe storage of incarcerated individuals. The byproduct of the warehouse is the exaggerated feeling of being forgotten. The reduction/elimination of rehabilitative programming combined with the dramatic increase in prison populations due to mass incarceration leaves many incarcerated individuals craving scant or non-existent opportunities to educate and better themselves. For example, Virginia's incarceration rates are higher than the national average, and from 2015 to 2019 the average daily population among Virginia's 40 or so prisons was approximately 30,000 (Prison Policy Initiative, 2020; VADOC, 2020). There were several inside students in my course who had completed every class and training program that was offered at the prison and were enrolled in correspondence courses outside of the prison. Incarcerated individuals are "hungry" for opportunities to learn and have educational and social experiences. Much of the feedback from inside students involved wanting "more." The students wanted more challenging class material, a more advanced study of criminological phenomena, more topics, more time discussing each topic, and more class days per week.

In addition to the deprivations of intellectual stimulation resulting from mass incarceration, the inside students also expressed appreciation for the social opportunities to interact with individuals from the outside. One inside student commented that it was a relief to come to class and interact with classmates who were not embedded in a prison subculture because he did not have to question what the other students were trying to get from him. One of the activities I designed for the course was inside/outside discussion questions. At the beginning of the semester, I had every student write discussion questions about either life on the inside or outside of prison. Each class day, I would pick one inside discussion question and one outside discussion question. This allowed more social exchange where students were free to share aspects of their lives on the inside or on the outside with each other, learn about each others' experiences, and gain empathy for one another.

It was largely through this exercise and group discussion work that much of the interpersonal learning and exchange took place. For the inside students, it was a new opportunity for learning, and particularly for discussion about criminology and criminal justice. Even though a number of them had taken college courses before, this was their first criminal justice course. Most of the inside students were very passionate about injustice and reform in/of the system. In class discussion and assignments, they were able to blend the academic terminology and concepts of mass incarceration with their firsthand experiences of the system. Although most had educated themselves about criminal justice practice and research, I also had a few inside students who did struggle academically. For example, I worked with one student who essentially only knew how to copy from the textbook when writing papers at the beginning of the semester, but by the end of the course he produced a 25-page handwritten reflection on the course.

Much of the focus of this reflection has been on the inside students, but I think the outside students benefited from this course experience even more than the inside students. As indicated above, many of the inside students had taken college courses before, so this was not a new experience; however, most, if not all, of the outside students had never been inside a prison before and certainly had not interacted with incarcerated individuals on such a personal level. The ultimate value of the course for the outside students was to be able to understand mass incarceration and incarcerated individuals on more than just an abstract level (see Perez & Leon, 2020). One of the first questions that the inside students asked the outside students was about our check-in procedures to the facility. The outside students immediately talked about how nervous they were being searched and how undignified and intrusive it felt. Finally, one of the outside students realized the point of the question and said, "wow, you guys have to go through that every day."

The demographic differences and similarities between the inside and outside students were also illustrative of the scope of mass incarceration for the outside students. Racial disparities in Virginia are greater than the national average. According to the Prison Policy Initiative (2020), the incarceration rate of Black people in Virginia is almost four times greater than that of white people. The outside students had learned about racial disparities in imprisonment rates but were able to fully grasp the concept when seven out of ten of the inside students were African American. The fact that the prison was located in a remote and rural part of Virginia with a zero percent African American population (according to the 2020 census) further demonstrated the concepts of warehousing and mass incarceration.[2] In contrast, the outside students were able to identify with some of the inside students based on their similarity in age. Although I do not know the exact ages of all the inside students, there were students who were quite youthful in the course alongside students who had grandchildren. When one of the inside students had his 21st birthday on a class day, the outside students realized there were individuals incarcerated who were younger than they were.

Class discussions also served to reinforce the criminological influences of social disadvantage and inequality. The inside students shared openly about their experiences with poverty, discrimination, substance use/abuse, victimization, and exposure to violent-experiences largely foreign to upper middle class outside students. One inside student shared with the class how two young children in his family had been killed by neighborhood gun violence. The same student also described how he and his father were both cocaine addicts and reflected with the class on the biological and social influences on his own addiction. One of the most impactful discussions about the role and influence of disadvantage among the inside students occurred on Halloween day. I asked students to discuss and share memories about Halloween growing up. One inside student said he never had a good Halloween. He was either alone or was beaten up by older neighborhood children who stole his Trick or Treat candy. Several outside students wrote about this particular discussion in their final reflection papers.

The course experience and direct exposure to facets of mass incarceration were also a good lesson in humility and privilege for the instructor, as well. I was a bit naïve and underprepared for the type of interactions that I had with the students. For those anticipating delivering a course of this nature on their own in the future, I would offer some guidance. The following two suggestions represent things I believe were partial failures on my part or things I would like to have done differently.

1 Ensure a system for offering course credit to the inside students prior to the beginning of the course. This was the biggest source of contention with the inside students. It is important to recognize their academic work on the same level as the outside students. This involves setting up an application process, a credit/class designation, and finding funding to pay the tuition for the inside students. After the first meeting with the inside students, I immediately began this process and ultimately had it completed by the last day of class. University offices and support structures, including community engagement/outreach and the adult degree program, were instrumental in achieving this timely goal.
2 Recognize and minimize ways that course policies, rules, and languages draw distinctions between inside and outside students. The credit issue above was a primary illustration of this. There were ways that I succeeded in treating the students equitably. There were other ways that I could improve, and there were institutional and university rules and policies beyond my control that inhibited this. Facility rules about name use (only last names) was a major inequity that constantly distinguished inside from outside students. I would recommend having a frank discussion with the inside students alone about ways that this can be accomplished, as well as a recognition that facility rules prohibit much of what I want to accomplish. My own pride got in the way here, as I never wanted to seem like I was "passing the buck" or blaming someone else for an unpopular decision. More open and honest communication from the beginning would have eased the tension all around.

The following suggestions are based on decisions or actions that were particularly successful in the course design and delivery.

1 Flexibility in course structures and individual approach/personality is important. When delivering a class at a correctional institution, class can be cancelled or dismissed with little or no notification. There were multiple occasions where we waited an hour or more for the inside students to be released from count/lockdown. I also had to revise my course plans on numerous occasions because of the facility interruptions or the natural flow of class discussion (see Leon & Perez, 2019).
2 Be selective about the outside and inside students. I was able to pick both the inside and outside students for the course. For the outside students, I had a brief application process where they had to provide faculty references, explain why they wanted to be in the course, and sit down with me for an interview. This ensured that I admitted students who were mature and responsible enough to manage the requirements and expectations of a course of this nature. For the inside students, I was sent a writing sample from all

applicants to help make my choice. I was conscious to avoid selecting students solely on the best written pieces, but rather drew from a variety of writings in terms of educational/academic skill.

In conclusion, after reflecting on this course experience, it was simultaneously the most challenging and most rewarding experience of my career. For those of us on the outside, it made the abstract classroom concept of "mass incarceration" a concrete reality.

Notes

1 This course was not affiliated with the Inside-Out Prison Exchange Program.
2 The outside students were also all white. Only one student of color applied for the course, but was unable to meet the eligibility requirements of the correctional facility.

References

Irwin, J. (2005). *The warehouse prison: Disposal of the new dangerous class.* Roxbury Publishing, Los Angeles, CA.

Leon, C.S., & Perez, G. (2019). Reading "Women Don't Riot" after the riot: Creating a University-Prison Collaboration. *Journal of Prison Education and Reentry, 5*(2), 144–156.

Perez, G., & Leon, C.S. (2020). Bonds beyond bars: Impact of an Inside-Out Prison Exchange Program. *The Journal of Correctional Education, 71*(3), 33–53.

Prison Policy Initiative. (2020). *Virginia Profile.* https://www.prisonpolicy.org/profiles/VA.html

Virginia Department of Corrections. (2020). *State Responsible Offender Population Trends FY2015–2019.* https://vadoc.virginia.gov/media/1473/vadoc-offender-population-trend-report-2015-2019.pdf

14

REFLECTION INSIDE-OUT

A Transformative Experience

Kaelyn Sanders

In 1997, Dr. Lori Pompa founded the Inside-Out Prison Exchange Program as a single course at Temple University. Inside-Out's purpose was to bring campus-based students together with incarcerated students for a semester-long, prison-based course. The course cultivated a transformative learning experience through student dialogue and discussion. Since its inception, Inside-Out has expanded into an international program that allows students to address criminal justice issues beyond the duration of the class (The Inside-Out Center, n.d.). As an undergraduate student, I was fortunate enough to take part in the Inside-Out Prison Exchange Program, and it not only changed the course of my academic interests but also my personal surrounding incarcerated individuals and the carceral system more broadly. This chapter serves as a recollection and reflection on my time spent in the program and how it still impacts me today. I hope after reading this chapter you understand why programs like Inside-Out are important and beneficial for both inside and outside students.

During my undergraduate studies, I signed up for the Inside-Out class at my university to fulfill a degree requirement. I had heard about Inside-Out before but was unsure of what to expect because despite having incarcerated family members; I had never been to a prison before. My class took place in a women's prison about 30 minutes away from our campus. We met with the women once a week for two hours and mainly focused on globalization. Initially, I expected the class to focus on criminal justice-related topics, but our instructor made it clear that she did not choose such topics because the women lived and breathed criminal justice every day they were in prison. So, she did not want to add to that. Once my instructor shared her reasoning, I understood why the class was on another topic, especially since we still learned about women's experiences in prison without directly asking. I was surprised at how much they were willing to share with us, but I believe that was a result of the bonds we created with them over the course of the semester.

I remember initially feeling excitement and nervousness about starting the class. Unfortunately, our first two course sessions were canceled because my professor had personal emergencies. Missing the first two sessions did not change much; however, we were unable to get a full tour of the prison facility because of this. The class structure was fluid. Typically,

DOI: 10.4324/9781003274292-18

we would read a news story and discuss them as a class. Also, every week, we would write journal entries after the class reflecting on the session, and at the end of the semester, we turned in our final journals. The final class project for the course was a group project on a topic of our choice, and although it would appear difficult to do a group project with incarcerated students, it was not difficult at all. My group's project was on marijuana legalization, and the inside students in my group were always on top of their project sections and handwrote many notes for us to add to the final presentation. I can honestly say it was one of the best group projects I participated in and at no point was I worried we would not do well. Working with these women on a project allowed them to show their responsible, dedicated, and intelligent side, which is something the prison environment often hampers or posits as nonexistent.

Alongside my nervousness, I recall feeling extra worried about how the inside women in the class would perceive me and wanted to ensure that I did not give the impression that I was judging them or their stories. I hoped to learn about their experiences and perspectives, and I imagined that they were accustomed to being vilified for their "inmate" label. So, I was vehemently intentional about showing respect for them as my peers in the classroom and respect for their voices. I was concerned about their level of comfortability with us (the outside students) being there more than I was about my safety or comfortability. Reflecting on the class, I cannot recall a single instance where I felt unsafe, and the class's overall structure was perfect because we learned about globalization and had space to connect with the inside students personally.

Because Inside-Out takes place inside a prison facility, I believe fostering connections between the inside and outside students is one of the most important tasks to ensure that everyone feels comfortable in the environment. If not for the comfortable and safe atmosphere, I am not sure if I would have enjoyed the experience as much as I did. There were times when I even forgot we were in a prison facility because I was so engaged in the class and group conversations. Still, reality always settled in at the end of class time when the inside students had to line up to be taken back to their units, and we, outside students, got back in our cars to go home.

Throughout the course, I reflected on my positionality as a young Black woman in college coming into this space. Since Black women are disproportionally imprisoned (Willingham, 2011), I knew that, to some degree, I might relate to some of the women there simply because I am a Black woman. I knew that there was a chance I would even meet some women from the same city as me, which did happen with one woman in my group. We grew up only about 15 minutes away from each other, which highlighted that there are likely more similarities than differences between me and the inside students. Knowing this eased my nerves and made the environment more comfortable. One thing I did not consider was my age compared to the inside students. I expected most of the women to be in their 30s or 40s, which the majority were, but one woman I connected with was only a few years older than me. We bonded a lot over our favorite shows, music, and makeup products. There were many times during the semester when she would tell me that she could not wait to get out because she wanted to go get her hair and nails done.

Another one of my first recollections during the program is being told by a corrections officer not to believe what the women say because they are manipulators. At the time, I was naïve to some correctional actors' stereotypical perspectives of the women they supervise, so this did not strike me as problematic. As I reflect on it, I realize that it seemed irrelevant and unnecessary to make a gross generalization of that kind regarding the women. It almost seemed like they were trying to foster a "us vs. them" mentality. Although we all know manipulators exist, it is crucial to think about the context of this statement's situation. Referring to incarcerated women in this manner does more harm than good because it hinders the women from being able to craft an unbiased narrative of who they are aside from their justice involvement. Telling this to college students, some of whom may be entering a prison facility for the first time, is especially dangerous because it could taint the way they view their incarcerated classmates.

Aside from that initial comment, my overall experience in the course was phenomenal, and I gained an inside perspective of what it is like to be a woman in prison. At the beginning of the class, we had large group discussions, and on our first day, we did a "speed meeting" exercise where an outside student talked with an inside student for a couple of minutes and then switched partners. The speed meeting activity helped lessen some of the nerves and anxiety on everyone's part. We focused on talking about our likes and dislikes, which helped form a constant realization that maybe we are more similar than we are different.

After the first few weeks, we split into groups based on our final project groups. I was in a group with one other outside student and four inside students. Three of the four women in my group were in their 30s, and the other woman was in her early 20s. Throughout the remainder of the semester, I grew close to the women in my group. However, after a couple of weeks of being in groups, one woman stopped showing up to class because she found out she was not one of the students receiving college credit and felt it was not worth her time anymore. I believe she was not receiving credit due to a limit on the number of inside students that received credit per class. Priority for college credit was given to people nearing their parole date. Unfortunately, I never saw her again, but I did ask the other women in my group to tell her hello when they saw her. Even though I wish she stayed in the class, her reasoning is valid, and I also would feel upset if I was told after the fact that I was not getting credit. I am unsure of whether this rule has changed since then, but I would hope all women are able to get credit now.

A similar occurrence happened with another woman in my group. For about two weeks, she was not in class because she had gotten into a fight and was in segregation. When she returned, she told us about the fight and how she was disappointed in herself for even letting the situation occur. I cannot recall the exact details of her story, but I remember the fight being about another woman in the prison saying something that upset the woman in my group. She also told us that being in segregation was hard, and I remember her saying something along the lines of, "The only thing worse than being in prison is waking up still in prison." While recounting her time in segregation, she seemed emotional as I noticed tears welling up in her eyes, but she never let them fall. When she shared this with us, I felt upset and angry for her because I understand that misconduct is not tolerated, but I also doubt segregation is the best or correct consequence for misconduct. Even now, when reflecting on this conversation, I still feel anger and sadness for her because I vividly remember the expressions on her face when recounting her experience. What happened to her never felt right to me, but I also felt helpless beyond providing a listening ear and support.

Things went as planned, meaning we were on track with our planned course schedule, for the remainder of the semester, and no more of my group members missed any classes. Frequently, we had a good portion of class time where we just sat and talked with one another to learn about each other. This is where I learned the women's ages and that I grew up in the same city as one of the women in my group. I also got to learn about their family life. One woman had two teenage daughters that she talked about a lot with us, especially since her oldest daughter was getting ready to graduate high school, and she knew she would not be able to attend the graduation. Not being able to attend her daughter's graduation hurt her because she wanted to be there, and her pain was visible even without any words having to be said, which made it easy to empathize with her. She also told us that sometimes her daughters would send her photos on the tablet she had access to, which made her happy because she still felt connected to them.

However, she also shared with us that her daughters often told her that her incarceration affected their mental health and upset them, which is understandable. Having an incarcerated parent is hard, especially when they have been gone for many years with many more years to go, and research has consistently documented the harmful effects of parental incarceration (Wakefield & Wildeman, 2018). Knowing this I reflected on what it must be like to only be able to see or talk to your parent every so often for a limited amount of time. It is understandable why it has such an effect on parents and their children, as it would be hard to maintain a strong relationship even if you are regularly speaking with them and visiting. I am also sure that many people would not feel empathy for her because they blame her for being in prison rather than trying to understand that regardless she is still a mother who loves her children.

On our last day of class, I also recall her telling the other outside student in our group and me that one of the reasons she loved coming to class was because we would talk to her about things going on in the outside world, and she would go back and talk to her daughters about those same things. When she told us this, she was crying as it was our last day with them in the class, and we all pretty much knew without saying that it was unlikely we would see each other again. The other two women in our group were also visibly sad, and I was too. I did not want the semester to end as I'd learned so much from these women and bonded with them.

The woman closest to my age and I got close because we had similar personalities and interests and were of the same race/ethnicity. I specifically remember one conversation about her fear of going up for parole. She mentioned that her "prison mom" had been incarcerated for over 30 years and was denied parole each time she went up. Because of this, she worried that the board would deny her due to the crime she committed years ago when her time came for parole. This conversation stuck with me because I never thought about how nerve-wracking the parole process could be. It motivated me to conduct a qualitative study of women on parole about their experiences with the process. Without the insight from the woman in my class, I would have never considered that part of their experience in the justice system. So, I wish I could thank her for that. Also, on our last day, we took photos together and heard Piper Kerman speak about her experiences while incarcerated and provide advice to the women. Unfortunately, the corrections officer who was supposed to email us our photos never did, and we never got an answer as to why. So, we were unable to receive those photos, which was upsetting. Despite this disappointment, my inside-out experience was terrific overall. I still think of the girls in my group often and wonder how they are doing.

When reflecting on this experience, many things were different from my initial expectations. I never thought that the bonds I created with the women would grow so strong and influence my research and scholarship. It shows that there is more to people's stories, and if you take the time to listen, you will see that you are more similar than you are different. The opportunity to consider the voices of people affected most by prisons was profoundly impactful. The women in my group and I enjoyed many of the same things, shared many of the same beliefs, and most importantly, we cared about each other enough to be saddened at the end of our semester. Also, one of the women even shared that when we did the "speed meeting" exercise, she was nervous about how we would view her and feared being judged for being incarcerated. Still, she said that we never once made her feel bad about her current situation. I was relieved to know that we had managed to foster a space of safety for her in this regard.

Through this experience, I gained a different and more positive viewpoint on incarcerated people. Although my opinions were not necessarily negative before because I have system-impacted family members, it is different when it comes to strangers. It is often easier to judge them. However, I felt more compelled to advocate for these women and incarcerated individuals generally. I was shocked to learn what their days looked like inside and how much of a mental and emotional toll the pains of imprisonment took on them. This experience helped strengthen my belief that there must be other ways to provide consequences that do not further harm anyone.

Another takeaway from this experience was my desire to learn more about incarcerated women's experiences. When we think about jails and prisons, we often think about them in the context of men's experiences. Therefore, I wanted to further my understanding of women's perspectives, which is why this experience is directly linked to the current work I do now as a doctoral student. Withal, the Inside-Out Prison Exchange Program experience was pivotal for me. It not only shaped my research interests but also my personal beliefs about the necessity of prisons and the harm they cause. I highly recommend that anyone take advantage of this program if it is available to you. If you decide to participate, remember to go in with an open mind and try to see how you can relate to the inside students rather than how you differ. I am optimistic that doing so will allow you to develop a more informed perspective.

References

The Inside-Out Center. (n.d.). *About Us*. Retrieved February 2, 2022, from https://www.insideout-center.org/about-inside-out.html#hashLink2

Wakefield, S., & Wildeman, C. (2018). How parental incarceration harms children and what to do about it. *National Council on Family Relations*, *3*(1), 1–6.

Willingham, B. C. (2011). Black women's prison narratives and the intersection of race, gender, and sexuality in US Prisons. *Critical Survey*, *23*(3), 55–66.

SECTION IV

Youth and Families

Mass incarceration has a profound impact on youth and families. The United States incarcerates youth at a higher rate than any other developed country (Barnert et al., 2017). Imprisonment negatively affects their education, health, and familial bonds. In addition, mass incarceration impacts families by taking away partners, parents, and caregivers; this creates fractured homes. This phenomenon can lead to single-parent households or force children into foster care, which is consequential for children and their caregivers. Almost half of incarcerated adults are parents to children under the age of 18 (Wang, 2022). These children face many developmental and emotional challenges as they cope with a family member being imprisoned (Wang, 2022). This section of the reader examines the consequences of mass incarceration on youth and families.

This section comprises two realities and two reflections. Russell and colleagues examine policies and practices associated with youth confinement in their chapter, "The Juvenile Justice System's Role in the Persistence of Mass Incarceration in America." Next, Caputo-Levine and Guitar-Judd discuss the far-reaching impact of mass incarceration on families in a rural community in their chapter, "At the Breaking Point: The Impact of Mass Incarceration on Families." The section concludes with two reflections. Heather Mooney reflects on her experience in a so-called therapeutic boarding school in her chapter, "Transported to the Troubled Teen Industry." The last reflection is authored by two sisters, LeAnna T. Luney and Maya Luney-Ballew, who share their story of having their father incarcerated in "Musings on School Communities, Information Evasion, and the Children of Incarcerated Parents."

References

Barnert, E. S., Dudovitz, R., Nelson, B. B., Coker, T. R., Biely, C., Li, N., & Chung, P. J. (2017). How Does Incarcerating Young People Affect Their Adult Health Outcomes? *Pediatrics*, *139*(2), e20162624. https://doi.org/10.1542/peds.2016-2624

Wang, L. (2022, August 11). *Both sides of the bars: How mass incarceration punishes families.* Prison Policy Initiative. Retrieved December 22, 2022, from https://www.prisonpolicy.org/blog/2022/08/11/parental_incarceration/

DOI: 10.4324/9781003274292-19

15

THE JUVENILE JUSTICE SYSTEM'S ROLE IN THE PERSISTENCE OF MASS INCARCERATION IN AMERICA

Kristan N. Russell, William Ash-Houchen, Shantaé M. Motley, and Vineeth Vijayan

LEARNING OBJECTIVES:

Upon successful completion of this chapter, students will be able to:

1 Identify the historical factors that precipitated and contributed to the increased confinement of youth in the United States.
2 Discuss the ways in which public reactions impact policy and decision-making within the juvenile justice system.
3 Explain how school district and legal practices (i.e., waivers to adult court) might relate to confinement trends.

Introduction

In 2019, youth accounted for approximately 1 in every 13 arrests for murder and aggravated assault in the United States (OJJDP, 2020). Given the severity of such offenses, many of these youth experienced confinement in the juvenile or adult systems. Evidence suggests that incapacitating youth increases their risk of recidivism (Walker & Herting, 2020), which is exacerbated if the incarceration occurs within the adult system (Bishop, 2000). As a result, highly punitive practices opting for detention placement rather than diversion to alternative programming could further contribute to the revolving door within the criminal justice system. The conversation around mass incarceration is often focused on the adult population. However, given the considerations outlined above, those who wish to comprehensively understand the precipitants of mass incarceration must consider the criminalization and confinement of youth.

Historically, youth were subjected to punishment with little differentiation from adults in the United States (Merlo et al., 2016). This led to youth being imprisoned alongside adults. The creation of juvenile courts and policies to better protect children and adolescents contributed to a shift from punitive to more rehabilitative approaches to youth offending. Today, youth who are adjudicated and detained are held in juvenile-specific facilities called detention centers.

DOI: 10.4324/9781003274292-20

Early and sustained interaction with the juvenile justice system is related to later interaction with the adult criminal justice system (Christle et al., 2005). The school-to-prison pipeline is an important consideration when discussing the relationship between youth adjudication and future recidivism in the adult system. From 2005 to 2013, many states enacted statutes aimed at reducing youth prosecution in adult courts and their placement in adult prisons. Eleven states have limited the placement of youth in adult jails and prisons, while another eleven states have made the laws that allow the transfer or waiver of youth to adult court more stringent in an effort to keep youth in juvenile courts (Howell et al., 2017).

The United States differs in many ways from other countries in the treatment of justice-involved youth. Efforts at promoting and integrating restorative justice principles are mandated by the Council of Europe and the United Nations (Laird, 2021). Countries like Austria divert up to fifty percent of suitable cases to out-of-court mediation or through informal negotiations between the perpetrator and victim through a mediator (Muncie, 2005). Within New Zealand and Australia, restorative justice has been well established as the driving force for the rehabilitation of juveniles (Muncie, 2005). Outside of a Western and European context, efforts to reduce carceral sentences for juveniles have promulgated in Africa, based on reconciliation. These efforts have not been replicated to the same extent in the United States, in the face of pressure from policymakers to be 'tough on crime.' (Carter, 2020). This has led to increases in waivers from juvenile court to adult court, as well as harsher punishments for youth adjudicated in the system (Merlo et al., 2016).

In this chapter, we will discuss (a) punitive and rehabilitative approaches in the youth justice system and their impact on confinement trends, (b) public reaction to youth behavior that has influenced policy, (c) the school-to-prison pipeline, (d) waivers to transfer youths to adult court and their potential relation to confinement trends, and lastly (e) recent efforts to reduce youth confinement.

Punishment vs. Rehabilitation in the Juvenile Justice System

The pressure policymakers face to be 'tough on crime' has led to harsher punishments for youth and has moved the juvenile justice system to heavily rely on punishment. The criminal justice system is designed to be punitive with the implication that it would prevent individuals from committing additional crimes and persuade others that committing crimes is not worth the punishment. The nature of design for the criminal justice system differs from the juvenile justice system. From the inception of the juvenile court system, it was designed to be a balanced system of rehabilitation and punishment (Bernard & Kurlychek, 2010; Butts & Mears, 2001; Feld, 1999; Mears et al., 2015). The belief is that a rehabilitative design for youth can keep them from progressing into a life of crime. An individual's brain is still forming until the age of 25, causing youth and emerging adults to lack rational decision-making skills (Mears et al., 2015; Tanenhaus, 2004). Over time rehabilitation became the forefront of the juvenile justice system, creating the association between rehabilitating youth and punishing adults (Fagan & Zimring, 2000; Mears et al., 2015; Tanenhaus, 2004).

The directing doctrine of the juvenile justice system is *parens patriae* which is Latin and translates to 'the state as parent' (Mears et al., 2007, 2015). The juvenile court was designed with the belief that it would act as a surrogate parent and provide services that would best serve youth in the system (Butts & Mitchell, 2000; Mears et al., 2015). Emphasis on rehabilitation was derived from the hope that it could save youth from the harmful effects and experiences of the adult justice system (Mears et al., 2015; Tanenhaus, 2004). The juvenile court has fallen short of providing youth with dispositions that provide both treatment and punishment, therefore not effectively redirecting youth from offending. Part of this shortcoming is due to 'tough on crime' approaches which criminalize youthful offending without effective rehabilitation. The criminalization of youth often leads to them encountering the adult criminal justice system, which leads to higher incarceration rates

Understanding that these factors lead to higher incarceration rates is not enough; policy changes are necessary to help reduce these rates and move back to the 'rehabilitation first' mentality regarding youth. The courts' willingness to utilize developmental science research that examines the risk-taking behavior of adolescents is promising (Monahan et al., 2015; Scott, 2013). If decision-makers are willing to consider the effect of imposing harsh punishments on youth during juvenile crime policymaking, it could serve to reduce incarceration rates (Monahan et al., 2015; Scott, 2013).

Panic and Public Policy

The juvenile justice system pendulum swung from rehabilitative to punishment oriented for youth because of media panic and incorrect hypotheses. In the late 1980s and early 1990s, the media sensationalized crime, focusing on tragic stories of victims to generate visceral and emotional responses by the public (Dowler, 2003; Pizarro et al, 2007). These public reactions led to strong, punitive rhetoric toward crime by the public, political leaders, and many other famous figures. During this time of heightened concern, John J. Diulio introduced a hypothesis about youth crime which quickly pervaded U.S. society (Equal Justice Initiative, 2014). This hypothesis, often referred to today as a crime myth, was based on the narrative that youth crime was increasing, paving the way for a new generation of supposed impulsive and violent young people dubbed 'superpredators' (Kappeler & Potter, 2005). It should be noted that the suggestion that youth crime was rapidly rising was incorrect and that youth crime was dropping at unprecedented rates (Sickmund & Puzzanchera, 2014). The narrative of superpredators furthered racial biases, associating this moniker with African American youth (Allen & Whitt, 2020). The prevalence of youth crime was further distorted by media reporting (Pizarro et al., 2007). Despite this, the idea of superpredators was met with rapid support and heralded in the introduction and implementation of many 'tough on crime' policies.

Given the role of youthful risk-taking behavior, impulsivity, and general psychosocial maturity, most youth will age out of harmful behavior. This is often referred to as a desistance trajectory or a pathway to non-offending (Mulvey et al., 2004). Alternatively, some youth persist in offending, often referred to as life-course persistent trajectories (Sampson & Laub, 2003), though it is a very small proportion of offending youth overall. These youth are those that concern the public and drive punitive policy that is exceedingly disproportionate to their representation in the system overall (Laub & Sampson, 2001).

Researchers have found it difficult to meaningfully distinguish youth with desistance vs. life-course persistent trajectories due to the considerable variation amongst the group and the dynamism of factors within this process (Mulvey et al., 2010). This may contribute to furthered support for 'tough on crime' legislation and practices. Policies that emphasize punishment over treatment result in a higher number of youth being incarcerated (Sickmund & Puzzanchera, 2014), further contributing to the mass incarceration issue in American society. To disrupt this pipeline, policymakers need to take the effects of present punitive legislation into consideration and consider promoting a shift back to rehabilitative practices that emphasize evidence-based treatment, support, and resources to keep youth out of the system for long term.

School-to-Prison Pipeline

An effective way to disrupt the pipeline to mass incarceration caused by public panic is to address the issue of the school-to-prison pipeline. The relationship between the justice system and the education system is complicated. Education is a strong predictor of financial stability, while lack of education is a strong predictor of encountering the justice system (Autor et al., 2008; Owens, 2017). Communities stricken by poverty are usually riddled with high crime rates and disorganization, adversely affecting the educational achievement of the youth raised in those communities (Katz & Turner, 2008; Ludwig et al., 2013; Owens, 2017; Sharkey et al., 2014).

The use of School Resource Officers (SROs), who were placed in schools for safety, order, and improvement of community relationships (Ttofi & Farrington, 2011; Wilson & Lipsey, 2007) may also play a role in the incarceration rates of youth. Research shows the use of SROs in schools has resulted in law enforcement handling misbehaving students through means like arrest, rather than parents or school officials addressing the issue. Resultantly, the use of these officers within the schools and their relationship to youth justice system contributes to what is now known as the *school-to-prison pipeline* (Owens, 2017; Wald & Losen, 2003). Various factors contribute to this pipeline including SRO presence, being under-funded and under-resourced, adjudicating youth for status offenses, and abiding by zero-tolerance policies within schools.

The school-to-prison pipeline affects millions of youths a year. During the 2011–2012 academic year, 35 million students were given detention, 1.9 million were suspended more than once, and about 130,000 were expelled from school (Mallett, 2017; U.S. Department of Education, 2014). This is due to the zero-tolerance policies that punish even the most minor incidents with harsh sanctions. Several studies have shown higher levels of adult offending behavior by former students who were suspended while in school (Hemez et al., 2020). As the number of suspensions and contact with law enforcement increases for school-aged youth, so does the likelihood of them being incarcerated, contributing to high incarceration rates.

The pipeline can be eradicated without putting students, school officials, and the community at risk. Policy changes can be implemented to move the pendulum from a punitive nature to a rehabilitative nature in the juvenile justice system and the education system (Mallett, 2017). Modifying zero-tolerance policies and increasing community assistance can lead to inclusion and rehabilitation of youth. Further, schools should avoid using SROs for disciplinary scenarios that do not require law enforcement involvement. Importantly, policymakers must increase funding given to schools to support resources and staff to address status offending, mental health, substance use, and other behavioral problems through evidence-based practices.

Transfer of Youth to Adult Court

Just as the education system pipelines youth into the juvenile justice system, the juvenile justice system also pipelines youth into the criminal justice system. An assessment of the contributing role of the juvenile justice system to mass incarceration necessitates an examination of a key interface – transfer of youth to adult courts. Public policy has played an outsized role in the patterning of the public's perception and orientation toward the juvenile justice system historically. As a codifying example, the rise in violent crime in the early 1990s results in numerous political maneuvers resulting in legislation facilitating the transition of juveniles to adult courts (McCord et al., 2001). The United States is a world leader in punitiveness (Muhammad, 2022). The underlying philosophy of the juvenile justice system differs from the adult justice system in that it understands juveniles as less culpable, and therefore less deserving of adult punishments (Merlo et al. 2016; Rattan et al., 2012).

Not all youth are guaranteed to have their case processed in the juvenile system. In the United States, there are multiple circumstances in which youth can be tried as an adult, each of which is accompanied by a different type of waiver. *Judicial waivers* (also known as judicial discretion) are when the juvenile court judge ultimately decides whether a transfer is appropriate. *Discretionary waivers* (also known as prosecutorial discretion or direct file) are another type of waiver in which these transfer statutes provide the prosecution discretion to file certain cases in adult court. The scope and parameters of that discretion vary across states. *Automatic waivers* (also known as statutory exclusion or mandatory waivers) are used by many jurisdictions to exclude certain offenses from juvenile court jurisdiction based on the nature of the charges, the youth's age, and/or their previous record. *Presumptive waivers* provide a rebuttable to the presumption that transfer to adult court is proper in certain cases (e.g., based on the child's type of offense or age) (Merlo et al. 2016). Many states use the approach of 'once an adult, always an adult,' determining that once a youth is transferred and tried as an adult, the youth will be prosecuted as an adult for further offenses. Reverse waivers permit certain jurisdictions to enact 'reverse waiver' provisions that allow the youth to argue in adult court for return to juvenile court

Due to the 'tough on crime' policies enacted in the 1990s, more youth began receiving convictions in adult courts, which is problematic as youth charged with a crime and sent to an adult prison have the same or increased risk of reoffending (Merlo et al. 2016). As a result, youth handled in the adult system are more likely to serve additional prison sentences, further contributing to the incarcerated population. Although 23 states have enacted legislation aimed at reducing the flow of juveniles to criminal court over the last decade, recent Bureau of Justice Statistics data indicates that approximately 200,000 youth under the age of 18 are prosecuted, sentenced, and incarcerated in the adult system each year (Carson & Golinelli, 2013). Although this program was initially designed to address the most severe (violent) and chronic youth committing crimes, its growth diluted the pool of transferred juveniles and cast a wide net, including "a broad range of young people who are neither very serious nor particularly chronic' (Bishop & Frazier, 2000, p. 265).

Recent Trends in Youth Confinement

The widening net allowing juveniles to be transferred into the adult system is an issue in youth confinement that is being addressed country-wide, but it is not the only confinement issue that is being addressed. Efforts to reduce disparity and decrease confinement within the juvenile justice system have included movement toward evidence-based practice and risk assessment, better portioning of services for specific justice-involved youth (e.g., girls), statutory changes, and increased efforts at diversion (Merlo et al., 2016). The Juvenile Justice and Delinquency Prevention Act (JJDPA) and its amendments were passed in 1974 to ensure justice-involved youth receive the minimum punitive sentencing option in juvenile courts. Diversion and diversion efforts represent critical intervention opportunities for the juvenile justice system, most often taking either an informal or formal approach. Informal diversion refers to discretionary decisions made by police, probation officers, judges, or others to let the youth out of the system, dismiss cases, not make an arrest, etc. Formal diversion, on the other hand, represents decisions by social workers, judges, and others to shift juveniles away from the formal processing and more toward services and programming (Schlesinger, 2018).

Efforts at diversion have demonstrated some success thus far. For example, teen courts and youth tribunals allow a modified courtroom structure wherein teens will act as juries, and with judicial approval, mete out appropriate punishment for minor offenses (Merlo et al., 2016). World events have allowed changes to the structure and processes of the juvenile justice system in the United States. The COVID-19 pandemic, for example, has limited opportunity for many types of delinquency, with larger amounts of time spent at home, many businesses and schools open in limited or virtual-only formats, and a lack of opportunity to spend time with potentially peers (Buchanan et al., 2020). While the full effects of the COVID-19 epidemic on the juvenile justice system cannot be discerned entirely yet, some early research suggests that arrest has been utilized as a last resort, reserved for only serious and violent charges. As fewer juveniles were arrested, fewer entered detention facilities. Many states, such as North Carolina, Illinois, Maine, and Maryland, took significant steps to reduce the number of detained juveniles at the start of the COVID-19 outbreak, representing a drop of up to 24% in detained juvenile populations (Buchanan et al., 2020).

In efforts to reduce adjudication in adult courts, some states have made strides toward increasing the age through which an individual could be adjudicated in juvenile court, with several states allowing juvenile court adjudication to continue up through age 20, and some extending the age further to 24. One prominent example is Vermont, which is set to become the only state to raise the maximum age an individual may attain before moving into adult court to above 18, though these efforts have recently met with political opposition (NCSL, 2021). As the social problem of youth incarceration is intricately related to the school-to-prison pipeline, Texas Senate Bill 1707 also marked an important change, delineating the role of school police officers as excluding routine school discipline; legislation of this type can help in closing one of the primary inflow routes of the school-to-prison pipeline and reduce youth confinement in the United States (S.B. No. 1707, 2019).

Several states have implemented larger sets of recent reforms to their respective juvenile justice systems (Sanders, 2021), with Connecticut and Ohio providing instructive cases. Connecticut, for example, has abolished youth detention for violation of court orders related to status offenses. Further legislation has moved status offense cases to non-judicial handling, increased support services for youth, and eliminated pre-trial detention for children at risk. The last two secure facilities for juveniles closed in Connecticut in 2016 and 2018, respectively. Finally, RECLAIM Ohio incentivizes local courts to plan and house community-based programming, with a specific focus on funding the counties that have committed the most youth to the state system. Significant reductions were observed in youth detention admissions in these specific counties over a ten-year period, with additional funding targeting mental health and substance use treatment in the community (Sanders, 2021).

Conclusion

Youth account for a considerable proportion of offending in the United States. As a result, young persons with justice system involvement will experience arrest, adjudication [...] many will experience arrest, adjudication, and detention, while others will be transferred to the adult justice system. Juvenile justice system contact is associated with future contact with the adult justice system (Christle et al., 2005). Many individuals currently incarcerated in the United States may have found themselves following this pathway. Thus, to address the mass incarceration problem, policymakers and stakeholders must consider how to disrupt the funneling that is taking place between the juvenile and adult systems. To address mass incarceration in the United States, we must recognize the contributing role of the juvenile justice system. This is demonstrated by the following key takeaways from this chapter and recommendations for how to improve:

1 The juvenile justice system was originally designed to be rehabilitative in nature; however, politics and other external influences have contributed to punitive policies and decision-making. Harsh punitive sanctions result in more youth incarceration. Thus, it is recommended that policies aim to require diversion options such as treatment and resources when they have been demonstrated to be more effective alternatives. Juvenile and family court judges should also be well-educated on best practices for youth, so they can recommend appropriate sanctions when given discretion.
2 Youth adjudicated to detention, especially for less severe and status offenses, are at a heightened risk for continued offending and justice system contact. Resultantly, it is recommended that judges and policies aim for treatment and rehabilitation whenever possible, especially with less severe and status offending, to ensure the best possible long-term outcomes for youth.
3 Contact with SROs can further contribute to youth being known to law enforcement and can increase their chances of justice system contact, especially in cases where SROs are involved in disciplinary actions within the school system. As such, it is recommended that SRO duties are clearly outlined within policies and do not include disciplinary action. Furthermore, schools should be better funded and resourced to be able to provide adequate services to youth for status offending, mental health, substance use, and other behavioral issues, rather than seeking assistance from SROs or implementing zero-tolerance policies.
4 When transferred to the adult criminal justice system, youth are at an increased risk of reoffending, committing more serious offenses, and returning to the justice system after release. As such, it is recommended that whenever discretion is possible, judges and other decision-makers should aim to keep the youth within the juvenile system.
5 Disproportionate contact for Black people and people of color exists at all points of juvenile justice system processing and within school disciplinary actions that contribute to the school-to-prison pipeline. Mass incarceration cannot be fully addressed without these biases being identified and rectified.

Understanding the role of youth incarceration in the United States is key to disrupting mass incarceration. While youth who engage in harmful behaviors only make up a portion of the incarcerated population, and not all will end up in the adult system; they do serve as a significant contributor to the overall issue of mass incarceration within the United States. Those who aim to address mass incarceration would be remiss not to consider the role of youth not only in how they relate to the issue, but also as an opportunity as a potential point of intervention and prevention strategies. Disrupting the school-to-prison pipeline, emphasizing rehabilitation over punishment, reforming policies affecting youth, and recognizing the issues that exist within the juvenile system can help move the needle in the right direction.

Discussion Questions:

1 Under what circumstances do you feel it is appropriate and necessary to transfer a youth to the adult court system? What are the benefits of doing so for the state and for the youth? What are the potential consequences of doing so for the state and for the youth?
2 There is a considerable debate surrounding the use of school resources officers. On one hand, their presence may contribute to the criminalization of disciplinary issues within school and increased justice system contact by students, particularly for students of color. On the other hand, in the wake of recent school shootings (e.g., Sandy Hook Elementary in Newtown CT, Stoneman Douglas High School in Parkland FL, and Robb Elementary in Uvalde, TX), many argue for the need for increased law enforcement presence within schools for the safety and protection of students and staff. Consider each argument with supporting or refuting evidence. Further, discuss what you believe the role and duties should be for school resources officers.
3 Legislative waivers require youth to be automatically transferred to the adult court system when certain offenses are committed, taking away judicial discretion to make individualized decisions based on each case. Do you support this form of waiver, why or why not?
4 Zero-tolerance policies, police presence in schools, lack of resources, and underfunding may all contribute to the school-to-prison pipeline. Staffing, resource, and financial issues were all exacerbated by the COVID-19 pandemic. Given the current state of schools, what do you believe are the best strategies for disrupting the school-to-prison pipeline? What factors need to be present for these strategies to be implemented and effective?

References

Alexander, M. (2010). *The new Jim Crow: Mass Incarceration in the Age of Colorblindness*. New York: New Press.

Allen, T. T., & Whitt, A. (2020). An examination of the relationship between media exposure and fear of victimization: Implications of the superpredator narrative on juvenile justice policies. *Juvenile and Family Court Journal, 71*(4), 23–34.

Autor, D. H., Katz, L. F., & Kearney, M. S. (2008). Trends in US wage inequality: Revising the revisionists. *The Review of Economics and Statistics, 90*(2), 300–323.

Bernard, T. J., & Kurlychek, M. C. (2010). *The cycle of juvenile justice*. Oxford University Press.

Bishop, D. M. (2000). Juvenile offenders in the adult criminal justice system. *Crime and Justice, 27*, 81–167. https://doi.org/10.1086/652199

Bishop, D., & Frazier, C. (2000). Consequences of transfer. In J. Fagan & F. R. Zimring (Eds.), *The changing borders of juvenile justice: Transfer of adolescents to the criminal court* (pp. 227–276).

Buchanan, M., Castro, E. D., Kushner, M., & Krohn, M. D. (2020). It's F**ing Chaos: COVID-19's impact on juvenile delinquency and juvenile justice. *American Journal of Criminal Justice, 45*(4), 578–600. https://doi.org/10.1007/s12103-020-09549-x
Butts, J. A., & Mears, D. P. (2001). Reviving juvenile justice in a get-tough era. *Youth & Society, 33*(2), 169–198.
Butts, J. A., & Mitchell, O. (2000). Brick by brick: Dismantling the border between juvenile and adult justice. *Criminal Justice*, 2, 167–213.
Carson, E. A., & Golinelli, D. (2013). Prisoners in 2012: Trends in admissions and releases, 1991–2012. Washington, DC: Bureau of Justice Statistics.
Carter, M. D. (2020). Bending the arc toward justice: The current era of juvenile justice reform in Georgia. *Georgia Law Review, 54*(4), 1133–1167. http://pvamu.idm.oclc.org/login?url=https://search.ebscohost.com/login.aspx?direct=true&db=a9h&AN=144574950
Christle, C. A., Jolivette, K., & Nelson, C. M. (2005). Breaking the school to prison pipeline: Identifying school risk and protective factors for youth delinquency. *Exceptionality, 13*(2), 69–88. https://doi.org/10.1207/s15327035ex1302_2
Dowler, K. (2003). Media consumption and public attitude toward crime and justice: The relationship between fear of crime, punitive attitudes, and perceived police effectiveness. *Journal of Criminal Justice and Popular Culture, 10*(2), 109–126.
Equal Justice Initiative. (2014, April). *The superpredator myth, 20 years later.* Retrieved from www.eji.org
Fagan, J., & Zimring, F. E. (Eds.). (2000). *The changing borders of juvenile justice: Transfer of adolescents to the criminal court.* University of Chicago Press.
Feld, B. C. (1999). *Bad kids: Race and the transformation of the juvenile court.* Oxford University Press.
Hemez, P., Brent, J. J., & Mowen, T. J. (2020). Exploring the school-to-prison pipeline: How school suspensions influence incarceration during young adulthood. *Youth Violence and Juvenile Justice, 18*(3), 235–255.
Howell, J. C., Wilson, J. J., Sickmund, M. H., Hodges, N. J., & Howell, M. Q. (2017). Caught in the act: States doing some things right in juvenile justice. *Juvenile and Family Court Journal, 68*(4), 25–42. http://pvamu.idm.oclc.org/login?url=https://search.ebscohost.com/login.aspx?direct=true&db=edshol&AN=edshol.hein.journals.juvfc68.25
Kappeler, V. E., & Potter, G. W. (2005). *The mythology of crime and criminal justice* (4th ed.). Long Grove, IL: Waveland.
Katz, B., & Turner, M. A. (2008). Rethinking US rental housing policy: A new blueprint for federal, state, and local action. In N. P. Retsinas & E. S. Belsky (Eds.), *Revisiting rental housing: policies, programs, and priorities* (pp. 319–358).
Laird, R. (2021). Regional international juvenile incarceration models as a blueprint for rehabilitative reform of juvenile criminal justice systems in the United States. *The Journal of Criminal Law and Criminology, 111*(2), 571–603. http://pvamu.idm.oclc.org/login?url=https://search.ebscohost.com/login.aspx?direct=true&db=edsjsr&AN=edsjsr.48614947
Laub, J. H., & Sampson, R. J. (2001). Understanding desistance from crime. In M. Tonry (Ed.), *Crime and justice: A review of research* (Vol. 28, pp. 1–69). Chicago, IL: University of Chicago Press.
Ludwig, J., Duncan, G. J., Gennetian, L. A., Katz, L. F., Kessler, R. C., Kling, J. R., & Sanbonmatsu, L. (2013). Long-term neighborhood effects on low-income families: Evidence from moving to opportunity. *American Economic Review, 103*(3), 226–31.
Mallett, C. A. (2017). The school-to-prison pipeline: Disproportionate impact on vulnerable children and adolescents. *Education and Urban Society, 49*(6), 563–592.
McCord, J., Widom, C. S., Crowell, N. A., & National Research Council (U.S.). (2001). *Juvenile crime, juvenile justice.* Washington, DC: National Academy Press.
Mears, D. P., Hay, C., Gertz, M., & Mancini, C. (2007). Public opinion and the foundation of the juvenile court. *Criminology, 45*(1), 223–257.

Mears, D. P., Pickett, J. T., & Mancini, C. (2015). Support for balanced juvenile justice: Assessing views about youth, rehabilitation, and punishment. *Journal of Quantitative Criminology*, *31*(3), 459–479.

Merlo, A. V., Benekos, P. J., & Champion, D. J. (2016). *The juvenile justice system: Delinquency, processing, and the law* (8th ed.). Pearson.

Monahan, K., Steinberg, L., & Piquero, A. R. (2015). Juvenile justice policy and practice: A developmental perspective. *Crime and Justice*, *44*(1), 577–619.

Muhammad, K. (2022). The foundational lawlessness of the law itself: Racial criminalization & the punitive roots of punishment in America. *Daedalus*, *151*(1), 107–120. https://doi.org/10.1162/daed_a_01892

Mulvey, E. P., Steinberg, L., Fagan, J., Cauffman, E., Piquero, A. R., Chassin, L., & Losoya, S. H. (2004). Theory and research on desistance from antisocial activity among serious adolescent offenders. *Youth Violence and Juvenile Justice*, *2*, 213–236.

Mulvey, E. P., Steinberg, L., Piquero, A. R., Besana, M., Fagan, J., Schubert, C., & Cauffman, E. (2010). Trajectories of desistance and continuity in antisocial behavior following court adjudication among serious adolescent offenders. *Development and Psychopathology*, *22*(2), 453–475. https://doi.org/10.1017/S0954579410000179

Muncie, J. (2005). The globalization of crime control – the case of youth and juvenile justice: Neo-liberalism, policy convergence and international conventions. *Theoretical Criminology*, *9*(1), 35–64. http://pvamu.idm.oclc.org/login?url=https://search.ebscohost.com/login.aspx?direct=true&db=edshol&AN=edshol.hein.journals.thcr9.4

NCSL (2021). *Juvenile age of jurisdiction and transfer to adult court*. National Conference of State Legislatures. Retrieved 08/22 from https://www.ncsl.org/research/civil-and-criminal-justice/juvenile-age-of-jurisdiction-and-transfer-to-adult-court-laws.aspx

OJJDP (2020, November 16, 2020). *OJJDP statistical briefing book: Juvenile arrest rate trends*. United States Department of Justice. Retrieved 05/01 from http://www.ojjdp.gov/ojstatbb/crime/JAR_Display.asp?ID=qa05200&selOffenses=1

Owens, E. G. (2017). Testing the school-to-prison pipeline. *Journal of Policy Analysis and Management*, *36*(1), 11–37.

Pizarro, J. M., Chermak, S. M., & Gruenwald, M. A. (2007). Juvenile "super-predators" in the news: A comparison of adult and juvenile homicides. *Journal of Criminal Justice and Popular culture*, *14*(1), 84–94.

Rattan, A., Levine, C., Dweck, C., & Eberhardt, J. (2012). Race and the fragility of the legal distinction between juveniles and adults. *PLoS One*, *7*(5), e36680. https://doi.org/10.1371/journal.pone.0036680

Sampson, R. J., Laub, J. H. (2003). Desistance from crime over the life course. In: Mortimer, J. T., Shanahan, M. J. (eds) Handbook of the life course. Handbooks of sociology and social research. Boston, MA: Springer. https://doi.org/10.1007/978-0-306-48247-2_14

Sanders, C. (2021). *State juvenile justice reforms can boost opportunity, particularly for communities of color* (Policy Brief). Center on Budget and Policy Priorities. https://www.cbpp.org/research/state-budget-and-tax/state-juvenile-justice-reforms-can-boost-opportunity-particularly-0

S.B. 1707, 86th Session. (2019). https://capitol.texas.gov/BillLookup/Text.aspx?LegSess=86R&Bill=SB1707

Schlesinger, T. (2018). Decriminalizing racialized youth through juvenile diversion. *The Future of Children*, *28*(1), 59–82. http://pvamu.idm.oclc.org/login?url=https://search.ebscohost.com/login.aspx?direct=true&db=edsjsr&AN=edsjsr.26641547

Scott, E. S. (2013). Miller v. Alabama and the (past and) future of juvenile crime regulation. *Law & Inequality*, *31*, 535.

Sharkey, P., Schwartz, A. E., Ellen, I. G., & Lacoe, J. (2014). High stakes in the classroom, high stakes on the street: The effects of community violence on student's standardized test performance. *Sociological Science*, *1*, 199.

Sickmund, M., & Puzzanchera, C. (2014). *Juvenile offenders and victims: 2014 national report*. Pittsburgh, PA: National Center for Juvenile Justice.
Tanenhaus, D. S. (2004). *Juvenile justice in the making*. Oxford University Press.
Ttofi, M. M., & Farrington, D. P. (2011). Effectiveness of school-based programs to reduce bullying: A systematic and meta-analytic review. *Journal of Experimental Criminology*, *7*(1), 27–56.
U.S. Department of Education. (2014). *Indicators of school crime and safety, 2014*. Washington, DC: National Center for Education Statistics, Institute of Education Services.
Wald, J., & Losen, D. J. (2003). Defining and redirecting a school-to-prison pipeline. *New Directions for Youth Development*, *2003*(99), 9–15.
Walker, S. C., & Herting, J. R. (2020). The impact of pretrial juvenile detention on 12-month recidivism: A matched comparison study. *Crime & Delinquency*, *66*(13–14), 1865–1887. https://doi.org/10.1177/0011128720926115
Wilson, S. J., & Lipsey, M. W. (2007). School-based interventions for aggressive and disruptive behavior: Update of a meta-analysis. *American Journal of Preventive Medicine*, *33*(2), S130–S143.

16

AT THE BREAKING POINT

The Impact of Mass Incarceration on Families

Deirdre Caputo-Levine and Diamond Guitar-Judd

LEARNING OUTCOMES:

Upon successful completion of this chapter, students will be able to:

1 Identify the impacts of mass incarceration on families.
2 Describe the ways in which race, ethnicity, social class, place, and age can shape individuals' experiences of mass incarceration.

Imagine moving to a foreign country and being expected to know everything about that country's customs, culture, laws, and language the minute your feet hit the ground. Family members of system-involved individuals go through this as they adapt to the carceral system. During the era of mass incarceration, the carceral system has emerged as a social structural force shaping family life in the United States. A recent survey (Enns et al., 2019) found that 45% of Americans have had an immediate family member who was incarcerated in jail or prison, and approximately 14% reported that the immediate family member was imprisoned for more than one year. Mass incarceration imposes many costs on system-involved families, including the loss of relationships, stigma, isolation, increased poverty risk, and a higher likelihood of experiencing chronic health conditions. These collateral costs are distributed along intersections of inequality.

In this chapter, we utilize an intersectional approach to explore how the family experience of mass incarceration is shaped by factors such as race, social class, and place. In addition, the chapter will incorporate a discussion of the lived experience of family member incarceration within Idaho, a state dominated by rural communities and small cities. One of the co-authors, Diamond Guitar-Judd, a system-involved wife and mother, has been instrumental in developing a support group for families in Idaho dealing with incarceration.

The Carceral State and Mass Incarceration

The carceral state is the set of practices and institutions focused on communities seen as problematic (Gottschalk, 2015; Schoenfeld, 2018). The prisons and jails are only the most

DOI: 10.4324/9781003274292-21

visible part of a carceral state that includes courts, prisons, jails, community corrections, juvenile justice, and police officials involved in state-level social control (Gottschalk, 2015; Schoenfeld, 2018). The operations of all levels of the carceral state impact family life.

Aspects of the carceral state preexisted the era of mass incarceration, such as institutions for people designated as "defective" and other facilities associated with the Eugenic Movement, and the public mental hospitals used to house problematic populations (Harcourt, 2010). Mass incarceration is the *process* that shifted the mode of action of the carceral state to the penal system. It does so by acting upon the bodies of individuals who are part of the problem population. In that sense, mass incarceration is also a *set of experiences* that individuals, families, and communities have as they negotiate the machinery of the carceral state. These experiences are shaped by race, social class, gender, and place.

What Is Intersectionality? Why Is It Important?

Intersectionality is a theoretical perspective and analytical tool which originated in the lived experiences of Black women who were activists and scholars (Carbado et al., 2013; Hill Collins and Bilge, 2016). Scholars often use intersectional approaches to study how aspects of social identities such as race, gender, social class, disability, and sexuality shape individual and group experiences of inequality within institutions. The carceral state has involved the increasing use of mechanisms of punishment and the use of prison to manage marginalized populations. As such, the families of system-involved people are likely to experience oppression along multiple axes of their identities. For example, an African American child living in the South Bronx with an incarcerated father shares some common experiences with a Shoshonean grandmother caring for her grandchildren on the Fort Hall reservation while her daughter is imprisoned. However, they face particular challenges because of race, age, and their communities' location.

As a framework of analysis, intersectionality requires us to recognize that aspects of individuals' identities may act as a disadvantage or an advantage. System-involved families may experience "intersectional invisibility" (Purdie-Vaughns and Eibach, 2008) when their identities do not match those of the "prototypical members" of their identity groups. For example, people impacted by mass incarceration are often understood as men under correctional supervision. As a result, the experiences of partners, children, and other family members of incarcerated persons have often vanished from view within both official and activist discourses. Intersectional invisibility can affect access to resources and services.

The Intersectionality of Incarcerated Families

The dynamics of mass incarceration are inherently intersectional. Mass incarceration is structured in ways that draw from communities based on race, ethnicity, social class, and place. In the 1980s and the 1990s, mass incarceration as a process and an experience was concentrated in working class and poor urban communities, and among young Black men (Travis et al., 2014). The concentration of incarceration in urban communities of color skewed the demographics of the prison and destabilized communities (Clear, 2007). In 2017, even after declining Black and Hispanic incarceration rates, these communities were significantly overrepresented within the state and federal systems (Gramlich, 2019). Although the number of Native Americans incarcerated is small, Native communities have experienced higher rates of incarceration in comparison to racial groups other than African Americans (Carson, 2021).

For much of the era of mass incarceration, scholars have envisioned rural communities as sites of prison building rather than incarcerated persons' home communities (see King et al. (2004) for example). However, Eason et al. (2017) point to the importance of rural counties as communities that prisons draw from, as well as locations of prisons. The geographic dynamics of mass incarceration have been shifting since incarceration rates peaked in 2009. In a comparison of disaggregated incarceration rates for 38 states, Becket and Beach (2021) found that the overall decline masked an increase in incarceration rates in rural counties. The shift in incarceration has been driven by changes in prosecution, as rural and suburban prosecutors were more likely to file cases as felonies than urban prosecutors (Pfaff, 2018). Jails in rural counties in Southern, Midwestern, and Western states have been identified as key drivers of mass incarceration (Vera Institute, 2017). Although often majority white, rural communities have become increasingly diverse; in 2020, 24% of rural residents were people of color (Rowlands and Love, 2021). Simes (2018) has also identified small cities as sites in which mass incarceration has become concentrated.

Rural communities and small cities present particular challenges for families of system-involved individuals. These communities have higher levels of acquaintance density – because of community size, members are more likely to know each other, facilitating the spread of discrediting information. This can compound the experience of stigma experienced by family members (Easterling and Feldmeyer, 2017). Accessing services can be difficult in small cities and rural environments and may necessitate significant travel.

The experience of having an incarcerated parent is mediated by factors that include race, ethnicity, and social class. Longitudinal analyses have found racial disparities in exposure to the incarceration of family members – with Black children born in 1990 having approximately eight times the risk of experiencing paternal incarceration than white children born in 1990 (Wakefield and Wildeman, 2011). A recent analysis found that African American children (11%) are almost twice as likely as white children (6%) and Latinx children (6.4%) to have a parent who is incarcerated (Cramer et al., 2017). Social class is influential in shaping children's exposure to family member imprisonment. Children whose families are living in poverty (12.5%) are more than three times as likely to have a parent incarcerated as children living in families that have incomes of at least twice the poverty level (3.9%) (Cramer et al., 2017).

Intersectional invisibility plays a key role in structuring the experience of system-involved families within Native American communities. Native communities consistently have the second highest incarceration rate in state and federal prisons (BJS, 2021b). Because Native communities are small, the raw numbers of Native people incarcerated are small. Thus, there are few statistics (Wang, 2021) and relatively little research on the impact of mass incarceration in Native communities. Native women are significantly overrepresented in the incarcerated population (Wang, 2021); this is problematic due to the significant impact of maternal incarceration on families. A study of risk and protective factors experienced by a sample of Alaska Native/American Indian and non-Native children in Alaska found that the Native children were more likely to experience parental incarceration (Austin et al., 2020). System-impacted families in Native communities may not have access to the same degree of assistance, particularly mental health services (Turanovic and Rodriguez, 2017), as other families.

How Mass Incarceration Has Shaped Family Life

The families of people who are system-involved are exposed to many severe strains. When Diamond, a co-author of the chapter, was thrown into the system in Idaho ten years ago, she had no clue what it meant.

> Before we met, my now-husband had already served 14 years between incarceration and community supervision. He had tried to warn me about how hard and backward things were, but I thought he was exaggerating. It wasn't until he received a technical violation and was sent back to prison that I began to understand that he had sugarcoated what being system-involved was like. After he was taken into custody by his supervising officer, I asked the officer what I needed to do. The answer I was given made my skin crawl, "Walk away now! He's a waste of skin and air." When I didn't walk away, this same supervising officer called me derogatory names, even accusing me of criminal activity. After that encounter, I made it my mission to make sure no other human would feel as lost and disrespected by an employee of the criminal justice system.

In 2014, Diamond worked with Denise Tyler, another system-impacted family member, to develop a fact-based support service for families. Over the last eight years, Diamond and the other participants in the group have supported more than 700 system-impacted family members, made reliable contacts within the Idaho Department of Corrections, held a town hall meeting with criminal justice employees, and mentored dozens of incarcerated citizens. Unfortunately, reoccurring themes have continued to pop up during their work with incarcerated people and their families. Four of the most concerning are (1) a lack of transparency within the Department of Corrections, (2) inconsistent and callous practices among department staff, (3) inadequate medical and mental health care, and (4) support systems that do not promote rehabilitation. Each of these concerns leads to prison work for family members.

Prison Work

Many of the strains that Diamond identifies are part of what Arditti et al. (2021) classifies as "prison work." Prison work is a form of labor, usually performed by women who care for incarcerated family members or people in reentry and reintegration. This labor occurs on top of childcare and other work that family members perform. It can involve arranging visits to jail or prison, negotiating relationships with children for incarcerated persons, trying to keep track of a loved one's physical and mental health care needs and treatment, and giving rides to parole or probation appointments. In Idaho, the family members who were part of Diamond's support group have taken on the responsibility for monitoring their family member's physical and mental health care. Under Corizon, the IDOC's prior health care provider, it was not uncommon for requests for medical appointments to go ignored for weeks. Even with medical power of attorney and emergency contact forms filled with the department, medical providers and department staff often refuse to communicate with external support systems. When the IDOC changed providers, the new provider scrambled to catch up because records were missing and incomplete. This lack of medical care is causing incarcerated individuals to suffer for years, only to be adequately taken care of after release and after the medical issues have caused severe problems.

Prison work can also be understood more broadly as the "emotional costs" of caring for an incarcerated person (Arditti et al., 2021). Mothers and grandparents must decide how much contact children should have with incarcerated parents based on children's needs and preferences. Prison work also involves walking a fine line to maintain healthy boundaries with an incarcerated person. Diamond argues that this consists of providing support in terms of commissary and advocating for their loved ones, but also not overreaching. Negotiating and maintaining boundaries is a critical element of prison work. She recommends against frequently calling correctional facilities to fix all of a loved one's issues, instead focusing on enabling them to use the available procedures to address concerns and issues that they are having. By learning to use these procedures, they learn conflict management skills, which gives them a foundation for navigating the outside world. It also gives them the building blocks needed to become independent and self-sufficient, which is required to make appointments, apply for jobs and housing, and handle the other everyday life stressors. Monetary support can be problematic. Sending commissary money can cut into a family's budget, making it hard to get through the month. There are also implications for the incarcerated person who may experience violence if others see them as having money or who may experience relapse if they can purchase drugs.

Prison work does not stop when family members leave the prison or jail. People returning from prison can bring the institution home with them in the form of the carceral habitus (Caputo-Levine, 2013), a set of ways of being adapted to the necessities of the carceral environment and are resistant to change. These behaviors, which include snap responses to perceived disrespect and a need to exert control, can lead to conflict within the family and community. Additionally, people who are in the process of reintegration may be fearful and may have difficulty navigating day-to-day interactions. Family members often have to assist the individual and mediate interactions.

Uncertainty

Diamond identifies uncertainty as an important factor shaping the experiences of the people participating in her support group. In Idaho, this starts at sentencing as a felony conviction results in a unified sentence consisting of a fixed and indeterminate time frame. The incarcerated person can be granted parole and given a tentative release date, subject to class completion and approval of a parole plan. This process has been complicated for people who are incarcerated in the out-of-state facility, as the facility case managers are confused about procedures for the Idaho parole hearings, and case managers did not complete the required planning packets before hearings. In addition, family members have contacted Diamond's support group for information on transitional housing and employment as case managers had not provided it. As a result, family members are stressed because they do not know when their loved ones are returning home and cannot make adequate plans.

When family members are released to community supervision, the conditions can be a continued source of stress. One may assume that the rules of parole supervision are clear-cut, with consistent definitions. However, this is not the case. For example, one common special condition of parole in Idaho is that a parolee is not to enter an intimate relationship without permission from their supervising officer. Unfortunately, some supervising officers can take this rule to an extreme, interpreting it to forbid spending unsupervised time with a current spouse or having children within a pre-approved established relationship. Those questioning this interpretation can be threatened with or receive a parole violation. This same type of social control may be used when an impacted individual questions why the supervising officer is not following department policies that are publicly accessible. The level of uncertainty experienced by family members adds to the strains caused by single-parenting and the lower income levels experienced by mothers with incarcerated partners (Craigie, 2021).

Stigma

One of the most significant stresses experienced by families is "courtesy stigma," (DeShay et al., 2021) which results from being associated with an individual who is understood as bearing a stigmatized characteristic such as a criminal conviction. Stigma is discomfort or shame that leads to fear and self-isolation. This stigma affects family members in several ways. First, it can lead to family members receiving negative labels that can impact access to resources and potentially inhibit the development of friendships and other social networks. This makes mutual aid groups for family members particularly important. Stigma can lead family members to experience disenfranchised grief (Arditti, 2012) as the relationship with the incarcerated person changes and may be severed. Because of the social disapproval accompanying incarceration, it can be challenging to reach out and share this loss experience with others. There are also no grieving rituals recognizing family members' grief and helping them mark the transition. The isolation that accompanies disenfranchised grief compounds the trauma associated with family member incarceration. The trauma of losing a family member to incarceration is complicated by the fact family members are experiencing "ambiguous loss" (Arditti, 2005). The incarcerated individual is not present, but they are not wholly absent. Family members can see them, but only by visiting jail or prison – sites that can be frightening and involve shame. Family members can communicate via phone calls and letters, but these can be expensive and may not be private. There is also no way of predicting how the situation will resolve, in what state the loved one will return. The ambiguity is problematic because it halts coping and complicates decision-making (Boss, 2007), freezing the relationship. Relationships may wither and die, even when all parties wish for the relationship to continue.

Children's Experiences

In 2016, 2.04% of children under the age of 18 had at least one parent incarcerated in state or federal prison (Maruschak, 2021). On a daily basis, approximately 2.7 million children have a parent incarcerated in prison or jail (Ghandnoosh et al., 2021). These numbers do not include children with family members under the supervision of community corrections or the juvenile court or who have other family members incarcerated in jail or prison. In addition, there is evidence that the incarceration of parents increases the imprisonment of children as adults (Burgess-Proctor et al., 2016). Burgess-Proctor et al. (2016) found this relationship to be most robust for maternal incarceration. This is of particular concern as the incarceration rate of women has increased by more than 525% between 1980 and 2020 (Sentencing Project, 2023). In addition, the ten states with the highest female incarceration rates have higher proportions of rural populations, and rural populations have difficulty accessing services.

Family member incarceration has been found to function as an adverse childhood experience (ACE). ACEs are traumatic experiences including child maltreatment and neglect and family member incarceration that have been associated with long-term adverse outcomes, including mental health problems, chronic physical illnesses, chemical dependency, and incarceration (Boullier and Blair, 2018; Finkelhor, 2020). The posited connection between experiences and outcomes is "toxic stress," a state of sympathetic nervous system overactivity that leads the body to respond as if it is constantly under threat (Boullier and Blair, 2018). Experiencing ACES impacts a child's ability to feel secure in their environment and successfully bond with caregivers. ACES that lead to the loss of the relationship with a parent can increase a child's "vulnerability to later adversity" (Arditti, 2012, 184). ACES are intersectional in nature, with ACE scores related to race, gender, and social class (Mersky et al., 2021). Thus, the children at the highest risk for exposure to family incarceration are also at elevated risk for other ACES.

The incarceration of family members triggers a snowball effect of disadvantage that operates on individual and group levels. Parental imprisonment has negative impacts across multiple aspects of life. Nesmith and Ruhland (2008) found that children who experienced parental incarceration felt the need to manage the emotions of stressed caregivers. The children took on additional responsibilities in the home and shared more adult worries about their caregiver, the household, and the well-being of the incarcerated parent. For some children, this experience approached "adultification," in which children undertake roles and responsibilities outside the norms of contemporary understandings of childhood (Burton, 2007). School officials may not understand the behavior of children who experience adultification, interpreting it as disrespectful or aggressive to adults and leading to conflict in educational settings (Burton, 2007). Studies of children who have incarcerated siblings are relatively rare, but Meek (2008) found that children reported that they worried about their brothers and worried that teachers would find out about their siblings' being in prison. Children were concerned about labeling, a fear that may not be misplaced given Dalliare et al.'s findings (2010) that teachers' knowledge of a student's incarceration can lead to decreased expectations. There is evidence that parental incarceration is associated with an increased risk of depression and alcohol abuse, lower levels of education, and reduced earning potential through young adulthood (Mears and Siennick, 2016). These findings are potentially mediated by childhood experiences of family hardship related to parental incarceration (Foster and Hagen, 2015). Foster and Hagen (2015) argue that the state policies of neglect interact with experiences of parental incarceration to produce social exclusion. They point to the relationship between paternal incarceration and low educational attainment levels among children, leading to adverse intergenerational outcomes such as incarceration in the second generation. Adverse intergenerational outcomes may also be tied to intergenerational trauma, especially within the context of intersections of oppression.

Mass Incarceration and Intergenerational Trauma

The concept of intergenerational trauma connects mass incarceration as a process and an experience to the histories of colonization, genocide, and slavery within the United States. Intergenerational or historical trauma is used to describe a "cumulative emotional and psychological wounding, over the lifespan and across generations, emanating from massive group trauma experiences" (Brave Heart, 2003, 7). It is the result of a "dislocation… from land, families, and communities" (Dennison et al., 2014, 1093). Intergenerational trauma draws from the experiences of Holocaust survivors (Wiseman et al., 2006), Native

American communities (Brave Heart, 2003), and Indigenous communities in Australia (Dennison et al., 2014, 1093).

The analogy we present is far from perfect. However, there are some potentially valuable parallels, and we hope it stimulates discussion. In BIPOC communities, mass incarceration may, as a set of experiences, have had a similar impact to the residential school era in Native American communities (Barker et al., 2019; Wilk et al., 2017). The residential schools in the United States and Canada removed Native American children from their families and communities in an attempt to assimilate the children into white social norms (Woolford, 2015). The curricula were intended to teach children how to engage in farming and domestic labor. Children were not allowed to speak their language or engage in cultural ceremonies. In the United States, the schools operated between 1878 and 1934, and in Canada, the last school closed in the 1990s. The state removed multiple generations of Native children from their families and communities. Children experienced a range of traumas, including physical and sexual abuse as well as spiritual abuse (Wilk et al., 2017). The trauma then followed children as they grew and returned to their homes.

Mass incarceration has been concentrated among young people of color, particularly those from African American and Native American communities, who return to their communities with earlier trauma experiences compounded by the prison experience. This is then transmitted to families and children through a combination of strain, social stigma, and state policies of neglect. In both cases, ongoing intergenerational effects have been documented (Barker et al., 2019; Foster and Hagan, 2015; Wilk et al., 2017). In African–American and Native American communities, the experiences of mass incarceration are tied to the experiences of slavery, displacement, and genocide.

Conclusion

As both a process and an experience, mass incarceration has shaped the lives of families in the United States. The impacts of family member incarceration are destabilizing and long-lasting. Diamond's summation of her experiences with the carceral state expresses this.

> When I started this journey almost ten years ago, it was the most terrifying thing I had ever been through. As I learned the ins and outs of the system, I realized that I never wanted anyone to feel like I did for the first few months. Although my husband has completed his sentence, we are both still dealing with the emotional and mental side effects of his time served. This journey is one that I wouldn't wish on anyone because it will make or break you, which is why I will never stop educating others on the "invisible" sides of incarceration.

This "make or break" experience and the labor that comes with it are not evenly distributed throughout the population. Although the dynamics of mass incarceration are in flux, the intersectional nature of mass incarceration continues. The experience of family member incarceration is shaped by race, gender, social class, and geographical location. Families impacted by the carceral system are generally from marginalized social groups. Diamond argues that incarcerated persons, returning citizens, and their families start in a ditch and have to dig their way out with only a spoon. Returning citizens bring their prison experiences home, causing strains and traumas to family members. Family members expend precious resources engaging in prison work and providing care for their loved ones before and after incarceration. Families are left under-resourced and stressed, with children at increased risk for participation in juvenile delinquency, thus setting the stage for a new cycle of mass incarceration.

Mass incarceration is concentrated among working-class African American and Native American communities, and it impacts the ability of these stressed communities to buffer members from strains. Moreover, in these communities, the lived experience of the carceral state adds layers to the experiences of discrimination, colonization, genocide, and assimilation that communities of color have experienced, leading to the intergenerational transmission of trauma. Trauma that is rooted in experiences related to race, incarceration has been found to compound trauma that results from other stressors such as poverty, loss of a parent, or difficulty in school (Aguiar and Halseth, 2015).

Intervention in the cycle of mass incarceration is possible. However, it requires an understanding of the intersectional nature of the impact of mass incarceration on families. Research into the needs of impacted families has the potential to identify ways to provide support for families and interrupt the intergenerational transmission of adverse outcomes. However, this research must be conducted in ways that value the cultural knowledge and strength of impacted families. Townsend et al. (2019) point to the importance of empowering families by using community-based participatory research (CBPR), a methodology that engages families in planning and conducting research. CBPR is rooted in principles of intersectionality and capacity building (Muhammad et al., 2018). This approach allows participants to identify community needs, strengths, and problems that need to be addressed and researchers to learn about the frameworks of necessity that the participants face. More importantly, CBPR creates a set of procedures which can be used to develop a respectful dialogue between researchers and community members.

Discussion Questions:

1. How do categories such as race, ethnicity, social class, and place shape the way that a family experiences mass incarceration? Provide a concrete example of a family (use an example from a film or reading or have the students develop a hypothetical family) and discuss how the members of the family experience their intersectionality.
2. What interventions might help to decrease the likelihood of intergenerational transmission of incarceration? (Ask the students to think about different levels – individual, family, community, and society.)

Works Cited

Aguiar, W., & Halseth, R. (2015). *Aboriginal Peoples Historic Trauma: The Processes of Intergenerational Transmission*. National Collaborating Centre for Aboriginal Health. https://www.ccnsa-nccah.ca/Publications/Lists/Publications/Attachments/142/2015-04-28-AguiarHalseth-RPT-IntergenTraumaHistory-EN-Web.pdf.

Arditti, J. A. (2005). Families and Incarceration: An Ecological Approach. *Families in Society, 86*(2), 251–260.

Arditti, J. A. (2012). Child Trauma Within the Context of Parental Incarceration: A Family Process Perspective. *Journal of Family Theory & Review*, *4*(3), 181–219.

Arditti, J. A., McGregor, C., Dennison, S., Johnson, S., & Besemer, K. (2021). Maternal Mediation in the Context of Fathers' Incarceration and Reentry. *Family Relations: An Interdisciplinary Journal of Applied Family Science*, *70*(2), 146–161.

Austin, A. E., Gottsfredson, N. C., Marshall, S. W., Halpern, C. T., Zolotor, A. J., Parrish, J. W., & Shanahan, M. E. (2020). Heterogeneity in Risk and Protection Among Alaska Native/American Indian and Non-Native Children. *Prevention Science*, *21*(1), 86–97.

Barker, B., Sedgemore, K., Tourangeau, M., Lagimodiere, L., Milloy, J., Dong, H., DeBeck, K. (2019). Intergenerational Trauma: The Relationship Between Residential Schools & The Child Welfare System Among Young People Who Use Drugs in Vancouver Canada. *Journal of Adolescent Health*, *65*(2), 248–254. DOI: 10.1016/j.jadohealth.2019.01.022.

Beckett, K., & Beach, L. (2021). The Place of Punishment in Twenty-First-Century America: Understanding the Persistence of Mass Incarceration. *Law & Social Inquiry*, *46*(1), 1–31.

Boss, P. (2007). Ambiguous Loss Theory: Challenges for Scholars and Practitioners. *Family Relations*, *56*(2), 105–110.

Bouillier, M. & Blair, M. (2018). Adverse Childhood Experiences. *Paediatrics and Child Health*, *28*(3), 132–136.

Brave Heart, M. Y. H. (2003). The Historical Trauma Response Among Natives and Its Relationship with Substance Abuse: A Lakota Illustration. *Journal of Psychoactive Drugs*, *35*(1), 7–13. DOI: 10.1080/02791072.2003.10399988.

Burgess-Proctor, A., Hurbner, B., & Durso, J. M. (2016). Comparing the Effects of Maternal and Paternal Incarceration on Adult Daughters' and Sons' Criminal Justice System Involvement: A Gendered Pathways Analysis. *Criminal Justice and Behavior*, *43*(8), 1034–1055.

Burton, L. (2007). Childhood Adultification in Economically Disadvantaged Families: A Conceptual Model. *Family Relations*, *56*(4), 329–345. DOI: 10.1111/j.1741-3729.2007.00463.x.

Caputo-Levine, D. (2013). The Yard Face: The Contributions of Inmate Interpersonal Violence to the Carceral Habitus. *Ethnography, 14*(2), 165–185.

Carbado, D., Crenshaw, K. W., Mays, V. M., & Tomlinson, B. (2013). Intersectionality: Mapping the Movements of a Theory. *Du Bois Review*, *10*(2), 303–312.

Carson, E. A. (2021). *Prisoners in 2020 – Statistical Tables*. Washington, DC: Bureau of Justice Statistics.

Clear, T. R. (2007). *Imprisoning Communities: How Mass Incarceration Makes Disadvantaged Neighborhoods Worse*. New York: Oxford University Press.

Craigie, T. A. (2021). Men's Incarceration and Women's Labor Market Outcomes. *Feminist Economics*, *27*(4), 1–28. DOI: 10.1080/13545701.2021.1942510.

Cramer, L., Goff, M., Peterson, B., & Sandstrom, H. (2017). *Parent-Child Visiting Practices in Prisons and Jails*. Washington, DC: Urban Institute.

Dallaire, D., Ciccone, A., & Wilson, L. (2010). Teachers' Experiences with and Expectations of Children with Incarcerated Parents. *Journal of Applied Developmental Psychology*, *31*(4), 281–290.

Dennison, S., Smallbone, H., Stewart, A., Freiberg, K., & Teague, R. (2014). 'MY LIFE IS SEPARATED': An Examination of The Challenges and Barriers to Parenting for Indigenous Fathers in Prison. *British Journal of Criminology*, *54*(6), 1089–1108. DOI: 10.1093/bjc/azu072.

DeShay, R., Vieraitis, L. M., Copes, H., Powell, Z. A., & Medrano, J. (2021). Managing Courtesy Stigma: Women and Relationships with Men in Prison. *Criminal Justice Studies*, *34*(3), 251–267.

Eason, J., Zucker, D. & Wildeman, C. (2017). Mass Imprisonment across the Rural-Urban Interface. *The Annals of the American Academy of Political and Social Science*, *672*(1), 202–216.

Easterling, B. A., & Feldmeyer, B. (2017). Race, Incarceration, and Motherhood: Spoiled Identity among Rural White Mothers in Prison. *The Prison Journal*, *97*(2), 143–165.

Enns, P., Yi, Y., Comfort, M., Goldman, A. W., Lee, H., Muller, C., Wakefield, S., Wang, E., & Wildeman, C. (2019). What Percentage of Americans Have Ever Had a Family Member Incarcerated? Evidence from the Family History of Incarceration Survey (FamHIS). *Socius: Sociological Research for a Dynamic World*, *5*(1), 1–45.

Finkelhor, D. (2020). Trends in Adverse Childhood Experiences (ACEs) in the United States. *Child Abuse & Neglect, 108*. DOI: 10.1016/j.chiabu.2020.104641.

Foster, H., & Hagen, J. (2015). Punishment Regimes and the Multilevel Effects of Parental Incarceration: Intergenerational, Intersectional, and Interinstitutional Models of Social Inequality and Systemic Exclusion. *Annual Review of Sociology, 41*, 135–158.

Ghandnoosh, N., Stammen, E., & Muhitch, K. (2021). *Parents in Prison*. Washington, DC: Sentencing Project.

Gottschalk, M. (2015). *Caught: The Prison State and the Lockdown of American Politics*. Princeton, NJ: Princeton University Press.

Gramlich, J. (2019). *The Gap between the Number of Blacks and Whites in Prison Is Shrinking*. Retrieved from https://www.pewresearch.org/fact-tank/2019/04/30/shrinking-gap-between-number-of-blacks-and-whites-in-prison.

Harcourt. B. (2010). Neoliberal Penality: A Brief Genealogy. *Theoretical Criminology, 14*(1), 74–92.

Hill Collins, P., & Bilge, S. (2016). *Intersectionality* (1st ed.). New York: Polity.

Kang-Brown, J., & Subramanian, R. (2017). *Out of Sight: The Growth of Jails in Rural America*. New York: Vera Institute.

King, R. S., Mauer, M., & Huling, T. (2004). An Analysis of the Economics of Prison Siting in Rural Communities. *Criminology & Public Policy, 3*(3), 453–480.

Maruschak, L. M., Bronson, J., & Alper, M. (2021). *Parents in Prison and Their Minor Children*. Washington, DC: Bureau of Justice Statistics.

Mears, D. P., & Siennick, S. E. (2016). Young Adult Outcomes and the Life-Course Penalties of Parental Incarceration. *Journal of Research in Crime and Delinquency, 53*(1), 3–35. DOI: 10.1177/0022427815592452.

Meek, R. (2008). Experiences of Younger Siblings of Young Men in Prison. *Children & Society, 22*(4), 265–277. DOI: 10.1111/j.1099-0860.2007.00108.x.

Mersky, J. P., Choi, C., Lee, C. P., & Janczewski, C. E. (2021). Disparities in Adverse Childhood Experiences by Race/Ethnicity, Gender, and Economic Status: Intersectional Analysis of a Nationally Representative Sample. *Child Abuse & Neglect, 117*. DOI: 10.1016/j.chiabu.2021.105066.

Monazzam, N., & Budd, K. (2023, April 3). Incarcerated Women and Girls. Sentencingproject.org. Retrieved April 25, 2023, from https://www.sentencingproject.org/fact-sheet/incarcerated-women-and-girls/

Muhammad, M., Garzón, C., Reyes, A., & The West Oakland Environmental Indicators Project. (2018). Understanding Contemporary Racism, Power, and Privilege and Their Impacts on CBPR. In N. Wallerstein, B. Duran, J. Oetzel, & M. Minkler (Eds.), *Community-Based Participatory Research for Health: Advancing Social and Health Equity* (pp. 47–59). San Francisco, CA: John Wiley & Sons, Inc.

Nesmith, A., & Ruhland, E. (2008). Children of Incarcerated Parents: Challenges and Resiliency, in Their Own Words. *Children and Youth Services Review, 30*(10), 1119–1130.

Pfaff, J. F. (2018). Criminal Punishment and the Politics of Place. *Fordham Urban Law Journal, 45*(2), 571–593.

Purdie-Vaughns, V., & Eibach, R. (2008). Intersectional Invisibility: The Distinctive Advantages and Disadvantages of Multiple Subordinate-Group Identities. *Sex Roles, 59*(5), 377–391.

Rowlands, D., & Love, H. (2021, September 28). Mapping *Rural* America's *Diversity* and *Demographic Change*. Brookings.edu. Retrieved April 25, 2023, from https://www.brookings.edu/blog/the-avenue/2021/09/28/mapping-rural-americas-diversity-and-demographic-change/

Schoenfeld, H. (2018). *Building the Prison State: Race and the Politics of Mass Incarceration*. Chicago, IL: University of Chicago Press.

Simes, J. (2017). Place and Punishment: The Spatial Context of Mass Incarceration. *Journal of Quantitative Criminology, 34*(2), 513–533.

Townsend, T. G., Kramer, K., & Hendy, G. A. (2019). Empowering Incarcerated Parents of Color and Their Families Using Community-Based Participatory Research. In J. M. Eddy &

J. Poehlmann-Tynan (Eds.), *Handbook on Children with Incarcerated Parents: Research, Policy, and Practice* (2nd ed., pp. 251–266). Cham: Springer Nature.
Travis, J., Western, B., & Redburn, S. (2014). *The Growth of Incarceration in the United States: Exploring Causes and Consequences*. Washington, DC: National Research Council.
Turanovic, J. J., & Rodriguez, N. (2017). Mental Health Service Needs in the Prison Boom: The Case of Children of Incarcerated Mothers. *Criminal Justice Policy Review*, *28*(5), 415–436.
Wakefield, S., & Wildeman, C. (2011). Mass Imprisonment and Racial Disparities in Childhood Behavioral Problems. *Criminology & Public Policy*, *10*(3), 793–817.
Wang, L. (2021). *The U.S. Criminal Justice System Disproportionately Hurts Native People: The Data, Visualized*. Retrieved from https://www.prisonpolicy.org/blog/2021/10/08/indigenous peoplesday/#:~:text=In%20jails%2C%20Native%20people%20had,was%20less%20than%20 one%20percent.
Wilk, P., Maltby, A., & Cooke, M. (2017). Residential Schools and the Effects on Indigenous Health and Well-Being in Canada—A Scoping Review. *Public Health Reviews*, *38*(8), 1–23. DOI: 10.1186/ s40985-017-0055-6.
Wiseman, H., Metzl, E., & Barber, J. P. (2006). Anger, Guilt, and Intergenerational Communication of Trauma in the Interpersonal Narratives of Second Generation Holocaust Survivors. *American Journal of Orthopsychiatry*, *76*(2), 176–184. DOI: 10.1037/0002-9432.76.2.176.
Woolford, A. (2015). *This Benevolent Experiment: Indigenous Boarding Schools, Genocide, and Redress in Canada and the United States*. Lincoln, NE: University of Nebraska Press.

17

REFLECTION

TRANSPORTED TO THE TROUBLED TEEN INDUSTRY

Heather E. Mooney

I first learned about youth rights (or the lack thereof) when I stayed at a runaway shelter in tenth grade. I wasn't so much homeless, as escaping domestic violence, and a household with parents who had co-occurring disorders. All I knew is that I didn't feel safe and couldn't stay at my friend's house after my mother threatened to charge my friend's mom with harboring a runaway. It wasn't always like this. Somewhere in my teen years things started shifting from the concerted cultivation of my suburban lifestyle, as I learned and questioned more about the world and my parents. The evolution of my curiosity and expression became "troubled" by high school. I was troubled because I was skipping classes, fighting with my parents, questioning authority, dressing differently, dying my hair, struggling with the deceptions and hypocrisy of this world, smoking cigarettes, and drinking alcohol. The social construction of my "troubles" was very much due to my social location (white, upper-middle class, cis female, queer) as friends in adulthood would laugh as I recanted my high school years stating from their social vantage point everything I went through was pretty "normal".

By the start of my junior year, I didn't go home much anymore, mostly crashing with older high school friends. This decision was the last straw for my parents. They were uncomfortable with me staying away, so in November they enticed me by offering my drivers license and instead, ambushed me at home with teen "escorts" (aka teen transporters). In a process that has been likened to legalized kidnapping, teens are woken up in their beds often around 3–5 am by two escorts who tell them they can take them the "easy way or the hard way" (read: restraints). I was told if I resisted further, they would handcuff me. My mother said "this is tough love" before the transporters pushed me into the minivan. It was clear there was no way to escape. This is when I realized I had no rights as a youth, as my parents signed me over to this ex-cop team who drove me literally kicking and screaming, across multiple state lines. The transporters told me nothing except how great my parents were and how this is the best for me as a "bad" kid. The involuntary "intervention" of transporting was traumatic, and I was never told where I was going, or for how long. There is no debriefing or processing of the transport, so I was just dropped off like a package to start the degradation ceremonies[1] of intake at a therapeutic boarding school (TBS).

DOI: 10.4324/9781003274292-22

Like others, this TBS was a behavior modification program, which started out with a few months of wilderness therapy before earning your way onto the secure campus full of year-round schooling, surveillance, and intensive (but mostly ineffective and troubling) group therapy. Such schools are a staple of the troubled teen industry (TTI), which also includes various private total institutions[2] like outdoor behavioral health (aka wilderness therapy) programs, residential treatment centers, religious academies, and rehabilitation (addiction/recovery) "ranches". Despite decades of concerning exposes and investigations, the industry has little regulation and no definitive number of youths who are involuntarily subjected to it. However, recent estimates of the "troubled teen" population exceed the number of juveniles held in public facilities nationally.

The intake process involved some of the worst humiliation and fear. I didn't know where I was exactly or if I'd ever see any of my friends back home again. The school conducted a strip search in this little wood shack out back on the property. I was on my period at the time, so I got to expose my nude body and my menses to all the staff, which was beyond mortifying as a young woman. It was a classic degradation ceremony, where you lost all your clothing (my prized silver vinyl pants!), identity, everything that you thought you knew about yourself was stripped away. They even dyed my bright traffic cone orange hair to brown (but it never did quite lose the orange hue in the right sunlight). I was assigned uniform wilderness wear and equipment that was regularly accounted for during daily shakedowns of all your belongings. For the next 16 months, I was under constant surveillance, rules, and regulations including strict dress codes. No sex (with self or others), no drugs (including caffeine), no violence (to self or others), no swearing, no TV, news, or internet (this was the late 1990s so cool kids had beepers not cell phones), no music or images that glorified breaking any of the rules. I confronted total powerlessness, and lack of rights as a child. I learned my body was the province of your parents, these institutions, those in authority, and the only place of sovereignty remained in the mind. Even, that you had to hang on to in the face of the four 12-hour long intensive secretive therapy workshops conducted with our groups essential to completing the program.

Having small comfort zones and being wildly vulnerable was integral to making it through. I learned acts of resistance, and how to lie to survive. In my subsequent research, I realized I adapted in the same ways incarcerated women did, buying in, bluffing, or flying under the radar. I lived the Thomas Theorem – what people perceive to be true (even if it isn't) will be real in its consequences. My mother was fully convinced I was sexually active (because I thought safe sex was sweet and carried condoms around, really for friends). Counselors fixated on that – most girls were assumed to be victims of sexual assault/abuse and forced to discuss this as if it were the ultimate reason for their delinquency. Pestered for months by counselors, I gave in and made up a story about losing my virginity, not ready but forced and cried over it and then finally the counselors and my mother were satisfied. Parents' word was regarded as the gospel; besides, staff knew who was paying the bills there and the customer was always right. Our program was based on techniques that came from CEDU[3] (a founding TBS in the TTI), inspired by Synanon, known for its controversial "attack therapy". This type of group therapy incorporates confrontational interactions between staff and students, often where verbal abuse or humiliation is used. TBSs fit the standards of totalistic teen treatment, this programmatic framework often mitigates or conflicts with building appropriate therapeutic alliances with staff or even peers since you were instructed to tell on yourselves and others.

Academics and friends were my respite from the therapy, and I was fortunate to have some outstanding teachers and new friends, who provided some of the greatest insights, inspiration, and human moments throughout the program. It was these connections and the friends I made there that made all the difference to me. Informally in some of the girls' dorms, I'd have late night discussions with my roommates (between night guard checks) where we confided in one another while enjoying our pooled junk food from the weekly concessions closet. Here we had the real group therapy sessions, about emerging and current sexuality in meaningful and deep ways. I learned that pretty much everyone masturbated, had siblings or cousins experiment sexually with them, or more severe forms of sexual abuse or assault by family, close friends, or acquaintances. Here we supported one another, took care to see them, listened, laughed, cried, and loved one another as we were. I've never known people so different yet similar, openly, fiercely exposed in my life.

Our program, like the rest of the TTI, taught conformity and compliance. I was not subjected to over-prescription of pills, but many were. Therapy was experienced quite contentiously and controlling for most students. Girls were punished more harshly and shamed. Long-term coping skills for managing mental health and substance abuse were lacking. Like Elliot Currie's work on troubled middle class youth's experiences in treatment programs, I found the pejorative assumption (that I was the problem), reigned in our program (2005). Currie's book "Road to Whatever" pointed out the larger social context, family structures, and social forces affecting the teens were constantly disregarded or downplayed, and they were forced to fight for their own agency in a system that pathologized any resistance (2005). Therapy focused on me as the sole problem in my family, not my parents, not that they should have divorced then (it took another fraught ten years to happen) nor was the treatment modalities or facility questioned. I never received a full psychological evaluation nor diagnosis to be admitted, in fact the first one I took was only a few years ago. I learned that success was more about my performance of upper-middle class, whiteness, feminine norms and ensuring I'd complete high school in a way that didn't disrupt my classed destiny of college.

The experience of attending a TBS, while nicer in amenities, was psychologically still experienced as the pains of imprisonment. The biggest difference is the lack of collateral consequences and a high school degree, which maintained my class and race privilege by obscuring my deviant past. Aftercare was a joke, and a plan to mitigate regression once back home fell apart within a few months. I nearly instantly moved out on my own, dropped out of the college selected for me, and started my own gap year, all I wanted was pleasure and freedom. Others also struggled: not long after graduating, my first friend (Jake) committed suicide by shooting himself. We had gone through wilderness together and he was a smart, sweet, and sensitive guy, who made drugs from his chemistry knowledge and had some deeply disturbing family dynamics. I feel like the program failed him. Sadly, from then on, it became a regular bulletin appearing unannounced. With the advent of social media, I was able to join an alumni group for my reform school, as I like to refer to it. Then as Ashley, another attendee shared it, was "just like crazy" that so many people kept passing away: "I just keep seeing the [web] page with like RIP, RIP, RIP." Essentially, every other year for the last 22 years since I went to reform school, peers keep passing away, mostly from drug overdoses or suicide. It breaks my heart every time and is the reason I study this topic.

Once you experience the total loss of autonomy, individuality, and rights by being remanded to a total institution, there's an understanding and instant connection to anyone else who has experienced that as well. It shifts your consciousness and connection to others. I and other attendees find that we are very sensitive to power dynamics and any infringement on our rights. I found solidarity and understanding with convict criminologists, and as of late with scholar survivors of coercive confinement as we finally published initial findings of our research on the TTI. The Breaking Code Silence movement proliferated in 2020, with Paris Hilton and many TTI survivors speaking out and actively working to create legislative changes. While TTI attendees remain a hidden population, this social movement is creating a groundswell of individuals coming forward with testimony, research, and advocacy for industry accountability. Now called Unsilenced, this non-profit "the voice of youth rights", introduced federal legislation in 2022 to stop institutional child abuse. But challenging a profitable and unregulated industry, especially for marginalized groups, will require an immense cultural and political shift. Not only does the United States remain the only industrialized nation to not ratify the United Nations Convention on the Rights of the Child (due to dominant religious and political forces), but it also remains one of the only places in the world that will sentence youth to lifelong imprisonment. The deeply entrenched culture of punishment and exclusion for "incorrigible" youth across any social locations in the United States remains a formidable obstacle in advancing youth justice.

Notes

1 Degradation ceremonies are processes by which individuals are stripped of their identity for resocialization; in this case of initiation to a total institution also to make youth more accepting of external control (Garfinkel 1956).

2 TTI facilities embody the four major characteristics of a total institution. First, youth are totally dependent on the facility for their livelihood (work, eating, and sleeping). Second, youth live completely within the facility and in constant intimate company of others. Third, teens are always supervised and on regimented schedules. Finally, everything youth engage in is to fulfill the mission of the institution, i.e., reform problem teens (Goffman 1961).

3 CEDU Educational Services (1967–2005) was founded by a former Synanon member, inspired many TTI program spin offs and "is widely credited with founding the private therapeutic schools industry" (Rosen 2021, p. 90).

References

Currie, Elliott. (2005). *The Road to Whatever: Middle-class culture and the crisis of adolescence*. New York: Macmillan.

Garfinkel, Harold. (1956). "Conditions of successful degradation ceremonies." *American Journal of Sociology*, *61*(5), 420–424.

Goffman, Erving. (1961). *Asylums: Essays on the Social Situation of Mental Patients and Other Inmates*. Garden City, NY: Anchor.

Rosen, Kenneth. (2021). *Troubled: The Failed Promise of American's Behavioral Treatment Programs*. New York: Little A.

18

REFLECTION

MUSINGS ON SCHOOL COMMUNITIES, INFORMATION EVASION, AND THE CHILDREN OF INCARCERATED PARENTS

LeAnna T. Luney and Maya T. Luney-Ballew

A federal judge convicted our father of armed bank robbery when we were six-years and five-years old, and our baby sister one-year old (Luney, 2019). Our reflection contributes to nuanced frameworks of mapping the effects of parental incarceration, which involve intergenerational, intersectional, and interinstitutional (Foster & Hagan, 2015; Giordano et al., 2019) approaches. Specifically, our collective narrative[1] on information evasion (IE) propels discourse on the stigma of parental incarceration (Murray et al., 2012; Siegel & Luther, 2019; Turney & Goodsell, 2018), and the social exclusion children face when a parent is imprisoned (Cochran et al., 2018; Eddy & Poehlmann-Tynan, 2019; Johnson & Easterling, 2012). IE occurs when we avoid sharing vital information with dependents – the children of incarcerated parents, in this case – that impacts their psychosocial sustainability and survival. We use IE to conceptualize the harmful impact that children withstand when adults exclude them from life altering conversations, decisions, and actions. We demonstrate how children with incarcerated parents process trauma within school communities and a culture of silence and stigma.

Through storytelling, intersectional analysis, and sisterhood, we share our unique and collective narrative as two Black womxn and femmes who grew up in a rural and predominantly white school system in the (physical) absence of our incarcerated father. We call school practitioners to implement abolitionist teaching and scholars to incorporate storytelling on the educational, psychosocial, and emotional lifeworlds of children with incarcerated parents. In sharing our experiences with IE, we hope to accentuate the minutiae of mass incarceration and how we – and others – survive its impact.

Information Evasion *Writ Large*: Silence, Stigma, and Social Cues and Community Customs

Adult Silence

Colloquially, we were positioned to "stay in a child's place." We were not afforded the privilege of asking questions, making our own decisions, operating with full autonomy, or

DOI: 10.4324/9781003274292-23

accessing pivotal information regarding us or the adults in our lives. As a result, we were left uninformed and confused as our father moved through the federal penal system during the swell of privatized prisons in the late 1990s and early 2000s. All we had known was he was there, then gone. We were lost in the shuffle of whispering adults who fell silent in our presence, impromptu sleepovers at elders' and community members' homes, and erratic daily operations, which were emblems of our family and community moving in secrecy to adjust to the loss of a social deity.

I was in preschool when our dad first disappeared. I remember a family friend dropping us off at school and when we got into the gym, the son of another family friend, from the same government housing complex, eagerly met us at the door with a newspaper. I found it strange that he held a newspaper in his hand because it was my understanding that newspapers were reserved for the elderly. This boy was known for being in grown folks' business and that particular day would be nothing different. As he approached the group of us walking in, he eyed my sister and I, making it clear that what he was about to share with the class would immeasurably impact us. As he proceeded, he shared the news of our father being on the run from law enforcement and his arrest. I did not believe him; the other children did. This taught me one of the hardest lessons of living with an incarcerated parent: children suffice as avenues of information while adults fall silent from the pressure of carceral stigma.

I do not recall anyone from school asking about our new family structure. Perhaps no one noticed, except when our mother signed us up to join a school program for students who had divorced parents. This was how our mother notified us that she and our father divorced. She disclosed their annulment shortly after I inquired, "Why am I in a group with kids whose parents are divorced?" I found it bizarre that the school district allowed us to join the program without considering our thoughts on our parents' marriage and familial structure. In my mind, participating in a program – which was not successful in helping me process my parents' divorce, let alone processing my father's incarceration – confused and irritated me. I felt all the more ashamed finding out about the divorce in this way and having no one to talk to about the root issue of my shame: my father's incarceration. A disconnect occurred between my community, the school programmers, and myself, reinforcing the silence around my father's incarceration. The social cues and stigma that we faced were rooted in silence. If adult topics were brought up in school settings, silence was the default.

Stigma (in Our Moments of Greatness)

No one told us, "Don't tell anyone that your dad is in prison" because they did not have to. From an early age, we understood the equation of doing something bad + getting caught = going to jail. We held the misconception that people who went to jail or prison were bad people, not people who happened to do a bad thing. And so, we constantly policed our words and actions to prevent further embarrassing the family, which became rather extreme and then *normal* for us. This not only meant enrolling in and completing advanced placement courses, but excelling in them; not only playing various sports, but being star athletes; and not only signing up for student clubs and organizations, but fulfilling leadership roles, all while being little Black girls in a predominantly and historically white school system. I wholeheartedly believe that we did so much, and did so much so well, because we fought against the community customs and messages telling us we were not enough as children of an incarcerated parent.

I had become quite the basketball player by my junior year of high school. Though most of my experiences as a student-athlete remain positively memorable, one haunts me. The night of a major win on our home floor, some friends decided to take me out. We went to a local park on the river. We arrived late and knew that the park was closed, but we did not cause trouble so we did not see the harm in staying for a while. Not long after we arrived, a cop approached us. There were no lights or sirens, just words. It was typical for strangers to know who I was as one of the only Black girl athlete stars in the small town. This particular night, the cop who stopped us not only knew my name, but knew about my father's incarceration. His line of questioning began with "What are y'all doing out here?" and "Has anyone been drinking?" Asking my friends and I to leave the park he said to me, "You played very well tonight, Maya. Your dad would be proud." I immediately froze. How odd was it that this stranger suddenly talked to me about my dad in the middle of a park on a Friday night? I knew that I had to perform well on the court and that would lead to a smidgeon of fame; however, I had no idea that anyone would make the connection between my father and I and be so comfortable making it known to me. This was one of the only times in my life that a stranger referenced my father and his absence. I was flooded with every negative emotion surrounding parental incarceration, including guilt, shame, fear, unworthiness, and hypervisibility. The stigma of being the child of an imprisoned parent negatively looms over you, even in our moments of greatness.

Social Cues and Community Customs

We learned that sharing information about our father being imprisoned was unworthy of discussion from a family whose mother helped us get to and from school and extracurriculars. As we ate dinner on a school night, the son of a family friend told us about our father being jailed as if it were commonplace dinner conversation. Unfortunately, we had not known where our father was, and this was the first we heard of his whereabouts. Our family friend – the boy's mother – quickly hushed him, signaling him to hold his tongue because we – the impacted children – nor the other children at the table need not know or talk about imprisoned parents.

This lesson rang true through school-community customs, demonstrated by our peers' heedless and ignorant parents. We remained unfit for heteronormative family types (although we eventually had a stepfather) because of our mother's perpetual mark of single motherhood. Her husband and the father of her three children, who had been physically and emotionally present, was serving a 40 year sentence. My father no longer frequented school events or escorted me to the bus stop. Throughout my life, I missed out on father-daughter dances, having him cheer me on at sporting events, and seeing him in the stands for choir productions and talent shows. The most memorable community custom where my father's absence impacted me was Eighth Grade Night for my volleyball team. It is habitual that the school community celebrates eighth graders, alongside their parents, at the last home game of the season. White people at the event asked me if a random man was my father, as they had never seen him before. The man was not my father; he was my friend's father. The people saw the only Brown man in the room and attributed that to my Blackness. I felt hypervisible, misunderstood, and angry at their ignorant racism and my father's absence. I now understand that the disregard about our incarcerated father befell the entire school community because of a lack of communal care for Black girls existing outside of heteronormative familial structures.

Our Call to Action

Utilizing educational performance as a measure of mass incarceration's impact on children must include first-hand accounts centering the psychosocialization and emotionality of parental incarceration with intersectional analyses accounting for socially constructed factors around anti-Black gendered racism, capitalism, and rural disenfranchisement. We offer the concept IE to demarcate consequences of parental incarceration within the context of silence, stigma, and social cues and community customs, as there remains a clear disconnect between schools and communities pertaining to the aftermaths of IE. Furthermore, our school systems perpetuate IE, as they understand students' home life through culturally incompetent and inaccessible networks; underservice multiple marginalized families because of inattentive and careless programming; and preserve the school-to-prison pipeline through a lack of care for the psychosocial and affective realities of children with incarcerated parents, and Black girls specifically. We situate IE as harm against children and a catalytic source of trauma.

We believe that educational institutions hold the power to disrupt and abolish mass incarceration because of the intimate connection between penal and school systems (Alexander, 2012; Love, 2019; Morris, 2016; Ritchie, 2017). Although both communities and schools perpetuate IE, our recommendations focus on the power that educational institutions must yield in our fight against mass incarceration. We call all actors of school communities to mitigate IE against the children of incarcerated parents and create solutions to manage the impact of mass incarceration by demanding that school leaders work from an abolitionist teaching framework.

Educational communities surveil, track, and disservice Black children (Love, 2019; Morris, 2016; Ritchie, 2017), which is why we believe that school leadership must become abolitionists to mitigate IE and other harms against children who mass incarceration overburdens. Abolitionist teaching provides an intersectional framework to understand the conditions making IE prevalent in school communities, allowing us to fight injustice alongside our students in the struggle for their humanity. Abolitionist teaching guides schools in redressing harm they perpetuate against the children of incarcerated parents. By adopting abolitionist teaching and praxis, school leaders center their most vulnerable students – such as Black girls in white and rural school systems who have incarcerated parents – to systemically transform educational policy, programming, and interactions.

To students whose parents are enduring incarceration in prisons, jails, mental facilities, immigration detention centers, and other carceral institutions: seek the information withheld from you. Use it to humanize your realities, disrupt systems, transform the world, and talkback (hooks, 1989) against IE and mass incarceration; all while granting yourself the grace that the world has denied you.

Note

1 Throughout this piece, we *collectively* speak from personal points of view. We hold differing perspectives of our father's incarceration, and experienced events both together and separately. We feel it important to tell our lived experiences with parental incarceration and IE interchangeably using the "I" and "we," "my" and "our," making no distinction between which author is narrating to stress the fact that our stories are always, already, weaved into one another through our sisterhood and shared realities within a school community.

References

Alexander, M. (2012). *The New Jim Crow: Mass Incarceration in the Age of Colorblindness*. New York: The New Press.

Cochran, J. C., Siennick, S. E., & Mears, D. P. (2018). Social exclusion and parental incarceration impacts on adolescents' networks and school engagement. *Journal of Marriage and Family*, *80*(2), 478–498. https://doi.org/10.1111/jomf.12464

Eddy, J. M., & Poehlmann-Tynan, J. (Eds.). (2019). *Handbook on Children with Incarcerated Parents: Research, Policy, and Practice*. New York: Springer Nature.

Foster, H., & Hagan, J. (2015). Punishment regimes and the multilevel effects of parental incarceration: Intergenerational, intersectional, and interinstitutional models of social inequality and systemic exclusion. *Annual Review of Sociology*, *41*(1), 135–158. https://doi.org/10.1146/annurev-soc-073014-112437

Giordano, P. C., Copp, J. E., Manning, W. D., & Longmore, M. A. (2019). Linking parental incarceration and family dynamics associated with intergenerational transmission: A life-course perspective. *Criminology (Beverly Hills)*, *57*(3), 395–423. https://doi.org/10.1111/1745-9125.12209

hooks, B. (1989). *Talking Back: Thinking Feminist, Thinking Black* (Vol. 10). Boston, MA: South End Press.

Johnson, E. I., & Easterling, B. (2012). Understanding unique effects of parental incarceration on children: Challenges, progress, and recommendations. *Journal of Marriage and Family*, *74*(2), 342–356. https://doi.org/10.1111/j.1741-3737.2012.00957.x

Love, B. L. (2019). *We Want to Do More Than Survive: Abolitionist Teaching and the Pursuit of Educational Freedom*. Boston, MA: Beacon Press.

Luney, M. (2019). True life: I'm serving a 40-year sentence too. *San Francisco Bay View: National Black Newspaper*. https://sfbayview.com/2019/04/true-life-im-serving-a-40-year-sentence-too/

Morris, M. W. (2016). *Pushout: The Criminalization of Black Girls in Schools*. New York: The New Press.

Murray, J., Farrington, D. P., & Sekol, I. (2012). Children's antisocial behavior, mental health, drug use, and educational performance after parental incarceration: A systematic review and meta-analysis. *Psychological Bulletin*, *138*(2), 175–210. https://doi.org/10.1037/a0026407.

Ritchie, A. J. (2017). *Invisible No More: Police Violence Against Black Women and Women of Color*. Boston, MA: Beacon Press.

Siegel, J.A., & Luther, K. (2019). Qualitative research on children of incarcerated parents: Findings, challenges, and future directions. In: Eddy, J., Poehlmann-Tynan, J. (eds) *Handbook on Children with Incarcerated Parents*. Springer, Cham. https://doi-org.ezproxy.uky.edu/10.1007/978-3-030-16707-3_11

Turney, K., & Goodsell, R. (2018). Parental incarceration and children's wellbeing. *The Future of Children*, *28*(1), 147–164. https://doi.org/10.1353/foc.2018.0007

SECTION V
Impacts and Consequences

Depriving an individual of their freedom is not the only form of punishment in the era of mass incarceration. Mass incarceration has a far-reaching impact that extends beyond prison's walls. There are collateral consequences that negatively impact health, communities, families, and quality of life. What rights do justice-impacted individuals have when they are released from prison? How does being incarcerated impact employment, housing, voting rights, and other civil liberties? What about families, children, and communities? These questions and others are examined in the Impacts and Consequences section of the book.

This section begins with Warner and Michaels' "Collateral Consequences: The Intended and Unintended Burdens of Incarceration." The authors examine formal and informal collateral consequences of imprisonment. Aseltine continues this discussion by examining voting laws that impact justice-involved people in her chapter "The Racial History and Contemporary Impacts of Felon Disenfranchisement."[1] Next, Tiana M. Herring's chapter examines the impact of Covid-19 on incarcerated individuals in "Trapped in an Epicenter: COVID-19's Impact on People Incarcerated in Prisons." The section concludes with a reflection by April Terry that focuses on the impact of punitive responses to juvenile behavior.

Note

1 As referenced in the Introduction, language is fluid and dynamic. The word "Negro" is not an acceptable term in contemporary language to describe Black or African American people. Its inclusion in Aseltine's chapter is from laws established or speeches made at the turn of the twentieth century.

DOI: 10.4324/9781003274292-24

19

COLLATERAL CONSEQUENCES

The Intended and Unintended Burdens of Incarceration

Cody Warner and Nikki Michaels

LEARNING OUTCOMES:

Upon completion of the chapter, students will be able to:

1 Overview ambiguities in the definition of collateral consequences.
2 Provide examples of common types of formal and informal collateral consequences.
3 Demonstrate how collateral consequences intersect with other forms of inequality.

Introduction

In 2016, Crystal Mason attempted to join more than 136 million U.S. citizens casting a vote in the Presidential Election. She was told by a poll worker in her Texas voting precinct that she was not on a list of registered voters. As a result, like more than two million other voters that year, Crystal cast a provisional ballot that would first be reviewed to determine eligibility. Crystal was not on the list of eligible voters because, at the time, she was serving a three-year term of supervised release from federal jurisdiction stemming from a 2011 tax fraud conviction. In the state of Texas, where Crystal lives, it is illegal to vote while you are serving a criminal sentence of any kind (jail, prison, probation, or parole). According to prosecutors, by attempting to vote while under federal supervision, Crystal had committed a felony, and she was convicted and sentenced to five years in prison. Crystal maintains she was unaware of her ineligibility, and in May of 2022 the Texas court of criminal appeals ordered a lower court to reconsider her case (Cheng, 2022).

Crystal's case has parallels that may not be immediately evident with the experiences of "Tony", an interviewee in Harding's (2003) study examining decisions to disclose a criminal status on employment applications. In recounting his interview experiences, Tony noted that,

> I can see it in their facial expressions...They kind of look at me kind of funny like it alters their opinion about me, so I'm kind of skeptical about all of that now...If it comes

DOI: 10.4324/9781003274292-25

down to another interview, I don't think I'll be telling them about no convictions or nothing.

(Harding, 2003, p. 581)

The decision to not disclose his record was not something that Tony anticipated, but was a risk worth taking after initial struggles to gain employment after prison.

The experiences of Crystal and Tony are unified by a couple of features. First, each had a prior felony conviction resulting in a criminal record, an experience shared by as many as 100 million American citizens (Vallas & Dietrich, 2014). And second, each experienced consequences of their criminal record in life outcomes unrelated to the original offense or punishment. That is, each experienced *collateral consequences* stemming from their felony convictions. But the nature of the impact varied. Crystal's consequences were formalized by laws making it illegal in Texas to vote while on probation. Tony's consequences were more informal, driven by the perceptions and stereotypes that potential employers have of applicants with a criminal record. This chapter discusses these collateral consequences of incarceration, focusing on both formal and informal policies, laws, restrictions, and outcomes that are linked to criminal convictions. However, given the myriad ways that the term collateral consequences has been used, we start by defining this chapter's central concept.

The research community has utilized a number of phrases to capture the types of formal consequences experienced by Crystal. The American Bar Association (ABA), for instance, considers these to be collateral consequences, defined as "legal and regulatory sanctions and restrictions that limit or prohibit people with criminal records from accessing employment, occupational licensing, housing, voting, education, and other opportunities" (ABA, 2013, p. 1). Elsewhere, these legal and regulatory sanctions have also been termed "invisible punishments" (Travis, 2002), "hidden sentences" (Kaiser, 2016), and "collateral sanctions" (Whittle, 2018). The phrasing is different, but united by the intentional and formal nature of these laws and policies.

But the term collateral consequences has also been used to capture unintended outcomes connected to legal punishment as experienced by Tony (Kirk & Wakefield, 2018). These are also sometimes called the social consequences of mass incarceration. They stem directly from a conviction, but not triggered by that conviction in a formal manner. We follow the suggestion by Kirk and Wakefield (2018) that this varied terminology be united under the label of collateral consequences. They are collateral in the sense that they are extraneous or supplemental to original punishments. And they have consequences that serve to chip away at core components of citizenship and full societal participation. Thus, collateral consequences are (1) formal laws, policies, and restrictions that are the direct result of a criminal conviction, and (2) informal impacts of criminal justice contact on individuals, their families, and their communities.

Formal Collateral Consequences

Once convicted of a felony offense, individuals receive their formal punishment and join the 6.34 million American residents under correctional supervision at any given time, including more than two million incarcerated in jails and prisons (Minton, 2019). What may not be immediately clear is that these felony convictions also trigger a number of other laws, policies, and restrictions that we refer to here as *formal collateral consequences*. Such consequences have been termed collateral sanctions because they are formalized into law and other administrative policies (Whittle, 2018). They have also been termed hidden punishments because their impact is not immediately clear (Kaiser, 2016). It is only when recently incarcerated individuals start the reentry process that many of the more than 40,000 formal collateral consequences become apparent.

Interested readers should consult the National Inventory of the Collateral Consequences of Conviction for more information on the breadth and scope of formal collateral consequences, and here we overview some of the primary and most consequential (https://niccc.nationalreentryresourcecenter.org/). This includes legal financial obligations, employment and occupational licensing, higher education, public assistance, and voter disenfranchisement. The nature of this information has become widely available due to the proliferation and accessibility of criminal databases where criminal record information is easily searched by public, private, and commercial entities (Alexander, 2012).

Legal Financial Obligations

Formal punishments of probation or incarceration also generally entail legal fines and fees. The amount of the fine is established via a jurisdiction's criminal code, but these legal financial obligations become formal collateral consequences for two reasons. First, there are a number of fees that are unrelated (or collateral) to the fine for the offense. These include surcharges to support criminal justice agencies, costs for a public defender, and fees to raise funds for victim restitution or other justice programming (Harris, 2016). In many cases, these discretionary fees are applied to all justice-involved individuals and the true amount is not known until sentencing is completed. Second, legal financial obligations often grow and outlast the original punishment. The costs of supervision elements such as drug treatment and testing, electronic monitoring, and even the costs of community supervision itself are often passed along to individuals under correctional supervision (Harris, 2016). Furthermore, legal debt can be subject to interest and late payment penalties, creating additional growth and long-term debt burdens for many justice-involved individuals who have legal debt highly disproportionate to income.

Employment and Occupational Licensing

Legal debt is particularly problematic in the context of employment and occupational licensing restrictions, one of the most common and diverse formal collateral consequences of incarceration (Kaiser, 2016). Some occupations are banned for those with felony convictions, especially public-facing positions such as public officials, teachers, and law enforcement officers. Positions involving contact with children, the elderly, or other vulnerable groups are also often banned via blanket policies. Other occupations are blocked off because of licensing restrictions. Diverse occupations from barbers to plumbers to lawyers can and do use a criminal record as a disqualification for licensing requirements. Furthermore, other formal collateral consequences can impact the ability to work. For example, working in security or private investigation is compromised in jurisdictions that deny access to firearm possession based on felony convictions. Jobs that require driving, such as moving or delivery services, would be compromised in jurisdictions that restrict a driver's license based on conviction status.

Higher Education

Attending college has long been viewed as a key mechanism of upward social mobility, but a criminal record can put college out of reach. At the application stage, most colleges and universities ask applicants to self-disclose their criminal history. A recent review of criminal history requirements for college applications found that 79.6% of private institutions and 58.1% of public institutions ask applicants to self-disclose their criminal record (Stewart & Uggen, 2020). The rationale behind these questions, according to surveys of college administrators, is to ensure campus safety, but they can work to exclude those with a criminal record. In many cases, applicants who disclose a criminal record are asked to provide additional information or documentation. This hurdle can thus contribute to increased attrition in the application process. Once admitted, a felony record can also complicate the ability to pay for college. If, while receiving financial aid, an individual receives a drug conviction, they can be ineligible for further aid for either set periods of time (as long as three years) or contingent on completing approved chemical dependency programs (Uggen & Stewart, 2014). Thus, even though people in prison have been found to average less than a high school education, a criminal record is a barrier in attempting to build social and human capital through higher education.

Public Assistance

The ability to work following incarceration takes on additional relevance because a criminal record can result in the loss or denial of several forms of public assistance. When the United States took a tough-on-crime turn starting in the 1970s, a variety of new policies accompanied harsh new punishments that worked to reduce or eliminate access to public assistance across domains such as housing and food (Wacquant, 2009). For example, signed into law by President Clinton in 1996, the Housing Opportunity Program Extension Act established a "one strike and you're out" policy to grant public housing authorities the ability to evict entire households based on the criminal activities of household members. In addition, these policies are often aimed specifically at people convicted of drug offenses. The Personal Responsibility and Work Opportunity Reconciliation Act of 1996 called for a lifetime ban on SNAP (Supplemental Nutrition Assistance Program) and TANF (Temporary Assistance for Needy Families) assistance for those with felony drug convictions. Readers should note that many of these policies have been revised in recent years. The Obama Administration ended conviction-based restrictions on access to public housing, and states have the option to opt out of SNAP and TANF restrictions. That said, as of 2015, 12 states fully enforce the TANF ban and nine states fully enforce the SNAP ban. Another 25 states have modified the ban to allow access to benefits under certain circumstances. As noted by Mauer (2015), individuals in states like Arkansas and Florida can receive TANF if they were convicted for possessing drugs, but are banned with drug manufacturing or distribution convictions. In other states, access to benefits can be reinstated after completion of drug treatment or following a waiting period. Despite these modifications, thousands of individuals are denied benefits for food every year because of past felony convictions, and many still believe that public housing is off-limits because of a criminal record (Kirk, 2018).

Voting Rights

Formal collateral consequences also chip away at core elements of citizenship and full societal participation, best illustrated by considering restrictions on voting rights following a felony conviction. In just two states, Maine and Vermont, persons in prisons are able to vote. All other states have some combination of voting restrictions in place, ranging from no voting only while incarcerated in prison (17 states) to no voting in prison or under community supervision (20 states), to no voting continuing past the completion of a sentence of incarceration or community supervision (11 states). In some of these states, such as Wyoming, individuals have to wait a certain number of years before they can apply to vote again. In others, such as Florida, individuals cannot vote until all fines and fees have been paid. And in some states, such as Tennessee, individuals have to formally apply to have their voting rights restored. As a result of these various restrictions, recent estimates suggest 5.17 million people were disenfranchised due to a felony conviction as of 2020 (Uggen et al., 2020). Much like other formal collateral consequences, felon disenfranchisement creates exclusion during a time period when social integration is so important.

Informal Collateral Consequences

The examples above are all considered formal consequences of criminal justice contact because they are put in place by legal and regulatory mechanisms. But incarceration and other forms of criminal justice contact have informal collateral consequences as well, and these unintended consequences can create obstacles to successfully completing the post-prison reentry process. A large body of research has developed to explore informal collateral consequences, and we focus here on some of the common research outcomes, including the labor market, health, housing and mobility, and relationships and families.

Employment and Earnings

Employment struggles after prison are one of the most widely cited and well-known informal collateral consequences of incarceration, but readers should know that that research does not consistently find a labor market penalty (see Apel & Ramakers, 2019). Those who enter prison already have poor labor market prospects, so it can be difficult to determine if or how incarceration builds on these pre-existing disadvantages. Statistically, this is referred to as a problem of selection, and research in this area has focused considerable attention on controlling for background disadvantages and creating appropriate control groups to use as a statistical comparison. Across data sources, research using survey data has found the most consistent evidence that incarceration is associated with labor market struggles. Research in this area has found that individuals who have been incarcerated are 10–20% less likely to work than their non-incarcerated peers, and report wages that are between 5% and 30% less than their non-incarcerated peers (Apel & Ramakers, 2019).

It is useful to think about post-prison labor market struggles through a combination of supply- and demand-side explanations. A supply-side explanation would note that those who have been incarcerated are objectively less employable than those who have not due to an erosion of both human and social capital. Time behind bars is time out of the labor market, and this can impact human capital through gaps in work history or loss of job skills. While incarcerated, individuals are separated from their social networks, damaging the elements of social capital that many rely on to obtain employment. A demand-side explanation, on the other hand, shifts the focus to employers. Here, research using the paired-tester (or audit) tradition has consistently demonstrated that formerly incarcerated individuals are at a distinct labor market disadvantage. Under this approach, otherwise equal individuals apply for the same job, with the only difference being that one indicates a past conviction and the other does not. The groundbreaking work of Devah Pager (Pager, 2003) showed that job applicants with a criminal record are about half as likely as their peers with no criminal record to receive a callback about a job. Pager reached this conclusion after sending matched pairs of job applicants to apply for entry-level jobs who varied on only two conditions: (1) a criminal record and (2) applicant race. Because the applicants were otherwise similar, the reduced employment prospects are likely driven by stigma and discrimination due to the criminal label. Prospective employers may see a criminal record and form impressions about an individual's perceived level of trustworthiness, reliability, or dangerousness.

Health

The intersection of a number of social and structural forces means that those who are incarcerated display poor physical and mental health profiles. For example, 21% of people in incarcerated in state and federal prisons have ever had an infectious disease, compared to 4.8% of the general population. Chronic health conditions, such as hypertension and diabetes are also elevated in prison populations (Maruschak, 2015). Mental health outcomes are no better, as 37% of incarcerated individuals have a history of mental health problems and 14% meet the requirements for serious psychological distress (three times the rate of the general population) (Bronson, 2017). On top of these pre-existing health disparities, research consistently finds that many health outcomes are worse after prison than before prison (Massoglia & Pridemore, 2015). It likely comes as no surprise, then, that incarceration is linked to early mortality, and this is especially the case during the time period shortly after release. A study of people released from prison in Washington State found that their mortality rate is 3.5 times higher overall than the general population, and 13 times higher during the first two weeks following release from prison (Binswanger et al., 2007). The leading cause of death among people released from prison is drug overdoses, although homicide and suicide play a role as well (Massoglia & Pridemore, 2015).

As with employment, documenting whether incarceration directly damages health is problematic given pre-existing health issues of those who become incarcerated. That said, three pathways have been developed linking incarceration to poor health (see Massoglia & Pridemore, 2015). First, because prison concentrates those in poor health, incarceration can directly compromise health via increased exposure to infectious disease. The day-to-day conditions of prisons, including overcrowding, poor ventilation, and shared hygiene facilities create ideal conditions for disease transmission. Second, incarceration is a stressor both in the short and long term, and stress is negatively associated with health. Incarceration is an acute stressor that requires dramatic life changes in a short period of time. It remains an acute stressor because of prison conditions such as overcrowding or threats of victimization. Incarceration is also a long-term stressor driven by extended prison terms and the social stigma of a criminal record. Third, incarceration may lead to poor health by disrupting prosocial bonds with friends and family members that contribute to more stable health outcomes.

Housing and Neighborhoods

One of the central questions for those exiting prison is: where will I sleep tonight? Stable housing is considered by many to be a cornerstone of successful reentry following prison, but an experience of incarceration has been shown to compromise secure and stable housing. Formal collateral consequences can limit access to public housing, probation and parole restrictions often require approval of housing arrangements, and labor market difficulties can impact the ability to pay for housing. On top of all of this, a criminal record is often used as grounds for exclusion in the private rental market, especially given the proliferation and ease of access to criminal background checks. Thus, the informal consequences of incarceration on housing are likely grounded in stigma and discrimination against those with a criminal record.

Like the labor market, researchers have long-used the paired-tester study to document discrimination in housing. While most of this research has focused on race and ethnicity, the method has also been used to explore the impact of a criminal record. Evans and Porter (2015), for instance, found a staggering difference in rental access by criminal record. Those who admitted to a criminal record were invited to see a rental property 43% of the time; in contrast, those without a record received an invite in almost every instance. Housing remains a precarious issue even once secured. Research focusing on post-incarceration housing and residential outcomes shows that a past history of incarceration is associated with elevated rates of residential mobility and a higher likelihood of residence in poor and disadvantaged neighborhoods (Remster & Warner, 2018). This ultimately contributes to elevated rates of homelessness among those with a history of incarceration. Current estimates suggest that between 4.7% and 11.4% of individuals released from prisons rely on homeless shelters in the first two years after release (Remster & Warner, 2018). Rates of homelessness are estimated to be ten times greater among the formerly incarcerated compared to the general public (Couloute, 2018).

Families and Children

So far, this chapter has focused on the collateral consequences among those who directly experience incarceration. But another group, termed legal bystanders, experience incarceration indirectly through their connection to the incarcerated person (Comfort, 2007). Chief among these legal bystanders are the partners and children of the incarcerated. Multiple studies, for instance, have shown that incarceration increases the likelihood of divorce and relationship dissolution, driven in-part by relationship problems including economic strain, declines in affection, and increases in relationship violence (Siennick et al., 2014). Female partners of incarcerated men have been found to have a greater risk of a major depressive episode, and their partner's incarceration decreases their own life satisfaction (Wildeman et al., 2012).

Children with an incarcerated parent have also been found to experience collateral consequences. Based on current estimates, about 3%, or 2.1 million, children have an incarcerated parent (Western, 2006), and about half of incarcerated parents report that their child lived with them prior to incarceration (Geller, 2013). A broad range of (mostly negative) outcomes have been linked to the incarceration of a parent, with most research focused on father incarceration. For instance, father incarceration has been linked to declines in school readiness, increases in special education placement, and early grade retention (Turney & Haskins, 2014). Father incarceration has also been linked to child mental health and behavioral problems, with research documenting increases in both externalizing problems (such as aggression and delinquency) and internalizing problems (such as anxiety and depression)

(Wakefield & Wildeman, 2014). Parental incarceration has also been linked to an increased risk of infant mortality (or death within the first year of life), suggesting that incarceration of parents compromises aggregate patterns of population health (Wakefield & Wildeman, 2014). Like the health of those directly incarcerated, these health and well-being consequences for partners and children are not intended but commonly accompany the incarceration of their family member.

Conclusion: The Intersections of Collateral Consequences

Current estimates suggest that as many as 100 million Americans may have a criminal record, meaning that wide swaths of our population are potentially subject to the exclusionary impact of formal and informal collateral consequences. In addition, these collateral consequences do not exist in a vacuum but rather intersect with other systems of stratification and inequality in the United States. This occurs through both the intersections of formal and informal collateral consequences, but also the intersections of collateral consequences and other forms of social inequality.

Formal and informal collateral consequences often feed off and compound on one another. As noted above, incarceration restricts the ability to work in certain occupations, especially those involving direct contact with children or the elderly. Other formal collateral consequences can also compromise employment, including driver's license or firearms restrictions. This is further compounded by the informal collateral consequences on employment, with occupational restrictions existing alongside discrimination by potential employers. And employment can be further complicated by the poor health and unstable housing commonly experienced in the aftermath of incarceration.

Collateral consequences can thus intersect to create social inequalities. But they can also intersect with existing social inequalities to create more damaging outcomes. The most widely cited work here are the employment studies of Devah Pager (2003), described above. Overall, a criminal record reduced the likelihood of a callback by 50%, but these patterns were also stratified by race. In one of the more striking examples of the intersection of race and criminal justice, Black applicants *without* a criminal record (14% callback rate) were less likely than white applicants *with* a criminal record (17% callback rate) to be called back about a job application.

It also is not difficult to see how these individual patterns intersect with aggregate trends in incarceration to deepen structural inequalities in the United States. Incarceration is concentrated in disadvantaged communities and communities of color, and even with recent declines in incarceration the Black and Hispanic imprisonment rates are 5.1 and 2.4 times the white rate, respectively. Black and Hispanic communities thus experience the disproportionate burden of formal and informal collateral consequences. To the extent that these consequences have mostly negative outcomes, then collateral consequences likely contribute to wide and enduring racial/ethnic inequalities. Scholars have argued strongly that the American system of punishment was built up to replace the social welfare state, acting as a controlling institution over disadvantaged and marginalized communities (Alexander, 2012). The collateral consequences of incarceration contribute to the perpetuation of disadvantage and marginalization in these same communities.

Finally, we hope to convey to readers that this is not a complete accounting of formal or informal collateral consequences. For instance, many jurisdictions restrict civic participation (e.g., serving on a jury) due to felony convictions, meaning jury service is restricted among those with some of the most direct criminal justice experience. A conviction and spell of incarceration is a drastic and consequential life-course transition, and the combined effects of the almost countless formal and informal consequences of incarceration can relegate individuals, primarily Black and Brown males, to a form of second-class citizenship typified by discrimination and social exclusion (Alexander, 2012). Collateral consequences limit social engagement during a period when returning citizens are encouraged or required to engage. The interviewee Tony attempted to find legitimate employment, a common requirement for those on community supervision. Crystal Mason attempted to vote and participate in the democratic process. Even as prison populations start to decline in the United States, the collateral consequences of incarceration stand in the way of successful reintegration.

Discussion Questions:

1 Collateral consequences are sometimes called "hidden" because they're not apparent or known at the time of sentencing. If you were a judge, would you punish differently if you knew the various post-incarceration collateral consequences different individuals would experience?
2 Formal collateral consequences are often triggered by laws and policies separate from the legal or criminal code. Addressing collateral consequences thus requires more diverse and varied action at local, state, and national levels. What formal collateral consequences do you think should be targeted for reform to achieve the biggest gains in successful outcomes following incarceration?

References

ABA. (2013). *National Inventory of the Collateral Consequences of Conviction*. Chicago, IL: American Bar Association. https://nicc.csgjusticecenter.org

Alexander, M. (2012). *The New Jim Crow: Mass Incarceration in the Age of Colorblindness*. New York: The New Press.

Apel, R., & Ramakers, A. (2019). Impact of Incarceration on Employment Prospects. In B. M. Huebner & N. A. Frost (Eds.), *Handbook of the Consequences of Sentencing and Punishment Decisions* (Vol. 3, pp. 85–104). New York: Routledge.

Binswanger, I. A., Stern, M. F., Deyo, R. A., Heagerty, P. J., Cheadle, A., Elmore, J. G., & Koepsell, T. D. (2007). Release from Prison—A High Risk of Death for Former Inmates. *New England Journal of Medicine*, *356*(2), 157–165. https://doi.org/10.1056/NEJMsa064115

Bronson, J. (2017). *Indicators of Mental Health Problems Reported by Prisoners and Jail Inmates, 2011-12* (p. 17). Washington, DC: Bureau of Justice Statistics.

Cheng, A. (2022). *Crystal Mason Thought She Had the Right to Vote. Texas Sentenced Her to Five Years in Prison for Trying*. New York: American Civil Liberties Union. https://www.aclu.org/issues/voting-rights/fighting-voter-suppression/crystal-mason-thought-she-had-right-vote-texas

Comfort, M. (2007). Punishment Beyond the Legal Offender. *Annual Review of Law and Social Science*, *3*(1), 271–296. https://doi.org/10.1146/annurev.lawsocsci.3.081806.112829

Couloute, L. (2018). *Nowhere to Go: Homelessness among Formerly Incarcerated People*. Northampton, MA: Prison Policy Project. https://www.prisonpolicy.org/reports/housing.html

Evans, D. N., & Porter, J. R. (2015). Criminal History and Landlord Rental Decisions: A New York Quasi-Experimental Study. *Journal of Experimental Criminology*, *11*(1), 21–42. https://doi.org/10.1007/s11292-014-9217-4

Geller, A. (2013). Paternal Incarceration and Father–Child Contact in Fragile Families. *Journal of Marriage and Family*, *75*(5), 1288–1303. https://doi.org/10.1111/jomf.12056

Harding, D. J. (2003). Jean Valjean's Dilemma: The Management of Ex-Convict Identity in the Search for Employment. *Deviant Behavior*, *24*(6), 571–595. https://doi.org/10.1080/713840275

Harris, A. (2016). *A Pound of Flesh: Monetary Sanctions as Punishment for the Poor*. New York: Russell Sage Foundation.

Kaiser, J. (2016). Revealing the Hidden Sentence: How to Add Transparency, Legitimacy, and Purpose to Collateral Punishment Policy. *Harvard Law & Policy Review*, *10*, 123.

Kirk, D. S. (2018). The Collateral Consequences of Incarceration for Housing. In *Handbook on the Consequences of Sentencing and Punishment Decisions* (pp. 53–68). New York: Routledge.

Kirk, D. S., & Wakefield, S. (2018). Collateral Consequences of Punishment: A Critical Review and Path Forward. *Annual Review of Criminology*, *1*(1), 171–194. https://doi.org/10.1146/annurev-criminol-032317-092045

Maruschak, L. M. (2015). *Medical Problems of State and Federal Prisoners and Jail Inmates, 2011-12* (p. 23). Washington, DC: Bureau of Justice Statistics.

Massoglia, M., & Pridemore, W. A. (2015). Incarceration and Health. *Annual Review of Sociology*, *41*(1), 291–310. https://doi.org/10.1146/annurev-soc-073014-112326

Mauer, M. (2015). *A Lifetime of Punishment: The Impact of the Felony Drug Ban on Welfare Benefits*. Washington, DC: The Sentencing Project.

Minton, T. D. (2019). *Correctional Populations in the United States, 2019 – Statistical Tables* (p. 15). Washington, DC: Bureau of Justice Statistics.

Pager, D. (2003). The Mark of a Criminal Record. *American Journal of Sociology*, *108*(5), 937–975.

Remster, B., & Warner, C. (2018). Residential Insecurities and Neighborhood Quality Following Incarceration. In B. M. Huebner & N. A. Frost (Eds.), *Handbook on the Consequences of Sentencing and Punishment Decisions* (Vol. 3, pp. 69–84). New York: Routledge.

Siennick, S. E., Stewart, E. A., & Staff, J. (2014). Explaining the Association between Incarceration and Divorce. *Criminology*, *52*(3), 371–398. https://doi.org/10.1111/1745-9125.12040.

Stewart, R., & Uggen, C. (2020). Criminal Records and College Admissions: A Modified Experimental Audit. *Criminology*, *58*(1), 156–188. https://doi.org/10.1111/1745-9125.12229.

Travis, J. (2002). Invisible Punishment: An Instrument of Social Exclusion. In M. Mauer & M. Chesney-Lind (Eds.), *Invisible Punishment: The Collateral Consequences of Mass Imprisonment* (pp. 15–36). New York: New Press.

Turney, K., & Haskins, A. R. (2014). Falling Behind? Children's Early Grade Retention after Paternal Incarceration. *Sociology of Education*, *87*(4), 241–258. https://doi.org/10.1177/0038040714547086

Uggen, C., & Stewart, R. (2014). Piling on: Collateral Consequences and Community Supervision. *Minnesota Law Review*, *99*, 1871.

Uggen, C., Larson, R., Shannon, S., & Pulido-Nava, A. (2020). *Locked Out 2020: Estimates of People Denied Voting Rights Due to a Felony Conviction*. Washington, DC: The Sentencing Project.

Vallas, R., & Dietrich, S. (2014). *One Strike and You're Out: How We Can Eliminate Barriers to Economic Security and Mobility for People with Criminal Records*. Center for American Progress. https://cdn.americanprogress.org/wp-content/uploads/2014/12/VallasCriminalRecordsReport.pdf

Wacquant, L. (2009). *Punishing the Poor: The Neoliberal Government of Social Insecurity*. Durham, NC: Duke University Press.

Wakefield, S., & Wildeman, C. (2014). *Children of the Prison Boom: Mass Incarceration and the Future of American Inequality*. New York: Oxford University Press.

Western, B. (2006). *Punishment and Inequality in America*. New York: Russell Sage Foundation.

Whittle, T. N. (2018). Felony Collateral Sanctions Effects on Recidivism: A Literature Review. *Criminal Justice Policy Review*, *29*(5), 505–524. https://doi.org/10.1177/0887403415623328

Wildeman, C., Schnittker, J., & Turney, K. (2012). Despair by Association? The Mental Health of Mothers with Children by Recently Incarcerated Fathers. *American Sociological Review*, *77*(2), 216–243.

20

THE RACIAL HISTORY AND CONTEMPORARY IMPACTS OF FELON DISENFRANCHISEMENT

Elyshia Aseltine

LEARNING OUTCOMES:

Upon completing the chapter, readers will be able to:

1 Describe the use, impact, and arguments made for and against felon disenfranchisement.
2 Analyze the significance of race in the historical origins and continued practice of felon disenfranchisement.
3 Describe how prison gerrymandering enhances the political impact of felon disenfranchisement.

There are various rights and social benefits that people may lose once convicted of a criminal offense. These losses are referred to as "collateral consequences," and they negatively impact many aspects of a person's life, including their ability to obtain employment, housing, education, and public benefits; as well as, to parent their children, to maintain/obtain citizenship, and to participate in the political process (i.e., to run for office, or to vote) (Chesney-Lind & Mauer, 2003).

The focus of this chapter is on "felon disenfranchisement," which is the loss of the right to vote because of a criminal conviction. The first section of the chapter describes felon disenfranchisement, where it is used, who is impacted by it, and what impact it has on political participation. The second section of the chapter focuses on justifications and criticisms of felon disenfranchisement, especially those related to its racially disparate impact. The last section considers the ways in which prison gerrymandering exacerbates the effects of felon disenfranchisement.

Felon Disenfranchisement: Its Use and Its Impact

Criminal conviction is the only means "other than age or mental infirmity, by which states continue to disenfranchise their citizens" (Schrader, 2009, p. 1313). Only in Vermont, Maine, and Washington, DC are all eligible citizens, regardless of criminal history or current incarceration status, allowed to vote. In all other US jurisdictions, people

DOI: 10.4324/9781003274292-26

incarcerated for felonies cannot vote. While prohibiting incarcerated people from voting is the most common state-imposed restriction, the incarcerated population comprises just one-fourth of the country's total disenfranchised population. Twenty-seven states expand disenfranchisement laws to prohibit voting by all those who are under any form of state supervision, including probation and parole. Three-fourths of those who are unable to vote because of disenfranchisement laws currently live in the community rather than in prison (Chung, 2021). Eleven states further expand voting restrictions to some or all of those who have completed their terms of incarceration and/or community supervision. The "post-sentence" population comprises approximately 58% of the total disenfranchised population (Chung, 2021). In 2022, Virginia and Kentucky have the most restrictive felon disenfranchisement policies—all those with felony convictions are permanently disenfranchised. (Recently, governors in both states have used their executive powers to restore the voting rights of at least some of their previously disenfranchised citizens.) The US is unique in its pervasive use of disenfranchisement. Many of the world's democracies have condemned the use of blanket criminal disenfranchisement policies (Katzenstein et al., 2010).

A growing trend in felon disenfranchisement practices is to prevent the re-enfranchisement of people who have unpaid legal financial obligations (LFOs) (Meredith & Morse, 2017). Most people with felony convictions have incurred some legal debt (Harris et al., 2010). Florida, Alabama, Arizona, and Tennessee each condition the restoration of voting rights on the full repayment of LFOs (Chung, 2021). LFOs can include any conviction-related costs (e.g., restitution, fines, and fees), as well as other non-criminal debts (e.g., child support payments) (Chung, 2021). Poor people and Black people are the least likely to be eligible to restore their voting rights because of LFO payment requirements (Meredith & Morse, 2017; Morse, 2021).

The Disenfranchised Population

Felonies are those crimes which can result in a prison sentence of one year or more; not all who are convicted of felonies will serve time in prison—some will serve their sentence in a local jail, others will be sentenced to probation, and the rare person will only pay fines (Shannon et al., 2017). While felonies include the most serious crimes such as murder, rape, arson, and robbery, many crimes about which we may be more ambivalent—e.g., drug crimes and some property crimes—are also felonies (Denham, 2019). The "proliferation of felony offenses means that a felony designation [today] may or may not correspond to our intuitive sense of what counts as a serious crime" (Sigler, 2013, p. 1741). Interestingly, a conviction for electoral fraud (typically a misdemeanor offense) would not subject a person to the loss of their voting rights.

There are about 5.17 million disenfranchised people in the US—one of out every 44 adults (Uggen et al., 2020). States vary in terms of the number of people convicted of felonies and in the strictness of their disenfranchisement laws. In Alabama, Mississippi, and Tennessee, more than 8% of the adult population (one out of every 13 people) is disenfranchised. Though Florida no longer permanently prohibits all those with a felony record from voting, it still leads the nation in total number of people who are unable to vote—over 1.1 million (Uggen et al., 2020).

People of color and, increasingly women, are most impacted by disenfranchisement practices. In total, 1.8 million Black citizens are banned from voting—approximately one out of 16 Black adults in the US. This problem is especially severe in Alabama, Florida, Kentucky, Mississippi, Tennessee, Virginia, and Wyoming, where more than one in seven Black adults are disenfranchised. In 34 states, the Latinx population is also disproportionately disenfranchised (Chung, 2021).

Women in many states are experiencing higher rates of disenfranchisement, in large part because their conviction and incarceration rates are "exploding" (Gentithes, 2019, p. 433). Approximately 1.2 million women are disenfranchised. Because of higher rates of incarceration, Black and Latinx women are more likely than white women to lose their voting rights (The Sentencing Project, 2022). Importantly, women are more likely than men to be imprisoned for drug or property offenses (Gentithes, 2019).

The Impact of Felon Disenfranchisement on Political Participation

Since 2000, there has been a growing amount of research on the impact of felon disenfranchisement on voter registration and turnout, and on election outcomes. Most studies are counter-factual, meaning they are empirical tests of what *might have* happened should all or some of those with felony convictions been allowed to vote. Researcher's decisions about how best to assign a political party to directly impacted people and/or how to create reasonable estimates about their likelihood of voting at all have important consequences for study results (Shineman, 2020). Some studies suggest that felon disenfranchisement has had a decisive impact on numerous national and state elections (Manza & Uggen, 2004, 2008; Uggen & Manza, 2002), while others find negligible impact of disenfranchisement on election outcomes (Burch, 2012; Klumpp et al, 2019; White & Nguyen, 2022). Another set of studies considers indirect effects of felon disenfranchisement policies on similarly situated "nonfelon" voters. Felon disenfranchisement reduces the voting likelihood of Black "nonfelons" in the state (Bowers & Preuhs, 2009; King & Erickson, 2016). This effect has also been found in Black neighborhoods with higher concentrations of "lost voters" (i.e., disenfranchised individuals with a history of participating in elections) (Morris, 2021). A final set of studies considers voting notification and restoration practices (Meredith & Morse, 2014; Shineman, 2020). These studies consistently reveal significant misinformation about the voting capabilities of directly impacted people, as well as onerous and confusing voting rights restoration processes (Jackson, 2017; Selin, 2019; Sigler, 2013).

Decreased political participation of those with felony convictions is consistent with other research about the impact of criminal justice system contact on political behavior. Contact with the criminal justice system in general—even arrests that do not result in formal charges—decreases a person's likelihood to vote, to participate in civic organizations, and to trust the government (Lerman & Weaver, 2014; White, 2022).

Thus far, empirical studies on voter effects of disenfranchisement offer little hope for making a compelling argument to abandon disenfranchisement policies. There is limited evidence re-enfranchisement would make a difference in elections outcomes, that those who do have their rights restored are likely to vote, that the impact of disenfranchisement laws can effectively be separated from the larger effects of any contact with the criminal justice system, or that those who are unable to vote view restoration as an urgent priority (Petersilia, 2003). For many, the most compelling arguments against felon disenfranchisement are rooted in concerns about its impact on racial equality and on our democracy.

Justifications and Critiques of Felon Disenfranchisement

Supporters of disenfranchisement see the practice as "self-inflicted—a matter of choices made, not burdens inherited" (Katzenstein et al, 2010, p. 1038). Losing the right to vote is a logical and appropriate consequence of a person's decision to engage in crime. People decide to engage in crime because of their individual characteristics and propensities, rather than because of social pressures or unequal societal arrangements. As important, advocates of the felon disenfranchisement also view the processes of creating and applying criminal laws as rationally motivated—while racism may have influenced past criminal justice practices, today's policies emerge out of an earnest and natural desire to address problematic and harmful behavior. Unless clear racial animus can be demonstrated in the construction or application of today's criminal justice laws, any racially disparate impact is an unfortunate, but unintended outcome.

Missing from much of the conversation in support of felon disenfranchisement (including opinions that emerge from the courts) is a meaningful engagement with our racial history and the disparate racial impacts of disenfranchisement practices. For those who support disenfranchisement, "the racialized character of felony disenfranchisement [is] a straightforward matter of individual choice and irresponsibility" (Katzenstein et al., 2010, p. 1038). The "individual choice" narrative allows for the easy dismissal of the racial history of disenfranchisement laws and an outright rejection of the ways in which contemporary practices continue to be influenced by entrenched constructs about racial propensities to engage in crime (Brewer & Heitzig, 2008).

Racism and Felon Disenfranchisement

Public opinion research reveals the subtextual racial meaning embedded in disenfranchisement practices. Studies consistently reveal that racial prejudice is a driving factor in the support of felon disenfranchisement policies (Shineman, 2020). Though most Americans support re-enfranchisement for those who are no longer in prison (Dawson-Edwards, 2008), support for re-enfranchisement is also influenced by race; re-enfranchisement support wanes amongst those who hold the strongest beliefs about racial propensities for criminality. This relationship is strongest amongst those who identify as liberal/moderate and who are less punitive (Chiricos et al., 2012).

Critics view felon disenfranchisement laws as "one of the last and most entrenched barriers to universal suffrage" and as "[a] deeply racialized problem" (Nelson, 2013, p. 111). The laws are seen as one strategy in a suite of practices that are purposefully designed to limit Black political participation. This suite includes both historical practices (e.g., poll taxes, literacy tests, "eight-box" laws, property tests, understanding clauses, grandfather clauses, white primaries, and lynching) and contemporary ones (e.g., voter identification laws, efforts to limit polling places/times, etc.) (Shah & Smith, 2021).

The Racial History of Felon Disenfranchisement Laws

The current race-neutral framing of felon disenfranchisement laws belies the reality that these laws "remain socially and culturally embedded in the discriminatory actions of the past" (Behrens et al., 2003, p. 568). In many discussions, including most notably those that occur in the courts, contemporary disenfranchisement laws have been "'whitewashed' to eliminate any indication of racial motivation (Schaefer & Kraska, 2012, p. 306).

Felon disenfranchisement laws were most likely to be passed during the Reconstruction period following the Civil War (Behrens et al., 2003). Many of these laws were developed in a piecemeal fashion with new qualifying offenses—offenses assumed to be associated with Black people—being added over time (Kelley, 2017). The adoption of disenfranchisement laws also coincided with the growth of the Southern Black incarcerated population—the percentage of the nonwhite prison population nearly doubled between 1850 and 1870 (Behrens et al., 2003). A more in-depth discussion of three states' efforts (i.e., Mississippi, Virginia, and Alabama) reveals the racial underpinnings of felon disenfranchisement laws.

Mississippi first passed disenfranchisement laws in 1869. During the 1890 convention, the state changed the language from disenfranchisement for "any crime" to disenfranchisement for a narrower list of crimes which were stereotypically associated with Black people. This "selected crime" model served as a model for other states (Kelley, 2017, p. 3). In fact, in many states, the most serious crimes (e.g., murder, rape) were not punished with disenfranchisement because the assumption was that this would eliminate too many potential white voters. The discriminatory intent of Mississippi's disenfranchisement laws was clear to the Mississippi Supreme Court six years later:

> [Black people] had acquired or accentuated certain particularities of habit, of temperament and of character, which clearly distinguished it, as a race, from that of whites... Restrained by the federal constitution from discriminating against the negro race, the convention discriminated against its characteristics and the offenses to which its weaker members were prone... Burglary, theft, arson, and obtaining money under false pretenses were declared to be disqualifications, while robbery and murder, and other crimes in which violence was the principal ingredient, were not.
>
> *(Ratliff v. Beale as cited in Shapiro, 1993, p. 541)*

In *Williams v. Mississippi* (1989), the US Supreme Court considered Mississippi's felon disenfranchisement laws. While the court recognized the racist intent of Mississippi's law, it ultimately determined that the law did not produce discriminatory results: the US Supreme Court concluded that Mississippi's disenfranchisement laws do not on their face discriminate between the races, and "it has not been shown that their actual administration was evil, only that evil was possible under them" (Shapiro, 1993, footnote 21).

Virginia first utilized felon disenfranchisement laws during slavery to limit free Black people in the state from voting. During the Virginia State Conventions of 1829–1830, "Once the conclusion was reached that free black [people] were prone to criminal conviction and subsequent incarceration, the framers inserted a phrase allowing for disenfranchisement for 'infamous crime'" (Gibson, 2015, p. 2). By 1845, free Black people represented about 6% of the non-slave population in the state but over 40% of those incarcerated in the state's penitentiary (Gibson, 2015).

Post slavery, Virginia continued to utilize disenfranchisement laws to control Black voters in the state. During the 1906 Convention in Virginia, Congressman Carter Glass stated,

> We are here to discriminate to the very extremity of permissible action under the limitation of the Federal Constitution, with a view to the eliminating of every negro voter who can be gotten rid of legally, without materially impairing the numerical strength of the white electorate.
>
> *(Schaefer & Kraska, 2012, p. 307)*

After specific "race-prone" crimes were identified and disenfranchisement laws were on the books, the state published lists of those barred from voting. These lists were sent to polling places in majority-black precincts; poll workers were required to consult the list prior to allowing someone to vote (Gibson, 2015).

During the 1901 Alabama Constitutional Convention, Delegate Freeman stated, "Everybody knows that this Convention has done its best to disenfranchise the negro in Alabama" (Shapiro, 1993, p. 548). Debates amongst delegates about which offenses to include/exclude were recorded in the official record, with determinations about what to include being made according to their perceived impact on reducing Black political participation. Though felon disenfranchisement laws have been challenged in all states that have them, Alabama's disenfranchisement laws were the only ones to be successfully challenged in the US Supreme Court. In *Hunter v. Underwood* (1985), the Supreme Court held Alabama's disenfranchisement laws to be unconstitutional because there was clear evidence that racial discrimination was a motivating factor behind the enactment of the law (Nelson, 2013).

The Legal Landscape of Felon Disenfranchisement: Intentionality and Structural Racism

The US Supreme Court has consistently held that felon disenfranchisement is constitutional, concluding that there is "an express textual warrant for denying the right to vote to those convicted of crimes" included in Section 2 of the 14th Amendment (Beeler, 2018, p. 1071). This "penalty clause" allows for the abridgement of voting rights because of "participation in rebellion, or other crime." The US Supreme Court's decision in the seminal case, *Richardson v. Ramirez,* has made felon disenfranchisement "statutorily unassailable" (Nelson, 2013, p. 162). States do not have to provide a compelling reason for denying people with felony convictions the right to vote; the courts sanction felon disenfranchisement as a "nonpenal exercise" and an appropriate expression of a state's rightful ability to make determinations about voting eligibility (Schaefer & Kraska, 2012; Sigler, 2013).

The *Hunter* decision is often identified as the primary legal barrier to challenging felon disenfranchisement laws of today. In *Hunter,* the court established the criteria for future challenges of such laws: such laws will only be held unconstitutional if it can be proven that they were designed to intentionally limit voter participation by race; evidence of racially disparate impact is not enough. This has been an unachievable expectation, even in post-*Hunter* Alabama. Post *Hunter,* "with only cosmetic changes and a new legislative history," Alabama's current disenfranchisement laws remain immune from legal challenges (Katz, 2007, p. 55).

Legal challenges focused on the racism of felony disenfranchisement have rarely benefitted from such explicit language on the record as was the case in Alabama; as a result, most legal challenges to disenfranchisement laws have failed to meet the court's "intentionality" requirement (Katzenstein et al., 2010). Our courts regularly consider felon disenfranchisement laws as "detached from [their] racially biased history… and [from their racially disparate] modern-day consequences" (Schaefer & Kraska, 2012, p. 312). By requiring plaintiffs in felon disenfranchisement cases to demonstrate that such laws were written explicitly with racial animus, the courts "have provided [effective] cover for legislation with neutral language but discriminatory effects" (Burmila, 2017, pp. 74–75). In arguing that only overt discrimination is of legal concern, the courts have effectively limited legal claims that felon disenfranchisement is an expression of structural racism:

> Long after overt discrimination diminishes, there still exists an array of social, economic, and legal arrangements, constructed during a time of explicit hatred, that work to the disadvantage of racial minorities. Where racial prejudice is kept alive by hate, structural racism thrives under conditions of conscious and *unconscious indifference to these historical realities and their contemporary consequences.*
>
> *(Schaefer & Kraska, 2012, p. 313, emphasis added)*

Felon disenfranchisement is not a unique case in this regard. The individualist and race-neutral assumptions of its advocates are used to justify many examples of racial bias and disadvantage within the criminal justice system (and beyond). The criminal justice system may serve as the perfect cover for color-blind expressions of racism. Relying on the criminal justice system to sort the good from the bad "provides the color-blind regime the perfect set of codes to describe racialized patterns of alleged crime and actual punishment without ever referring to race" (Brewer & Heitzig, 2008, p. 633). Unconscious beliefs about crime as a natural phenomenon among certain groups need never be exposed. The discussion can remain one of crime and "criminals" rather than one of racists and racism; felon disenfranchisement is seen as an acceptable form of punishment for "bad" people, rather than a state-sanctioned practice that reinscribes racist ideas and (re)produces racial inequalities.

Prison Gerrymandering

Though many jurisdictions have been relaxing their disenfranchisement practices in the last 20 years (Ewald, 2009), only one place (Washington, DC) has changed their laws to allow incarcerated people to vote. Felon disenfranchisement, combined with the practice of prison gerrymandering, has additional political consequences for our democracy.

Every ten years, the federal government is constitutionally mandated to take a full count of the nation's population (the US Census). The "actual enumeration" of people in the US determines apportionment of congressional representatives; at the state level, Census counts are used to determine legislative seats, electoral district lines, and, in some cases, budget allotments (Ebenstein, 2017; Remster & Kramer, 2018). While much of the Census process is prescribed by federal law, there is some discretion afforded the Census Bureau in its collection of data, including the practical interpretation of the "usual residence rule." The "usual residence rule" requires that people be counted where they "live and sleep most of the time." For most of our history, Census-takers have counted people in prison toward the population where the prison is located, rather than their original home communities (Drake, 2011). Because of the small size of our prison populations for much of our history, this practice did not raise much controversy. In the current context of mass incarceration and felon disenfranchisement, however, this practice has become more politically consequential (Skocpol, 2017).

The US Supreme Court has interpreted the Equal Protection Clause of the Fourteenth Amendment to mean that states must abide by the "one-person, one vote principle." This means that states are expected to draw congressional districts with populations that are as close to equal as possible. The understanding is that equal population is the basis of equal representation (Skocpol, 2017). While there is a good deal of leeway given to the states on what factors (beyond population size) may be taken into consideration when creating districts, the general expectation is that district sizes differ from each other by no more than 10%—this is called the "safe-harbor rule" (Ebenstein, 2017).

Prison-building, especially in the era of mass incarceration, has been a rural phenomenon. At least 350 rural counties have acquired prisons since 1980 (Stachulski, 2019). Rural areas house approximately 20% of the US population but about 40% of our incarcerated population (Skocpol, 2017). Rural jurisdictions are overwhelmingly white; however, those who fill our prisons are disproportionately drawn from urban communities of color. Prison gerrymandering is the practice of assigning prison residents to count toward the population of white, rural jurisdictions rather than the racially diverse, urban areas where they lived prior to incarceration. As a result of prison gerrymandering, white, rural jurisdictions' populations are inflated, entitling them to more representation than they would otherwise be allotted and urban, minority communities are deprived of the political representation they deserve. The result is "a thumb on the [political] scale for white, rural interests" (Skocpol, 2017, p. 1488).

States are not required to use Census data when making districting or funding decisions (Stachulski, 2019). Several states (New York, Delaware, California, and Maryland) have passed legislation that requires incarcerated people to be allocated to their previous residence for redistricting purposes (Skocpol, 2017). But many jurisdictions do not make such accommodations. In Texas, for example, Dallas County convicts approximately 15% of the state's population but imprisons none (Skocpol, 2017). In Illinois, Cook County (which includes Chicago) supplies 60% of the incarcerated population but houses less than 1% (Skocpol, 2017). In Pennsylvania, Philadelphia supplies 40% of the people in state prisons but only 1% are housed within the city (Ebenstein, 2017). Because of felon disenfranchisement laws that prohibit incarcerated people in most states from voting, "[p]risons house dense agglomerations of nonvoters" (Skocpol, 2017, p. 1476). In jurisdictions where prisons are located, incarcerated people are "in effect 'ghost constituents,' whose interests can be ignored by their representatives with little fear of electoral repercussions" (Ebenstein, 2017; Skocpol, 2017, p. 1484).

Political power is shifted between voters in jurisdictions with prisons and those without. It is possible to have two districts of equal numbers that could vary dramatically in terms of the actual proportion of eligible voters within their boundaries. As a result, those who reside in the areas with higher prison populations will have more political influence than those in other similarly sized districts with fewer incarcerated people. For example, prior to the passage of Maryland anti-prison gerrymandering legislation, in Somerset County County 64% of the population in the county's First Commission District was incarcerated. This resulted in each resident in that district having 2.7 times as much influence as residents in other county districts (Wood, 2014). The most extreme example comes from a local ward in Anamosa, Iowa. Ninety-six percent of the ward is comprised of incarcerated people. In the 2005 city election, the winner of the seat prevailed with just two write-in votes—one from his wife and one from his neighbor (Stachulski, 2019).

Apportioning incarcerated people to the area in which they are incarcerated is a discretionary practice. The Census Bureau makes exceptions to the "usual residence rule" for US personnel living abroad (Suber, 2014) and for children who attend non-collegiate boarding schools (Drake, 2011). Juveniles housed in juvenile detention centers, however, are counted as residents of the facility. Though it is not a perfect comparison, some analogize current practices with the "three-fifths compromise" for counting enslaved people—in both cases, people (slaves and incarcerated people) are counted as a part of the population when it is politically advantageous for others to do so but are simultaneously denied the opportunity to participate in political processes (Skocpol, 2017).

Conclusion

In his dissent in *Richardson*, Justice Marshall pointed out that the "or other crime" addition to the Fourteenth Amendment appeared to be "inexplicably tacked on" after being sent to a joint committee for revisions. There is no clear historical record of why it was added, what exactly is meant by the phrase "other crime," or whether the authors explicitly intended for people convicted of any crime to be able to lose their right to vote. Rather than be distracted by this ambiguous addition, Marshall argues, we should focus on the more unequivocal purpose of the Fourteenth Amendment—to prevent the disenfranchisement of Black voters (Schrader, 2019). Advocates of the abolishment of felon disenfranchisement laws are making similar appeals.

We now know about the racial history of disenfranchisement laws, their (direct and indirect) racially disparate impacts, and even the racial antipathy associated with continued support of such laws—one might hope that this would be enough evidence to make a compelling case for their abolishment. As we know, the *Hunter* decision offers little hope for using these arguments in the courts. As such, some advocates have shifted their focus toward winning the "hearts and minds" of voters to change laws through voter referendums. This strategy has had some positive effects in the last twenty years or so, but not for reasons we might think. According to Katzenstein et al. (2010), a commissioned focus group analysis in Florida found that support for re-enfranchisement was mostly driven by a race-neutral belief that people should be able to vote once they have paid back their debt to society. Arguments that focused on the "diminished rights of racial minorities or appealing to the language of rights at all" failed to inspire the public (Katzenstein et al., 2010, p. 1041). Some researchers have argued that drawing attention to racial disparity in criminal justice (e.g., incarceration, police stops, etc.) has the opposite intended effect—rather than inspire the public to fight inequality, it causes people to become more supportive of the disparity-causing policies (Hetey & Eberhardt, 2018). This may be the most disheartening conclusion of all: the most effective strategy for dismantling policies like felon disenfranchisement that are clearly rooted in a racist past and that have clear racially disparate consequences today is to continue to pretend that racism does not exist.

Discussion Questions:

1. Is it possible to have "race-neutral" felon disenfranchisement laws in the US? Why or why not?
2. Should states be required to count incarcerated people in their home communities when making redistricting decisions? Why or why not?
3. What do you think would be the most promising strategy for advocates who wish to abolish felon disenfranchisement laws?

References

Beeler, C. (2018). Felony disenfranchisement laws: Paying and re-paying a debt to society. *University of Pennsylvania Journal of Constitutional Law*, *21*, 1071–1104.

Behrens, A., Uggen, C., & Manza, J. (2003). Ballot manipulation and the "menace of Negro domination": Racial threat and felon disenfranchisement in the United States, 1850–2002. *American Journal of Sociology*, *109*(3), 559–605.

Bowers, M., & Preuhs, R. R. (2009). Collateral consequences of a collateral penalty: The negative effect of felon disenfranchisement laws on the political participation of nonfelons. *Social Science Quarterly*, *90*(3), 722–743.

Brewer, R., & Heitzig, N. (2008). The racialization of crime and punishment. *American Behavioral Scientist, 51*(5), 625–644.

Burch, T. (2012). Did disfranchisement laws help elect President Bush? New evidence on the turnout rates and candidate preferences of Florida's ex-felons. *Political Behavior, 34*(1), 1–26.

Burmila, E. M. (2017). Voter turnout, felon disenfranchisement and partisan outcomes in presidential elections, 1988–2012. *Social Justice Research*, *30*(1), 72–88.

Chesney-Lind, M., & Mauer, M. (Eds.). (2003). *Invisible punishment: The collateral consequences of mass imprisonment.* New York: The New Press.

Chiricos, T., Padgett, K., Bratton, J., Pickett, J. T., & Gertz, M. (2012). Racial threat and opposition to the re-enfranchisement of ex-felons. *International Journal of Criminology and Sociology*, *1*, 13–28.

Chung, J. (2021). *Voting rights in the era of mass incarceration: A primer*. The Sentencing Project, https://www.sentencingproject.org/publications/felony-disenfranchisement-a-primer/

Dawson-Edwards, C. (2008). Enfranchising convicted felons: Current research on opinions towards felon voting rights. *Journal of Offender Rehabilitation, 46*(3–4), 13–29.

Denham, B. E. (2019). Attitudes toward legalization of marijuana in the United States, 1986–2016: Changes in determinants of public opinion. *International Journal of Drug Policy*, *71*, 78–90.

Drake, J. C. (2011). Locked up and counted out: Bringing an end to prison-based gerrymandering. *Washington University Journal of Law & Policy*, 37, 237–265.

Ebenstein, J. A. (2017). The geography of mass incarceration: Prison gerrymandering and the dilution of prisoners' political representation. *Fordham Urban Law Journal*, *45*(2), 323–372.

Ewald, A. C. (2009). Criminal disenfranchisement and the challenge of American federalism. *Publius: The Journal of Federalism*, *39*(3), 527–556.

Gentithes, M. (2019). Felony disenfranchisement & the Nineteenth Amendment. *Akron Law Review*, *53*(2), 431–444.

Gibson, H. A. (2015). Felons and the right to vote in Virginia: A historical overview. *The Virginia News Letter*, *91*, 1–9.

Harris, A., Evans, H., & Beckett, K. (2010). Drawing blood from stones: Legal debt and social inequality in the contemporary United States. *American Journal of Sociology*, *115*(6), 1753–1799.

Hetey, R. C., & Eberhardt, J. L. (2018). The numbers don't speak for themselves: Racial disparities and the persistence of inequality in the criminal justice system. *Current Directions in Psychological Science*, *27*(3), 183–187.

Hunter v. Underwood, 471 U.S. 222 (1985).

Jackson, T. A. (2017). Dilution of the black vote: Revisiting the oppressive methods of voting rights restoration for ex-felons. *University of Miami Race & Social Justice Law Review*, *7*, 81–106.

Katz, D. M. (2007). Article I, Section 4 of the Constitution, the Voting Rights Act, and restoration of the congressional portion of the election ballot: The final frontier of felon disenfranchisement jurisprudence. *Journal of Law & Social*, *10*, 47–79.

Katzenstein, M. F., Ibrahim, L. M., & Rubin, K. D. (2010). The dark side of American liberalism and felony disenfranchisement. *Perspectives on Politics*, *8*(4), 1035–1054.

Kelley, E. (2017). *Racism & felony disenfranchisement: An intertwined history*. Brennan Center for Justice. https://www.brennancenter.org/sites/default/files/publications/Disenfranchisement_History.pdf

King, B. A., & Erickson, L. (2016). Disenfranchising the enfranchised: Exploring the relationship between felony disenfranchisement and African American voter turnout. *Journal of Black Studies*, *47*(8), 799–821.

Klumpp, T., Mialon, H. M., & Williams, M. A. (2019). The voting rights of ex-felons and election outcomes in the United States. *International Review of Law and Economics*, *59*, 40–56.

Lerman, A. E., & Weaver, V. M. (2014). *Arresting citizenship*. Chicago, IL. University of Chicago Press.

Manza, J., & Uggen, C. (2004). Punishment and democracy: Disenfranchisement of nonincarcerated felons in the United States. *Perspectives on Politics*, *2*(3), 491–505.

Manza, J., & Uggen, C. (2008). *Locked out: Felon disenfranchisement and American democracy*. Oxford, UK: Oxford University Press.

Meredith, M., & Morse, M. (2014). Do voting rights notification laws increase ex-felon turnout? *The Annals of the American Academy of Political and Social Science*, *651*(1), 220–249.

Meredith, M., & Morse, M. (2017). Discretionary disenfranchisement: The case of legal financial obligations. *The Journal of Legal Studies*, *46*(2), 309–338.

Morris, K. (2021). Neighborhoods and felony disenfranchisement: The case of New York City. *Urban Affairs Review*, *57*(5), 1203–1225.

Morse, M. (2021). The future of felon disenfranchisement reform: How partisanship and poverty shape the restoration of voting rights in Florida. *California Law Review*, *109*, 1143–1197.

Nelson, J. S. (2013). The First Amendment, equal protection, and felon disenfranchisement: A new viewpoint. *Florida Law Review*, *65*(1), 111–172.

Petersilia, J. (2003). *When prisoners come home: Parole and prisoner reentry*. Oxford, UK: Oxford University Press.

Ratliff v. Beale, 74 Miss. 247, 265-66 (1896).

Remster, B., & Kramer, R. (2018). Shifting power: The impact of incarceration on political representation. *Du Bois Review: Social Science Research on Race*, *15*(2), 417–439.

Richardson v. Ramirez, 418 U.S. 24 (1974).

Schaefer, B. P., & Kraska, P. B. (2012). Felon disenfranchisement: The judiciary's role in renegotiating racial divisions. *Race and Justice*, *2*(4), 304–321.

Schrader, J. B. (2009). Reawakening privileges or immunities: An originalist blueprint for invalidating state felon disenfranchisement laws. *Vanderbilt Law Review*, *62*(4), 1285–1314.

Selin, J. L. (2019). The best laid plans: How administrative burden complicates voting rights restoration law and policy. *Missouri Law Review*, *84*(4), 999–1036.

Shah, P., & Smith, R. S. (2021). Legacies of segregation and disenfranchisement: The road from Plessy to Frank and voter ID laws in the United States. *RSF: The Russell Sage Foundation Journal of the Social Sciences*, *7*(1), 134–146.

Shannon, S. K., Uggen, C., Schnittker, J., Thompson, M., Wakefield, S., & Massoglia, M. (2017). The growth, scope, and spatial distribution of people with felony records in the United States, 1948–2010. *Demography*, *54*(5), 1795–1818.

Shapiro, A. L. (1993). Challenging criminal disenfranchisement under the Voting Rights Act: A new strategy. *The Yale Law Journal*, *103*(2), 537–566.

Shineman, V. (2020). Restoring voting rights: Evidence that reversing felony disenfranchisement increases political efficacy. *Policy Studies*, *41*(2–3), 131–150.

Sigler, M. (2013). Defensible disenfranchisement. *Iowa Law Review*, *99*, 1725–1744.

Skocpol, M. (2017). The emerging constitutional law of prison gerrymandering. *Stanford Law Review*, *69*(5), 1473–1539.

Stachulski, F. (2019). Prison gerrymandering: Locking up elections and diluting representational equality. *University of Illinois Law Review*, *2019*(1), 401–428.

Suber, S. (2014). The senseless census: An administrative challenge to prison-based gerrymandering. *Virginia Journal of Social Policy & the Law*, *21*(3), 471–505.

The Sentencing Project. (2022). *Incarcerated women and girls*. Available from https://www.sentencingproject.org/publications/incarcerated-women-and-girls/

Uggen, C., & Manza, J. (2002). Democratic contraction? Political consequences of felon disenfranchisement in the United States. *American Sociological Review*, *67*(6), 777–803.
Uggen, C., Larson, R., Shannon, S., & Pulido-Nava, A. (2020). *Locked out 2020: Estimates of people denied voting rights due to a felony conviction*. The Sentencing Project. https://www.sentencingproject.org/publications/locked-out-2020-estimates-of-people-denied-voting-rights-due-to-a-felony-conviction/
White, A. R. (2022). Political participation amid mass incarceration. *Annual Review of Political Science*, *25*, 111–130.
White, A., & Nguyen, A. (2022). How often do people vote while incarcerated? Evidence from Maine and Vermont. *The Journal of Politics*, *84*(1), 568–572.
Wood, E. L. (2014). *Implementing reform: How Maryland & New York ended prison gerrymandering*. https://digitalcommons.nyls.edu/cgi/viewcontent.cgi?referer=&httpsredir=1&article=1002&context=fac_other_pubs

21

TRAPPED IN AN EPICENTER

COVID-19's Impact on People Incarcerated in Prisons

Tiana M. Herring

LEARNING OUTCOMES:

Upon completing the chapter, readers will be able to:

1 Generalize prison responses to the pandemic and their impacts on incarcerated people and their families.
2 Explain why pre-pandemic conditions in prisons heightened the risk of COVID-19 behind bars.
3 Identify and evaluate the effectiveness of policies implemented during the pandemic.
4 Examine the ways in which the pandemic has and has not had a long-lasting effect on mass incarceration in the United States.

The nature of mass incarceration in the United States provided the perfect conditions for a deadly virus to spread rampantly behind bars resulting in a devastating toll on the lives of incarcerated people and their families. Even before the World Health Organization declared a pandemic, criminal justice advocates were sounding the alarms about how deadly a pandemic could be for incarcerated people and providing suggestions for slowing the spread of a virus (Blakinger & Schwartzapfel, 2020; Wagner & Widra, 2020a). Prisons could have used the pandemic as an opportunity to rectify some of the problems with mass incarceration, such as overcrowding (Carson, 2020); the economic burden placed on families to cover the costs of phone calls (Wagner & Jones, 2019) and other exorbitant costs associated with incarceration (Raher & Herring, 2021); and the social harms of removing people from their families, communities, and support systems (Wang, 2022b). Instead, departments of corrections (DOCs) allowed the pandemic to heighten the stakes of the already fatal flaws in the U.S. prison system.

The purpose of this chapter is to summarize a range of prison system responses to the pandemic, and the impact these actions had on people incarcerated in prisons. While the pandemic doesn't have a clear end date at the time of writing this chapter, most of the data presented is from March 2020 to July 2021 due to availability of data. The chapter begins by discussing the extent to which prisons followed public health guidance, from wearing

DOI: 10.4324/9781003274292-27

masks to reducing the number of people in prison. Next, I outline the policy changes prisons implemented during the pandemic focusing on changes that affected the physical and mental wellbeing of incarcerated people. Then, the chapter discusses mass testing procedures, infection rates, and mortality rates. Finally, there is a brief section about how the pandemic affected incarcerated people's families.

Following Public Health Guidance

From the beginning of the pandemic, prison systems struggled to adequately implement public health recommendations intended to reduce the spread of the virus. One of the reasons this may have been difficult is because many prison systems hadn't given adequate thought to what their prison response plan would be in the event of a pandemic. While DOCs couldn't have predicted COVID-19 would exist years in advance, it's *not* unrealistic to expect prisons systems to have emergency plans in place for a variety of potential disasters. As Savilonis (2014) explains, investigations into prisons that have had major disasters reveal very few had emergency plans in place and correctional staff were not trained to handle these crisis situations. By having to create a plan from scratch, prison systems spent valuable time and energy drafting plans instead of focusing on the people in their care.

Wearing masks was a relatively simple way to mitigate the spread of COVID-19. Yet, an August 2020 survey of masking policies for incarcerated people and correctional staff found that 40% of state DOCs didn't require staff to wear masks (Widra & Herring, 2020). This was a particularly alarming finding given that correctional staff were regularly interacting with the outside world, and thus the vectors for bringing COVID-19 into the prisons. The survey also revealed only 30% of prison systems required incarcerated people to wear masks. The dual failures by DOCs to implement masking requirements and enforce them (Lewis, 2021) endangered incarcerated people and the general public.

Social distancing was also difficult for prisons to implement given the sheer number of people in prisons as a result of mass incarceration. Ten prison systems, including the Bureau of Prisons, were operating at or above 100% of their rated capacity during the pandemic (Widra, 2020). All other prisons, with the exception of Maine, were operating at 75% of their rated capacity or higher. With 1.2 million people housed in nearly full facilities, it's unsurprising that DOCs were unable to enforce social distancing measures. The only real possibility was if prisons decreased their populations substantially. For the most part, this didn't happen.

Population Reduction Efforts

Decarceration has been a fixture of mass incarceration reform efforts for years because of the United States' disproportionate use of incarceration compared to the rest of the world (Widra & Herring, 2021). Since so many prison systems were operating at or near their maximum capacities before the pandemic (Carson, 2020), public health experts recommended prisons to release people to prevent the spread of the virus. Elderly and otherwise medically vulnerable populations were perhaps obvious suggestions for release but advocates also recommended states to release people who were nearing the ends of their sentences and those with a "low likelihood" of committing another serious crime (Wagner & Widra, 2020b). While prison populations did decrease, the reductions were relatively modest, and they were not due to prisons releasing people to the safety of their communities (Sawyer, 2022).

Changes in Prison Populations

By the end of 2020, prison populations dropped 15% relative to the population in December 2019 (Carson, 2021). This prison population reduction was almost entirely due to a decrease in prison admissions, not as a result of people being released from prisons. Prisons actually released *fewer* people in 2020: there was a 10% decrease in the number of people released in 2020 compared to 2019. Admissions dropped 40% over the same time due to changes in court proceedings, trial delays, and some state prison systems refusing jail transfers to prevent the spread of COVID-19. More grimly, at least part of the reduction in the population can also be attributed to an increase in deaths in prison: compared to 2019, there was a 46% increase in the number of people who died in prisons in 2020.

Population reductions varied greatly by prison system. New Jersey decreased their prison population by 42% from March 2020 to June 2021, making it an outlier compared to the rest of the country (Herring & Sharma, 2021). For context, the state with the second greatest prison population reduction over the same time was Illinois which decreased its population by 27%. On average, prison systems reduced their prison populations by 16%.

Release Mechanisms

States had many options for releasing people from prison. Some of the recommended policy changes included accelerating releases, approving people for medical and/or compassionate release, releasing people imprisoned for minor offenses, or suspending incarceration for technical parole and probation violations.

While the first three release policies were used fairly often with 43%–50% of prison systems implementing at least one of these reforms, only 20% of states suspended incarceration for technical violations (Herring & Sharma, 2021). This could have been an easy and effective tool to prevent returns to prison considering many technical violations wouldn't be considered a crime if the person wasn't on parole. However, by not changing this policy, people on parole were at risk of reincarceration for relatively minor mishaps like missing curfew or failing to pay parole fees, which can range from $10 to $208 per month (Fines and Fees Justice Center and Reform Alliance, 2022).

Parole boards could have also contributed to prison population reduction efforts by allowing people who had served their minimum sentences to serve the rest of their terms in their communities. A Prison Policy Initiative study found that over half of the thirteen states studied had either no change or a reduction in the percentage of parole hearings that resulted in parole approval from 2019 to 2020 (Herring, 2021). Only two states, Oklahoma and Iowa, held more hearings in 2020 than in 2019, meaning fewer people were even given the opportunity to have their case heard by the parole board despite the dire situation in prisons. Between the decrease in the total number of parole hearings and the number of approvals across the board, only four states approved more people for parole in 2020.

Policy Changes Implemented Inside of Prisons

Instead of releasing people, one of the first actions prison systems took in response to the pandemic was to change the way incarcerated people functioned within prisons, including changing policies related to physical health and socialization with people inside and outside of prisons.

Policies Affecting Physical Health

Even before the pandemic, people in prisons were not healthy compared to the general population. People in state prisons are 2 times as likely to have been diagnosed with asthma, 5.6 times as likely to have had Hepatitis C, and 6.5 times more likely to have met the criteria for substance use disorder in the year before they were admitted to prison (Wang, 2022a). Prisons also generally lack adequate health care, perhaps in part because there are no set standards for care (McCann, 2022). Many prison systems hire health care professionals who have had their licenses suspended or restricted and are ineligible to work in "free world" medical settings (Blakinger, 2021). Additionally, prisons often do not have the means to provide reproductive health care or regular specialized care for people with chronic illnesses (McCann, 2022). Thus, incarcerated people likely went into the pandemic with untreated health problems.

Medical co-pays in prisons contribute to the unhealthy environment. Before the pandemic, all but eleven states charged medical co-pays typically between $2 and $5 (Herring, 2020b). Incarcerated people typically earn $0.14–$0.63 hourly, with many not receiving compensation at all (Sawyer, 2017); as such, these co-pays extremely expensive. During the pandemic, all prison systems except Nevada's modified their co-pay policies to encourage incarcerated people to seek treatment for COVID-19 if necessary (Herring, 2020b).

Most states stopped charging medical co-pays only for people with respiratory, flu-related, or COVID-19 symptoms. While suspending co-pays for people with these symptoms was certainly better than doing nothing, prisons could have done better by not charging co-pays at all since many COVID-19 symptoms aren't respiratory or flu-related. One state even publicly threatened to charge people for disingenuously reporting symptoms to bypass the co-pays (Indiana Department of Correction, 2020). The fear of being charged when trying to determine whether one is possibly infected with a deadly virus only serves to prevent people from seeking help until it's too late. Bizarrely, the Federal Bureau of Prisons implemented their first co-pay policy modification (suspension of co-pays for COVID-19-related symptoms) in March 2021—a year after the pandemic started—and they rolled back the change after only three months (Herring, 2022).

Medical co-pay suspensions varied throughout the pandemic with some states improving their policies over time and others returning to restrictive policies despite rising cases. Twelve states suspended all co-pays at some point during the pandemic. From March 2020 to December 2021—when COVID-19 cases in prisons peaked—at least three states had rolled back these suspensions. At the beginning of the pandemic, 49 states had changed their policies in some way and by February 2022, only 22 states still had their COVID-19 co-pay changes in place (Herring, 2022).

Another way prisons aimed to improve incarcerated people's physical health was by providing them with free hygiene products to promote frequent handwashing and general cleanliness. Before the pandemic, incarcerated people were expected to buy their own hygiene products. One study found that people in prison spent an average of $89 on hygiene products per year (Raher, 2018). Twenty-eight prison systems provided incarcerated people with soap or hand-sanitizer free of charge at some point during the pandemic (Herring & Sharma, 2021). Soap alone, without changing the cleanliness of facilities (Blakinger & Schwartzapfel, 2020) or requiring staff wear masks, ultimately wasn't enough to ensure incarcerated people would be safe from COVID-19.

Policies Affecting Mental Wellbeing

The pandemic marked a change in the way incarcerated people interacted with each other and their loved ones outside of prison. In recent years, DOCs have erected barriers to communication between incarcerated people and their families. From phone calls to electronic messaging on tablets (which alone are exorbitantly expensive), the costs of maintaining meaningful ties have increased and the burden is placed on families. Even physical mail is becoming subject to privatization as DOCs choose to adopt mail scanning policies that often result in incarcerated people receiving low-quality, blurry, and often colorless letters and photos (Armstrong, 2021).

To facilitate communication with family and friends, no-cost phone calls were widely implemented. By July 2021, 43 states and the Federal Bureau of Prisons had provided an option for incarcerated people to talk to their loved ones on the phone or via video call without charge (Herring & Sharma, 2021). In April 2020, the average length of these free calls was 7.5 minutes per call or 10 minutes free per week (Herring & Widra, 2020). After temporarily suspending fees for phone and video calls, Pennsylvania decided to implement a free, permanent video calling program. This change, in conjunction with the option for families to visit in person, is a great way to promote family connection which has been shown to decrease an incarcerated person's likelihood of returning to prison (Wang, 2021).

Despite the importance of meaningful interaction for all humans, a common response to the pandemic was to restrict the movement of incarcerated people through lockdowns. To be clear, these lockdowns were nothing like the early pandemic "lockdowns" people who weren't incarcerated experienced: while people in the "free world" had entertainment, the ability to go on walks, and phones to keep them connected to the world, prison lockdowns in many instances confined people to their cells for up to 23 hours a day, took away their ability to socialize, and prevented them from partaking in programming opportunities (Shapiro, 2020).

One of the more abysmal attempts to socially distance incarcerated people was to place them in solitary confinement to prevent the spread of the virus. These measures may have temporarily halted the spread of COVID-19 behind bars, but this was done at the expense of people's long-term cognitive functioning, quality of life, and life expectancy. Research has shown that long periods without human interaction result in the part of the brain that plays a major role in memory physically shrinking. Solitary confinement has also been associated with a greater risk of premature death after release, and the development of a specific psychiatric syndrome characterized by symptoms like severe panic attacks; difficulties with thinking, concentration, and memory; paranoia; and delirium (Herring, 2020a). In trying to contain an uncontainable virus, prisons may have created a new lifelong problem for incarcerated people.

Vaccinations

On average, 65% of people incarcerated in prisons had been vaccinated by July 2021 (Herring & Sharma, 2021). North Dakota, New Jersey, and Oregon had the highest vaccination rates with over 85% of their incarcerated populations receiving the vaccine. A handful of states—Montana, Nebraska, New York, Florida, Arkansas, and Iowa—had vaccination rates below 50%. For context, more than 50% of the population in every state is fully vaccinated (Mayo Clinic, n.d.). Some of this failure to vaccinate more people is due to poor education surrounding the vaccine. Many incarcerated people distrust the prison system and corrections officers. In order to promote vaccine acceptance, prisons should have gone beyond creating flyers by bringing in experts and trusted community members to have a conversation about the vaccine. With more intensive educational measures, at least incarcerated people would have had the opportunity to make an educated decision about whether to receive the vaccine instead of rejecting it due to misinformation or a lack of information.

Infection Rates, Mass Testing, and Mortality Rates

The real test of the measures DOCs took is evidenced by the infection and death rates. It may be unsurprising that, as a result of the policies mentioned above, death and infection rates inside prisons were extremely high compared to those outside prisons. By April 2021, a third of people in prisons had contracted COVID-19, more than three times the rate of infections in the general U.S. population at the time (Burkhalter et al., 2021). Additionally, 2,700 people in prison had died of COVID as of July 2021 (Herring & Sharma, 2021).

Infection Rates

The virus spread rampantly in prisons resulting in some prison systems having infection rates as much as 13.7 times higher than in the general population as of July 2021 (Herring & Sharma, 2021). The highest COVID-19 infection rate in prisons was 82%. In comparison, the highest COVID-19 infection rate in the general population was 14%.

These high infection rates didn't only impact incarcerated people and the prison staff. A study from late 2020 found that COVID-19 spread quicker in areas with more people incarcerated (Hooks & Sawyer, 2020). The researchers estimated that in just three months, mass incarceration led to 560,000 additional COVID-19 cases across the country. Thus, as DOCs failed to implement effective policies to prevent the spread of the virus, infections from incarcerated people had a ripple effect into surrounding communities. Responding more efficiently and effectively to the virus would have been beneficial for everyone.

In all but three states, infection rates were higher in prisons than they were in the general population (Herring & Sharma, 2021). (The three exceptions were Georgia, Mississippi, and Alabama; based on news reports from Georgia and Mississippi (Boone, 2020; Griesbach & Turcotte, 2021) low infection rates in these states may be evidence of testing rate deflation which will be discussed in the following section.) In the remaining prison systems, infection rates ranged from a low of 1.5 times the general population in Indiana to a high of 13.7 times the general population in Hawaii. Michigan had the highest infection rate, which is likely attributable to their mass testing policies.

It's possible that some of the summary numbers reported in this section are undercounts given the effect mass testing has on infection rates. Even if the numbers presented were completely accurate—meaning prison systems didn't miss positive cases, whether intentionally or not—it's clear that incarcerated people were at an extremely high risk of contracting COVID-19 compared to what their risk of infection would have been if they were released. While the risk of infection was bad enough given the possibility of long-term health complications (and a lack of adequate health treatment), incarcerated people were also at a higher risk of death as a result of COVID-19.

Mass Testing

COVID-19 testing procedures varied by prison system in ways that impact our interpretation of infection and death rates. As tests became more widely available, some prison systems started implementing mass testing strategies. This meant that everyone was tested, regardless of whether they were showing symptoms or had been in direct contact with someone who tested positive. Some states tested everyone regularly, while other states would initiate mass testing only if a facility received a certain number of positive results. Generally, this was a smart policy because it meant that asymptomatic cases, or cases in which people had symptoms that varied from the "normal" COVID-19 symptoms, were identified. It allowed prisons to have a better understanding of the scope of the virus behind bars. Mass testing also meant, however, that these prisons were more likely to detect infection, leading to higher positivity rates.

One way to determine which states conducted widespread testing in prisons is by looking at test rates per 1,000 people incarcerated in prisons. Prison systems with testing rates at or above 1,000 per 1,000 people in prison indicate that they were likely administering at least one test per person. Conversely, testing rates below this rate indicate not everyone in prison had been tested. By only testing people who had symptoms or were in prolonged contact with confirmed positive cases, there's a greater chance of missing positive cases and thereby deflating overall infection rates. Other tactics may have also been utilized to manipulate infection rates. For example, before mass testing began in Arizona, there were reports from both staff and incarcerated people that in one of the state prisons, officials instructed incarcerated people to refuse testing to maintain artificially low infection rates (Jenkins, 2020).

Early pandemic data from July 2020 show there was a median testing rate of 327 per 1,000 in the 40 states with available testing data and the BOP. Six states—Maryland, Massachusetts, Michigan, Minnesota, Vermont, and Wisconsin—had testing rates greater than 1,000 per 1,000 people incarcerated in prisons (Lemasters et al., 2020). Minnesota had the highest testing rate with 1,531 tests per 1,000 people in prisons. On the other end of the spectrum, there were 10 states with testing rates below 100 tests per 1,000 people in prisons. This means that less than 10% of the prison populations in these states were being tested. Hawaii, Mississippi, New Hampshire, Alabama, and Illinois had the lowest testing rates with below 25 tests per 1,000 people in prison.

Mortality Rates

By July 2021, nearly 2,700 people in prison had died as a result of contracting COVID-19 (Herring & Sharma, 2021). Vermont was the only state spared from a prison death attributable to the virus. Most prison systems had higher mortality rates compared to the general population; the average prison COVID-19 mortality rate was 1.6 times that of the general population.

Compared to infection rates, there were more prison systems that fared better than the general population in terms of the rate of COVID-19 deaths in their facilities. Thirteen jurisdictions had lower mortality rates inside of prisons than in the general population (Herring & Sharma, 2021). That leaves a majority of states with a greater rate of deaths inside of prisons. Most people who died of COVID-19 in prisons weren't sentenced to death, but it was the ultimate sentence they received. Based on the data, there's a chance their lives could have been spared had more people been released while there was still time to prevent the spread.

COVID-19 from the Outside

While incarcerated people experienced the worst of COVID-19 behind bars, their family members were also greatly impacted by DOCs' responses to the pandemic. Knowing that one's family member is at a greater risk for contracting COVID-19 behind bars, and the fear of them potentially dying without being able to see them, was hard enough for loved ones of incarcerated people. Prisons exacerbated these pains, however, by releasing little information online at a time when in-person visits weren't possible and phone calls were limited. The UCLA Law COVID Behind Bars Data Project released a series of scorecards giving states letter grades based on the availability of COVID-19 data on their websites (DeWolf et al., 2021). In their final report from July 2021, more than 80% of prison systems received failing grades. In addition to the lives lost in prisons, incarcerated people experienced great losses within their families, with some reporting they weren't even permitted to see their family members on video calls before they passed (Lewis, 2021). Ultimately, prisons only made the loneliness and sadness of the pandemic worse.

Conclusion

All prisons took different approaches to responding to the pandemic, but none of them did enough to protect incarcerated people. Prison systems had extremely high infection rates, and almost all saw people in their care die. Prisons simply weren't prepared to protect the 1.2 million people in their care. The DOCs' failures aren't due to a lack of options—there were many more responses available for prisons to implement that were ignored.

While the virus doesn't discriminate based on race or class, the current criminal legal system in the United States does. Black, Hispanic, and Native American people are overrepresented in prisons. There are more people over 55 years old than there are people aged 18–24 even though research shows that, as people get older, they're less likely to recidivate (Wang et al., 2022). Forty percent of people in state prisons didn't have a job in the month before their arrest and the last available data (Rabuy & Kopf, 2015) reveals that working-aged people in prisons made less than $20,000 per year on average before they were incarcerated. There unfortunately isn't comprehensive data available on all the incarcerated people who have died as a result of COVID-19. It's safe to assume, though, that given the overrepresentation of people of color and poor people in prisons, they are likely also overrepresented in the infections, deaths, and devastation.

Discussion Questions:

1. Based on the UCLA Law COVID Behind Bars Data Project, more than 80% of prison systems received failing grades for their handling of the Covid-19 pandemic. What are some actions prisons could have taken to improve the conditions for incarcerated individuals?
2. What are lessons learned for the future from the handling of the Covid-19 pandemic in prisons?

References

Armstrong, M. (2021, August 9). *Prisons are increasingly banning physical mail.* Slate. https://slate.com/technology/2021/08/prisons-banning-physical-mail.html

Blakinger, K. (2021, July 1). *Prisons have a health care issue — and it starts at the top, critics say.* The Marshall Project. https://www.themarshallproject.org/2021/07/01/prisons-have-a-health-care-issue-and-it-starts-at-the-top-critics-say

Blakinger, K., & Schwartzapfel, B. (2020, March 6). *When Purell is contraband, how do you contain coronavirus?.* The Marshall Project. https://www.themarshallproject.org/2020/03/06/when-purell-is-contraband-how-do-you-contain-coronavirus

Boone, C. (2020, August 21). *CDC: Prison COVID-19 cases undercounted without mass testing.* The Atlanta Journal-Constitution. https://www.ajc.com/news/coronavirus/cdc-prison-covid-19-cases-undercounted-without-mass-testing/GGIZ2FS6KREW5JKQS4IEIQVKJY/

Burkhalter, E., Colon, I., Derr, B., Gamio, L., Griesbach, R., Klein, A. H., Issawi, D., Mensah, K. B., Norman, D. M., Redl, S., Reynolds, C., Schwing, W., Seline, L., Sherman, R., Turcotte, M., & Williams, T. (2021, April 10). Incarcerated and infected: how the virus tore through the U.S. prison system. *New York Times.* https://www.nytimes.com/interactive/2021/04/10/us/covid-prison-outbreak.html

Carson, E. A. (2020, October). *Prisoners in 2019.* Bureau of Justice Statistics. https://bjs.ojp.gov/content/pub/pdf/p19.pdf

Carson, E. A. (2021, December). *Prisoners in 2020 – Statistical tables.* Bureau of Justice Statistics. https://bjs.ojp.gov/content/pub/pdf/p20st.pdf

DeWolf, L., Rajeshwar, P., & Tyagi, E. (2021, March 17). *Missing the mark: Data reporting & quality scorecard.* U.C.L.A. Law COVID Behind Bars Data Project. https://uclacovidbehindbars.org/blog/scorecard

Fines and Fees Justice Center and Reform Alliance. (2022, May). *50 state survey: Probation & parole fees.* Fines and Fees Justice Center. https://finesandfeesjusticecenter.org/content/uploads/2022/05/Probation-and-Parole-Fees-Survey-Final-2022-.pdf

Griesbach, R., & Turcotte, M. (2021, January 28). Mississippi prison officials tout low rates of covid. The reason may be fewer tests. *New York Times.* https://www.nytimes.com/2021/01/28/us/mississippi-prisons-covid.html

Herring, T. (2020a, December 8). *The research is clear: Solitary confinement causes long-lasting harm.* Prison Policy Initiative. https://www.prisonpolicy.org/blog/2020/12/08/solitary_symposium/

Herring, T. (2020b, December 21). *Prisons shouldn't be charging medical co-pays – especially during a pandemic.* Prison Policy Initiative. https://www.prisonpolicy.org/blog/2020/12/21/copay-survey/

Herring, T. (2021, February 3). *Parole boards approved fewer releases in 2020 than in 2019, despite the raging pandemic.* Prison Policy Initiative. https://www.prisonpolicy.org/blog/2021/02/03/parolegrants/

Herring, T. (2022, February 1). *COVID looks like it may stay. That means prison medical copays must go.* Prison Policy Initiative. https://www.prisonpolicy.org/blog/2022/02/01/pandemic_copays/

Herring, T., & Sharma, M. (2021, September 1). *States of emergency: The failure of prison system responses to COVID-19.* Prison Policy Initiative. https://www.prisonpolicy.org/reports/states_of_emergency.html

Herring, T., & Widra, E. (2020, April 8). *Tracking the statements of Departments of Corrections on the COVID-19 virus.* Prison Policy Initiative. https://www.prisonpolicy.org/blog/2020/04/08/virus-statements/

Hooks, G., & Sawyer, W. (2020, December 15). *Mass incarceration, COVID-19, and community spread.* Prison Policy Initiative. https://www.prisonpolicy.org/reports/covidspread.html

Indiana Department of Correction. (2020, November 1). *COVID-19 preparedness and response plan.* https://www.in.gov/idoc/files/IDOC-COVID19-Preparedness-Plan-11-1-2020.pdf

Jenkins, J. (2020, August 21). *Yuma inmates allege prison officials ordered them to refuse covid-19 testing to keep numbers down.* KJZZ 91.5. https://kjzz.org/content/1611602/yuma-inmates-allege-prison-officials-ordered-them-refuse-covid-19-testing-keep

Lemasters, K., McCauley, E., Nowotny, K., & Brinkley-Rubinstein, L. (2020). COVID-19 cases and testing in 53 prison systems. *Health & Justice, 8*(24), n.p. https://doi.org/10.1186/s40352-020-00125-3

Lewis, N. (2021, April 22). *How we survived covid-19 in prison.* The Marshall Project. https://www.themarshallproject.org/2021/04/23/how-we-survived-covid-19-in-prison

Mayo Clinic. (n.d.). *U.S. COVID-19 map: What do the trends mean for you?.* Retrieved July 16, 2022, from https://www.mayoclinic.org/coronavirus-covid-19/map

McCann, S. (2022, June 29). *Health care behind bars: Missed appointments, no standards, and high costs.* Vera Institute of Justice. https://www.vera.org/news/health-care-behind-bars-missed-appointments-no-standards-and-high-costs

Rabuy, B., & Kopf, D. (2015, July 9). *Prisons of poverty: Uncovering the pre-incarceration incomes of the imprisoned*. Prison Policy Initiative. https://www.prisonpolicy.org/reports/income.html

Raher, S. (2018, May 24). *The company store: a deeper look at prison commissaries*. Prison Policy Initiative. https://www.prisonpolicy.org/reports/commissary.html

Raher, S., & Herring, T. (2021, November 9). *Show me the money: Tracking the companies that have a lock on sending funds to incarcerated people*. Prison Policy Initiative. https://www.prisonpolicy.org/blog/2021/11/09/moneytransfers/

Savilonis, M. A. (2014, January 1). *Prisons and disasters*. Law and Policy Doctoral Theses. https://melissasurette.com/wp-content/uploads/2015/08/Prisons-and-Disasters.pdf

Sawyer, W. (2017, April 10). *How much do incarcerated people earn in each state?* Prison Policy Initiative. https://www.prisonpolicy.org/blog/2017/04/10/wages/

Sawyer, W. (2022, January 11). *New data: The changes in prisons, jails, probation, and parole in the first year of the pandemic*. Prison Policy Initiative. https://www.prisonpolicy.org/blog/2022/01/11/bjs_update/

Shapiro, J. (2020, June 15). *As covid-19 spreads in prisons, lockdowns spark fear of more solitary confinement*. NPR. https://www.npr.org/2020/06/15/877457603/as-covid-spreads-in-u-s-prisons-lockdowns-spark-fear-of-more-solitary-confinemen

Wagner, P., & Jones, A. (2019, February 11). *State of phone justice: Local jails, state prisons and private phone providers*. Prison Policy Initiative. https://www.prisonpolicy.org/phones/state_of_phone_justice.html

Wagner, P., & Widra, E. (2020a, March 6). *No need to wait for pandemics: The public health case for criminal justice reform*. Prison Policy Initiative. https://www.prisonpolicy.org/blog/2020/03/06/pandemic/

Wagner, P., & Widra, E. (2020b, March 27). *Five ways the criminal justice system could slow the pandemic*. Prison Policy Initiative. https://www.prisonpolicy.org/blog/2020/03/27/slowpandemic/

Wang, L. (2021, December 21). *Research roundup: The positive impacts of family contact for incarcerated people and their families*. Prison Policy Initiative. https://www.prisonpolicy.org/blog/2021/12/21/family_contact/

Wang, L. (2022a, June 22). *Chronic punishment: The unmet health needs of people in state prisons*. Prison Policy Initiative. https://www.prisonpolicy.org/reports/chronicpunishment.html

Wang, L. (2022b, August 11). *Both sides of the bars: How mass incarceration punishes families*. Prison Policy Initiative. https://www.prisonpolicy.org/blog/2022/08/11/parental_incarceration/

Wang, L., Sawyer, W., Herring, T., & Widra, E. (2022, April 13). *Beyond the count: A deep dive into state prison populations*. Prison Policy Initiative. https://www.prisonpolicy.org/reports/beyondthecount.html

Widra, E. (2020, December 21). *Since you asked: Just how overcrowded were prisons before the pandemic, and at this time of social distancing, how overcrowded are they now?* Prison Policy Initiative. https://www.prisonpolicy.org/blog/2020/12/21/overcrowding/

Widra, E., & Herring, T. (2020, August 14). *Half of states fail to require mask use by correctional staff*. Prison Policy Initiative. https://www.prisonpolicy.org/blog/2020/08/14/masks-in-prisons/

Widra, E., & Herring, T. (2021, September). *States of incarceration: The global context 2021*. Prison Policy Initiative. https://www.prisonpolicy.org/global/2021.html

22

REFLECTION

PUNITIVE RESPONSES TO JUVENILE BEHAVIOR

Narratives from a Juvenile Correctional Facility Worker

April N. Terry

The U.S. is now entering the fourth decade "detached" from the 1990s era consumed by the "superpredator"—a term used to describe a cohort of youth, specifically, Black boys, who were said to be a generation of violent teenagers regularly engaged in criminal behavior (Gluck, 1997). While research has documented the inaccuracies in such predictions (Cohen & Spinak, 2018), the U.S. has continued to incarcerate youth at alarming rates, with most studies highlighting biased practices (Rovner, 2021). In some instances, youth are incarcerated for low-level offenses while disparities exist for youth-of-color. For girls, many are incarcerated for non-violent behaviors including status-level offenses. While rates of juvenile incarceration have declined since the moral panic of the 1990s, troubling trends remain (The Sentencing Project, 2021), including incarcerating youth to be "rehabilitated" as community-based resources may be unavailable. This is especially true in rural states, including the Midwestern state where I worked as a master's level psychologist and am now an academic in a criminal justice department.

The current chapter focuses on my observations and experiences working as a psychologist across one state providing psychosexual evaluations on youth, as well as within the state's only juvenile correctional facility (JCF) housing both boys and girls. These narratives are told from my personal accounts in this role, coupled alongside my current position as an academic, where I regularly engage in research at this same facility. This chapter blends my first-hand experiences with research on mass incarceration of youth in the U.S.

I first began my professional work in juvenile corrections completing statewide community psychosexual evaluations on youth adjudicated of sexual offenses and before the disposition hearing (sentencing phase for adults). The goal was simple—provide evidence-based guidance to courts on matching youths' risks with their needs, while avoiding incarceration unless deemed necessary. Unfortunately, at times, courtroom stakeholders held different opinions, ones that centered on beliefs such as incarcerating *all* youth for *any* sexual offense, even when against best-practice standards. At the time of my employment, approximately 40% of the incarcerated boys' population were there due to sexual offenses while most girls were incarcerated for technical violations. I was told by individuals completing pre-sentence investigations that they could not support my recommendations for

DOI: 10.4324/9781003274292-28

community-based recommendations, as they knew how their judge would be more punitive so they tailored their reports to align with this known outcome. I watched many young people stripped of their community lives, positive supports, and school involvement to be incarcerated in their state's maximum custody JCF. Once there, I heard correctional officers refer to these youth as "chomos" (child molesters) and question why a new administrator would house all youth with sexual offenses together (adhering to best-practices in having access to services), asking, "Who is this idiot?"

In addition to stereotypes of juveniles who commit sexual offenses, broader cultural beliefs of youth delinquency have also shaped our education system. As the school-to-prison pipeline has shown, youths-of-color, those with cognitive, behavioral, and/or mental health needs, managing lives of intergenerational poverty, are met with punitive school measures. Their behavioral responses to their cumulative disadvantage results in school systems punishing their survival skills by relying on the juvenile justice system. The school-to-prison pipeline is only minutely detached from the 1990s panic regarding the coming of the superpredator. Before these youth reach the JCF, some spend upwards of one year in local jails and detention facilities, even though policies prohibit this holding time. During this time, the population of incarcerated youth was comparable to the state average with approximately 80% youth-of-color and 20% white youth. This Midwestern state does not break down race further than Black, white, and "other" youth. The average age of an incarcerated youth was around 16–17 years of age but as young as 10. Individuals 18 years of age, but adjudicated as juveniles, remained in adult jails—environments that subjected them to numerous forms of victimization (Valentine et al., 2019).

After a few years in this role, I moved away from my community work and took a position as a psychologist within this facility. As the newest psychologist, I was assigned to the girls' unit as all other clinical staff refused to work with them. Clinical staff regularly referenced intentional efforts to avoid working on the "girls' side" as they believed this to be too time consuming and required them to respond to "drama." Yet, much like adult statistics and national averages, the girls represented only around 10–11% of all incarcerated youth in this Midwestern state. The stigma of working with girls and women extended throughout this JCF and new employee training did not offer information to contradict these gender stereotypes. Correctional staff likely hold misconceptions regarding boys' behaviors and the ideals surrounding the need for mass incarceration of the "superpredator." Additionally, some support cultural beliefs surrounding the adultification of young Black girls—a term less frequently cited in academic literature and absent in most training curriculums. Adultification refers to viewing Black children, including Black girls, as more adult and less innocent than their white counterparts (Epstein et al., 2017). Even my formal education had not equipped me with this knowledge or prepared me for this work. No one told me that incarcerated girls would share stories of chronic abuse and neglect, followed by maladaptive coping skills (e.g., self-harm, running away, and using substances), and ultimately, a system that criminalized their responses to their victimization. The girls shared accounts of poly-victimization, followed by a community infrastructure that ignored their signs and overt requests for help. Poly-victimization meant many girls reported multiple types of abuse (Turner et al., 2010), most commonly, they discussed sexual and physical abuse and the viewing of domestic violence. They subsequently found themselves behind bars, under the guise of correcting and protecting them. While incarcerated, the trauma continued from strip searches to isolation. During one research interview with an incarcerated girl, she shared with me that she feared the dark and being locked in her cell reminded her of childhood abuse where she was locked in a closet. *All* girls I worked with had some abuse in their pasts. My experience was the lack of awareness for these issues could be partially explained by lack of in-house training. Staff were provided minimal information on culturally aware, trauma-informed, and developmentally appropriate information to best respond to the behaviors of incarcerated youth.

From my time in a JCF, I quickly learned you cannot address one's delinquent behaviors without first addressing their traumas, as the trauma creates a pathway to offending behavior. Communities, and especially rural towns, suffer from systemic issues supporting a desperate and ill-informed approach to managing delinquent behavior (Terry, 2018). In my Midwestern state, many community stakeholders do not recognize girls' responses to abuse and neglect but are quick to label their behavior as non-conforming. In my later work as an academic, judges would share that they sent girls into placements as a means of "protecting" them—a harmful practice that further supports the mass incarceration of children. They believed removing girls from their communities would help change girls' behavior. Decision-makers mistakenly think facilities have much to offer; yet, I question how it is acceptable to serve dinner at 4:30 pm, and how it is tolerable to see live cockroaches on someone's food—an actual event I witnessed on one occasion while conducting research. The conditions are deployable, and I doubt these were observed as exceptions to the norm.

The professionals supporting the incarceration of youth are the ones labeling these behaviors as criminal, rather than recognizing them as responses to chaotic environments. Unfortunately, this practice is not supported in research and is also damaging—calling this cruel and unusual punishment would be accurate. When decision-makers view overt behaviors (e.g., fighting and running away) as delinquent, they ignore the underlying issues driving the behavior and inadvertently support the maintenance of mass incarceration. Without serious attention to welfare needs, communities are only providing a temporary band-aid to a youth's circumstances (Goshe, 2019). As these youth age, many take another pipeline into adult prisons as rehabilitative services fall short of offering a holistic approach including youth, their families, and community institutions. Once under correctional supervision, a revolving door allows for juvenile incarceration to serve as a bootcamp for adult mass incarceration.

To provide context, my Midwestern state ranked fifth in the U.S. for youth incarceration rates prior to a massive juvenile justice reform bill in 2016 (KDOC, 2015). A 2014 cost study reported a $100,000+ bill to retain a juvenile for one year (KDOC, 2015). One component of the reform bill was to make it more difficult to send youth to the JCF and to reduce the lengths of incarceration. This reform promised $8,000,000 for community-based services (Christie & Bowman, 2016); however, as of 2022, much of these funds have not been secured by community agencies and the state reallocated $21 million of these funds to cover other needs while currently promising to "return" the funding. While the pendulum swings between get-tough approaches and zero-tolerance policies to the belief that correctional facilities offer rehabilitative services to youth, the reality is, detained youth receive minimal programming. Facilities serve to warehouse kids after removing them from their homes.

In both of my professional roles, I have witnessed the incarceration of *many* low-and moderate-risk youth. During the 2015 state review, it was found that many detained youths were low-and moderate-risk youth based on the nationally validated risk assessment tool; again, girls were usually deemed a much lower risk than boys. Due to this lower level of need, they did not qualify for services as the research has documented the damaging effects of mixing low-risk youth with high-risk youth (Lovins & Latessa, 2013). Research has also shown the importance of those incarcerated retaining bonds with community supports (Martinez & Abrams, 2013). Yet, in this Midwestern state, some youths are over six hours away from their hometowns. Even those families interested in seeing their loved one may be prevented due to the cost and time-intensive nature of their travels. COVID-19 increased barriers to retaining community and family supports as my Midwestern state, and others, paused all visitation during a time when incarcerated populations needed connection the most. These issues could be fully avoided by recognizing the harms of incarcerating youth and building institutional capacity to address the needs of youth within their communities.

When politicians make decisions regarding the policies and practices pertaining to juvenile delinquency, some may do so without the guidance of evidence-based practices. As an academic, I ask my students the following question, "How many times have you seen a politician say they want to get soft on crime?" I have yet to have a student provide an example of hearing this first-hand. Yet, preventative approaches such as mentoring programs have shown promise in providing community-based, low-cost interventions that target psychological, social, and behavioral concerns (Raposa et al., 2019). Community programs such as Functional Family Therapy (FFT) and Multisystemic Therapy (MST) represent prevention programs found to be effective in both cost and crime reduction (Lee et al., 2012). FFT is an evidenced-based intervention for at-risk youth and families that provides support in clinical settings as well as the home, schools, mental health facilities, and even for youth under the supervision of child welfare services and probation (Alexander & Robbins, 2019). With MST, therapists also work within the home, schools, and communities, to provide tools to caregivers to help at-risk youth reduce system-involvement and improve family and community dynamics. While these approaches are applied after youth have been identified as at-risk or delinquent, it is a step in the right direction—toward an approach of reducing the negative impact of detaining youth. According to some, programs should expand on the "what works" literature. It all starts with changing organizational culture by identifying the types of changes needed, developing programs to engage staff in the change, align all systems and processes, and model this from executive staff down to field workers (Alvesson & Sveningsson, 2015).

In conclusion, this chapter centered on the unforgiving policies and practices that allow for the criminalization of youth's behavior rather than understanding delinquency as a public health issue. Punitive practices may not be obvious as they remain couched in rehabilitative efforts and juvenile reforms. The incarceration of any youth is problematic and should be taken seriously. Local and broader decision-makers should rethink the juvenile justice system entirely, moving away from practices that support removing youths from their communities, and implement robust community-based resources that seek to restore relationships between at-risk youths and their communities.

References

Alexander, J. F., & Robbins, M. (2019). Functional family therapy. In Lebow, J. L., Chambers, A. L., & Breunlin, D. C. (eds). In *Encyclopedia of couple and family therapy* (pp. 1232–1240). Cham: Springer International Publishing.

Alvesson, M., & Sveningsson, S. (2015). *Changing organizational culture: Cultural change work in progress*. New York: Routledge.

Christie, J., & Bowman, R. (2016). *Senate Bill 367: Components and impacts of the bill.* Crime and Justice Institute.
Cohen, L., & Spinak, J. (2018). Busting the "juvenile super-predator" myth. In Henning, K., Cohen, L., & Marrus, E. (eds.) In *Rights, Race, and Reform* (pp. 269–284). New York: Routledge.
Epstein, R., Blake, J., & González, T. (2017). *Girlhood interrupted: The erasure of black girls' childhood.* Center on Poverty and Inequality: Georgetown Law. Retrieved from https://genderjusticeandopportunity.georgetown.edu/wp-content/uploads/2020/06/girlhood-interrupted.pdf
Gluck, S. (1997). Wayward youth, super predator: An evolutionary tale of juvenile delinquency from the 1950s to the present. *Corrections Today, 59*(3), 63–66.
Goshe, S. (2019). How contemporary rehabilitation fails youth and sabotages the American juvenile justice system: A critique and call for change. *Critical Criminology, 27*(4), 559–573.
Kansas Department of Corrections (KDOC). (2015). *Cost study of youth residential centers for juvenile offenders: Pursuant to Senate substitute for House Bill 2588.* Retrieved from https://www.doc.ks.gov/publications/juvenile/yrc.
Lee, S., Aos, S., Drake, E., Pennucci, A., Miller, M., & Anderson, L. (2012). *Return on investment: Evidence based options to improve statewide outcomes, April 2012 update.* Olympia, WA: Washington State Institute for Public Policy.
Lovins, B., & Latessa, E. (2013). Creation and validation of the Ohio Youth Assessment System (OYAS) and strategies for successful implementation. *Justice Research and Policy, 15*(1), 67–93.
Martinez, D. J., & Abrams, L. S. (2013). Informal social support among returning young offenders: A metasynthesis of the literature. *International Journal of Offender Therapy and Comparative Criminology, 57*(2), 169–190.
Raposa, E. B., Rhodes, J., Stams, G. J. J., Card, N., Burton, S., Schwartz, S., Yoviene Sykes, L. A., Kanchewa, S., Kuperschmidt, J., & Hussain, S. (2019). The effects of youth mentoring programs: A meta-analysis of outcome studies. *Journal of Youth and Adolescence, 48*(3), 423–443.
Rovner, J. (2021, July 15). *Black disparities in youth incarceration.* The Sentencing Project. Retrieved from https://www.sentencingproject.org/publications/black-disparities-youth-incarceration/
Terry, A. N. (2018). *Dirt roads to justice and Heartland girls: Coercive sexual environments in nonmetropolitan communities.* Kansas State University.
The Sentencing Project. (2021, May). *Fact sheet: Trends in U.S. corrections.* Retrieved from https://www.sentencingproject.org/publications/trends-in-u-s-corrections/
Turner, H. A., Finkelhor, D., & Ormrod, R. (2010). Poly-victimization in a national sample of children and youth. *American Journal of Preventive Medicine, 38*(3), 323–330.
Valentine, C., Restivo, E., & Wright, K. (2019). Prolonged isolation as a predictor of mental health for waived juveniles. *Journal of Offender Rehabilitation, 58*(4), 352–369.

SECTION VI
Reentry

Approximately 95% of incarcerated individuals will one day be released from prison. More than 600,000 individuals are released from federal and state prisons every year (Carson, 2018). This does not include the nine million that are churned through jails every year. But it doesn't stop there, two out of three formerly incarcerated individuals are rearrested within three years for new offenses or technical violations (Alper et al., 2018). A justice-involved individual must overcome many challenges and obstacles for successful reentry, including housing, employment, institutional support, and societal stigma, just to name a few. This section of the reader covers some of the realities of what life is upon reentering society and one's community.

The section begins with Becker and Liu's "Reuniting Justice-Involved Fathers to Their Families – The Impact on Desistance." They examine how the construction of a father identity serves as a turning point for formerly incarcerated men to veer away from crime. The reentry section continues with "The Role of Faith-Based Organizations in Re-Entry" where Beláňová and colleagues examine the potential for recidivism reduction through faith-based organizations. Next, Troshynski and Willis discuss their work with a non-profit organization that provides services to formerly incarcerated people and what influences successful reentry in "Embracing Hope: Stories of Successful Reentry Experiences." The reentry section concludes with a reflection by Emily Sorenson, a director of a reentry program, discussing her experiences in "The Reality of Reentry."

References

Alper, M., Durose, M. R., & Markman, J. (2018). *2018 update on prisoner recidivism: A 9-year follow-up period (2005–2014)*. Washington, DC: Bureau of Justice Statistics.
Carson, E. A. (2018). *Prisoners in 2016 (NCJ 251149)*. Washington, DC: Bureau of Justice.

DOI: 10.4324/9781003274292-29

23

REUNITING JUSTICE-INVOLVED FATHERS TO THEIR FAMILIES – THE IMPACT ON DESISTANCE

Patricia Becker and Lin Liu

LEARNING OUTCOMES:

Upon successful completion of this chapter, students will be able to:

1 Explain desistance and explore why it is an important area of research.
2 Understand the role that fatherhood plays in one's desistance process.

Introduction

The United States remains the world's leader in incarceration, with over 6.6 million adults under some form of correctional supervision in the United States (Kaeble & Cowhig, 2018). In 2016 alone, roughly 430,000 individuals were released from both state and federal prisons (Kaeble & Cowhig, 2018). Research has found that stable and gainful employment, healthcare, housing resources, and family support are major catalysts to desistance from crime (e.g., Lattimore & Visher, 2009; Liu & Bachman, 2021; Visher & Travis, 2011). A smaller body of studies reported that parenthood exerted a protective effect against recidivism (e.g., Breen, 2014; Stone & Rydberg, 2019). Of particular concern for families is that more than half of those imprisoned are parents, with an estimated 1.7 million children having a parent behind bars either in federal or state prison (Glaze & Herberman, 2013). Black and Latino families experience this at a much higher rate than other racial/ethnic groups, with an estimated four in ten Black fathers and two in ten Hispanic fathers serving time in prison (Glaze & Herberman, 2013). The main purpose of this chapter is to enhance our knowledge of how incarceration structures the relationships between fathers and their children, and in turn, how this relationship impacts the desistance process over a 20-year period.

Despite the current markedly high number of post-incarcerated fathers experiencing reentry, research efforts focused on the link between reclaiming fatherhood and desistance are relatively limited. Although there have been numerous studies on the identity and cognitive change and desistance (Bachman et al., 2016; Paternoster & Bushway, 2009), the majority of these studies focused on post-incarcerated mothers or individuals with no

DOI: 10.4324/9781003274292-30

children. We know very little about how the fatherhood role and commitment to parenting among reentering individuals affects their progression of reentry. Furthermore, extant studies examining parenthood often use a binary variable "having children or not" to capture parenthood and quantify the effect of this binary variable on recidivism (e.g., Breen, 2014; Monsbakken, Lyngstad, & Skardhamar, 2013; Stone & Rydberg, 2019). Thus, quantitative results provide limited information about the process and experience of identity change and how the fatherhood role intersects with one's identity transformation. Our understanding of desistance among returning fathers is hampered by few studies focusing on identity transformation and the narratives that reflect how individuals perceive this experience. The present chapter adds to the literature by utilizing qualitative data from in-depth interviews with post-incarcerated fathers to explore how and why they reclaimed a father identity as well as its impact on their desistance.

Constructing a Pro-Social Self

Originally conceptualized as a clear "end-point" or "event," scholars have transitioned to understanding desistance as a process where individuals decrease and then eventually cease criminal behaviors. The research on desistance not only provides intellectual contributions but also yields implications for intervention practice and policymaking. With the findings on desistance, policymakers can develop rehabilitation programs to promote the desistance among those who once had contact with the justice system. These programs help justice-involved individuals sever a criminal past and equip them with personal and social assets needed for a healthy and productive life. While previous scholars (Sampson & Laub, 1993) have focused on the role of external and structural forces, more recent theorizing (Giordano et al., 2002; Maruna, 2001; Paternoster & Bushway, 2009) has underscored the internal and agentic processes such as identity and cognitive transformations. More recent theorizing about desistance has explored the cognitive process individuals experience that precipitates desistance. Paternoster and Bushway (2009) developed a theoretical formulation to explain desistance, which they titled the Identity Theory of Desistance (ITD). Paternoster and Bushway argue that each justice-involved individual faces failures (i.e. they get arrested and incarcerated) and as long as they view these failures as (1) something out of their control (i.e. having a self-serving bias) and (2) isolated incidents, they will continue to engage in anti-social behaviors. However, when individuals perceive their offending behaviors as causing more pain than pleasure, and they realize the failures they are experiencing are because of their own behaviors, rather than something out of their control, they begin participating in steps to change their identity to one that aligns itself with more pro-social values (Paternoster et al., 2015).

This newly emerging prosocial identity, Paternoster and Bushway (2009) argue, prompts a change in the individual's preferences away from anti-social activities like criminal behavior or the "party life" (Shover, 1996), toward more prosocial behaviors like legitimate work and positive relationships with friends and family. Paternoster and Bushway (2009) claimed that it is the collection of these internal changes in one's identity and preferences that encourages behavior that conforms with a pro-social identity. This desistance theory, unlike others, hypothesizes that identity change is necessary for desistance to occur, that identity change must come before prosocial opportunities can arrive and be successfully used, and that desistance can occur even in the absence of conventional turning points.

Fatherhood and Desistance

Prior research investigating parenting and desistance has largely relied on the role of motherhood (e.g., Bachman et al., 2016; Giordano et al., 2002; Kreager et al., 2010). Of those studies that do explore the impact of fatherhood on desistance, there appear to be inconsistencies between quantitative and qualitative findings. Quantitative findings indicate that adolescent fathers are more likely to continue their delinquent behaviors than adolescent nonfathers (Pirog-Good, 1988; Springarn & DuRant, 1996; Stouthamer-Loeber & Wei, 1998; Unruh et al., 2003; Wei et al., 2002). One possible explanation for this finding is that these studies are only including fatherhood as an independent variable, rather than focusing more closely on the lived experiences of fathers to understand their perceptions of their fatherhood roles and how this may or may not have impacted their decision-making.

There have been a few qualitative studies that have examined the lived experiences of fatherhood and most find the role decreases criminal offending. For example, being a good father was consistently described as strong motivation for desistance from criminal behavior by adolescents (Shannon & Abrams, 2007; Wilkinson et al., 2009). Similarly, in Shannon and Abrams (2007) analysis, justice-involved youth fathers discussed school, work, and taking care of their children as motivations for desisting from crime.

Although fatherhood can act as a turning point leading to desistance, this may be far from an involuntary process. Edin, Nelson and Paranal's (2004) found that fatherhood did act as a turning point in the lives of men with criminal histories. However, fatherhood in their study led to several trajectories, including disruption of parent–child bonds, rebuilding of parent–child bonds, and deterrence from further crime. Although the combination of fatherhood and crime did not lead to desistance in every case, this study identified that paternal bonds could lead to change in criminal behavior. Relatedly, Moloney and colleagues (2009) qualitative study revealed that the transition to fatherhood did not automatically lead to lasting changes in behavior. Similar to justice-involved mothers, there were structural and material barriers that constrained the men's abilities to fully embrace their new father identities and desist from crime (Moloney et al., 2009).

While extant literature has been equivocal about the effects of fatherhood and desistance, there have been few attempts to examine the salience of parenting in this process. In this chapter, we present evidence that the role of "father" often offers drug and justice-involved men a chance for redemption, a chance to salvage strained relationships, a path through which justice-involved fathers can potentially reimagine themselves (Giordano et al., 2002) and a mechanism to build and maintain their prosocial identity (Paternoster & Bushway, 2009).

Methods

For this study, we conducted a secondary analysis of an existing qualitative dataset, the NIJ-funded Roads Diverge: Long-term Patterns of Relapse, Recidivism, and Desistance for a Re-Entry Cohort dataset (Bachman et al., 2013). This dataset includes extensive, one-on-one interviews with 293 adults who had lengthy substance misuse and criminal histories and who were released from prison in the early 1990s. The interviews were conducted between 2010 and 2011. Of the 293 respondents, a total of 187 were men. From those 187 men, 151 self-reported having children at the time of this interview, which served as the final sample for this chapter.

Results

Among respondents in our sample, 70 identified as white, 71 identified as Black, six identified as Hispanic, and four identified as Asian. Additionally, the majority of respondents (80.7%) reported having children. Also, the majority (57.8%) of respondents reported using illegal substances during the past 12 months, yet fewer were still engaging in other illegal activity (40%).

For the majority of the desisting fathers in our sample, the engagement in parenting responsibilities solidified a newly formed prosocial identity and increased the likelihood of desistance. The fathers in our sample who desisted and whose progress was linked to an aspiration to be a better parent described their parenting role as having provided a platform upon which they could maintain and enhance their new prosocial identities. Their parenting roles, however, took on different forms which are explored in detail below.

Another Chance: Parenting

The vast majority of fathers had children either before or during their criminal careers. As such, some of the respondents described getting *another chance* with fatherhood. Importantly, these narratives illuminate how they had always loved their children, but their addictions prevented them from performing their fatherhood roles. Getting another chance at fatherhood was thus a significant source of strength throughout their desistance effort. Bryson's story illustrates this second chance with fatherhood well. He declared that he would not go back to prison because he knew what it felt like to be incarcerated while his children needed him. Although it was his feared self of dying inside prison and getting older that propelled his desistance process, he detailed how hard it was not being there for his children and how having another chance with them kept him on the right track:

> I guess I'm getting older and I just don't want the you know, I don't want to go back to prison at all, I mean last time I was in there for that little over a year I mean it was harder than the 11 and a half I served the first time, mainly because I had kids and I knew I wasn't out there with them, taking care of them, you know.

Similar to Bryson, Charlie described his struggles with addiction and his journey back to his children. He lost contact with them for many years while he was incarcerated, however, when asked how he was able to maintain his sobriety he responded:

> I just got to the point where I wanted some different stuff. Some of the stuff I used to have coming up before drugs. I want to spend time with my son, my daughters versus using my time up to go out, sit around and do some dumb stuff. I took those steps to get there man.

Other respondents described gaining another chance with fatherhood by having children later in life. Charles described his second chance:

> I: So where are you at in life now? Do you have temptations to use and cravings and stuff and if so is that stuff you talk about in your sessions at this place? What's keeping you from using now?

> R: If I drink again I'm going to end up going to prison, spending a lot of money again, or I'll get another DUI and I mean I've been locked up so many times in my life I've missed so much of my daughters growing up time and I don't want to miss that with my son. There has been a few times where I almost just said the heck with it I'm going to go get drunk but somebody is watching over me because somebody won't let me do it.
> I: What stops you?
> R: Thinking about my son, thinking about the relationship that will be gone with my son if I get in trouble again.

The majority of these fathers described the heart break that severing ties with their children caused during periods of incarceration. For example, Cole knew he had to make a change after his last incarceration. He described the torture of having his oldest son visit him in prison: "To see me behind a glass where I can't touch him or feel him, so we came to some type of agreement where, just leave him home I'll talk to him over the phone, you know what I mean?" He goes on to detail how he lost a chance of bonding with this son because of his addictions, and how he was granted another chance with his youngest:

> My little one was conceived when I was out. That was a good feeling, I got to see everything, the labor, the growing of the stomach and you know the up late night feedings and that's the stuff I missed from my first son when I was incarcerated so it kind of like brought me closer to my family when I got home and had that second one and it all played a part.

These narratives describe *another chance* with fatherhood that respondents experienced. Their *another chance* occurred in two ways: respondents reconnected with their children or they had children later in life. Whether it was the shame of seeing their children while behind bars or the lost time and broken relationships, their journey back to fatherhood proved to be a significant source of strength throughout their desistance effort.

Another Chance: Grandparenting

One avenue that allowed desisting fathers another chance at parenting was the role of grandparent. The majority of respondents who were grandfathers talked unequivocally about how this role positively impacted their desistance effort. Respondents frequently expressed love for their grandchildren and how their very existence solidified their prosocial identity by giving them a new legacy that they did not want to lose. For example, when asked to identify something that has helped keep him clean, Ken offered the following: "My grandkids allow me to be, feel I have some self-worth in life." Like Ken, Jason described how important his grandchildren were to his desistance:

> I still have my wife and I still have my children, I feel like I've got something to hold on too… And I wouldn't wanna lose that by yanno doing something like that to them, and I've got little grandkids now that look up to their papa yanno like, and what are they gonna look like if they are looking for papa and papa in jail. What am I gonna tell my grandson or granddaughter that I'm in prison, you get what I'm saying, they're my backbone, it's not like I'm just doing it for them, but yes I'll say that yes I'm doing it for them.

At the end of his interview, Jason was asked what he would say to anyone struggling with addiction and wanting to get clean, he responded:

> I would say to them, if I was gonna tell them anything, get some, I mean find something in, in this world, the way it is even though the times are rough like it is today, find something that you really love and really care about and hold onto it. That helped me, it works it really does, like I said as being as old as I am and my grandkids, I live for them.

Vince knew he had to make a change in his life when he became frustrated with having to watch his grandchildren grow up from behind bars. He was filled with embarrassment and shame for not being the grandfather he wanted to be. He described:

> R: One thing, I know that I'm getting older and I look back at my kids and they're getting older and I realize that the amount of grandkids I have, it really hurt me to have my daughters bring my grandkids to a prison to visit me.
> I: Wow.
> R: So that's another factor, I don't want to see another like that and I don't want to be in no situation like that. So, I know in order for me to not be in a situation like that I had to change a lot of my behaviors and that's the main one I hadn't changed.

Supporting Paternoster and Bushway's (2009) Identity Theory of Desistance, the grandfather respondents who desisted identified a number of purposeful changes in their preferences, the processes through which they came to those choices, and how these manifested from a transformed identity (Kerrison & Bachman, 2016). The majority began to see themselves as someone with a family instead of an "addict" or "offender." More importantly, they reflected on how the harm they caused had real consequences. Ben shared:

> It got to a point where I really couldn't hide it ya know what I mean? And I got tired of them being hurt by what I was doing, so I had to start thinking about other people other than myself. I had to start thinking about how it's going to affect them if I go back, I got a grandson today, too. Yea man he's 1, so it's my oldest daughter's son so I think I gotta, I gotta look at it like the bigger picture. I've been broke, but I refuse to go out and do something crazy... But I'm saying that it's like a mindset that my mindset now is different than it was before. It's just certain things... That's how serious you gotta take your recovery. That's how serious you gotta take your freedom and that's what makes a difference in my life today that I'm not selfish like I used to be. And I really didn't know that I was hurting anybody but me ya know what I mean? If I'm getting high that's me, it's my body I'm not really hurting nobody... I had to change that sort of thinking man I had to think about my daughters I had to think about my grandson I had to think about my wife, I had to think about me, I'm tired of going to jail.

Although it was their initial feared self that propelled them on their desistance journey, some respondents explained that their continued desistance was directly linked to their fear of losing contact with their grandchildren. When asked what has kept him clean all these years, Brett described a fear of losing custody of his grandchildren who live with him and his wife:

> The two oldest ones live with us now, because their father won't take care of them. That's another thing about a positive part of life growing up. I'm taking care of my grandchildren now, and I'm giving them everything... I'm raising my grandchildren because if I don't take care of them, nobody will.

These narratives reveal how grandparenting positively impacted the desistance process for these men. For the majority, the embarrassment, shame, and fear of losing contact with their grandchildren proved immensely impactful for respondents. However, fulfilling both the fatherhood and grandfather role came *after* these men found the strength and agency to achieve a "non-offender" identity.

Conclusion

The primary purpose of this study was to shed light on the underlying role that fatherhood and identity transformation play in the desistance process for justice-involved men who were entrenched within the criminal justice system throughout their parenting years. The narratives and stories told by the majority of the respondents supported the reality that with addiction comes a lifetime struggle characterized by relapses regardless of formal or informal punishments (Anglin et al., 2009). Even with numerous experiences of incarceration and treatment, a little more than half of the men, despite being fathers, were still misusing substances and nearly one quarter self-reported engaging in other criminal behaviors ten years after a baseline release in the mid-1990s.

The findings revealed a complex relationship between fatherhood and desistance. For the vast majority of the men interviewed, fatherhood did not initiate desistance, but rather assisted with maintaining and bolstering desistance efforts after agentic identity transformation. Although most fathers experienced numerous periods of incarceration and treatment, when they successfully desisted from both crime and substance misuse, stepping back into the role as father or grandfather was extremely important in solidifying their desistance. Men in the sample experienced additional chances with fatherhood that allowed them to confirm their identities as fathers. These second chances occurred in a number of ways: (1) reconnecting with children later in life, (2) having another child, or (3) reconnecting as grandparents.

In addition to advancing conversations around fatherhood and desistance, this chapter also has important implications for policy. There needs to be policies and programs aimed at providing fathers, particularly those from disadvantaged backgrounds, with resources that support a pro-social fatherhood role that is accessible. Policies and initiatives should focus on paternal involvement with children (Anderson & Letiecq, 2005). In particular, programs that value connectedness, communication, and relationships can support alternative constructions of masculinity that do not focus on financial providing (Bond, 1999; Roy & Dyson, 2010). For example, community-based and culturally competent programs and policies are less likely to reject justice-involved men who want to (re)connect with their children, while promoting support for alternative expressions of pro-social fatherhood roles (Roy & Dyson, 2010).

Additionally, policies must encompass restorative justice initiatives to support mediation and reconciliation forums for justice-involved individuals and their family members (Bachman et al., 2016). These initiatives may prove extremely beneficial to family members who may have been directly victimized or negatively impacted by the decisions and behaviors of justice-involved individuals (Miller, 2011). Ultimately, policies and programs that incorporate the characteristics outlined above may prove extremely beneficial in creating new conceptualizations of what it means to be good men generally, and good fathers specifically, when faced with a number of collateral consequences and stigmas due to race, class, and criminal record.

In sum, the stories described by the men interviewed are representative of today's justice-involved population where long arrest histories, numerous incarcerations, and extensive substance misuse are a troubling reality. The overwhelming majority of respondents described leaving prison or treatment only to return to neighborhoods rife with crime and drugs where gainful employment and affordable housing were nonexistent. (Re)Inclusion into their families was only one of the many hurdles these men endured. However, reconnecting with children proved to have a significant impact on their desistance efforts.

Although this chapter filled several critical gaps found within the theoretical work on desistance from crime and substance misuse, we believe that the most important takeaway is that this work (re)affirms the fact that justice-involved individuals' behavior is not fixed. Rather, their behavior can and does change. So why do our laws and society in general operate under the framework "once a criminal always a criminal?" This social isolation, stigmatization, and less than citizenship mentality is detrimental for those navigating this reality and goes against the democratic ideals that are supposedly the foundation of America (Kerrison, 2014).

We hope that the findings in this chapter encourage thought-provoking conversations and continued theorizing regarding the relationship between desistance and fatherhood.

Discussion Questions:

1 Describe the ways in which justice-involved fathers received *another chance* at parenting.
2 From their narratives, what motivated justice-involved fathers to refrain from misusing substances or engaging in anti-social behaviors?

References

Anderson, E. & Letiecq, B. (2005). Situating fatherhood in responsible fatherhood programs: A place to explore father identity. In Marsiglio, W., Roy, K. & Fox, G. L. (eds.), *Situated fathering: A focus on physical and social spaces* (pp.187–208). Boulder, CO: Rowman & Littlefield.

Anglin, M. D., Brown, B. S., Dembo, R., & Leukefeld, C. (2009). Criminality and addiction: Selected issues for future policies, practice, & research. *Journal of Drug Issues, 39*(1), 89–99.

Bachman, R., Kerrison, E. M., O'Connell, D., & Paternoster, R. (2013). Roads diverge: Long-term patterns of relapse, recidivism, and desistance for a cohort of drug involved offenders. Final Report for Grant #2008-IJCX-0017, National Institute of Justice, U.S. Department of Justice.

Bachman, R., Kerrison, E. M., Paternoster, R., Smith, L., & O'Connell, D. (2016). The complex relationship between motherhood and desistance. *Women & Criminal Justice*, *26*(3), 212–231.

Bond, M. (1999). Gender, race, and class in organizational contexts. *American Journal of Community Psychology*, *27*, 327–355.
Breen, A. V. (2014). Changing behavior and changing personal identity: The case of pregnant and parenting young women and antisocial behavior. *Identity*, *14*(1), 60–79.
Edin, K., Nelson, T. J., & Paranal, R. (2004). Fatherhood and incarceration as potential turning points in the criminal careers of unskilled men. In Patillo, M., Weiman, D. F. & Western, B. (eds.), *Imprisoning America: The social effects of mass incarceration* (pp.46–75). New York: Russell Sage Foundation.
Giordano, P. C., Cernkovich, S. A. & Rudolph, J. L. (2002). Gender, crime, and desistance: Toward a theory of cognitive transformation. *American Journal of Sociology*, *107*, 990–1064.
Glaze, L. E., & Herberman, E. J. (2013). *Correctional populations in the United States, 2012*. Washington, DC: Bureau of Justice Statistics.
Kaeble, D. & Cowhig, M. (2018). Correctional populations in the United States, 2016. *Bureau of Justice Statistics*, 1–14.
Kerrison, E. M. (2014). *The crux of context: An examination of how collateral consequences legislation impacts the desistance process* (Doctoral dissertation, University of Delaware).
Kerrison, E. M., & Bachman, R. (2016). Second-chance grandparenting: How a new and renewed identity impacts the desistance process. *Across the Spectrum of Women and Crime: Theories, Offending, and the Criminal Justice System*, 225–242.
Kreager, D. A., Matsueda, R. L., & Erosheva, E. A. (2010). Motherhood and criminal desistance in disadvantaged neighborhoods. *Criminology*, *48*(1), 221-258.
Lattimore, P. K., & Visher, C. A. (2009, December). *The multi-site evaluation of SVORI: Summary and synthesis*. Department of Justice. https://citeseerx.ist.psu.edu/document?repid=rep1&type=pdf&doi=877cdfb8a35c173910520b4f3a7cad32179de57a
Liu, L., & Bachman, R. (2021). Self-identity and persistent offending: A quantitative test of identity theory of desistance. *Journal of Offender Rehabilitation*, *60*(5), 341–357.
Maruna, S. (2001). *Making good: How ex-convicts reform and rebuild their lives*. Washington, DC: American Psychological Association.
Miller, S. L. (2011). *After the crime: The power of restorative justice dialogues between victims and violent offenders*. New York: New York University Press.
Moloney, M., MacKenzie, K., Hunt, G., & Joe-Laidler, K. (2009). The path and promise of fatherhood for gang members. *The British Journal of Criminology*, *49*(3), 305–325.
Monsbakken, C. W., Lyngstad, T. H., & Skardhamar, T. (2013). Crime and the transition to parenthood: The role of sex and relationship context. *British Journal of Criminology*, *53*(1), 129–148.
Paternoster, R., Bachman, R., Bushway, S., Kerrison, E., & O'Connell, D. (2015). Human agency and explanations of criminal desistance: Arguments for a rational choice theory. *Journal of Developmental and Life-Course Criminology*, *1*(3), 209–235.
Paternoster, R., & Bushway, S. (2009). Desistance and the "feared self": Toward an identity theory of criminal desistance. *Journal of Criminal Law and Criminology*, *99*(4), 1103- 1156.
Pirog-Good, M. A. (1988). Teenage paternity, child support, and crime. *Social Science Quarterly*, *69*(3), 527–546.
Roy, K. M., & Dyson, O. (2010). Making daddies into fathers: Community-based fatherhood programs and the construction of masculinities for low-income African American men. *American Journal of Community Psychology*, *45*(1–2), 139–154.
Sampson, R. J. & Laub, J. H. (1993). *Crime in the making: Pathways and turning points through life*. Cambridge: Harvard University Press.
Shannon, S. & Abrams, L. (2007). Juvenile offenders as fathers: Perceptions of fatherhood, crime and becoming an adult. *Families in Society: The Journal of Contemporary Social Services*, *88*(2), 183–191.
Shover, N. (1996). *Great pretenders: Pursuits and careers of persistent thieves*. Boulder, CO: Westview Press.

Spingarn, R. W., & DuRant, R. H. (1996). Male adolescents involved in pregnancy: Associated health risk and problem behaviors. *Pediatrics*, *98*(2), 262–268.
Stone, R., & Rydberg, J. (2019). Parenthood, maturation, and desistance: Examining parenthood transition effects on maturation domains and subsequent reoffending. *Journal of Developmental and Life-Course Criminology*, *5*(3), 387–414.
Stouthamer-Loeber, M., & Wei, E. (1998). The precursors of youth fatherhood and its effect on delinquency of teenage males. *Journal of Adolescent Health*, *22*, 56–65.
Unruh, D., Bullis, M., & Yovanoff, P. (2003). Community reintegration outcomes for formerly incarcerated adolescent fathers and nonfathers. *Journal of Emotional and Behavioral Disorders*, *11*(3), 144–156.
Visher, C. A., & Travis, J. (2011). Life on the outside: Returning home after incarceration. *The Prison Journal*, *91*, 102S–119S.
Wei, E., Loeber, R., & Stouthamer, M. (2002). How many of the offspring born to teenage fathers are produced by repeat serious delinquents? *Criminal Behavior and Mental Health*, *12*, 83–98.
Wilkinson, D., Magora, A., Garcia, M., & Khurana, A. (2009). Fathering at the margins of society: Reflections from young, minority, crime-involved fathers. *Journal of Family Issues*, *30*(7), 945–967.

24

THE ROLE OF FAITH-BASED ORGANIZATIONS IN RE-ENTRY

Andrea Beláňová, Tereza Trejbalová, and Jan Tomášek

LEARNING OUTCOMES:

Upon successful completion of this chapter, students will be able to:

1 Describe the role of faith-based organizations in providing re-entry services to released individuals and the organizations' potential for recidivism reduction.
2 Consider the benefits of and issues with faith-based re-entry services in the secular context of the criminal justice system.

Introduction

Mass incarceration in the United States continues to further disadvantage marginalized communities and, among other implications, leads to an increased need for the proper services to be provided to those released from prison. Re-entry programs attempt to fulfill this need by helping released individuals maintain their freedom – consequently mitigating the negative impacts of mass incarceration. These programs take numerous forms, from informal support groups to re-entry courts, but by integrating care that is both directly and indirectly religious with organized re-entry services, faith-based organizations (FBOs) transcend the largely corporeal nature of the criminal justice system.

Within these particular programs, forgiveness and shame work are considered key factors for system-impacted individuals' transformation. Oftentimes, FBOs portray faith as fostering an individual's sense of solidarity, resiliency, and confidence to serve as a source of motivation and ethics. Nevertheless, their religious nature can further marginalize individuals with a different value system. In this chapter, we explore the research related to FBOs and their potential role in recidivism and mass incarceration reduction. Additionally, we offer the case of the Czech Republic's FBOs. Given the country's high incarceration rate and its exceptionally irreligious environment, this case exemplifies the pros and cons of religious re-entry services in the secularized milieu of the criminal justice system.

DOI: 10.4324/9781003274292-31

Re-Entry, Desistance, and Religiosity

A release from prison and subsequent reintegration back into the community are oftentimes accompanied by significant challenges that can thwart a successful (i.e., crimefree) re-entry, such as stigmatization, or issues with finding stable employment and housing (see, for example, Durnescu, 2021). Despite the obstacles facing those released from prison, their return to crime is not inevitable. Research convincingly demonstrates that the majority of individuals will eventually cease their criminal engagement (Ward & Maruna, 2007) and their risk of recidivism will not be significantly different from that of the general population (Hanson, 2018). As such, the focus should be on factors that demonstrably contribute to those released ultimately going straight (Maruna et al., 2004). This approach, sometimes referred to as positive criminology (Ronel & Elisha, 2011) and based on the desistance paradigm (McNeill, 2006), is becoming increasingly more common in the current rehabilitation discourse.

Although a universally accepted definition of desistance has not yet been established, it is usually conceptualized as the long-term abstinence from criminal activities among those with a pattern of offending (Maruna, 2001). In any case, the consensus is that for most people engaging in criminal behavior, desistance is not a one-off event but a complex and oftentimes extensive process. In terms of different stages of desistance, primary desistance can essentially mean any time the individual stops committing crime, but a significant shift in identity is necessary for secondary desistance (Maruna & Farrall, 2004). Given the impact of other people's reactions on an individual and their self-perception, we can also speak of tertiary desistance that refers to external validation from others of one's change and acceptance into society (McNeill, 2015).

Several theoretical models emphasizing different types of desistance factors have been proposed. While some authors mainly emphasize the influence of the natural maturation of the individual (Rocque, 2017), others focus on social factors and note that certain life events (e.g., finding a life partner and starting a family, getting a stable job, or breaking away from a group of peers), can serve as turning points in a criminal trajectory (Laub & Sampson, 2001). However, the motivation of the person and their own initiative also play an important role. Therefore, desistance is also associated with significant changes of identity (Paternoster & Bushway, 2009) or life narratives (Maruna, 2001). Many criminologists believe that all these approaches have merit, and that desistance should be viewed as an interplay of relevant social and subjective factors that one is ready for and open to (Giordano et al., 2002).

One of the factors that have been examined as contributing to desistance, and therefore successful re-entry, is religiosity.[1] Since re-entry starts in prison, religiosity and participating in religious activities can play a key role for incarcerated individuals experiencing guilt, loneliness, and boredom (Denney, 2018; Jang et al., 2018; O'Connor, 2004). Individuals with sincere[2] motivations reported that religious involvement during their prison stay has positively changed them (e.g., finding hope and direction; Dammer, 2002).

Outside of an institution, quantitative and qualitative studies have documented religiosity as a protective factor through fostering prosocial behavior, providing moral guidance, and improving social relationships and mental health (Chambré, 2001; Jang et al., 2018; Jensen & Gibbons, 2002; Johnson, 2011; O'Connor et al., 1998; Walters-Sleyon, 2013; Willison et al., 2011). In terms of desistance specifically, the shame experienced after committing a crime in combination with religious faith has been effective in preventing recidivism (Jensen & Gibbons, 2002), suggesting the need to account for different interactions

(O'Connor, 2004; O'Connor et al., 1998). O'Connor (2004) further argues that the value of religiosity in desistance and re-entry goes beyond reducing recidivism and should consequently be considered in broader societal contexts as well. Regardless of the empirical support, some studies find little to no evidence that religiosity contributes to successful rehabilitation (e.g., Gerace & Day, 2010).

Religious ideas presuming the possibility of rehabilitation and restoration of the self serve as potential explanations for why religiosity can lead to prosocial outcomes (Walters-Sleyon, 2013). It can provide a framework for a complex personal transformation through preventing suicidal feelings and depression; offering new life purpose; and promoting forgiveness, responsibility, courage, psychological strength, and motivation to avoid criminal behavior and substance use (Walters-Sleyon, 2013; Willison et al., 2011; Wills et al., 2009). Skotnicki (1996) calls to include a dramatic transformative personal experience that leads to a change of one's identity and behavior – a "cognitive conversion" – into rehabilitation. Such transformation corresponds with religious conversion that changes an individual's life (Graddy & Ye, 2006; Jang et al., 2018; Maruna et al., 2006; Williams, 2016), as it allows an integration of disparate and shameful life events into an empowering, visionary narrative (Maruna et al., 2006).

As desistance also results from an accumulation of social bonds (Laub & Sampson, 2001), religion can act as a source of informal social control. Religious communities' focus on respect and compassion can meet the re-entering individuals' needs for forgiveness and redemption (Clear et al., 2000; Kewley et al., 2015). Moreover, accompanying activities engage re-entering individuals with an institution that reinforces their prosocial behavior and requires them to commit to a structured routine (Giordano et al., 2008; Graddy & Ye, 2006; Johnson, 2011; Stansfield, 2017; Williams, 2016; Wills et al., 2009). Regular participation in religious activities can then significantly increase one's social capital, peer support, sense of belonging, and even strengthen contact with one's own family (Bakken et al., 2014; Roberts & Stacer, 2016). According to Hallett and McCoy (2015), this aspect is particularly salient for individuals whose previous friends were predominantly engaged in criminal behavior and who have limited opportunities to use conventional social networks. Similarly, those who have committed some of the most serious crimes and are likely to be met with rejection and resentment from mainstream society may find these contacts especially important (Kewley et al., 2015). However, the extent to which these contacts alleviate the risk of subsequent recidivism varies. Although the religious community's assistance in solving practical problems or learning new patterns of behavior can be substantial, it can hardly ameliorate the wider social problems and economic disadvantages in some cultural contexts (Stansfield, 2017).

In sum, faith may become an effective tool for overcoming various obstacles that those re-entering face upon their release (Bakken et al., 2014). Religiosity can offer a key source of life's meaning, emotional capital, or the ability to cope with stress, which may also affect one's behavior in situations that used to trigger aggression (Giordano et al., 2008). It is vital to recognize that for some individuals, especially those who are particularly marginalized, faith can represent one of the few – if not the only – tools of desistance available (Mohammed, 2019). Its importance may continue to increase in the future as some traditional institutions that promote desistance continue to weaken, for example, declining popularity of marriage, decreased stability within social relationships, or a lack of legitimate employment opportunities (Bakken et al., 2014).

Faith-Based Organizations

Given the potential of religiosity for desistance and successful re-entry, FBOs are considered important as service providers with recidivism prevention strategies that include, for example, providing social services, urgent relief and moral guidance, mentoring, and assisting with administrative tasks after release (Graddy & Ye, 2006; Manuel & Glatzer, 2019; Walters-Sleyon, 2013). In terms of the role of religion, the concept of FBOs encompasses "any organization that refers directly or indirectly to religion or religious values, and functions as providers of basic, emergency social services, and as instigators of political action, mobilization and contestation" (Fridolfsson & Elander, 2012, p. 635). For example, faith can be intertwined with decision-making processes, interactions with clients and among staff, organizational ethics and structure, language, and program philosophy (Bowers Du Toit, 2019; Ebaugh et al., 2003; Kniss & Campbell, 1997; Williams, 2016). For these organizations, the term "faith" is preferred to "religion" to distinguish them from religiously motivated social help provided by different congregations (Chambré, 2001).

In their work with clients, FBOs usually provide a wide portfolio of services which might be less professionalized but more focused on areas left out by the public sector and on urgent needs, such as extreme poverty (Cloke & Beaumont, 2012; Fridolfsson & Elander, 2012; Graddy & Ye, 2006; Manuel & Glatzer, 2019). In contrast to secular organizations, FBOs promote nonmaterialistic values, value-based ethics, and a communitarian approach, as well as powerful narratives of individual transformation to offer hope of a second chance for released individuals (Jang et al., 2018; Walters-Sleyon, 2013; Williams, 2016). That is not to say that FBOs do not also utilize secular expertise (e.g., mental health services), but they tend to emphasize the postmodern concepts of individuality and humanism with faith being understood as an added value (Chambré, 2001; Ebaugh et al., 2003; Fridolfsson & Elander, 2012; Willison et al., 2011).

The added value of faith further encompasses the enthusiastic engagement of volunteers from local religious communities, who are motivated by faith, compassion, forgiveness, and *caritas* and *agape*[3] (Bowers Du Toit, 2019; Chambré, 2001; Cloke & Beaumont, 2012; Ebaugh et al., 2003; Gerace & Day 2010; Graddy & Ye, 2006; Manuel & Glatzer, 2019; O'Connor, 2004; Willison et al., 2011). Despite the benefits of their engagement, many clients do not choose these organizations because of their religious identity and thus the "faith factor" can sometimes have a marginalizing effect for potential clients and staff not sharing the same values. In some cases, faith can dominate the discourse at the expense of care and the organization may be at risk of becoming an "exclusionary subculture" (Cloke & Beaumont, 2012, p. 15; also see Ebaugh et al., 2003; Manuel & Glatzer, 2019; O'Connor et al., 1998).

Proselytization[4] can also become a salient issue for FBOs as organizations with an evangelical background, in particular, sometimes do not distinguish between religious and secular activities (Bowers Du Toit, 2019; Kniss & Campbell, 1997; Williams, 2016). However, the majority of FBOs are not coercive and keep religious activities optional (Willison et al., 2011). An interesting paradox arises in this case: Although institutionalized religions continue to lose their status in secularized countries, their service to the vulnerable populations (e.g., charity) is highly appreciated by the public (Manuel & Glatzer, 2019). Public perception of FBOs is particularly fundamental for their functioning and their access to public funds, resulting in faith being communicated according to the organization's approach (Chambré, 2001; Ebaugh et al., 2003; Graddy & Ye, 2006; Kniss & Campbell, 1997; Manuel & Glatzer, 2019).

The Czech Case: FBOs Meet Secularism

Undoubtedly, geographical context is crucial when considering religiosity, the role of FBOs, and the re-entry and desistance processes (Cloke & Beaumont, 2012). Specifically, the social structure and context of the region are crucial, as Stark (1996) suggests that religiosity of an individual must be "ratified" by their social environment to decrease their likelihood to reoffend. The Czech Republic is used as a case study, as the country presents unique characteristics in terms of low religiosity and high incarceration rates: The country has a rate of 177 incarcerated individuals per 100,000 residents, which is especially high when compared to the median rate of 73 in western European countries (Fair & Walmsley, 2021). Research has repeatedly revealed that many of those released from prison in the Czech Republic reoffend: In a sample of 808 people released from Czech prisons in 2012, 45% were reconvicted within two years (Tomášek & Rozum, 2018). Similarly, 40% of 642 parolees reoffended during their supervision (Rozum et al., 2008). Some of the major obstacles to re-entry in the Czech Republic are substance use, and financial problems, such as coping with one's debt or securing stable employment (Tomášek et al., 2016).

When the focus is shifted to religiosity in the Czech Republic, rapid growth of interest in religion was expected after the fall of communism in 1989 as the communist regime was strictly atheist and prohibited most religious activities. However, the process of church property restitution and a decision to separate the church from the state in 2013 created a further divide between mainstream and church discourses (Minarik, 2019). Currently, it is one of the most nonreligious and secularized nations in the world, where religious affiliation has been decreasing together with increasing mistrust in institutionalized religion (Pew Research Center, 2018). The country has been described as "religiously indifferent" or even "religiously illiterate" (Václavík et al., 2018).

The initial Czech faith-based re-entry efforts were mostly driven by the enthusiasm of religious individuals, rather than being a top-down decision by church officials (Nešpor & Hamplová, 2020). To this day, the provision of faith-based re-entry services in the country predominantly depends on individual initiatives that report success; however, no empirical data are available to support this assertion (Dirga & Váně, 2016). Most Czech FBOs nowadays offer services primarily to adult men, providing housing, material assistance, and social work/counseling (e.g., assistance with official communication, financial problems, substance use issues, and mental health support). These organizations are generally affiliated with local branches of the Roman Catholic Church, Protestant churches (Evangelical Church of Czech Brethren, Czechoslovak Hussite Church, Church of Brethren, or Silesian Evangelical Church of the Augsburg Confession), and a few evangelical bodies (Apostolic Church, Evangelical Methodist Church, and Salvation Army). The Czech branch of Prison Fellowship International (PFI; Mezinárodní vězeňské společenství or MVS in Czech) is introduced as an example of an organization with a Christian background.

PFI/MVS offers a broad spectrum of re-entry activities, such as in-prison individual sessions and support groups, mentoring upon release, organizing groups for the released individuals, activities for children from the impacted families, etc. Research examining activities similar to those of the PFI/MVS (characterized by accepting religious authority, charismatic prayer, and emphasizing peer support and individual spirituality) supports their effectiveness in preventing recidivism (see, e.g., Johnson, 2011). The organization is aware of the Czech socio-cultural milieu. For example, it largely downplays its religious character in its communication with the Czech Prison Service officials or in the media, especially in comparison to its internal communications (e.g., social media and newsletters). The organization's tendency to professionalize and engage in public policy suggests an effort to overcome the reputation of an organization that primarily promotes and actively uses faith. Aside from existing in a religiously indifferent country, the PFI/MVS also presents an interesting case due to its ecumenical nature with an engagement of highly motivated volunteers.

Volunteer recruitment occurs during lectures in small churches, appealing on providing direct help to those in need with a religious zeal. Most volunteers are mothers who get involved during their parental leave, transforming their personal faith into a socially beneficial activity. On the other hand, most clients are religiously indifferent and usually have no personal experience with religion, paralleling the general Czech population. They get in touch with the organization when seeking material support, or they get a recommendation, and the religious overtone may come as a surprise. Based on our field research, in many cases religion is the only interest that the volunteers and clients share due to their oftentimes differing lifestyles. Religiosity is a key aspect that serves as a reference point for the volunteers and their clients to frame their narratives with a shared language and allows them to set a common goal. If this reference point is disturbed, continued cooperation becomes challenging as evidenced by the following field note from our research in a group for released individuals (all examples used are from PFI/MVS):

> This evening a Newcomer appeared. After a motivating video about religion in prison, the group was asked to discuss it. The Newcomer was very critical: "These [religious] programs for prisoners and ex-prisoners are useless. Most attendees are not interested in religion, they come for a purpose, for food or cigarettes," he claimed. The whole group tried to correct him. The lecturer raised her voice to calm the group and provided arguments for intervening God. Finally, the Newcomer gave up by saying: "I can see that I don't belong here" and left.

The Newcomer's presence was uncomfortable for the group and once he started to doubt faith, the situation escalated. His arguments crossed the line, as without agreeing on faith's centrality their cooperation could not continue.

In the previous case, introducing specific language proved to be critical for the client's partaking. Language generally serves as a functional framework that helps to reshape the identity of the released individuals. Their pre-prison experiences are conceptualized as destructive products of the "old self." Crime and substance use are interpreted as the work of Satan or of "the dark side." Volunteers and clients alike portray the process of an individual's change as a battle between the good and bad that cannot be overcome without God's mercy. The efforts of volunteers and clients to use such narratives are apparent at the meetings. During our field visit, the volunteer reframed a client's language:

> The clients are sharing their news in a circle. Client A: "I am currently looking for a job, cannot find any. But my health improved! The last problem I had just disappeared."

> Mentor: "Because there were many people praying for you!" Client A: "Yes. Yes, it is a miracle. Miracles are happening to me all the time now [...]."

Yet clients are not passive and find their own ways to negotiate the presence of religion within the organization's activities. The strong emphasis on religious values, language, and morality can create tension between volunteers and clients within the organization. This tension usually manifests in clients' relief strategies or through microaggression. For example, during singing praises in a self-help group, one client would repeatedly take bathroom and cigarette breaks or start eating and texting. Humor was another form of relief among the clients:

> During a routine activity, a problematic situation appeared. Two men are unsuccessfully trying to deal with it. After some time, one of them utters with irony: "Hey, you know what is going to save us?" The second man reacts immediately with laughter: "God will save us."

The case of the Czech Republic illustrates how fundamental the national context along with political ideology, and socio-cultural milieu are when speaking of religiosity in re-entry (Garland et al., 2017). In many countries, social work is among the most appreciated activities of institutionalized religion as it continues to lose its influence in the Western world (Manuel & Glatzer, 2019). However, in highly secularized countries like the Czech Republic, religion- and faith-related activities are oftentimes ignored or otherwise disrupted. The organizations' potential to publicly increase the reputation of religion through charity work contrasts with conscious efforts to downplay organizations' religious identities in the overall irreligious national context (Nešpor & Hamplová, 2020), as evidenced by the example of the PFI/MVS.

Conclusion

The release from prison and reintegration into society are challenging processes that contribute to the return of many people to correctional facilities, further complicating issues related to mass incarceration. Securing stable housing, legitimate income, and health care are some of the most basic needs that are oftentimes not fulfilled in the lives of released individuals. These risk factors are to an extent balanced out by different protective factors: Literature on desistence suggests that, for example, surrounding oneself with prosocial individuals is conducive to one's disengagement in criminal activities (e.g., Laub & Sampson, 2001). Yet, the stigmatization and histories of formerly incarcerated individuals oftentimes impede their chances of building new prosocial relationships in the community. Re-entry programs can alleviate some of the struggles encountered by individuals released from prison and strengthen their protective factors through providing various services. This chapter offered an insight into the workings of re-entry FBOs to consider their strengths and weaknesses in aiding successful reintegration. Aside from commenting on these as they relate to the clients, the focus was also on structural obstacles that may arise in different environments, such as the religiously indifferent Czech Republic. More research is needed to establish the effectiveness of religiosity in preventing recidivism, but inquiries related to how culture shapes the way re-entry FBOs present themselves would also enrich the discourse.

Discussion Questions:

1 What are the advantages and disadvantages of FBOs when compared to secular organizations?
2 To what extent is the role of FBOs impacted by the role of religion in different regions? Discuss the examples of the USA, Czech Republic, Israel, Pakistan, India, China, and Thailand.

Notes

1 For the purposes of this text, religiosity is defined as a combination of religious belief, affiliation, and participation in activities.
2 The author defines "sincere" individuals as whose religious involvement is motivated by genuine interest (Dammer, 2002).
3 *Agape* is a Greek term for an unconditional love, and *caritas* is a Latin term referring to caring love for all.
4 Proselytization refers to an active attempt to convert individuals to a specific religion.

References

Bakken, N. W., DeCamp, W., & Visher, C. A. (2014). Spirituality and desistance from substance use among reentering offenders. *International Journal of Offender Therapy and Comparative Criminology*, *58*(11), 1321–1339. https://doi.org/10.1177/0306624x13494076
Bowers Du Toit, N. F. (2019). Does faith matter? Exploring the emerging value and tensions ascribed to faith identity in South African faith-based organisations. *HTS Theological Studies*, *75*(4), 1–7. https://doi.org/10.4102/hts.v75i4.5530
Chambré, S. M. (2001). The changing nature of "faith" in faith-based organizations: Secularization and ecumenisms in four AIDS organizations in New York City. *Social Service Review*, *75*(3), 435–455. https://doi.org/10.1086/322222
Clear, T. R., Hardyman, P. L., Stout, B., Lucken, K., & Dammer, H. R. (2000). The value of religion in prison. *Journal of Contemporary Criminal Justice*, *16*(1), 53–74. https://doi.org/10.1177/1043986200016001004
Cloke, P., & Beaumont, J. (2012). Conclusion: The faith-based organisation phenomenon. In J. Beaumont & P. Cloke (Eds.), *Faith-based organisations and exclusion in European cities* (pp. 265–279). Bristol: Bristol University Press, Policy Press.
Dammer, H. R. (2002). The reasons for religious involvement in the correctional environment. *Journal of Offender Rehabilitation*, *35*(3/4), 35–58. https://doi.org/10.1300/J076v35n03_03
Denney, A. S. (2018). Prison chaplains: Perceptions of criminality, effective prison programming characteristics, and the role of religion in the desistance from crime. *American Journal of Criminal Justice*, *43*(3), 694–723. https://doi.org/10.1007/s12103-017-9425-3
Dirga, L., & Váně, J. (2016). Postpenitenciární péče z perspektivy nábožensky založených organizací. In V. Černíková, J. Fristová & kol (Eds.), *Postpenitenciární péče – aktuální otázky* (pp. 104–112). Evropský ústav práva a soudního inženýrství, Hodon.
Durnescu, I. (2021). Work as a drama: The experience of former prisoners in the labour market. *European Journal of Criminology*, *18*(2), 170–191. https://doi.org/10.1177/1477370819838718
Ebaugh, H. R., Pipes, P. F., Saltzman Chafetz, J., & Daniels, M. (2003). Where's the religion? Distinguishing faith-based from secular social service agencies. *Journal for the Scientific Study of Religion*, *42*(3), 411–426. https://www.jstor.org/stable/1387743
Fair, H., & Walmsley, R. (2021). *World prison population list*, 13th edition. Institute for Crime and Justice Policy Research, London.

Fridolfsson, C., & Elander, I. (2012). Faith-based organizations and welfare state retrenchment in Sweden: Substitute or complement? *Politics and Religion*, *5*(3), 634–654. https://doi.org/10.1017/S1755048312000338
Garland, B., Wodahl, E., & Smith, R. G. (2017). Religious belief and public support for prisoner reentry. *Criminal Justice Policy Review*, *28*(9), 879–895. https://doi.org/10.1177/0887403415619985
Gerace, A., & Day, A. (2010). Criminal rehabilitation: The impact of religious programming. *Journal of Psychology and Christianity*, *29*(4), 317–325. https://dro.deakin.edu.au/view/DU:30031306
Giordano, P. C., Cernkovich, S. A., & Rudolph, J. L. (2002). Gender, crime, and desistance: Toward a theory of cognitive transformation. *American Journal of Sociology*, *107*(4), 990–1064. https://doi.org/10.1086/343191
Giordano, P. C., Longmore, M. A., Schroeder, R. D., & Seffrin, P. M. (2008). A life-course perspective on spirituality and desistance from crime. *Criminology*, *46*(1), 99–132. https://psycnet.apa.org/doi/10.1111/j.1745-9125.2008.00104.x
Graddy, E. A., & Ye, K. (2006). Faith-based versus secular providers of social services –Differences in what, how and where. *Journal of Health and Human Services Administration, 29*(3), 309–335. https://www.jstor.org/stable/25790696
Hallett, M., & McCoy, J. S. (2015). Religiously motivated desistance: An exploratory study. *International Journal of Offender Therapy and Comparative Criminology*, *59*(8), 855–872. https://doi.org/10.1177/0306624X14522112
Hanson, R. K. (2018). Long-term recidivism studies show that desistance is the norm. *Criminal Justice & Behavior*, *45*(9), 1340–1346. https://doi.org/10.1177/0093854818793382
Jang, S. J., Johnson, B. R., Hays, J., Hallett, M., & Duwe, G. (2018). Religion and misconduct in "Angola" prison: Conversion, congregational participation, religiosity, and self-identities. *Justice Quarterly*, *35*(3), 412–442. https://doi.org/10.1080/07418825.2017.1309057
Jensen, K. D., & Gibbons, S. G. (2002). Shame and religion as factors in the rehabilitation of serious offenders. *Journal of Offender Rehabilitation*, *35*(3–4), 209–224. https://doi.org/10.1300/J076v35n03_11
Johnson, B. R. (2011). The role of religious institutions in responding to crime and delinquency. In P. B. Clarke (Ed.), *The Oxford handbook of the sociology of religion* (pp. 857–876). Oxford University Press, Oxford.
Kewley, S., Beech, A. R., & Harkins, L. (2015). Examining the role of faith community groups with sexual offenders: A systematic review. *Aggression and Violent Behavior*, *25*(A), 142–149. https://doi.org/10.1016/j.avb.2015.07.016
Kniss, F., & Campbell, D. T. (1997). The effect of religious orientation on international relief and development organizations. *Journal for the Scientific Study of Religion*, *36*(1), 93–103. https://doi.org/10.2307/1387885
Laub, J. H., & Sampson, R. J. (2001). Understanding desistance from crime. *Crime and Justice*, *28*, 1–69. https://doi.org/10.1086/652208
Manuel, P. C., & Glatzer, M. (2019). "Use words only if necessary": The strategic silence of organized religion in contemporary Europe. In P. C. Manuel & M. Glatzer (Eds.), *Faith-based organizations and social welfare: Associational life and religion in contemporary Western Europe* (pp. 1–18). Palgrave Macmillan, Cham.
Maruna, S. (2001). *Making good: How ex-convicts reform and rebuild their lives*. American Psychological Association, Washington, D.C.
Maruna, S., & Farrall, S. (2004). Desistance from crime: A theoretical reformulation. *Kolner Zeitschrift fur Soziologie und Sozialpsychologie*, *43*, 171–194. https://doi.org/10.1007/978-3-322-80474-7_7
Maruna, S., Porter, L., & Carvalho, I. (2004). The Liverpool desistance study and probation practice: Opening the dialogue. *Probation Journal*, *51*(3), 221–232. https://doi.org/10.1177/0264550504045899
Maruna, S., Wilson, L., & Curran, K. (2006). Why God is often found behind bars: Prison conversions and the crisis of self-narrative. *Research in Human Development*, *3*(2&3), 161–184. https://doi.org/10.1080/15427609.2006.9683367

McNeill, F. (2006). A desistance paradigm for offender management. *Criminology & Criminal Justice*, 6(1), 39–62. https://doi.org/10.1177/1748895806060666

McNeill, F. (2015). Desistance and criminal justice in Scotland. In H. Croall, G. Mooney, & R. Munro (Eds.), *Crime, justice and society in Scotland* (pp. 200–216). Routledge, London.

Minarik, P. (2019). Post-communist church-state settlements in Central Europe: Why did it take so long in the Czech Republic. *Journal of Church and State*, 62(4), 654–670. https://doi.org/10.1093/jcs/csz083

Mohammed, M. (2019). Religiosity and desistance from crime. In S. Farrall (Ed.), *The architecture of desistance* (pp. 161–180). Routledge.

Nešpor, Z. R., & Hamplová, D. (2020). Irreplaceable church welfare in the least religious country: The case of the Czech Republic. In M. Glatzer & P. C. Manuel (Eds.), *Faith-based organizations and social welfare: Associational life and religion in contemporary Eastern Europe* (pp. 221–236). Palgrave Macmilian, Cham.

O'Connor, T. (2004). What works: Religion as a correctional intervention, Part I. *Journal of Community Corrections*, 14(1), 11–27. https://www.civicresearchinstitute.com/online/article.php?pid=9&iid=221

O'Connor, T., Ryan, P., & Parikh, C. (1998). A model program for churches and ex-offender reintegration. *Journal of Offender Rehabilitation*, 28(1/2), 107–126. https://doi.org/10.1300/J076v28n01_07

Paternoster, R., & Bushway, S. D. (2009). Desistance and the feared self: Toward an identity theory of desistance. *Journal of Criminal Law & Criminology*, 99(4), 1103–1156. https://scholarlycommons.law.northwestern.edu/cgi/viewcontent.cgi?article=7339&context=jclc

Pew Research Center. (2018, October 29). *Eastern and Western Europeans differ on importance of religion, views of minorities, and key social issues*. http://www.pewforum.org/wp-content/uploads/sites/7/2018/10/Eastern-Western-Europe-FOR-WEB-1.pdf

Roberts, M. R., & Stacer, M. J. (2016). In their own words: Offenders' perspectives on their participation in a faith-based diversion and reentry program. *Journal of Offender Rehabilitation*, 55(7), 466–483. https://doi.org/10.1080/10509674.2016.1216914

Rocque, M. (2017). *Desistance from crime: New advances in theory and research*. Palgrave Macmillan, New York.

Ronel, N., & Elisha, E. (2011). A different perspective: Introducing positive criminology. *International Journal of Offender Therapy and Comparative Criminology*, 55(2), 305–325. https://doi.org/10.1177/0306624X09357772

Rozum, J., Kotulan, P., & Tomášek, J. (2008). Účinnost dohledu u osob podmíněně *propuštěných*. Institut pro kriminologii a sociální prevenci. http://www.ok.cz/iksp/docs/348.pdf, Praha.

Skotnicki, A. (1996). Religion and rehabilitation. *Criminal Justice Ethics*, 15(2), 34–43. https://doi.org/10.1080/0731129X.1996.9992017

Stansfield, R. (2017). Drawing on religion in the desistance process: Paying attention to race and ethnicity. *Criminal Justice and Behavior*, 44(7), 927–945. https://doi.org/10.1177/0093854817699438

Stark, R. (1996). Religion as context: Hellfire and delinquency one more time. *Sociology of Religion*, 57(2), 163–173. https://doi.org/10.2307/3711948

Tomášek, J., Diblíková, S., & Scheinost, M. (2016). *Probace jako efektivní nástroj snižování recidivy*. Institut pro kriminologii a sociální prevenci. http://www.ok.cz/iksp/docs/438.pdf, Praha.

Tomášek, J., & Rozum, J. (2018). Recidivism as a measure of the effectiveness of sanctions: Experience from the Czech Republic. *Acta Universitatis Carolinae Philosophica et Historica*, XXIV(2), 9–22. https://www.ceeol.com/search/article-detail?id=641570

Václavík, D., Hamplová, D., & Nešpor, Z. R. (2018). Religious situation in contemporary Czech society. *Central European Journal of Contemporary Religion*, 2(2), 99–122. https://doi.org/10.14712/25704893.2018.6

Walters-Sleyon, G. (2013). Studies on religion and recidivism: Focus on Roxbury, Dorchester, and Mattapan. *Trotter Review*, 21(1), 22–48. https://scholarworks.umb.edu/trotter_review/vol21/iss1/4/

Ward, T., & Maruna, S. (2007). *Rehabilitation*. Routledge, London.
Williams, A. (2016). Spiritual landscapes of Pentecostal worship, belief, and embodiment in a therapeutic community: New critical perspectives. *Emotion, Space and Society*, *19*, 45–55. https://doi.org/10.1016/j.emospa.2015.12.001
Willison, J. B., Brazzell, D., & Kim, K. (2011). *Faith-Based corrections and reentry program: Advancing a conceptual framework for research and evaluation*. https://www.ojp.gov/pdffiles1/nij/grants/234058.pdf
Wills, J., Datta, K., Evans, Y., Herbert, J., May, J., & McIlwaine, C. (2009). Religion at work: The role of faith-based organizations in the London living wage campaign. *Cambridge Journal of Regions, Economy and Society*, 2(3), 443–461. https://doi.org/10.1093/cjres/rsp016

25

EMBRACING HOPE

Stories of Successful Reentry Experiences

Emily I. Troshynski and Carolyn Willis

LEARNING OUTCOMES:

Upon successful completion of this chapter, students will be able to:

1 Articulate how recidivism is defined by federal entities.
2 Become familiar with research on reentry including what impacts rates of recidivism.
3 Compare findings from reentry research to findings from a localized reentry evaluation.

Mass Incarceration and Reentry

Reentry is this process of formerly incarcerated individuals returning back to "general society or the community" (Silver, D'Amato, & Wooldredge, 2021, p. 2). Within the United States, every year, over 600,000 individuals from state prisons and ten million from county jails return home. In Nevada, the state where this research takes place, 23,000 people are incarcerated in prisons yearly and 38,000 are booked into local jails (Sawyer & Wagner, 2020). 79% of these individuals return to Clark County and to the larger Las Vegas metropolitan area.

Prior scholarship notes that the majority of persons released from incarceration – 68% within three years and 77% within five years – will be reincarcerated for a new crime (Alper, Durose, & Markman, 2018). Within Nevada, closer to 25% return to prison in less than a year (NDOC, 2020). Generally, recidivism is known as the tendency of a previously incarcerated person to re-offend. The National Institute of Justice states that:

> Recidivism is measured by criminal acts resulting in rearrests, reconviction or return to prison with or without a new sentence during a three-year period following the prisoner's release.
>
> *(see Buckley, 2021)*

Based on these general and federal definitions, most research outcomes related to reentry include a heavy focus on reductions in rates of recidivism.

DOI: 10.4324/9781003274292-32

Primarily, reentry research focused on quantitative data to analyze and/or predict rates of recidivism. Less qualitative scholarship has documented the reentry process as experienced by justice-involved persons returning home including what works to lower rates of recidivism and increase successful transitions post-incarceration. After summarizing relevant research on successes and challenges associated with reentry, this chapter documents conversations with clients and reentry programming staff at a local reentry organization, HOPE for Prisoners (HFP). Highlighting successful reentry experiences helps us better understand the multidimensional and structural issues associated with reentry, what it means to "embrace hope", and how experiential knowledge is paramount in cultivating a feeling of community.

Related Reentry Research

During the reentry process, formerly incarcerated persons navigate local, state, and federal practices, policies, as well as a range of social conditions (Silver, D'Amato, & Wooldredge, 2021). Challenges to reentry include obstacles that make it difficult to return to society. Avenues toward successful reentry include opportunities that have been shown to help facilitate reintegration and reduce recidivism. Prior reentry research has focused on the impacts of housing, employment, and family reunification.

Accessing safe and affordable housing is connected to acquiring vital services required for successful transitions. Barriers to housing include local regulations (zoning and ordinances), federal mandates (eligibility requirements), and probation/parole rules (prohibiting associating with persons convicted of felonies). Oftentimes, living with partners, friends, and family members is not an option. When housing is available, disclosure of criminal histories impacts opportunities to rent (Philips & Spencer, 2013). Limited rental history, deficient personal/employment references, and a shortage of security deposits create added challenges. These housing instability experiences have been linked to extreme rates of homelessness (Couloute, 2018), increased levels of recidivism (Lutze, Rosky, & Hamilton, 2014), and negative impacts on physical and mental health (Meltzer & Schwartz, 2016).

Maintaining a job is a hallmark in reducing rates of recidivism. Financial assistance reduces the likelihood of recidivism while stable employment and higher living wages are especially critical (Anderson, Nava, & Cortez, 2018). Depending on educational level, employment history/experience, and vocational skills, there are added challenges in finding, securing, and maintaining employment. Careers are limited because many are legally barred from employment within child-related and healthcare fields (Spjeldnes & Goodkind, 2009). These realities are compounded by employers' general misunderstandings about reentry and a reluctance to hire justice-involved individuals.

Previously incarcerated persons with close social ties to family members (and/or persons not blood/legally related) are more likely to successfully reintegrate. Family members are essential in providing much-needed financial and emotional support. Prior reentry studies have documented that almost half of released persons are "expected to rely on family as a source of support" (Berg & Huebner, 2011, p. 4). Therefore, sustaining and strengthening social relationships helps to reduce the risk of recidivism as well as reincarceration.

Notably, physical and mental health concerns often complicate housing, employment, and positive family reunification. Justice-involved individuals have higher rates of antisocial behavior, anxiety, and PTSD (Schappell, Docherty, & Boxer, 2016), as well as substance use/abuse histories (Wakefield & Uggen, 2010). These health conditions are difficult to manage when many are uninsured or lack access to medical and mental healthcare. These realities contribute to an increased need for emergency healthcare services in the future (Marlow, White, & Chesla, 2010).

Evidently, "successful" reentry is not as simple as measuring rates of recidivism. Success is, instead, related to availability and access to human needs in the immediate- (i.e., clothing, paperwork, and housing), short- (i.e., transportation and employment), and long-term (i.e., educational/training and physical and mental healthcare) as well as to the quality of social ties and human capital.

Localized Research: HOPE for Prisoners

Given Nevada's incarceration and recidivism rates, understanding reentry from the perspective of previously incarcerated persons returning home is crucial. A focus on a local reentry organization, HFP showcases conversations with seven reentry programming staff and 20 clients who have successfully completed the 18-month HFP reentry program. Findings document services that are most important in lowering rates of recidivism while promoting successful reintegration.

Site Location and Methods

HFP was birthed from the personal experiences of its Founder and CEO, Jon Ponder. As a three-time convicted individual, Jon served his last prison sentence at a maximum-security federal penitentiary. After completing his sentence, Jon was released to the Clark County, Nevada community where he was sentenced. Jon utilized his personal reentry experiences, and evidence-based perspectives, as well as leveraged relationships within the community, to build a reentry organization that centers on guiding individuals throughout their reentry journey.

HFP has been in operation since 2009 and offers reentry interventions and services to formerly incarcerated persons returning home. Services include both pre -and post-release case management, mentoring, family reunification, counseling, and workforce development services centered on educational and vocational training. HFP has provided reentry services to over 4,000 individuals and currently serves approximately 500 individuals yearly, the majority (85%) are males.

HFP receives funding from federal, state, and local agencies, as well as individual donations from members of the community. Funding opportunities have been provided by the Department of Justice, Department of Labor, and partnering organizations like the local Workforce Board. Based on prior federally funded program evaluations documenting an impressive 6.8% rate of recidivism for clients after 18 months, HFP stands out from other community-based reentry programs across the United States (Troshynski et al., 2016).

HFP aims to reduce recidivism, increase public safety, and develop opportunities within the community to facilitate the greatest probability of successful reintegration for individuals returning home after incarceration. Through a process of community transformation, HFP provides "hope" to justice-involved individuals and emphasizes the importance of empowering clients "where they are at". Clients utilizing HFP services are demonstratively referred to as "hopefuls". Placing the hopeful at the center of reentry programming – and their prior correctional labels, activities, and conditions a far second – is a hallmark of this non-profit organization.

Research Participant Information

As noted in Table 25.1, seven programming staff were interviewed and all identified as female. Information captured highlights the diversity among staff as it relates to age, race, ethnicity, educational background, involvement and prior experience with HOPE, languages spoken, and relationship status.

Table 25.2, highlights the attributes of hopefuls participating in the program. Clients interviewed (N = 20) had varying backgrounds as it relates to prior convictions, length of time served, age, race, ethnicity, relationship status, and education. Upon release, all clients were considered to be "high-risk" to re-offend and/or recidivate based on the Nevada Risk Assessment System (NRAS) tool. Importantly, these hopefuls have successfully completed the 18-month HFP program. Their insights into what works and what is still needed are paramount.

Findings – Services Connected to Successful Reintegration

Within the HFP framework, client and staff experiences define what "success" means for this organization. For example, all program staff members defined success as lowering rates of recidivism; yet, staff articulated that recidivism is intimately connected to client success in navigating and overcoming reentry challenges. Staff and clients noted the importance of securing safe and affordable housing, finding employment and planning for a career, having access to physical and mental health needs while maintaining sobriety, and welcoming pro-social family reunification. Hopefuls and staff also talked much about the importance of reflection, consistency, and accountability and how these are related to "changing mindsets" and "embracing hope".

TABLE 25.1 Program Staff Attributes

Program staff attributes	Number interviewed (N = 7)
Gender	Females (N = 7)
Age range	25–50 years (Average 38.33 years)
Relationship status	Single (N = 2)
	Long-term relationship or married (N = 5)
Race and ethnicity	White (N = 3)
	Black (N = 4)
	Hispanic, Latino or Spanish background (N = 1)
Languages spoken	English, Spanish, Samoan, or Creole
	50% spoke more than two languages listed above
Educational background	Graduate degree (N = 3)
	Some college experience or a high school diploma (N = 4)
Involvement with HOPE	Little over a year to well over five years (average of 3.5 years)
Prior experience with HOPE	Volunteer (N = 6)
	Mentor (N = 5)
	Teacher/trainer (N = 2)
	Prior clients/alumni (N = 2)
Worked full-time position at HOPE	Little over a year to three and a half years (average of 23 months).

TABLE 25.2 Hopeful Attributes

Hopeful Attributes	*Number of Hopefuls Interviewed (N = 20)*	*Percentage*
Gender	Males (N = 11)	55
	Females (N = 9)	45
Race and ethnicity	White (N = 12)	63
	Black (N = 4)	21
	Mixed or Other (N = 4)	21
	Hispanic, Latino/a, Spanish Background (N = 2)	10
Relationship status	Married (N = 1, Female)	5
	Separated or Divorced (N = 7)	35
	Single (N = 12)	60
Educational background	Graduate Degree (N = 2)	10
	Some College (N = 2)	10
	High School Graduate (N = 10)	50
	Some High School (N = 6)	30
Prior convictions	Two Priors (N = 17)	85
	Three or More Priors (N = 10)	50
Length of time served immediately prior to HFP	37 days to 72 months (6 years)	
Age range	Between 21 and 54 years	
	Female: Average 36	
	Males: Average 38	

Success with Housing – "Game Changer"

Housing provides an address, place to live, and sense of security. Having a safe and stable place to call home is integral for clients reintegrating back into the community. For staff, "reentry success" is articulated as,

> ... having resources, and more housing. When [clients] exit prison, they come home, and a lot of them don't have a home to go to. So they find themselves reverting to the criminal mentality of running the streets, selling drugs, and doing what they were doing previously. You know, survival mode. So, housing is so big. Housing and employment are interconnected.

Having knowledge and access to housing resources helps staff provide for clients' housing needs. This is a *"game-changer"* and directly impacts rates of recidivism and successful reintegration.

HFP facilitates clients' reentry experiences by making sure all staff are knowledgeable about available housing options within the local community. For HFP, success is often derived from partnering with different organizations offering emergency housing. One staff person mentioned, "*No matter the situation, everyone is still human... the importance of community partnerships is key*". Examples of maintaining collaborative connections include weekly community resource meetings where local entities are introduced to staff and provide overviews of services available. Staff found these meetings *"kept it fresh"* and *"keep us up-to-date"* on the types of housing services/programs available.

Regularly advocating for clients, staff also mentioned how they spend time in conversation with private residence owners willing to provide long-term housing to formerly incarcerated persons. Additionally, staff work closely with clients to seek out alternative housing options, fill out paperwork, and prepare interviews with landlords/property owners/managers to ensure clients have safe and secure housing options.

Despite these networking and advocating activities, finding, and securing safe housing was still the biggest reentry challenge noted by all staff members and clients interviewed. For example, when a hopeful has children, housing options are even more limited. As Phoebe, a client, mentioned:

> ...[HFP] gave me some resources for possibilities to rent to ex-felons. And honestly, they were not good areas because I have a thirteen-year-old daughter. She's in foster care and I'm getting her back in two weeks. So, I had to have housing... I had to have somewhere, you know, safe. So housing was a big obstacle for me.

It took Phoebe close to a year to find housing that she felt was safe enough for her daughter. During that time, HFP worked with her to ensure she secured employment and completed a financial literary course. This course helped Phoebe manage her finances, plan for larger security deposits, and, over time, increase her credit score. Phoebe mentioned these opportunities were *"the most useful"* for her because she was finally able to secure housing in a safe neighborhood.

Finding a safe, sober living space was also a noted reentry challenge. In discussing his success, Max, mentioned, *"HOPE for Prisoners has helped me. There's a teacher in one of the classes that recommended the sober living house to me. So HOPE helped with that"*. For HFP, success is acknowledged as clients secure safe and affordable housing that brings about healthy stability. As one staff mentioned, *"Safe stable housing helps instill the motivation for them to overcome additional challenges"*. Access to such housing is even more important for clients' child-care and/or maintaining sobriety.

Success with Employment – "They like my work"

HFP addresses employment challenges from a *"workforce development perspective"* whereby success in employment is connected to understanding clients' prior work history (if any), and unique trade/educational skill sets while addressing skill gaps or educational/training needs. Once staff understands a client's history, a plan is created to address any gaps, while finding them opportunities to apply to and interview for jobs.

One hopeful, Randy, mentioned HFP provided a better understanding of what to expect within the workforce. After being incarcerated for several years, the process of procuring employment was confusing. Randy explained,

> HOPE helped me with the know-how. Things that I kind of separated myself from in terms of like work or working. Like, the workplace environment, interviewing. That was really a big thing to learn.

HFP staff encourages clients to think about a *"long-term career"* instead of just a *"job for now"*. To secure career opportunities, staff and clients create goals for long-term success. As noted by program staff, *"it's more career-based employment than just mean-time jobs"*.

Even for clients experiencing unemployment or job changes due to COVID-19, HFP staff encouraged them to spend "downtime" educating themselves and enrolling in additional employment training courses. For example, at the time of the interview, one hopeful, Grant, was waiting for his employer to relocate him to another site location. Based on his long-term career goals, Grant also mentioned how he was taking advantage of classes offered at HFP:

> I'm unemployed until they [current employer] can relocate me somewhere else. But I like that job and they like my work. So I'll be going back to them because I'm doing the CDL training here [at HFP] as well.

To ensure clients secure employment with sustainable living wages, staff advocate for clients with employers in the community they regularly collaborate with. In talking about his and other hopefuls' success with employment, Matthew explained,

> ...That's how I gained employment. [HFP] work very closely with the company – hand in hand - and they [the company] took us in. Even knowing what we are. Because I'm a two-time felon. I could put in applications 'til I'm blue in the face and nothing's happening.

Matthew continued,

> Through HOPE, it was comforting knowing that "Hey, look, all you gotta do is go in to the interview." So they [company] know your background... your history, and – yeah - it's a definite answer.

Similarly, in talking about long-term career planning as a "big success", another hopeful, Tia, emphasized *"the importance of completing the training and doing well"*; the range of employment and training resources available/provided to her was the most impactful. Since training opportunities encourage participation and lead to clients securing training credentials, these workforce development avenues promote career pathway opportunities which, in turn, creates long-term sustainable financial independence.

Max also discussed how HFP helped him find employment opportunities that *"fit"* with his long-term goals and *"visions for the future"*. For Max, this planning was also connected to breaking previous cycles of criminal activity:

> Successes? Gaining and retaining employment. Having a vehicle. Just, you know, staying out of trouble... This last was my fourth time being in prison. It's a vicious cycle... just breaking that cycle... um, being a normal human being, you know?

After securing safe housing, gaining and retaining employment was an important "success story" for all hopefuls interviewed.

Maintaining Sobriety – "The hardest thing to do"

In assessing physical and mental healthcare needs, one of the biggest challenges for clients is to maintain sobriety while navigating their reentry process. Staff noted that *"drug and alcohol use challenges - as it relates to sobriety - are huge"*. All clients interviewed had prior experiences with alcohol and drug use and abuse and the vast majority (two clients did not have an addiction history) were invested in their sobriety. This was "*the biggest challenge*", for Grace:

> Really, the challenge is like..., when you first get out...Then you get out to nothing... all these rules and expectations to do this and maintain this. Find work and then work. Some people do. Some don't. At first, though, the hardest thing to do is stay sober.

Relatedly, Sonny discussed how he was previously enrolled in a treatment program, not associated with HFP, *"for substance abuse and then relapsed"*. In reflecting on his "*biggest success",* he highlighted access to treatment and impacts on sobriety,

> Hope for Prisoners had a good program. I did it for I think six weeks? And it's completely different from the one that I did before. I think it was easier to understand. I think it was better.

When asked to explain what made the HFP program "better", he said, "It was more in-depth about the reasoning that people 'use' and like their counselors have all like been there before. Which makes it easier to talk to them, you know?" Sonny mentioned how "what worked" for him was having therapists and counselors with experiential knowledge. This professional self-disclosure might have helped Sonny to connect, open up, be motivated by a potential role model, and maintain sobriety.

From an organizational perspective, success includes having qualified staff available to identify physical and mental health needs, barriers to accessing care, as well as triggers, and/or instances where clients may have relapsed. In thinking about client success with sobriety, staff discussed how clients are often *"triggered by the stressors – like change, shame, and environmental factors"* – concurrently associated with the reintegration process. To alleviate challenges, HFP refers clients to local treatment and counseling services. Additionally, hopefuls meet with professional therapists and counselors working at HFP. Lastly, HFP offers personal development classes to all clients. These aid hopefuls in identifying and managing stressors and triggers, while also incorporating pro-social/leisure activities.

Pro-Social Family Reunification – "Things changed!"

Access to legal services for child custody and child support issues are vital resources within a reentry program as navigating legal issues can be complicated. HFP clients are provided opportunities to work with family services and child support divisions to address child support issues. For individuals with child custody cases, staff work with governing agencies to provide updates on clients' participation in the HFP program. At times, the family reunification process can be fostered by the client's changed behavior. This usually occurs when hopefuls demonstrate a consistent change in behavior where family members can see they are moving towards a pro-social lifestyle and leaving the "old life" behind.

When asked about his success, Freddy articulated how this change impacted his relationship with both his son and grandson. After Freddy's son found out he was in HFP, he asked, "*So, you're really doing this?*" Freddy explained,

> I'm like yeah! I'm doing it! He [client's son] brought my grandkids around to see me. Before he wouldn't because I was, I was a beast. I was up there doing too much. So, when

> he had seen that pops had calmed down, he brought my grandson over. Things changed; you know?

When this level of change is attained, justice-involved persons are not only able to reestablish relationships, but also reassume roles often severed due to their previous lifestyles and experiences with incarceration.

As part of the programming services and resources available at HFP, family reunification classes and counseling are provided to clients. Phoebe discussed how she was in the process of getting her younger daughter out of foster care while rebuilding her relationship with her older daughter. She mentioned,

> We're repairing. I was gone a long time... now I'm back. So, you know just repairing our relationship. We're being healthy because we've had a lot of dysfunction.

When asked if HFP helped with family reunification, she said, *"Absolutely! We do family therapy through HOPE and they take care of it - the fare. Yeah, they're amazing. I love them"*. Success with family reunification adds another layer that solidifies a healthy prosocial reentry process where clients feel welcomed and part of a larger community where they are supported.

Changing the Mindsets of Community and Clients – "Doing different"

"Changing mindsets" is not just a phrase used within HFP; there are mechanisms in place encouraging hopefuls to be reflexive, plan, and think through their decisions. The pre- and post-release process include consistent goal setting throughout the 18-month program. Program staff received training in administering risk assessments, identifying challenges and needs, prescribing care, and providing case management services to clients. These trainings are paramount as they establish a framework to work alongside clients to create and address immediate, short- and long-term goals – spaced out and routed appropriately so as not to overwhelm clients. Staff and clients indicated that it is "easier" to participate in a program when expectations are clearly articulated, agreed upon, and administered with a level of care and consistency. Connected to client success, Zak explained:

> ...[Program staff] changed my mindset, my perspective on what success could look like, how I could still be me without having to do with those old things [criminal activities] that were detrimental to my success.

Randy echoed,

> I came out with a different mindset... I just felt like nothing got in my way. HOPE for Prisoners, what it was really good at – still is really good at – is giving you, emphasizing the idea of self-esteem, like morale.

Consistent and frequent one-on-one case management includes conversations with clients about their goals and accomplishments. Programmatic services help clients succeed in realizing, working towards, and attaining goals.

Throughout conversations, all 20 hopefuls mentioned how important resources were in changing routine behaviors and thoughts as well as how they understood what "success", for them, might look like. Grant also explained how HFP helped him to set goals, "*...be accountable, and think differently*". He continued,

> I'm doing different, especially since I'm trying to get this ball moving in the right direction. It's a lot of "stop thinking like that and think like this" ... just keep it going.

In thinking about measuring client success, staff also noted:

> ...at the end of the day, his [hopeful] mindset about committing crimes and not being involved with his family is way different. You can't put that on paper. There's no way to track that.

Conversations about helping hopefuls to "change their mindset" included a sincere focus and dedication to the use of person-centered language including "clients", "participants", "residents", "hopefuls", and "family". This humanizing language instills a sense of hopeful change and removes the stigma often associated with negative labels like "inmate," "ex-offender," or "felon." HFP staff noted, "*Words have meaning*" and are connected to positive experiences clients embrace as they begin to introduce, describe, and reinvent themselves while they reintegrate.

As noted previously, there are several ways to measure success throughout this multifaceted process known as reentry. For HFP, the most important measures are realized when clients complete the 18-month program, move towards self-sustainability, and embrace the opportunity to be a community member and give back. Clients often return as alumni of HFP and volunteer to be mentors to new hopefuls. This does not only signal "success" or "completion" of a program but provides a way for clients to transition to the role of a community mentor and remain connected to the larger organization and all its services and resources.

Discussion – Embracing Hope

Excerpts within this chapter highlight how reentry success is multilayered and includes overcoming structural, institutional, and personal challenges at different moments throughout the reintegration process. HFP incorporates a therapeutic organizational pre- and post-release reentry framework that embraces experiential knowledge derived from personal encounters with the justice system. Several administrators, staff, practitioners, and mentors have similar justice-involvement experiences relatable to hopefuls. These unique components are articulated below including how HFP encourages a holistic and humane reentry program that embraces hopefuls "where they are at" and commits to "walk beside them" on their reentry journey.

HOPE for Prisoners Is "Like family"

Over half of the programming staff (N = 4 or 57%) acknowledged their prior involvement with the criminal justice system has shaped the way they interact with clients and ultimately influenced their case management styles. One expressed, "*As a case manager, I reflect on my experiences... what I needed and implement it into my case management*" with clients. Another mentioned:

> My past experience with the criminal justice system has shaped how I case manage and interact with clients and staff since I had to navigate the system pre- and post-release. It has given me a better understanding of the challenges, fear, and uncertainty our clients experience on a daily basis. Because I am equipped with the knowledge, I am able to problem-solve and relate to client challenges differently.

By addressing individual-level risks and needs, providing support and reentry resources, and creating community, HFP provides avenues for client success to be attainable.

Importantly, not only are hopefuls successful individually, but they are successful together in a community that supports and embraces them. A staff and alum noted:

> While in the program, I never felt 'case managed.' It felt like family; I wanted to visit HOPE. There was a sense of community which was most important to me.

Clients, too, mention how HFP feels like a community or family. For example, Sonny mentioned,

> ...[HFP] helped with everything. Clothing, interviews. They helped me do a resume. They make you their family— like they helped me with Christmas for my kids. And they're all great!

When avenues for success are accessible – and when clients are cared for and treated like "family" – hopefuls feel empowered and become invested community members. These interpersonal organizational-dynamics further contribute to positive outcomes and successes. Freddy, another client, mentioned,

> I know they [HFP staff] do a really good job of keeping in contact. The frequency - in terms of how they reach out to you and constantly stay engaged with you - I think it's really vital for people reintegrating into society simply because some people coming out don't have anybody.

Not only is it important for clients to feel understood, cared for, and embraced as part of a larger organization and community, but it is also important to be able to meet other individuals who have succeeded in their own reentry journey.

HOPE for Prisoners Is "Seeing someone who made it"

All employees acknowledged that part of the success HFP derives comes from sharing their own personal reentry experiences with clients. This experiential knowledge facilitates honest and open interaction between staff and clients. For those staff/affiliated persons that have successfully reintegrated, sharing their stories motivates clients as they can "*see someone who made it*". These interpersonal connections provide clients with an understanding that they, too, can *"make it as well"*. For example, Matthew mentioned, *"She's [staff] been through a lot of the same things I have and she's experienced major changes and we talk about it"*. Freddy confirmed, *"I heard her [staff] story, and I realized something - that, if these people have done just as much time or more than I have, and they're successful, why can't I be?"*.

This experiential knowledge was also connected to reasons why clients believe the program is successful. Zak said,

> I think that's the basis of why they [HFP] are so successful. Because they're actually genuinely concerned, and they care about what they are doing. That's why people are finding success there because the proof is in the pudding. They actually walked the walk and don't just talk a bunch of crap. They are actually in it to win it, so to speak.

"Success" is not a one-size-fits-all model. These shared experiences create collective moments to embrace and celebrate while helping to identify reference points as to what success could look like. Discussing experiences and learning from one another provides opportunities for collaboration and the development of best practices at the local level. Having a safe space to talk about reentry also increases the frequency of contact between program staff, mentors, and clients. Functioning as a collaborative community, everyone is on the same page – this level of consistency promotes cohesiveness and stability needed throughout the reintegration process.

Conclusion

Many of the challenges and successes associated with housing, employment, and family reunification were analogous to those identified in prior research. Additional insights into "success" included routine behavior and cognitive changes (i.e., changing mindsets) as well as the importance of sharing and learning from justice-involved persons (i.e., experiential knowledge). These findings suggest that there is no "cookie-cutter" approach to reentry. As narratives herein indicate, there is also no "one way" to identify success. Lowering rates of individual-level recidivism is notable. However, recognition of the significance of structural factors external to an individual that impacts their recidivism is also important.

Connected to this, "success" is realized in differing ways depending on individualized reintegration experiences as well as client needs and goals – immediate-, short-, and long-term. Although the reentry process presents a myriad challenges, success occurs when a program provides individualized case management with access to a range of services and resources. Making sure every single client has a safe space to process, be reflexive, share stories, and engage in collaboration is important. Embracing hope, finding a sense of community where previously incarcerated persons feel like they belong, and providing a space to celebrate accomplishments together is also imperative.

Discussion Questions:

---

1. What are some of the challenges facing staff and hopefuls as they return home? How do they successfully overcome these challenges?
2. For staff and hopefuls, what makes for a successful reentry program/experience?

References

Alper, M., Durose, M. R., & Markman, J. (2018). *2018 Update on Prisoner Recidivism: A 9 Year Follow-Up Period (2005–2014)*. Bureau of Justice Statistics: Office of Justice Programs.

Anderson, A., Nava, N. J., & Cortez, P. (2018). The conduits and barriers to reentry for formerly incarcerated individuals in San Bernardino. *Journal of Prison Education and Reentry*, *5*(1), 2.

Berg, M. T., & Huebner, B. M. (2011). Reentry and the ties that bind: An examination of social ties, employment, and recidivism. *Justice Quarterly*, *28*(2), 382–410.

Buckley, D. (2021). *From Ex-offenders to Hopefuls: Exploring Changing Narratives and Personal Stories of Desistance* (Master's thesis, University of Nevada, Las Vegas).

Couloute, L. (2018). *Nowhere to Go: Homelessness among Formerly Incarcerated People*. Prison Policy Initiative.

Lutze, F. E., Rosky, J. W., & Hamilton, Z. K. (2014). Homelessness and reentry: A multisite outcome evaluation of Washington State's reentry housing program for high risk offenders. *Criminal Justice and Behavior*, *41*(4), 471–491.

Marlow, E., White, M. C., & Chesla, C. A. (2010). Barriers and facilitators: Parolees' perceptions of community health care. *Journal of Correctional Health Care*, *16*(1), 17–26.

Meltzer, R., & Schwartz, A. (2016). Housing affordability and health: Evidence from New York City. *Housing Policy Debate*, *26*(1), 80–104.

Nevada Department of Corrections (NDOC) (2020). Report available at: https://doc.nv.gov/uploadedFiles/docnvgov/content/About/Statistics/2018%20Recidivism%20Cohort.pdf

Philips, L. A., & Spencer, M. W. (2013). The challenges of reentry from prison to society. *Journal of Current Issues in Crime, Law and Law Enforcement*, *6*(2), 123–133.

Sawyer, W. & Wagner, P. (2020). *Mas Incarceration: The Whole Pie 2020*. The Prison Policy Initiative.

Schappell, A., Docherty, M., & Boxer, P. (2016). Violence and victimization during incarceration: Relations to psychosocial adjustment during reentry to the community. *Violence and Victims*, *31*(2), 361–378.

Silver, I. A., D'Amato, C., & Wooldredge, J. (2021). The cycle of reentry and reincarceration: Examining the influence on employment over a period of 18 years. *Journal of Criminal Justice*, *74*, 101812.

Spjeldnes, S., & Goodkind, S. (2009). Gender differences and offender reentry: A review of the literature. *Journal of Offender Rehabilitation*, *48*(4), 314–335.

Troshynski, E., Kennedy, M. A., Sousa, W. H., Madensen, T. D., & Willis, C. (2016). Prisoner reentry in Nevada: Final report on the hope for prisoners program. *University of Nevada Las Vegas, Center for Crime and Justice Policy, Research in Brief, CCJP, 1*

Wakefield, S., & Uggen, C. (2010). Incarceration and stratification. *Annual Review of Sociology*, *36*, 387–406.

26

REFLECTION

THE REALITY OF REENTRY

Emily Sorenson

Mass incarceration and reentry services are connected in a multitude of ways; one of the most obvious being that reentry programs assist previously incarcerated individuals with transitioning back into society. I'm here to say that after directing several reentry programs across the state of New York, funded by many sources and serving different subsets of the reentry population: reentry programs are being tasked with the impossible expectation of fixing a broken system – one that contributes to the phenomenon of mass incarceration we see nationwide.

Fundamentally, reentry programs provide support to previously incarcerated individuals upon reentering society, presumably after spending a substantial amount of time in prison. However, in more recent years, reentry programs have evolved. In fact, most of the reentry programs I currently oversee do not even require any incarceration time. Yet, all of the individuals we serve consistently present with the same needs, many of which are unrelated to their actual crimes and more related to the circumstances that led them to commit the crime in the first place.

We're talking criminogenic risk factors here, folks. The individuals we serve willingly come to our programs in search of mental health services, housing assistance, educational and occupational training, substance use counseling, and the list goes on. These are not needs that crop up over night when someone is arrested and released 12 hours later. Rather, these are needs that are present prior to the commission of the crime. These are needs that are persistent in communities and remain unaddressed.

I'm going to use one of my favorite clients to give you an example of what I'm talking about. I know I shouldn't have "favorite clients," but I do. His name is Gary*. I've known Gary for six years. When we first met in 2015, I was not working in reentry, but in therapeutic foster care.[1] Gary was 15 and living in a residential treatment facility after being removed from his biological mother's home. Gary transitioned into a foster home where I worked to bring stability and care into his life. This meant walking a 16 year old boy to high school every single morning at 7 am in downtown Rochester, NY just to see him run out the back doors of the school as I walked away. We did this song and dance for two years until Gary moved back to his mother's home and I moved on to a different job.

DOI: 10.4324/9781003274292-33

Fast forward to 2019. I'm managing a reentry office, and who walks into my new office after another arrest? Gary. Talk about a bittersweet moment. Here we went again, working day in and day out, with so much more support this go around. Our reentry programs linked Gary with GED classes, forklift licensure training, daily breakfast and lunch, a housing subsidy program, transportation, job placement, and mental health services. We even replaced his ID a total of *seven* times. There were new clothes bought, and donated household items when he moved into his first apartment, and Gary was truly grateful every step of the way.

As I write this, Gary currently resides in a New York State prison with a 4.5 year sentence after an attempted robbery charge.

But, why? Why, if Gary was given all of these supports, did he still end up incarcerated? The answer is exactly what links mass incarceration and reentry programs in the first place: unaddressed and, widespread, community needs. In Gary's story alone, we saw mental health needs, an unstable family life, unsuccessful education, a lack of positive peers ("criminal associates"), and (although not mentioned above), substance abuse. These are all criminogenic risk factors that went unaddressed for a majority of Gary's life that our reentry programs are not equipped to handle long term.

While it probably seems like I'm slighting the work reentry programs do, I'm certainly not. As I previously mentioned, I currently oversee multiple different reentry programs across New York State and don't foresee myself switching careers anytime soon. I've never seen a harder working set of staff in any field than I have in reentry. We're all in this work because we *believe* in it. We know that we're being dealt an impossible hand, but if it means that we can help the people we're so passionate about supporting even just a little, even if it's just replacing someone's ID (seven times), we're going to do it.

Reentry programs may need a different name before too long because what we're doing is certainly not a reentry issue. If the government and criminal justice agencies are serious about wanting to reduce recidivism and mass incarceration, a large majority of these needs can and should be taken care of prior to release. And for individuals that don't require a long stint of incarceration, let's start looking at what is truly getting in the way of their success prior to system involvement.

There is something to be said about practicing what we preach. Reentry program staff are consistently telling clients to be proactive instead of reactive. It's time we start doing the same.

*Name has been changed to protect individual's identity.

Note

1 "Therapeutic Foster Care is out-of-home care by foster parents with specialized training to care for a wide variety of children and adolescents, usually those with significant emotional, behavioral, or social issues or medical needs" (childwelfare.gov).

SECTION VII

Ending Mass Incarceration

"Mass Incarceration is the civil rights crisis of our time" (Chettiar and Raghavan, 2019, p. 95). There is a bipartisan consensus amongst policymakers and the general population that the U.S. cannot continue to over-incarcerate its people (Davidson, 2020). We have seen criminal justice reform efforts to end mass incarceration, such as reducing prison populations during COVID, closing prisons, decriminalizing certain offenses, and reforming sentencing guidelines. There are also debates about whether the system should be reformed or completely overhauled—abolished. What is prison abolition anyway? It is not closing prisons and letting people roam free. Prison abolition is a movement of people who want to imagine and create a society where prisons are no longer needed because we have found different ways to respond to social problems such as homelessness, poverty, and mental health (Davis, 2011). Bail reform, decarceration by releasing people from prison during COVID, and other examples could be understood as abolitionist perspectives. There are other ways to understand ending mass incarceration: ending extreme sentencing reforms, reforms that expand the right to vote to people on parole or incarcerated, limiting incarceration for probation and parole violations, and drug policy reforms are all examples of criminal justice reforms that have happened in the past year (Porter, 2022). The last section of the book examines the different means to end mass incarceration.

This final section begins with Kilmer and Antune's "Mass incarceration, reproductive injustice, and the need for abolitionist solutions." Kilmer and Antune discuss the importance of abolitionist alternatives to imprisonment as a method of supporting system-involved women and their reproductive autonomy. Gomez and Farr continue the discussion by reviewing the prison abolition movement as a form of resistance against racial injustices in their chapter, "Today's Lynching is Incarceration: Critical Race Theory, Mass Incarceration, and Prison Abolition." Next, Alia Nahra discusses the police abolition movement and its role in ending mass incarceration in "Enacting a World Beyond Policing." Following this chapter, Leslie Scott considers ending mass incarceration in her chapter "Decriminalizing Substance Use Disorders to Combat Mass Incarceration." The section concludes with Arne Kvernvik Nilsen's reflection, "Prisons We Do Not Deserve."

DOI: 10.4324/9781003274292-34

References

Chettiar, I., & Raghavan, P. (2019). *Ending Mass Incarceration: Ideas from Today's Leaders*. Brennan Center for Justice. Retrieved from https://www.brennancenter.org/sites/default/files/publications/2019_EndingMassIncarceration_digital.pdf

Davidson, J. (2020, January 12). Perspective|federal prison reform has bipartisan support. But it's moving slowly. *The Washington Post*. Retrieved December 23, 2022, from https://www.washingtonpost.com/politics/federal-prison-reform-has-bipartisan-support-but-its-moving-slowly/2020/01/08/81edfbd6-3268-11ea-898f-eb846b7e9feb_story.html

Davis, A. Y. (2011). *Are Prisons Obsolete?* New York: Seven Stories Press.

Porter, N. (2022). *Top Trends in Criminal Justice Reform, 2022*. The Sentencing Project. https://www.sentencingproject.org/fact-sheet/top-trends-in-criminal-justice-reform-2022/

27

MASS INCARCERATION, REPRODUCTIVE INJUSTICE, AND THE NEED FOR ABOLITIONIST SOLUTIONS

Ashley Kilmer and Maria João Lobo Antunes

LEARNING OUTCOMES:

Upon completion of this chapter, students will be able to:

1 Explain the concept of reproductive justice in relation to the experiences of incarcerated women in United States prisons and jails.
2 Analyze the use of abolitionist alternatives to incarceration as a response to criminal offending behavior while supporting women's reproductive autonomy.

Introduction

Reproductive justice is a theoretical framework born out of Black feminist thought in the 1990s to analyze the impact of intersecting systems of oppression that strip women of their autonomy and resources to decide if, and when they have children, the conditions under which they give birth, and the right to parent (Hayes, Sufrin, & Perritt, 2020). Many of the social factors that produce inequalities and injustices in relation to reproductive justice converge within the United States' system of mass incarceration. Carceral spaces are the antithesis of reproductive justice with an extensive history of denying people access to health care, and subjecting women to forced sterilization as well as forced birth. Sadly, the violation of incarcerated women's reproductive rights is more ordinary than exceptional. In this chapter, we use the reproductive justice framework as a critical lens to examine how the use of carceral punishment by the State amplifies the reproductive injustice experienced disproportionately by Black and brown women through the regulation of their bodies. As the incarceration rate of women continues to outpace that of men (Sentencing Project, 2020), the reach of the State in controlling the reproductive choices of system-impacted women expands as well. Efforts to reform sentencing practices and correctional policy within this system of punishment are not sufficient when women are still subjected to government mechanisms of dehumanization and control. Instead, we posit that abolitionist alternatives to imprisonment can more effectively address the circumstances that contribute to offending

DOI: 10.4324/9781003274292-35

behavior and repair harm produced by criminal behavior while promoting opportunities to empower and support system-involved women and their reproductive autonomy.

Additionally, we want to acknowledge at the start of this chapter that the research, policies, and cases reviewed often use the terms "woman" and "mother" and primarily reflect the perspective and experiences of cisgender women incarcerated in women's prisons. We also adopt this terminology throughout the chapter. However, we recognize that transgender individuals and other incarcerated people who do not identify with these labels, some of whom are imprisoned in men's facilities, also experience pregnancy, parenthood, and reproductive injustice. The framework of reproductive justice applies to everyone whose reproductive health and bodily autonomy are threatened by systems of oppression. Finally, when we began outlining the idea for a chapter on reproductive justice and mass incarceration, the possibility that *Roe v. Wade* (1973) would be struck down, while a genuine fear we shared, was not something we thought we would need to confront. Yet here we are. This decision, along with the experiences of incarcerated women discussed in this chapter, demonstrates the ongoing conflict between the State and women's reproductive rights, a conflict exacerbated by the violent and coercive foundation of the United States carceral system. Further, taken holistically, the impact of criminalizing reproductive choice will also affect those on probation and parole in states where abortion is now illegal and travel restrictions are imposed as part of supervision conditions (see Bertram & Sawyer, 2022 for a thoughtful discussion). The damage caused by striking down *Roe* will be profoundly felt within the criminal legal system and beyond.

The Rise of Incarcerated Women

The close of the 20th century saw a sharp increase in the number of incarcerated women, particularly at the end of the 1980s (see Figure 27.1). Mass incarceration, the product of ever-expanding law enforcement policies, the shift from indeterminate sentencing to mandatory minimums and three-strikes laws, the War on Drugs, and other release mechanisms impacted justice-involved individuals. However, the effect on women is far more deleterious. "As a minority group, women prisoners have been subjected to theory framing, management practices, and programs posited as gender neutral or derived or borrowed directly from those for men," (Baldry, 2010: 254). The needs of women in prison, often addressed as if like those of men, stem from the lack of attention, policy, and research attending to the unique needs of women (Van Voorhis, 2012). As Aranda-Hughes and colleagues (2021) state, "female offending populations are unique from men, in several ways," (51) not only regarding the types of crimes women commit but also the range of challenges and social problems experienced, including poverty, mental illness, child abuse, and drug and alcohol dependence.

According to the Sentencing Project (2020), the rate of female incarceration exceeded that of males, increasing more than 700% since the 1980s with over one million women under some form of correctional supervision. While the numbers have stabilized over the last 15 years, rates of imprisonment for women continue to overtake those of men.

Critically, the upward trends in women's incarceration are obvious, but what is particularly concerning is the significant difference across racial and/or ethnic groups. As seen in Figure 27.2, compared to Black and Latin women, the trends for white women are notably higher. Indeed, the numbers for Black and Latine women are moving downwards, with a steady decline over the last decade. A myriad of explanations may account for these variations

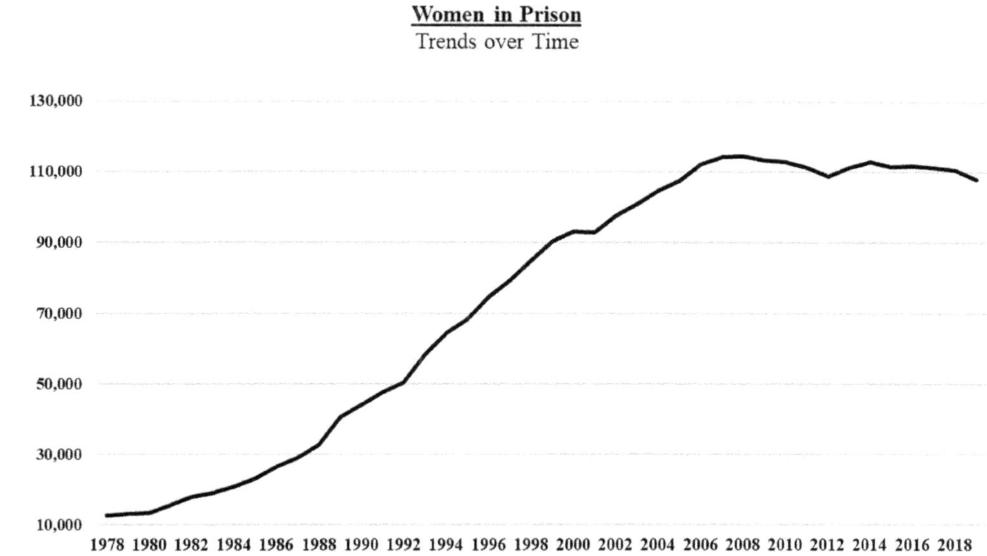

FIGURE 27.1 Women's Incarceration Trends 1978 to 2018.

Source: Bureau of Justice Statistics. Data generated using the Corrections Statistical Analysis Tool at www.bjs.gov

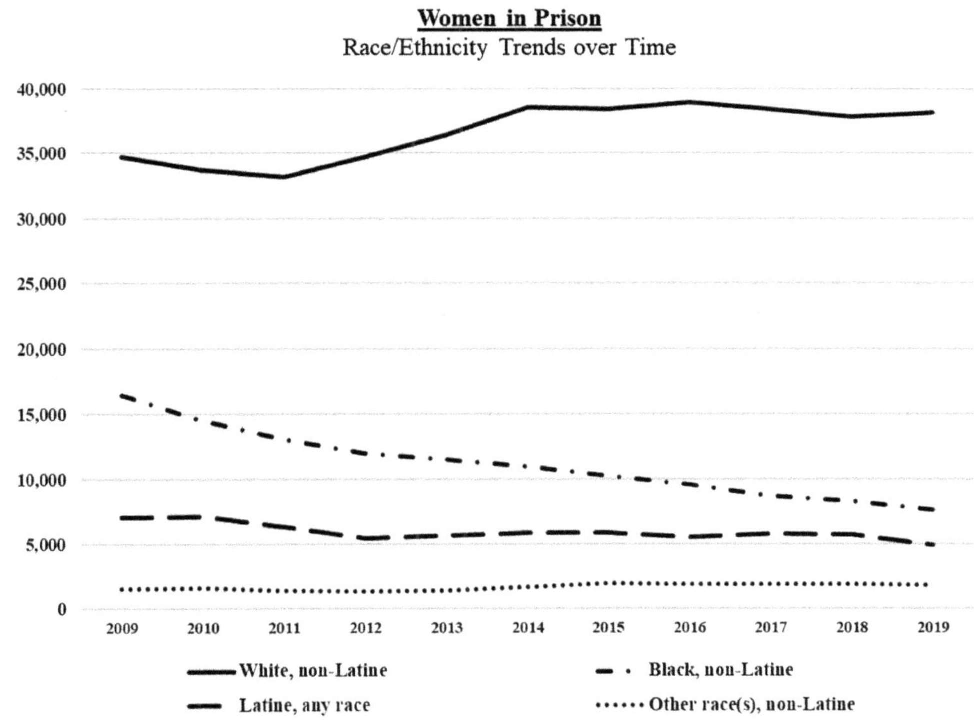

FIGURE 27.2 Racial and Ethnic Disparities in Women's Incarceration Trends.

Source: Bureau of Justice Statistics. Data generated using the Corrections Statistical Analysis Tool at www.bjs.gov

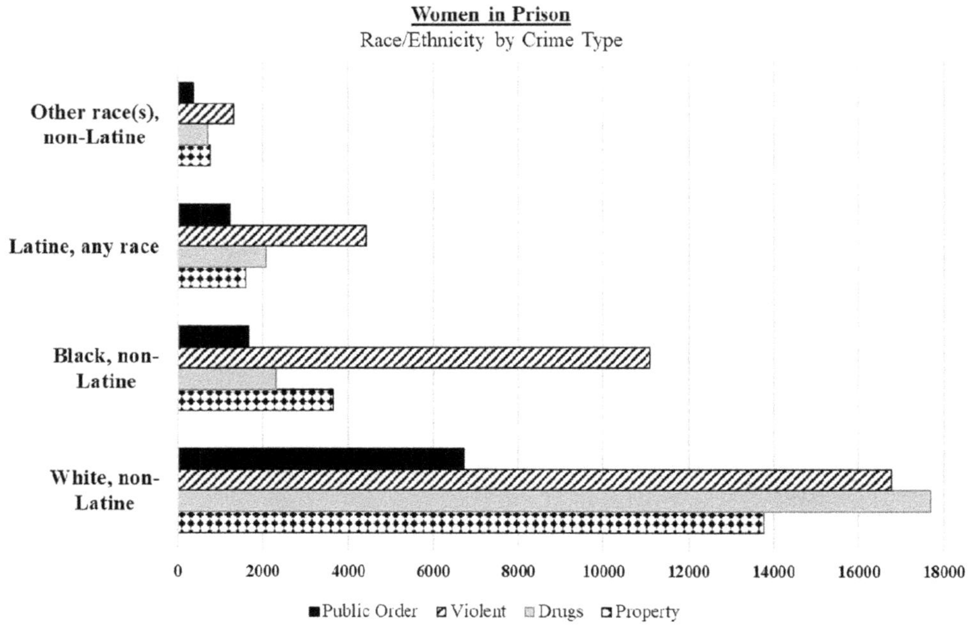

FIGURE 27.3 Women in Prison- Crime Type, Race and Ethnicity.

Source: Bureau of Justice Statistics. Data generated using the Corrections Statistical Analysis Tool at www.bjs.gov

including crime type, jurisdiction, or even just the fact that white women outnumber Black and Latine women in the general population. The crimes for which women are incarcerated also differ, such that men are much more likely to be institutionalized for violent crimes, while women are more likely to serve time for property, drug, and public-order offenses.

Studies can depict women as a monolith, likely to be sentenced for non-violent crimes, yet the data clearly tells a different story. Specifically, Figure 27.3 denotes the importance of acknowledging important race and ethnic differences which also speak to larger correctional issues like reproductive justice. Both Latine and Black women are more likely to be sentenced to carceral terms for violent crimes followed by property offenses. White women, however, are imprisoned for primarily drug crimes.

If we consider that close to 75% of incarcerated women are between the childbearing ages of 18 and 44, and a similar percentage are already mothers of minor children (Bronson & Sufrin, 2019; Friedman, Kaempf, & Kauffman, 2020), reproductive justice for women in prison is not only a need, but a right.

Reproductive Justice as an Analytical Framework

"Reproductive justice" as a framework for analyzing intersectionality (Crenshaw, 1989) and power in reproductive politics was coined by a collective of Black women in the mid-1990s to "recognize the commonality of our experiences and, from the sharing and growing consciousness, to build a politics that will change our lives and inevitably end our oppression" (Women of African Descent for Reproductive Justice, 1994 in Ross, 2017: 286). The reproductive justice framework moves beyond the narrow scope of reproductive rights, such as abortion care, focusing more broadly on the intersection of race, gender, and class to examine how reproductive relations and politics are defined and change over time, shaping social attitudes and public policy (Ross, 2017; Roberts, 2015; Ehrenreich, 1993). As a critical feminist framework, reproductive justice centers the voices of historically marginalized groups: Black women, queer people, and transgender and gender-nonconforming individuals (Ross, 2017), recognizing the relationship between theory and activism in the pursuit of social and reparative justice. Citing the inadequacy of existing feminist theory to provide the tools and conceptual space for Black women to express and organize based on their unique histories and experiences of oppression (Ross, 2017), reproductive justice provides a contemporary, intersectional, and critical framework for the creation of new self-definitions, theoretical discourse, and praxis (Luna & Luker, 2013).

The Reproductive justice framework is predicated on human rights emphasizing (1) choice in the conditions in which to have children; (2) choice to not have children through the use of birth control, abortion, or abstinence; and (3) parenting children in safe and healthy environments, absent of violence (Ross, 2017: 290; Luna & Luker, 2013). Reproductive justice also asserts that systemic forms of racial and economic inequality and structural violence shape and limit people's decisions about reproduction and parenting. For example, historically marginalized Black mothers struggling with poverty or drug addiction are more likely to be charged with child abuse and endangerment, incarcerated, and lose custody of their children compared to white mothers (Greene, 1991). These mothers are also subjected to greater State surveillance and control if receiving social benefits and are then denied access to those same benefits because of a criminal conviction (Roberts, 2011; Ehrenreich, 1993).

Over the last three decades, the reproductive justice framework has been used to examine forms of injustice and oppression within the areas of public health, parenting, psychology, social work, public policy, and art and has been centered in activism efforts in the United States and internationally (Sentencing Project, 2020; Baldry, 2010; Jahn et al., 2020). More recently, reproductive justice has been used to analyze and theorize on reproductive oppression and harm produced by the criminal legal system, particularly mass incarceration. In the United States, the loss of reproductive autonomy produced by imprisonment disproportionately harms Black women and other women of color, particularly those from historically marginalized and economically disadvantaged communities who are already vulnerable to having their reproductive choices restricted or controlled by the State (Roberts, 2011). Carceral spaces, often shrouded from public view, further exacerbate the stigmatization and vilification experienced by women, particularly mothers (Ehrenreich, 1993; Roberts, 2011), and facilitate the production of reproductive harm with relatively little public awareness or resistance.

Mass Incarceration and Reproductive Injustice

The imprisonment of women and the loss of bodily and reproductive autonomy is not a new form of State control; however, the rise of mass incarceration over the last several decades signifies more women funneled into the criminal punishment system and subjected to this particular iteration of governmental control (Hayes, Sufrin, & Perritt, 2020). Roberts

(1993) argues that reproduction has been wielded as an instrument of punishment by the State, targeting Black and brown women, grounded in a racial ideology that devalues, and is potentially threatened by their procreative capacity. While there are many instances of reproductive injustice within correctional settings, this section reviews contemporary examples that align with the three sets of human rights for reproductive justice previously identified: the right to decide whether to have children and under what conditions, the right to prevent or terminate pregnancy, and the right to parent children in an environment free from violence.

The Right to Decide Whether to Have Children and Under What Conditions

There is a paucity of data detailing the number of women who enter correctional settings while pregnant or who become pregnant during their incarceration (typically as a result of rape by correctional staff). However, it is estimated that approximately 4% of women entering prison confinement and 3–5% of women entering jail confinement are pregnant at the time of their incarceration (Sufrin et al., 2019; Bronson & Sufrin, 2019). Considerably less is known about rates of pregnancy in juvenile detention settings, but a recent study found that 3.3% of girls were pregnant at time of detainment (Kim et al., 2021). Most of these pregnancies result in a live birth (Sufrin et al., 2019), yet access to prenatal care or codified policy regarding care of pregnant women and delivery procedures are limited. A review by the American Civil Liberty Union (n.d.) of federal and state standards for pregnancy-related care found that only half of states have any policies on labor and delivery procedures or care for those with high-risk pregnancies and 12 states have no written policy.

Labor and delivery for pregnant incarcerated individuals is often a dehumanizing and powerless experience where the incarcerated have little, if any, autonomy over how they deliver their child, who is present during delivery, or decision-making regarding pain-management or emergency care. Perhaps the most well-known form of reproductive harm is the use of shackles or physical restraints during labor and delivery. At the time this chapter was written, 37 states and the Federal Bureau of Prisons had some level of restriction on the shackling of pregnant women, but states vary widely in their use of restraints or leave vaguely worded exceptions for "extraordinary circumstances" (King, 2018; Hernandez, 2022; DiNardo, 2017). In states with no codified restrictions, the use of shackles is routine and considered standard procedure (King, 2018), including handcuffing a woman's wrist or ankle to their hospital bed during labor and delivery, a practice that can exacerbate pain and injury and potentially place the mother and child's life at risk when time-sensitive movement of the patient or transfer to an operating room is required (Haber et al., 2022). Since instances of attempted escape or harm are exceptionally rare (Haber et al., 2022), shackling therefore serves no other purpose than control, reminding women of their carceral status in an act of dehumanization while they are most vulnerable.

A second example of reproductive injustice that violates the right of women to decide whether to have children is coercive sterilization, a practice rooted in racist and eugenicist ideology of the late 19th century as a means to rid society of crime and other forms of "moral deficiency" (Roberts, 1993). The historical narrative of Black motherhood as inherently problematic or burdensome to the State stems from Reconstruction-era social attitudes following the abolishment of slavery. When Black bodies were no longer viewed as a commodity for capitalist exploitation and instead perceived as a threat to white supremacy,

Black women were subjected to State surveillance, criminalization, and control of their reproductive choices (Roberts, 1993; Winters & McLaughlin, 2020). Sterilization has been presented as a "choice" to those convicted of crimes in exchange for sentencing reductions. However, the choice becomes coercive, especially for those where imprisonment means the loss of custody or access to children, housing, employment, or needed services (Winters & McLaughlin, 2020; Ferster, 1966). The decision to undergo sterilization becomes even more coercive for incarcerated women whose limited autonomy is further threatened by possible punitive consequences for noncompliance – or choice is removed entirely. In 2014, an investigation found that the California prison system performed tubal ligations on 144 women between the years 2005 and 2010 without required state authorization or patient consent (California State Auditor, 2014). While the findings led to California banning sterilization of incarcerated women in 2014, the hundreds of women whose cases are documented (and likely many more who are not), have lost their ability to choose if and when to have children.

The Right to Not Have Children Through Preventing or Terminating Pregnancy

The criminal legal system is not without irony, in that women who want to have children may be subjected to coerced sterilization and those who do not may be forced to through the denial of abortion care. Access to abortion care varies widely across state- and federal-level detention and correctional facilities (Sufrin et al., 2019). Additionally, state-level restrictions or bans on abortion further limit imprisoned women's reproductive choice to not have children. Considering the recent Supreme Court decision to overturn the Constitutional right to abortion, correctional systems in approximately half of the United States will be able to legally deny pregnant women access to abortion care, a reproductive justice issue that impacts tens of thousands of incarcerated women every year (Sufrin, Creinin, & Chang, 2009). Even when jails and prisons allow abortion access, correctional personnel may fail to provide pregnant individuals with timely information or authorization for abortion care, and policies may require imprisoned people to pay for their abortion, an expense few can afford (Sufrin et al., 2021). Access to abortion services becomes more precarious for incarcerated minors and those detained in immigrant facilities, as judicial approval is often required in addition to the other aforementioned barriers (Kim et al., 2021; Messing, Fabi, & Rosen, 2020; Hiemstra, 2021). In 2017, three unaccompanied minors detained by the Office of Refugee Resettlement (ORR) were denied access to abortion care by then head of ORR, Scott Lloyd, who was granted authorization to make all medical decisions for unaccompanied, immigrant minors. Lloyd initially dismissed legal concerns arguing that immigrant children do not have the right to abortion care because, "Constitutionally," they are not considered "people" (de Saint Felix, 2019: 420). Attempts to control girls' and women's bodily autonomy and rationalizations denying basic reproductive rights go so far as government officials arguing that in some instances, the personhood of these same girls and women is not "constitutionally" recognized and therefore they are undeserving of the protections afforded by the Bill of Rights.

The Right to Parent Children in Safe Environments Absent of Violence

Incarcerated mothers not only lose the right to choose their parenting environment but can be forced to expose their children to conditions that are potentially harmful to their health and well-being. Narratives abound of women giving birth alone in unsanitary cells or assisted by untrained correctional staff who refused to approve transportation to a hospital (Padilla, 2019; Livingston, 2019; Carlesso, 2019). Consider the case, in 2021 where an incarcerated pregnant woman in Florida had her repeated pleas to correctional staff ignored, resulting in the death of her prematurely born child due to medical complications (Pennix, 2021). While statistics on pregnancy outcomes in incarcerated populations are limited, available data indicate that adverse outcomes, including maternal or neonatal mortality, are rare (Sufrin et al., 2019). However, maternal distress during pregnancy and delivery, unsanitary conditions, and lack of access to medical care during and immediately following birth introduces unnecessary risk and trauma.

Following delivery, imprisoned mothers may have less than 24 hours with their newborn before the child is placed into the care of a family member, State custody, or placed for adoption (Franco, Mowers, & Lewis, 2020; Glaze & Maruschak, 2010). The near-immediate separation of parent and child, despite condemnation by the medical community and child development experts (Franco, Mowers, & Lewis, 2020), reflects deeply rooted assumptions that incarcerated women are bad mothers and undeserving of a relationship with their child (Roberts, 1993). It is not surprising then, that the United States is one of only a handful of nations globally that routinely separates incarcerated mothers from their newborn children (Friedman, Kaempf, & Kauffman, 2020). While it is standard practice internationally to allow newborns to reside with their mothers in prison nurseries, these programs are currently found in less than a dozen states in the U.S. (Friedman, Kaempf, & Kauffman, 2020; Schaefer-Riley, 2019). Incarcerated mothers are left with little opportunity to bond with their newborns and barriers to visitation, relationship dynamics, and State intervention can minimize the involvement of incarcerated mothers in the lives of their young children. Research has found that children of incarcerated mothers are more likely to experience adverse childhood experiences including exposure to interpersonal violence, abuse (Turney, 2018), housing instability (Smyth, 2012), and structural violence such as racial inequality and poverty (Rodriguez, Smith, & Zatz, 2009; Poehlmann, 2005; Miller, 2006). When incarcerated mothers are denied the right to parent their children in safe environments, their children are placed at greater risk of exposure to both interpersonal and structural forms of violence. In cases where children are placed into the legal custody of the State, incarcerated mothers have even less ability to exert any parental influence on how their child is cared for and upon their release, must face a myriad of legal and financial barriers to reunification of their children (Stone, Liddell, & Martinovic, 2017).

Reproductive Justice and Abolitionist Alternatives to Incarceration

The most common responses to the reproductive injustice experienced by incarcerated individuals who are, or can become, pregnant are calls for reform, some of which have been met with success. Following the investigation of forced sterilizations of incarcerated women in California, the state banned sterilizations unless an individual's life is in danger and they provide informed consent (S.B. 1135, 2014). After a years-long legal battle on access to abortion of undocumented individuals detained by Immigration and Customs Enforcement, the ORR adopted a policy that prohibits government officials from obstructing access to abortion care for unaccompanied minors in their custody (UAC Policy Memorandum 20-1, 2020). In recent years, states have also restricted the use of shackling during labor and delivery (Associated Press, 2022), expanded access to medical care during and following pregnancy (Michigan.gov, 2021), and expanded prison nurseries (Weinberg, 2022). At the federal level, U.S. senators introduced the "Justice for Incarcerated Moms Act" that provides incentives for states to restrict the use of shackling, provides funding for programs and research on maternal and infant health, and increases data collection and reporting on pregnancy and post-partum outcomes of incarcerated individuals (S.341, 2021). It should be noted that the current political climate regarding reproductive rights means state- and federal-level protections related to abortion care and long-acting reversible contraceptive access are vulnerable to changes in administrations, party control of national and state legislatures, agency leadership, and judicial opinion.

While reform efforts may reduce some of the unjust and inhumane treatment of pregnant individuals and incarcerated parents, they are insufficient for promoting reproductive justice for imprisoned people. We argue that reproductive justice is incompatible with incarceration and that reform cannot eliminate the oppression and violence, including historical and contemporary use of imprisonment to dehumanize and exploit Black bodies, foundational to the United States carceral system. Within such a system, the idea that women have the power to provide consent or make decisions about parenthood without coercion or implicit threats of punishment from State actors is unrealistic (Whatcott, 2018).

Additionally, mass incarceration, fueled by the criminalization of poverty and drug addiction in non-white communities (Roberts, 1993), serves primarily to expand State control over Black and brown bodies both during *and* following imprisonment (Hayes, Sufrin, & Perritt, 2020). Women, often resulting from gender- and race-based disparities and marginalization prior to incarceration, encounter greater housing, employment, and economic instability following incarceration compared to men (Garcia-Hallett, 2019). These challenges make it difficult for mothers to regain custody of their children and post-release supervision by the correctional system, social workers, or child protective services subject women to continued State surveillance and involvement in their parenting decisions (Garcia-Hallett, 2019; Roberts, 2011). Thus, the promotion of reproductive justice for historically marginalized women and pregnant people must include approaches that move away from incarceration, and other forms of coercive State intervention, and towards abolitionist alternatives.

We have long known that incarcerating people does not create safer communities and, instead, often exacerbates the sources of conflict and strain that contribute to crime (Steman, 2007; McLeod, 2015; Bagric, Hunter, & Svilar, 2021). Furthermore, when 75% of incarcerated women are mothers, the very act of imprisonment is an act of violence that separates a child from their parent, often resulting in trauma and negative short- and long-term consequences that persist beyond the duration of one's sentence. Responses to the harm produced by criminal activity that are grounded in abolitionist principles can address the inequalities and structural violence that contribute to crime in the first place and reduce future crime involvement (Davis, 2003; Bell, 2021). For example, reducing racial and gender gaps in employment and poverty can promote economic independence, improve housing stability, and empower women to freely make reproductive choices that best serve their needs. This would eliminate the role of the State in monitoring and controlling the decisions of women through their utilization of public assistance or legal system involvement.

We recognize that prison abolition is not a short-term solution to mass incarceration but there are alternatives to incarceration that reduce exposure to carceral sources of reproductive injustice. Community-based programs that allow mothers to reside with their children while receiving needed services and support and restorative justice responses that focus on repairing the harm caused by crime instead of inflicting punishment on the offending individual are two such approaches. One example is Drew House, an alternative-to-incarceration program for mothers with felony charges that prioritizes support instead of punishment (Smyth, 2012). Women and their children are provided apartments and receive on-site access to childcare and gender-responsive substance abuse and mental health treatment services with criminal charges dropped following successful completion, allowing women to move forward in their lives without a stigmatizing criminal conviction (Goshin & Byrne, 2011).

Conclusion

Increased incarceration of women, who disproportionately represent racially marginalized populations, has resulted in an ever-growing number of individuals subjected to a punishment system with a history of reproductive oppression and harm. The reproductive justice framework provides a useful lens through which we can examine the intersection of race, gender, class, and other aspects of identity and status on State control of women's reproductive and parenting decisions. Even with efforts to reform correctional policy related to reproductive healthcare and parenting, women cannot truly have reproductive autonomy in a carceral environment founded on the regulation and dehumanization of criminalized individuals. Instead, we advocate for renewed consideration of abolitionist alternatives to incarceration with a focus on addressing racial and gender inequity in areas of employment, education, housing, and healthcare. Not only do these factors have a greater impact on crime reduction than incarceration, but they can also empower women to make their own decisions about reproduction and parenting without State surveillance and coercion.

Discussion Questions:

1. What is Reproductive Justice and how does it apply both within and outside of carceral settings?
2. How do abolitionist alternatives to incarceration differ from reform of correctional policy and practices in the promotion of reproductive justice?

References

American Civil Liberty Union. (n.d.). State standards for pregnancy-related health care and abortion for women in prison. https://www.aclu.org/state-standards-pregnancy-related-health-care-and-abortion-women-prison-0

Aranda-Hughes, V., Turanovic, J. J., Mears, D. P., & Pesta, G. B. (2021). Women in solitary confinement: Relationships, pseudofamilies, and the limits of control. *Feminist Criminology*, 16(1), 47–72.

Associated Press. (2022, April 15). Tennessee Moves Bill Limiting Shackles on Pregnant Inmates. *U.S. News*. https://www.usnews.com/news/best-states/tennessee/articles/2022-04-15/tennessee-moves-bill-limiting-shackles-on-pregnant-inmates

Baldry, E. (2010). Women in transition: from prison to.... *Current Issues in Criminal Justice*, 22(2), 253–267.

Bertram, W. & Sawyer, W., (2022). What the end of Roe v. Wade will mean for people on probation and parole. https://www.prisonpolicy.org/blog/2022/06/30/roe/
Bronson, J., & Sufrin, C. (2019). Pregnant women in prison and jail don't count: Data gaps on maternal health and incarceration. *Public Health Reports*, 134(1_suppl), 57S–62S.
California State Auditor. (2014). Sterilization of female inmates: Some inmates were sterilized unlawfully, and safeguards designed to limit occurrences of the procedure failed. https://www.auditor.ca.gov/pdfs/reports/2013-120.pdf
Carlesso, J. (2019, March 4). Inmate who delivered baby in prison cell sues state for denying medical care. *The Connecticut Mirror*. https://ctmirror.org/2019/03/04/inmate-who-delivered-baby-in-prison-cell-sues-state-for-denying-medical-care/
Crenshaw, K. (1989). Demarginalizing the intersection of race and sex: A Black feminist critique of antidiscrimination doctrine, feminist theory and antiracist politics. *University of Chicago Legal Forum*, 1, 139–167.
Davis, A. Y. (2003). Are prisons obsolete?. Seven Stories Press.
de Saint Felix, S. (2019). Practicing pathology: The rhetoric of pathology in Jane Doe's struggle to obtain an abortion in federal immigration custody. *World Medical & Health Policy*, 11(4), 408–423.
DiNardo, C. (2017). Pregnancy in confinement, anti-shackling laws and the extraordinary circumstances loophole. *Duke Journal of Gender Law & Policy*, 25, 271.
Ehrenreich, N. (1993). Colonization of the womb, *Duke Law Journal*, 43, 492.
Ferster, E. Z. (1966). Eliminating the unfit—Is sterilization the answer?. *Ohio State Law Journal*, 27, 591.
Franco, C., Mowers, E., & Lewis, D. L. (2020). Equitable care for pregnant incarcerated women: Infant contact after birth—A human right. *Perspectives on Sexual and Reproductive Health*, 52, 211–215.
Friedman, S. H., Kaempf, A., & Kauffman, S. (2020). The realities of pregnancy and mothering while incarcerated. *Journal of the American Academy of Psychiatry and the Law*, 48(3), 365–375.
Garcia-Hallett, J. (2019). "We're being released to a jungle": The state of prisoner reentry and the resilience of women of color. *The Prison Journal*, 99(4), 459–483.
Glaze, L. E., & Maruschak, L. M. (2010). *Parents in prison and their minor children*. U.S. Department of Justice, Office of Justice Programs, Bureau of Justice Statistics. https://www.bjs.gov/content/ pub/pdf/pptmc.pdf
Goshin, L. S., & Byrne, M. W. (2011). Evaluation of a supportive housing alternative to incarceration for women charged with a felony and their children. *Evaluation*. https://shnny.org/uploads/DrewHouse_Report.pdf
Greene, D. L. (1991). Abusive prosecutors: Gender, race & class discretion and the prosecution of drug-addicted mothers. *Buffalo Law Review*, 39, 737.
Haber, L. A., Pratt, L. A., Erickson, H. P., & Williams, B. A. (2022). Shackling in the hospital. *Journal of General Internal Medicine*, 37(5), 1258–1260.
Hayes, C. M., Sufrin, C., & Perritt, J. B. (2020). Reproductive justice disrupted: Mass incarceration as a driver of reproductive oppression. *American Journal of Public Health*, 110(S1), S21–S24.
Hiemstra, N. (2021). Mothers, babies, and abortion at the border: Contradictory US policies, or targeting fertility?. *Environment and Planning C: Politics and Space*, 39(8), 1692–1710.
Hernandez, J. (2022, April). More states are restricting the shackling of pregnant inmates, but it still occurs. *National Public Radio*. https://www.npr.org/2022/04/22/1093836514/shackle-pregnant-inmates-tennessee
Kim, M., Sufrin, C., Nowotny, K., Beal, L., & Jiménez, M. C. (2021). Pregnancy prevalence and outcomes in 3 United States juvenile residential systems. *Journal of Pediatric and Adolescent Gynecology*, 34(4), 546–551.
King, L. (2018). Labor in chains: The shackling of pregnant inmates. *Policy Perspectives*, 25, 55.
Livingston, L. (2019, May 8). "It was horrifying," says woman who gave birth in Broward jail. *Local 10 News*. https://www.local10.com/news/2019/05/08/it-was-horrifying-says-woman-who-gave-birth-in-broward-jail/

Luna, Z., & Luker, K. (2013). Reproductive justice. *Annual Review of Law and Social Science*, 9, 327–352.

Messing, A. J., Fabi, R. E., & Rosen, J. D. (2020). Reproductive injustice at the US border. *American Journal of Public Health*, 110(3), 339–344.

Michigan.gov. (2021, October 19). Governor Whitmer expands maternal and post-partum healthcare for prisoners [Press Release]. https://www.michigan.gov/whitmer/news/press-releases/2021/10/19/governor-whitmer-expands-maternal-and-post-partum-healthcare-for-prisoners

Padilla, M. (2019, September 1). Woman gave birth in Denver jail cell alone, Lawsuit says. *The New York Times*. https://www.nytimes.com/2019/09/01/us/diana-sanchez-birth-denver-jail.html

Pennix, T. (2021, August 11). "I basically held my baby all night, until she died," mother forced to birth baby in jail. *CBS4 News*. https://mycbs4.com/news/local/i-basically-held-my-baby-all-night-until-she-died-mother-forced-to-birth-baby-in-jail

Poehlmann, J. (2005). Children's family environments and intellectual outcomes during maternal incarceration. *Journal of Marriage and Family*, 67(5), 1275–1285.

Roberts, D. E. (1993). Crime, race, and reproduction. *Tulane Law Review*, 67(6), 1945-1977.

Roberts, D. E. (2011). Prison, foster care, and the systemic punishment of black mothers. *UCLA Law Review*, 59, 1474–1500.

Roberts, D. E. (2015). Reproductive justice, not just rights. *Dissent*, 62(4), 79–82.

Rodriguez, N., Smith, H., & Zatz, M. S. (2009). "Youth is enmeshed in a highly dysfunctional family system": Exploring the relationship among dysfunctional families, parental incarceration, and juvenile court decision making. *Criminology*, 47(1), 177–208.

Ross, L. J. (2017). Reproductive justice as intersectional feminist activism. *Souls*, 19(3), 286–314.

S.341 – 117th Congress (2021–2022): Justice for Incarcerated Moms Act. (2021, February 22). http://www.congress.gov/

S.B. 1135, 2014 Reg. Sess. (Cal. 2014). https://leginfo.legislature.ca.gov/faces/billTextClient.xhtml?bill_id=201320140SB1135

Schaefer-Riley, N. (2019, March 22). On prison nurseries. *National Affairs*. https://www.nationalaffairs.com/publications/detail/on-prison-nurseries

Sentencing Project. (2020). https://www.sentencingproject.org/issues/women/

Smyth, J. (2012). Dual punishment: Incarcerated mothers and their children. *Columbia Social Work Review*, 10(1), 33–45.

Stone, U., Liddell, M., & Martinovic, M. (2017). Incarcerated mothers: Issues and barriers for regaining custody of children. *The Prison Journal*, 97(3), 296–317.

Sufrin, C., Beal, L., Clarke, J., Jones, R., & Mosher, W. D. (2019). Pregnancy outcomes in US prisons, 2016–2017. *American Journal of Public Health*, 109(5), 799–805.

Sufrin, C. B., Creinin, M. D., & Chang, J. C. (2009). Incarcerated women and abortion provision: A survey of correctional health providers. *Perspectives on Sexual and Reproductive Health*, 41(1), 6–11.

Sufrin, C., Jones, R. K., Beal, L., Mosher, W. D., & Bell, S. (2021). Abortion access for incarcerated people: Incidence of abortion and policies at US prisons and jails. *Obstetrics & Gynecology*, 138(3), 330–337.

Turney, K. (2018). Adverse childhood experiences among children of incarcerated parents. *Children and Youth Services Review*, 89, 218–225.

UAC Policy Memorandum 20-1 (2020). Medical Services Requiring Heightened ORR Involvement. Administration for Children & Families, Office of Refugee Resettlement. https://www.acf.hhs.gov/sites/default/files/documents/orr/garza_policy_memorandum.pf

Van Voorhis, P. (2012). On behalf of women offenders: Women's place in the science of evidence-based practice. *Criminology & Public Policy*, 11(2): 111–145.

Whatcott, J. (2018). No selves to consent: Women's prisons, sterilization, and the biopolitics of informed consent. *Signs: Journal of Women in Culture and Society*, 44(1), 131–153.

Weinberg, T. (2022, May 14). Missouri legislature passes bipartisan bill creating prison nursery for incarcerated moms. *Missouri Independent*. https://www.kcur.org/politics-elections-and-government/2022-05-14/missouri-legislature-passes-bipartisan-bill-creating-prison-nursery-for-incarcerated-moms

Winters, D. J., & McLaughlin, A. R. (2020). Soft sterilization: long-acting reversible contraceptives in the carceral state. *Affilia*, 35(2), 218–230.

28

"TODAY'S LYNCHING IS INCARCERATION"

Critical Race Theory, Mass Incarceration, and Prison Abolition

Yola Gómez and Paddy Farr

LEARNING OUTCOMES:

Upon successful completion of this chapter, students will be able to:

1 Gain foundation knowledge in the six tenets of critical race theory including (1) the ordinariness of racism, (2) racial interest convergence, (3) the social construction of race, (4) differential racialization, (5) intersectionality, and (6) the importance of narratives.
2 Learn to apply critical race theory to mass incarceration through a historical overview of the aftermath of reconstruction, the war on drugs, and neoliberalism.
3 Connect the critique of mass incarceration to the prison abolition movement and be able to describe three of its focuses including support for incarcerated individuals, organizing and advocacy for decarceration, and alternatives to mass incarceration through noncarceral program development.

Introduction

The United States has the highest prison population of any nation in history. Currently, of the 10.77 million people incarcerated globally (Fair and Walmsley 2021), the US incarcerates 2.2 million people, more than one out of five globally (Carson 2020; Zeng and Minton 2021). Often left out of this number of the incarcerated population, there is an additional 396,488 average daily detention of suspected undocumented migrants (ICE 2019). Given the current US adult population in the 2020 census of 258,343,281 (US Census 2020), that is 1 out of 100 people in the US are locked up, a number that has maintained since 2008 (Warren et al. 2008). Nevertheless, this still leaves out half of the correctional population. In addition to the incarcerated population, there are 3.89 million people on probation or parole, increasing the total correctional population to nearly 6.5 million people under supervision of the criminal justice system. All in all, that is nearly 1 out of 50 people in the US under correctional supervision. However, despite these terrifying numbers, these statistics do not provide the full picture. It is well-established that Black, Indigenous, and Latinx

DOI: 10.4324/9781003274292-36

people have the highest rates of incarceration (Nellis 2021). Without coming to terms with this injustice, investigations into mass incarceration are missing something central to the process. Grasping the centrality of race within mass incarceration, it is critical to look beyond the demographics of mass incarceration in order to elaborate how the development of the carceral system became as it is. In this chapter, the analytic of critical race theory provides the analytic for grasping how mass incarceration is a central tool of white supremacy. In particular, this chapter investigates how US carceral systems are direct products of slavery and neoliberalism. As a direction forward, the chapter argues the prison abolition movement continues a long legacy of resistance within the US against these racial injustices.

What Is Critical Race Theory?

Of late, critical race theory has become a much derided and divisive topic within contemporary US society. Beginning in 2020, a cadre of right-wing activists began an orchestrated attack on the study and dissemination of racial oppression. This has triggered both national- and local-level reactions. However, despite all the hype, critical race theory is based on a set of intuitive propositions regarding race and oppression. Put succinctly, critical race theory is a theoretical orientation concerned with the ways in which racial oppressions are concealed through color blind policies in the post-Civil Rights era. It is founded on the critical method set forth through critical legal studies (Crenshaw et al. 1995; Delgado and Stefancic 2012), a movement in legal scholarship that starts from a critique of formalism and objectivism in legal practice to identify the ways in which law making and law application are instruments of oppression (Unger 1983). As an extension of Critical Legal Studies into investigations of race, critical race theory encompasses multiple theoretical positions demonstrating ways in which the liberal rights and welfare function as a system of racial oppression: "as a critical orientation focused on structural inequalities arising from liberal post-civil rights politics, critical race theorists have demonstrated ways in which liberal equality has reinforced rather than dismantled white supremacy" (Farr 2021, 184). From this foundation of critique, critical race theorists have worked to uncover racism as experienced across racialized oppressions. In their text, *Critical Race Theory an Introduction*, Richard Delgado and Jean Stefancic (2012) outline six central tenets that form the theoretical premises of critical race theory. These six tenets present as theses and include (1) ordinariness of racism, (2) racial interest convergence, (3) social construction of race, (4) differential racialization, (5) intersectionality, and (6) narrativity (Delgado and Stepancic 2012). In addition to these six tenets of critical race theory, neoliberalism is defined below because of its importance to the following analysis of mass incarceration. Each of these theses plus neoliberalism are particularly well established within systems of mass incarceration. Thus, before moving on to a critical race analysis of mass incarceration, it is critical to fully grasp how these function. Focusing on the first five theses, a direct line is drawn between race and the history of slavery and neoliberalism.

Ordinariness of Racism

Within the US, "racism is ordinary, not aberrational" (Delgado and Stepancic 2012, 7). One side of this ordinariness of racism is from individual actors who hold bigoted beliefs and demonstrate discriminatory behavior against Black, Indigenous, and Latinx people. However, the other side of this ordinariness, the side most ubiquitous, is systems of power in which Black, Indigenous, and Latinx people are subject to violence and oppression. Both of these two sides are important for grasping racism within the US; however, investigating mass incarceration requires special focus on the side of systems. Within this context, the ordinariness of racism is illustrated through systems of policing, differential judgments, and incarceration. Each of these systems presents themselves as "colorblind," providing equal justice to all while at the same time they are enacted through clearly established racializations. Hence, "color-blind, or 'formal,' conceptions of equality" wherein phrases like all men are created equal are "expressed in rules that insist only on treatment that is the same across the board" and as such "can thus remedy only the most blatant forms of discrimination" (Delgado and Stepancic 2012, 7).

Social Construction

Despite the intuitive proposition that racism is ubiquitous in US systems, there is a parallel intuitive proposition that race is not a biological category. The Human Genome Project has well demonstrated this truth. As stated by evolutionary biologist Alan Templeton, "humans are an amazingly diverse species, but this diversity is not due to a finite number of subtypes or races," but instead, "the vast majority of human genetic diversity reflects local adaptations and, most of all, our individual uniqueness" (Templeton 2013). Nevertheless, race is something very real in our world. As witnessed within the systems of mass incarceration, wherein about 1 in 106 white adult men are in prison while 1 in 15 Black men and 1 in 36 Latinx men are in prison (Warren et al. 2008), race exists as a social reality through which power and punishment are organized. Hence, while indisputably not a fact of biology, it is something that exists in our world developed through a socially constructed concept: "race and races are products of social thought and relations" (Delgado and Stepancic 2012, 7).

Interest Convergence

Race is "not objective, inherent, or fixed, they correspond to no biological or genetic reality" but "rather, races are categories that society invents, manipulates, or retires when convenient" (Delgado and Stepancic 2012, 7). There are specific purposes for the social construction of race: it is the product of power as developed through the history of slavery and colonization. In short, interest convergence explains how the rights of People of Color only improve when they converge with the interests of whites. As such, the concept of race is a tool of white supremacy through which "white-over-color ascendancy serves important purposes, both psychic and material" (Delgado and Stepancic 2012, 7). As an origin point, in the 16th and 17th centuries, during the convergence of slavery and colonization, the Spanish and the British constructed the concept of race as a means to slavery of Black people and the colonization of Indigenous Americans (James and Burgos 2022). Hence, the European colonization of the Americas and the slave trade implemented the concept of racial difference in order to construct an interest convergence for a wide-scale genocide and expropriation that has developed the systems of mass incarceration maintained today.

Differential Racialization

At the same time that race is socially constructed and serves purposes of interest convergence, the concept of race also changes over time. Where racialization served specific purposes for slavery and colonization, different groups have been racialized in different ways at different times in history in order to meet specific needs. Known as the thesis of differential racialization, identifying these changing concepts of race draws "attention to the ways the dominant society racializes different minority groups at different times, in response to shifting needs such as the labor market" (Delgado and Stepancic 2012, 8). Demonstrated through changing needs within US labor and capitalism, some groups such as Irish and Italian people were once not included among white people but now are. At the same time, groups such as Latinx and Middle Eastern people have been included among white in demographic data but racially othered within social practice. Hence, as dynamics shift and needs change for the purpose of maintaining power, race likewise shifts and changes in order to accommodate.

Intersectionality

Further complicating the idea of race, people are not simply their race. Each and every person has multiple identities that intersect between gender, race, class, ability, sexuality, etc. These intersections affect the person's experience of the world. Furthermore, just as race is not an essential characteristic of a person, neither are these other identities. This thesis of intersectionality and anti-essentialism, coined by Kimberle Crenshaw, explains how because "no person has a single, easily stated, unitary identity" (Delgado and Stepancic 2012, 8), racialization is likewise problematized. Central to Crenshaw's insights, anti-essentialism and intersectionality arise directly from the concrete experiences of Black, Indigenous, and women of color involved in both the feminist movement and anti-racism, an experience and line of critique that developed in the 1960s and 1970s (Crenshaw 1989, 1991). Where Black, Indigenous, and women of color experience racism in the feminist movement, they likewise experienced sexism within the anti-racist movement, hence the title of Hull, Bell-Scott, and Smith's (1982) edited compilation, *All the Blacks are Men, All the Women are White, But Some of Us are Brave.*

Narrativity

From *Narrative of the Life of Frederick Douglass, An American Slave* (Douglass 1845) to Hull, Bell-Scott, and Smith's (1982) *But Some of Us Are Brave*, storytelling has played a central role in Black, Indigenous, and people of color sharing their experiences of racism and oppression. Identifying central trend narrativity in the history of struggle against white supremacy, critical race theory points to the importance of narratives presented by "a unique voice of color" in which different experiences of racism by different peoples are best described in their own voice "because of their different histories and experiences with oppression" (Delgado and Stepancic 2012, 8). These narratives are not mere stories but rather provide insights into the concrete forms of white supremacy thus developing significant social theories through the voice of the narrator. The stories told by survivors of mass incarceration, as witnessed within this book, have the power to teach us what we cannot see.

Neoliberalism

In the late 20th century, the US led a global change in economic policy toward a free market. This change was the result of economic theorists and policy makers turning toward neoliberalism. While not a tenet of critical race theory, neoliberalism is a critical term that must be grasped in order to comprehend the following discussion. Neoliberalism posits that the fewer restrictions there are placed on trade the more capital will be generated and the freer a society will become (Vallier 2021). However, this eliminating of restrictions on trade likewise entails the elimination of welfare programs, labor laws, and international barriers all of which decrease the ability to generate capital. In the late 20th and 21st centuries, neoliberalism in US economic policy has resulted in the steady backsliding of social welfare, the elimination of domestic labor protections, and the removal international restrictions to trade, a trend that has harmed Black, Indigenous, and Latinx people within the US and internationally. Delgado and Stepancic (2012) identify these changes in policy as increasing in the US while simultaneously triggering displacement of populations in the Global South. As a backdrop and the impetus for mass incarceration in the 21st century, neoliberalism provides the economic theory for the continuation of colonialism and slavery.

Application of Critical Race Theory to Mass Incarceration

US carceral systems are notoriously unequally distributed across races. As of 2019, whereas white people are held in prisons at a rate of 263 per 100,000, Black, Indigenous, and Latinx people are held in prisons at a rate of 1,446 per 100,000, 1291 per 100,000, and 757 per 100,000 (Carson 2020; Daniel 2020). Similarly, whereas white people are held in jails at a rate of 184 per 100, 000, Black and Indigenous people are held in jails at a rate of 600 per 100,000, 420 per 100,000 (Zeng 2021). This disproportionate rate is likewise witnessed in probation and parole statistics where Black people are "2.6 times as likely to be on probation, and nearly 4 times as likely to be on parole, as white people" and Indigenous people are "48% more likely to be on probation, and 77% more likely to be on parole, than their white counterparts" (Bradner et al. 2020, 6). From these statistics, the question is how did US carceral systems become this way?

From Slavery to the Prison System

Beginning with the first three theses discussed above—the ubiquity of racism, the social construction of race, and racial interest convergence—the function of US systems of mass incarceration is a descendent of systems established within the history of slavery and the aftermath of reconstruction. During the era of reconstruction, white and Black people participated together in "sweeping economic and political developments [of which] in that period did appear, at least for a time, to have the potential to seriously undermine, if not completely eradicate, the racial caste system in the South" (Alexander 2010, 29). However, the emancipation and abolition of slavery following the US Civil War was cut short. As established within the 13th Amendment of the US Constitution, "the 13th Amendment created a loophole for the continuation of slavery, which society has expanded and built off of for over 100 years to create what is now referred to as mass incarceration" (Pereira 2018, 52–53). Providing an exception to abolition, "slavery remained appropriate as punishment for a crime" (Alexander 2010, 31). This is clearly stated in the 13th Amendment which reads "Neither slavery nor involuntary servitude, *except as a punishment for crime whereof the party shall have been duly convicted,* shall exist within the United States, or any place subject to their jurisdiction."

In the aftermath of the 13th Amendment, it became common practice to place the incarcerated in unpaid conditions of labor. Known as convict leasing, "in which prisoners were contracted out as laborers to the highest private bidder," the exemption within the 13th Amendment established a means to maintain conditions of slavery for "tens of thousands of African Americans [who] were arbitrarily arrested during this period, many of them hit with court costs and fines, which had to be worked off in order to secure their release" (Alexander 2010, 31). This practice was eventually challenged in and upheld by the Supreme Court in 1871. In *Ruffin v. Commonwealth*, the Supreme Court states explicitly that while imprisoned, a person "is for the time being a slave, in a condition of penal servitude to the State, and is subject to such laws and regulations as the State may choose to prescribe." The prison system was designed as a means to target Black people recently emancipated returning them to the bonds of slavery. As such, the US carceral system is not merely a manifestation of but a central tool in the maintenance of white supremacy as interest convergence through the construction of race as a means to social control.

Becoming "the nation's first prison boom" (Alexander 2010, 32), the exception clause explicitly provided the state slave holder rights over the incarcerated maintaining the system of convict leasing over Black people (Pereira 2018). Over the course of the 20th century, the system of convict leasing evolved to become the contemporary system of prison labor (Alexander 2010). To this day, prison labor is practiced as a form of slavery: an incarcerated person is paid far below minimum wage, is not an employee, is not afforded labor rights, and much of their earnings must be used to pay for the costs of their incarceration (Alexander 2010). Simultaneous to these developments, Jim Crow laws mandating segregation became a strategy to enforce white supremacy through mass violence against Black people. At this site of criminal justice and mass violence, hate groups assembled of white citizens, the Ku Klux Klan being the most notorious, took on the role of enforcers through lynching, "committing castrations, killings, and the bombing of black homes and Churches" all with impunity (Alexander 2010, 37). Hand in hand, white supremacist terrorism and the criminal justice system together preserved the system of white supremacy held over from the ante-bellum period through Jim Crow.

From the reconstruction era until the Civil Rights Act of 1964 and the Voting Rights Act of 1965, the US carceral system formed a critical piece of the structural inequalities inherent within segregation (Alexander 2010). However, with the formal end of Jim Crow and the institutionalization of color-blind policies, racial injustice continued through "the racially sanitized rhetoric of 'cracking down on crime'—rhetoric that is now used freely by politicians of every stripe" (Alexander 2010, 42). The key moment in this process of transformation to color-blind policy in criminal justice reaffirming a white supremacist interest convergence comes with the "war on drugs" (Fornili 2018; Jeffers 2019; Travis, Western, and Redburn 2014). From the original coinage by Nixon to the contemporary era of mass incarceration, this transformation led to an explosion in the US carceral system in which the US prison population grew more than 400% (Farr 2021). Whereas there were 330,000 people in prison in 1980, this number ballooned to over 1,600,000 by the year 2009 (Schratz, DeBor, and Mauer 2018). This resulted in the imprisonment of 1 in 15 Black men (Warren et al. 2008). Alexander quotes Sasha Abramsky, "a black minister in Waterloo, Mississippi:"

> Today's lynching is a felony charge. Today's lynching is incarceration. Today's lynch mobs are professionals. They have a badge; they have a law degree. A felony is a modern way of saying, 'I'm going to hang you up and burn you.' Once you get that F, you're on fire.
>
> *(Abramsky quoted by Alexander 2010, 159)*

From Neoliberalism to Mass Incarceration

Parallel to the war on drugs, another war began, this time funded by the US government to secure military interests across Latin America (Grandin 2011; Rabe 2015). In the 1980s, a US-led process of neoliberalization and neocolonialism established systems of control over Latin America through aggressive military-based policies (Grandin 2011; Rabe 2015). As a function of these policies, the racialization of migrants, particularly those from Latin America, became a standard mode of migration enforcement (García 2017; Romero 2008; Sanchez and Romero 2010). Like the interest convergence of the war on drugs, a tough-on-crime approach to international migration grew from these neoliberal policies within the Global South (Farr 2021). These transformed policies have heavily effected migration, and between the years 1994 and 2019, the daily detention population of suspected undocumented migrants had grown from 6,785 to 47,000 (Reyes 2019). The majority of those detained within these centers are Indigenous and/or Latinx people; hence, while migrant detention like the war on drugs is formally color blind, the practice is directly connected back to a history of neocolonial military aggression and neoliberalism.

Through this system of migration enforcement, a wall is constructed along the southern border of the US while borders remain nearly open along the northern border. At these geographical sites, in a similar way to the color-blind policies developed within the war on drugs, "the documentation status of a migrant conceals the ways in which enforcement of migration targets communities of color" (Farr 2021, 10). While the concept of documentation is not directly connected to racialization, the practice of detention functions through the racialization of specific migrant populations, particularly Latinx people (García 2017; Romero 2008; Sanchez and Romero 2010). Demonstrating the thesis of differential racialization, these policies draw "attention to the ways the dominant society racializes different minority groups at different times, in response to shifting needs" (Delgado and Stepancic 2012, 8). Between these differential racializations, the formation of the war on drugs, neoliberalism, and neocolonialism results in the mass imprisonment of Latinx and Indigenous people. As stated above, whereas the rate of incarcerated white people is 261 per 100,000, Black and Indigenous people are the most highly incarcerated groups with rates of 1,240 per 100,000 and 1,291 per 100,000 (Daniel 2020; Nellis 2021). Although Latinx are imprisoned at rates of 349 per 100,000 (Nellis 2021), this does not account for the mass of Latinx migrants held in US detention which would drive this number up (Farr 2021).

Although interest convergence and differential racialization are well established within the history of mass incarceration, it is likewise important to problematize these simplifications. At the same time that race is a clear marker for higher rates of incarceration, so too is class with the majority of the incarcerated population coming from people living in poverty (Rabuy and Kopf 2015), gender with the explosion in the incarceration of women, sexuality with some of the highest rates of LGBTQ people incarcerated, and ability with a majority of incarcerated people presenting with mental or physical disabilities. Each of these identities affects the experience of incarceration in specific ways determining the experience of race in mass incarceration. Connecting to the thesis of intersectionality and anti-essentialism, this complication identifies how changing incarceration practices affect particular intersections of which women require special attention, the intersection of gender and race being strongly associated with increasing rates of incarceration. In the past 20 years, the population of women in prison and jail has increased from 26,326 in 1980 to 152,854 in 2020 plus 866,877 on probation or parole (Kajstura 2019; Sentencing Project 2022). As with the general incarcerated population, the majority of women in prison are Black and Latinx with rates 65 per 100,000 and 48 per 100,000 in comparison to rates for white women of 38 per 100,000 (Sentencing Project 2022).

Returning to the Abolition Movement

The US has a long history of collective struggle against racial oppression, and this begins with the historical abolition movement. Entrenched within the history of the US, this story begins not with the arrival of the Mayflower or Declaration of Independence but rather with white slave holders trafficking Africans to Virginia in 1619 (Hannah-Jones 2021). At the same time that this injustice begins, in opposition to slavery, abolition grew as a parallel movement against this genocide of Black people (Roberts 2019). The history of the movement for abolition of slavery provides a strong example for contemporary activist movements to challenge the systems of mass incarceration. While the dominant view in the US is that the abolition movement was a historical moment that ended with the Civil War, the abolition of slavery was ratified by Congress in 1865 via the 13th Amendment, just as through the 13th Amendment slavery never truly ended neither did the abolition movement (Alexander 2010; Roberts 2019). Whereas chattel slavery was followed by laws reestablishing white supremacy over Black people via Jim Crow and the birth of mass incarceration, so too has the fight for abolition continued on in new forms. Thus, Dorothy Roberts (2019) explains, because US carceral systems are shaped by the history of slavery and colonization, in the same way, opposition to US carceral systems is shaped by the history of the abolition movement.

Throughout the reconstruction and its aftermath, the abolition movement continued to operate as a means to emancipation from the bonds established through Jim Crow (Roberts 2019). Like the earlier incarnation of the abolition movement, the opposition to Jim Crow laws was led by a multiracial social movement aimed at tearing down the ongoing discrimination and oppression continued from slavery. Again paralleling the history of the abolition of slavery, the dominant view of Jim Crow is that the fight for civil rights ended with the ratification of the Civil Rights Act and the Voting Rights Act. However, as described by Alexander (2010), Jim Crow was also not truly abolished but instead reformed as a new Jim Crow within the US systems of mass incarceration. Whereas Jim Crow was followed by again reestablishing conditions of slavery over Black people, as an opposition to this continuation of slavery, the prison abolition movement likewise renewed as the movement for prison abolition (Roberts 2019). Like the movement for the abolition of chattel slavery and Jim Crow, contemporary organizations and collectives fighting for abolition are struggling at different front against mass incarceration but against the same enemy. Roberts writes:

> Prison abolitionists look back to history to trace the roots of today's carceral state to the racial order established by slavery and look forward to imagine a society without carceral punishment. Both are critical motivations for abolishing the prison industrial complex. The case for abolition that is grounded in history and politics provides a compelling framework for understanding the need to eradicate the entire carceral punishment system as well as for identifying strategies to accomplish that goal. Indeed, we can

see the extreme cruelty and degradation that characterize today's penitentiaries, police forces, and executions as the inevitable result of a racially subordinating system.

(Roberts 2019, 19)

Conclusion: Practical Proposals for Policy and Activism

Although the idea of prison abolition sounds radical and utopian, the ideas behind prison abolition are growing to become mainstream. Indeed the tide has begun to change in the US practice of mass incarceration resulting in the early rumblings of a decarceration process across both democratic and republican administrations. Four factors have been critical in the past decade in this decrease in mass incarceration (Farr 2021). Firstly, in 2010, US Congress passed the Fair Sentencing Act (S.1789) in order to decrease sentencing disparities for drug offenses. Second, in 2011, the US Supreme Court ruled against the state of California in *Brown v. Plata* mandating decreased crowding in California prisons. Third, in 2018, US Congress passed the First Step Act (S. 756) in order to further decrease incarceration for low-level crime. Finally, in 2020, US Congress the CARES Act (S. 3548) which included a provision to increase home confinement of incarcerated people populations aimed at decreasing COVID-19 in high risk population groups.

Nevertheless, the effect of these policies has remained negligible (Farr 2021), and at the current rate of decarceration, it will not be until 2093 that the incarcerated population is cut by 50% (Ghandnoosh 2018). Where critical race theory argues that "because racism advances the interests of both white elites (materially) and working-class people (psychically), large segments of society have little incentive to eradicate it" (Delgado and Stepancic 2012, 7), decarceration has failed because the interest convergence has maintained. It is this difficulty that the abolition movement places in its sights. Prison abolitionists have confronted mass incarceration on multiple different levels including support for incarcerated individuals, organizing and advocating for decarceration, and developing innovative programs as alternatives to mass incarceration. Although each of these forms of activism could take up many pages, these three approaches to prison abolition can be briefly described.

Firstly, activists work to provide support through letter writing, books to prison distribution, legal defense, and fund raising. Some of the groups fighting for abolition of prison and jails through support include Black and Pink, Audre Lorde Project, Anarchist Black Cross, Critical Resistance, and Incite among many others. Similarly, there are groups fighting for the abolition of migrant detention including No Mas Muertes, Mariposas sin Fronteras, and Puente Movement among many others. Second, because mass incarceration has created a system of unequal and unjust punishment, prison abolitionists call for decarceration efforts to decrease those locked up. As discussed above, at a national level, policy has begun to shift against mass incarceration and decarceration efforts have increased in an effort to decrease the number of those incarcerated. These successes have been accomplished through the efforts of activists who have tirelessly worked to advocate for policy changes and organized communities to demand change. Third, prison abolitionists have developed innovative programs as alternatives for mass incarceration. As an alternative to the system of punishment and mass incarceration, these efforts include programs in restorative and transformative justice, harm reduction-based drug and alcohol programs, and crisis support programs such as CAHOOTS as alternatives to police.

What each of the above forms of abolitionist practice demonstrates is that there are many ways for the movement for abolition of mass incarceration to operate. Each of these programs comes to the abolitionist movement without a final goal, but rather envision a continuing movement to change society. In the words of Dorothy Roberts, "while human freedom required slavery abolition then, today it requires the abolition of the prison industrial complex that has replaced slavery as the bulwark of racial capitalism" (Roberts 2018, 40).

Discussion Questions:

1 What are the six theses of critical race theory and how are these applied to mass incarceration?
2 How is the movement for prison abolition an answer to the difficulties posed by mass incarceration and how is this practiced?

References

Alexander, M. (2010). *The New Jim Crow: Mass Incarceration in the Age of Colorblindness.* New York: The New Press.

Bradner, K et al. (2020). *More Work to Do: Analysis of Probation and Parole in the United States, 2017–2018.* Columbia University Justice Lab. Accessed 6-13-2022 from https://justicelab.columbia.edu/sites/default/files/content/More%20Work%20to%20Do.pdf

Carson, E. A. (2020). *Prisoners in 2019. Bureau of Justice Statistics.* Accessed 6-13-2022 from https://bjs.ojp.gov/content/pub/pdf/p19.pdf

Crenshaw, K. W. (1989). "Demarginalizing the intersection of race and sex: A black feminist critique of antidiscrimination doctrine, feminist theory and antiracist politics." *University of Chicago Legal Forum 139*, 139–167.

Crenshaw, K. W. (1991). "Mapping the margins: Intersectionality, identity politics, and violence against women of color." *Stanford Law Review 43*(6), 1241–1299.

Crenshaw, K. W., Gotanda, N., Peller, G. and Thomas, K. (1995). *Critical Race Theory: The Key Writings that Formed the Movement.* New York: The New Press.

Daniel, R. (2020). "Since you asked: What data exists about Native American people in the criminal justice system?" *Prison Policy Initiative.* Retrieved 12-16-2020 from: https://www.prisonpolicy.org/blog/2020/04/22/native/

Delgado, R. and Stefancic, J. (2012). *Critical Race Theory: An Introduction.* 2nd ed. New York: New York University Press.

Douglass, F. ([1845] 2005). *Narrative of the Life of Fredrick Douglass, an American Slave.* New York: Signet Classics.

Fair, H. and Walmsley, R. (2021). "World prison population list thirteenth edition." *Institute for Crime & Justice Policy Research.* Retrieved 6-13-2022 from: https://www.prisonstudies.org/sites/default/files/resources/downloads/world_prison_population_list_13th_edition.pdf

Farr, P. (2021). "Toward a critical race analysis of the COVID-19 crisis in US carceral institutions." *Critical Social Policy* 42(2), 177–196. https://doi.org/10.1177%2F02610183211001495

Fornili, K. S. (2018). "Racialized mass incarceration and the war on drugs: A critical race theory appraisal." *Journal Addiction Nursing* 29(1), 65–72. https://doi.org/10.1097/JAN.0000000000000215

García, S. (2017). "Bridging critical race theory and migration: Moving beyond assimilation theories." *Sociology Compass 11*(6). https://doi.org/10.1111/soc4.12484

Ghandnoosh N (2018) Can We Wait 75 Years to Cut the Prison Population in Half? The Sentencing Project. Available at: https://www.sentencingproject.org/wp-content/uploads/2018/03/Can-we-wait-75-years-to-cut-the-prison-population-in-half.pdf

Grandin, G. (2011). *The Last Colonial Massacre: Latin America in the Cold War.* Chicago, IL: University of Chicago Press.

Hannah-Jones, N. (2021). *The 1619 Project: A new American origin story*. New York: WH Allen.
Hull, A., Bell-Scott, P. and Smith, B. (1982). *All the Women Are White, All the Blacks Are Men, but Some of Us Are Brave: Black Women's Studies*. New York: Feminist Press.
ICE (U.S. Immigration and Customs Enforcement). (2019). "Fiscal year 2018 ICE enforcement and removal operations report." Retrieved 1-21-2020 from: https://www.ice.gov/doclib/about/offices/ero/pdf/eroFY2018Report.pdf
James, M. and Burgos, A. (2022). "Race." In *The Stanford Encyclopedia of Philosophy*, Edward N. Zalta (ed.). Accessed 6-15-2022 from: https://plato.stanford.edu/archives/spr2022/entries/race/
Jeffers, J. L. (2019). "Justice is not blind: Disproportionate incarceration rate of people of color." *Social Work in Public Health 34*(1), 113–121. https://doi.org/10.1080/19371918.2018.1562404
Kajstura, A. (October 29, 2019). *Women's Mass Incarceration: The Whole Pie 2019*. https://www.prisonpolicy.org/reports/pie2019women.html
Nellis, A. (2021). *The Color of Justice: Racial and Ethnic Disparity in State Prisons*. The Sentencing Project. Accessed 6-13-2022 from: https://www.sentencingproject.org/publications/color-of-justice-racial-and-ethnic-disparity-in-state-prisons/
Pereira, S. (2018). "Mass incarceration: Slavery renamed," *Themis: Research Journal of Justice Studies and Forensic Science* 6(3). https://doi.org/10.31979/THEMIS.2018.0603
Rabe, S. G. (2015). *The Killing Zone: The United States Wages Cold War in Latin America*. London: Oxford University Press.
Rabuy, B. and Kopf, D. (2015). "Prisons of poverty: Uncovering the pre-incarceration incomes of the imprisoned." *Prison Policy Initiative*. Retrieved 5-28-2020 from: https://www.prisonpolicy.org/reports/income.html
Reyes, J. R. (2019). *Immigration Detention: Recent Trends and Scholarship*. New York: The Center for Migration Studies of New York (CMS). Retrieved 1-14-2020 from: https://cmsny.org/publications/virtualbrief-detention/
Roberts, D. (2019). "Foreword: Abolition constitutionalism." *Harvard Law Review 133*(1), 3–122.
Romero, M. (2008). "Crossing the immigration and race border: A critical race theory approach to immigration studies." *Contemporary Justice Review 11*(1), 23–37,
Sanchez, G. and Romero, M. (2010). "Critical race theory in the US sociology of immigration." *Sociology Compass* 4(9), 779–788. https://doi.org/10.1111/j.1751-9020.2010.00303.x
Schratz, D., DeBor, S. T. and Mauer, M. (2018). "Decarceration strategies: How 5 states achieved substantial prison population reductions." *The Sentencing Project*. Retrieved 5-8-2020 from: https://www.sentencingproject.org/wp-content/uploads/2018/09/Decarceration-Strategies.pdf
Sentencing Project (2022). Incarcerated Women and Girls. Retrieved 4-18-2023 from https://www.sentencingproject.org/fact-sheet/incarcerated-women-and-girls/
Templeton A. R. (2013). "Biological races in humans." *Studies in History and Philosophy of Biological and Biomedical Sciences* 44(3), 262–271. https://doi.org/10.1016/j.shpsc.2013.04.010
Travis, J., Western, B. and Redburn, S. (2014). *The Growth of Incarceration in the United States: Exploring Causes and Consequences*. Washington, DC: The National Academies Press. https://johnjay.jjay.cuny.edu/nrc/NAS_report_on_incarceration.pdf
Unger, R. M. (1983[1986]). *The Critical Legal Studies Movement*. Cambridge, MA: Harvard University Press.
US Census (2020). US Census. US Census Bureau. Accessed 4-18-2023 from https://www.census.gov/programs-surveys/decennial-census/decade/2020/2020-census-main.html
Vallier, K. (2021). "Neoliberalism." In *The Stanford Encyclopedia of Philosophy*, Edward N. Zalta (ed.). Accessed 10-10-2022 from: https://plato.stanford.edu/entries/neoliberalism/
Warren, J et al. (2008). *One in 100: Behind Bars in America 2008*. Pew Charitable Trust. Accessed 6-13-2022 from: https://www.prisonpolicy.org/scans/onein100.pdf
Zeng Z (2019) Jail inmates in 2017. US Department of Justice Office of Justice. Programs Bureau of Justice Statistics. Washington DC. Available at: https://www.bjs.gov/content/pub/pdf/ji17.pdf
Zeng, Z. and Minton, T. (2022). "Jail inmates in 2019." *Bureau of Justice Statistics*. Accessed 6-13-2022 from: https://bjs.ojp.gov/content/pub/pdf/ji19.pdf

29

ENACTING A WORLD BEYOND POLICING

Alia Nahra

LEARNING OBJECTIVES:

Upon successful completion of this chapter, students will be able to:

1 Articulate the reasons why traditional reforms have not solved the problem of over-policing.
2 Discuss steps taken by jurisdictions across the country to reduce their communities' reliance on police.
3 Begin to imagine the future steps required to create a world that does not rely upon criminalization.

Introduction

Earlier chapters in this volume have described the current system of mass incarceration in the United States, as well as the history of how the country became this way. By this point in the book, readers should understand the scope of the problem of over-incarceration. However, it is important to spend time discussing in-depth the multiple levers through which mass incarceration proliferates, as there are many decision-makers and policy choices that have led the country to where it stands today. It is also imperative to engage with solutions to these issues—if over-criminalization must be reversed, what system should be created to exist in its place?

This chapter focuses on the front end of the mass incarceration machine, policing. Police in America are law enforcers; but the wide discretion they are endowed with to maintain law and order widens the risk of (and opportunity for) the use of their authority to cause unnecessary harm. This harm is most often, and most calamitously, felt by people operating at the margins of society, those without the resources or opportunities to insulate themselves from unnecessary contact with police—and consequently, the broader criminal legal system. It is these communities, Black, brown, poor, and/or queer, that are most systemically subjected to structural oppression through the layering of disadvantage and targeted enforcement.

DOI: 10.4324/9781003274292-37

Harms of the Status Quo

A concrete example of the inequitable treatment perpetuated by the current policing system, which in turn contributes to mass incarceration, is the New York City Police Department's infamous stop-and-frisk policies. This form of discretionary policing has long been documented as disproportionately targeting low-income communities of color (Chronopoulos, 2017; Jones-Brown and Williams, 2021; Liebman and Dansky, 2016; Oberman and Johnson, 2016). The practice entangles huge amounts of people in the criminal legal system for minor infractions; as such, misdemeanors accounted for 77% of the city's criminal cases in 2019 (Butcher and Rempel, 2022). Black people were arrested for half of all misdemeanors in New York in that year, despite making up less than a quarter of the population (Butcher and Rempel, 2022; Oberman and Johnson, 2016). Similarly, Hispanic/Latinx individuals were arrested for 36.7% of New York City's misdemeanors in the same time period, 1.4 times their representation in the population (Butcher and Rempel, 2022; Oberman and Johnson, 2016). Despite assurances that this form of "broken windows" policing—which assumes that signs of deterioration and lack of order (e.g., broken windows, graffiti, and abandoned buildings) create an environment that encourages criminal behavior—discourages more significant harmful activity, the practice has the opposite effect (Kamalu and Onyeozili, 2018). Researchers have continuously demonstrated that heavily policing low-level offenses does not reduce more serious crimes and that refraining from prosecuting misdemeanors can lower the rate of reoffending; additionally, over-policing can actually have the effect of increasing crime by burdening communities and eroding the perceived legitimacy of the police (Butcher and Rempel, 2022; Jashnani et al., 2021; Kamalu and Onyeozili, 2018; Lieberman and Dansky, 2016; O'Brien et al., 2019; Steinberg and Albertson, 2016). So rather than alleviate crime or improve safety, stop-and-frisk policing has served to simply widen the net of mass incarceration by saddling individuals with unnecessary arrest records and removing people from their communities.

The material consequences of being arrested are vast, ranging from barriers to employment, education, and housing, as well as financial burdens due to fines, fees, and court appearances (Craigie et al., 2020; Kamalu and Onyeozili, 2018). Individuals with an arrest record often have difficulty finding employment, receiving bank loans, and gaining admission or financial aid for education due to background checks and internet searches (Geller and Fagan, 2019; Kamalu and Onyeozili, 2018). Arrests can result in students missing classes and exams, and in some cases, extreme educational harms, such as suspension or expulsion (Craigie et al., 2020; Jashnani et al., 2021). Unhoused people and individuals residing in unstable housing arrangements are especially vulnerable to losing their housing or shelter after an arrest, and in many places, one could be evicted from or lose future eligibility for public housing (Silva, 2015). Even without a conviction, people forced to pay bail or spend time in jail are subjected to a host of financial losses while additional court appearances create another significant burden as individuals may have to miss work, pay for childcare, and arrange transportation—sometimes for multiple court appearances after an arrest (Oberman and Johnson, 2016). Adults can also face long-term consequences resulting from discretionary arrests, including loss of parental rights, and immigrants may experience barriers to citizenship or deportation (Kamalu and Onyeozili, 2018; Make the Road NY, 2014). An arrest is no small incident.

Those subjected to police contact and arrests may also face internal consequences as a result of experiencing physical, verbal, and/or sexual abuse at the hands of the police and suffering the emotional impacts of these traumatic experiences. Countless people have been subjected to humiliating and dehumanizing treatment at the hands of police and jail officials, such as strip searches, being held in dirty cells, and denial of necessities like water, access to a bathroom, and medications (Jashnani et al., 2021). Individuals may also suffer bodily harm due to overly tight handcuffs, unsafe transportation without a seat or seatbelt, and injuries resulting from being brutalized by the arresting officers; police may additionally subject individuals to verbal abuse in the form of threats and ethnic, racial, religious, and sexual slurs (Jashnani et al., 2021). And, of course, there's the fact that police in America have killed over 1,000 people a year since 2014, and a *Buffalo News* database estimates that, on average, a law enforcement officer is caught engaging in sexual misconduct every five days (Knowles and Ritchie, 2021). This harm is real, pervasive, and almost certainly underreported. Finally, police violence can manifest in more amorphous ways, such as the inconvenience and dehumanization of unjustified stops and searches or the constant fear and stress imposed by extensive police surveillance of an individual or community.

Police contact is the first step toward being detained, so the link between policing and mass incarceration is clear. And yet, one need not actually become incarcerated to feel the negative effects of this engagement. It is the myriad penalties described above that reinforce the importance of considering policing as the front door to mass incarceration. The decision to stop, question, or arrest someone is often a discretionary choice made by an individual or group of police officers, and yet the detrimental impact on those targeted, as well as the people around them, can be lifelong and incredibly harmful.

Attempts at Reform

Despite the obvious harms enacted by the police, it can be challenging for policymakers and the public alike to imagine—and more importantly, implement—a different way of life. For most people, the existence of police is the norm, and Americans have been conditioned to expect that policing is the answer to social disorder or violence. But the police do not prevent crime (Baughman, 2020; Bump, 2020; Gruber, 2021; Henderson and Yisrael, 2021; Knowles and Ritchie, 2021). In fact, in many cases, they create it—for example, charges of resisting arrest, entrapment practices, or many misdemeanors that are unconnected to actual harm (Tinto, 2020). Over America's decades of mass incarceration, countless piecemeal reforms to the criminal legal system have been proposed, attempted, and sometimes even touted as successes. Yet the structure of policing in America has remained largely unchanged throughout—in fact, in many cases, these reforms have only strengthened and rewarded violent departments (Murakawa, 2020). Minneapolis, for example, had implemented a slate of "best practice" reforms years before its police force became infamous for its murder of George Floyd in May 2020; these earlier reforms were themselves prompted by "a long history of tension between [the Minneapolis Police Department] and Minneapolis communities" (Jannetta et al., 2019, 12). These modifications had little impact except for expanding the department's budget and further entrenching police power (Siegel, 2020). This is true also at the level of individual officers. Derek Chauvin, the policeman who knelt on Floyd's neck for nearly nine minutes, had been the subject of at least 17 previous misconduct complaints in his nearly two decades on the force, and yet these grievances did nothing to impede his career trajectory while the department-wide reforms continued to have no impact on its officers' violence (Dewan and Kovaleski, 2020). It is not the police who are forced to bear the consequences of the harm they cause, but rather the people and communities entangled in the system of mass incarceration because of it.

As a part of national uprisings in response to Floyd's murder, the phrase "defund the police" became part of common parlance more than ever before, bringing the long-standing project of police and prison abolition to the mainstream. Arrieta-Kenna (2020) provides a brief history of the police abolition movement, leading up to this popularization, and it is important to note that recent momentum has not been spontaneous. Many organizations and community leaders have been engaging in abolitionist work for a very long time. However, the concept of defunding or abolishing the police can be daunting and is often misunderstood. Scholar-activist Mariame Kaba (2020) has done much to simplify the movement for the mainstream public, but whether by ignorance or choice, many continue to dismiss the concept without engaging with its principles. These principles are intertwined with a broader goal of freeing the country from the prison industrial complex writ large, and there are many varying views on how to achieve such a transformation. But the core mission of police abolition is simple—replace the country's reliance on police with a more free, democratic, and humane society, investing in models of safety that center on community and well-being over punishment, surveillance, and control.

Defining Police Abolition

There is a simple framework for understanding the difference between "reformist reforms," which masquerade as system improvements but actually serve to further expand the power and breadth of policing, and abolitionist steps that reduce contact with the police and the reach of the institution of policing (Critical Resistance, 2020). The framework, created by abolitionist organization Critical Resistance, asks four questions when evaluating a proposed change: first, does the action reduce funding to police? In order to substantially reimagine public safety and build a world that does not rely on police, it is imperative that funding be invested in resources and services that better serve community needs. The second question is whether the proposed reform challenges the idea that police increase safety—because, as discussed above, the claim that police reduce crime or make communities safer is not true. Third, the organization asks: would this change reduce the tools, tactics, or technology at the disposal of police forces? Similar to the question of funding, many reforms that were initially imagined as ways to monitor or provide oversight of police have actually just given them more tools with which to oppress marginalized communities and disempowered people. And finally, the framework inquires: does the proposal reduce the scale of policing? This acts as a more comprehensive question, examining the intent and impact of a reform by digging into what will happen once it is implemented.

Reformist Reforms

The widespread use of body cameras is a perfect example of a misguided attempt at reform. Body cameras were initially proposed as a revolutionary change to police oversight and expanded accountability, allowing for the monitoring of an individual officer's actions at all times. But in practice, providing police officers with body cameras actually serves to expand the reach of policing and further legitimize the institution. At a practical level, their adoption has done little to slow the tide of police violence (Matsakis, 2020). Implementing body cameras additionally requires a huge increase in funding for police departments, both to purchase the equipment and to maintain an oversight, review, and storage procedure for footage. This reform does not reduce funding to police. Body cameras also provide the illusion of accountability, which further entrenches the idea that there is a difference between "good" and "bad" policing that can be easily exposed by visibility. Cameras furthermore increase the technology available for police, allowing for novel modes of surveillance and more tools that must be purchased to support the new infrastructure. Finally, body cameras do not reduce the scale or brutality of policing, instead perpetuating the idea that officers who do not act in ways that are visually appalling are less threatening or dangerous.

Large studies of police departments in Washington, D.C. and Milwaukee, Minnesota found that body cameras had little to no effect on officer behavior and use of force (Yokum et al., 2017). Police can always turn off body cameras and, even when footage is released, it often is used for surveillance of civilians or does not bring about the accountability sought by community members (Critical Resistance, 2020; Devich-Cyril, 2020). Body camera footage is also often hidden from oversight, and agencies tasked with investigating police misconduct consistently report difficulty obtaining evidence from them. In a 2019 memo, the Civilian Complaint Review Board in New York described extensive problems with conducting investigations involving body camera footage, including hundreds of unanswered requests for footage and at least one instance when the police department routinely denied the existence of footage that was then leaked to the press (Carayannis, 2019). In cases where camera footage has brought renewed attention to a case or some measure of accountability to officers, it is often bystander cell phone footage that prompts a public response, rather than body cameras worn by police.

The same evaluation framework can be applied to community policing initiatives, especially when run through an existing police force. At its core, community policing is a strategy that repeatedly assigns the same officers to be present within a small area of a jurisdiction. Understood most generously, community policing initiatives are proposed with the intention of familiarizing the officer or officers with a specific locality and its inhabitants (and vice versa) so that tensions might be reduced, and problems be solved more holistically. To take a more critical view, community policing is an insidious way to institute thorough surveillance of a particular neighborhood and target a precise subset of the general population, with the outcome of further entrenching the reach of mass incarceration. But regardless of the intention, these programs are a perfect example of a "reformist reform" that further entrenches police presence and power in subjugated publics.

Begin with question one of the framework—does introducing community policing reduce police funding? No. More officers would need to be hired to institute a police presence in various neighborhoods, and overtime budgets might need to be expanded to continuously send the same officers into the same places over long periods of time. So, this would further bloat police budgets. Question two—would introducing this change challenge the belief that police increase safety? Community policing espouses the idea that it is a lack of trust between cops and community that causes police violence, not the institution itself—further legitimizing the myth that better policing increases public safety. While the program might actually provide further evidence that police presence makes a community less safe if violence or harm increases after introduction, there is no benefit to introducing such an experiment with human lives. Question three—would this reduce the tools, tactics, or technology that the police can access? This initiative would add new tactics to the police repertoire, by expanding the responsibilities to which each officer is tasked (for example, if two officers are placed in a particular neighborhood, it becomes their responsibility to deal with most calls for service in that place, whereas in a prior system differing responsibilities were likely delegated to various precinct members) and by increasing the need for information systems to coordinate across neighborhoods (if the default is that a police force is spread across its jurisdiction, rather than centrally located within the precinct, the force will likely rely upon more technology to coordinate and communicate between officers). Therefore, the police would likely have to expand their technology and tactics when implementing a community policing program. Additionally, introducing such a system would, by definition, increase the points of contact that community members have with officers; in turn this would increase the likelihood of harm enacted by officers against individuals in the area. And finally, question four—would the reform reduce the scale of policing? As exemplified by the answers to the previous questions, community policing efforts are almost guaranteed to expand the scale of policing, particularly in communities of color and under-resourced neighborhoods within which the perceived breakdown of trust lies. The community policing enterprise is therefore an example of a reform that perpetuates, or at least facilitates, mass incarceration.

Abolitionist Steps to Reducing Harm

In contrast to the example of community policing, which clearly fails the Critical Resistance test, consider a proposal to suspend the use of paid administrative leave for officers being investigated for misconduct. Instead of paid leave, the proposal offers that officers should be suspended without pay while they are under investigation for misconduct (and, if complaints against them are substantiated, the officer should be fired). Such a change would diminish the cost burden of the department on a locality's budget; that money could instead be invested in community-based programs or other municipal priorities. So, this reduces police funding. Question two—would this shift challenge the idea that police increase public safety? Yes, by ceasing coverage of administrative costs incurred by officers perpetrating egregious harm and therefore ceasing to affirm that covering the costs of police being investigated is at part and parcel of doing the business of safety. Additionally, access to paid leave allows individual officers to engage in misconduct with little personal consequence and presumes that police violence is only unjustifiable in extreme circumstances. Therefore, suspending paid leave satisfies question three by reducing the tactics of violence and physical force at police disposal. And, finally, suspending the use of paid leave reduces the scale of policing and clears question four. Budgets reflect community values, so not financially supporting those who use excessive force is an indicator of reduced support for the institution. So, this reform, in contrast to body cameras or community policing, is a step toward reducing and eventually eliminating reliance upon police.

Proponents of police abolition are interested in developing strategies for responding to harm and enacting accountability that work to create living conditions that prevent, or at least drastically limit, harm from happening in the first place. This might look like sending mental health and/or social workers in response to personal crises; tasking trained civilians with conducting unarmed traffic patrols and responding to property offenses; implementing specialized resolution tactics for neighborhood and domestic disputes (such as restorative or transformative justice models); funding safer and more reliable public transit systems; and establishing school and community wellness centers (Vitale, 2020). In the future reality of a world without police, communities will have all of these supports available, and more. Mass incarceration will cease to exist because the system that creates it will be eliminated.

In some jurisdictions, policymakers have begun to experiment with these more impactful shifts away from policing. For example, in June of 2020, the government of Rochester, New York decided to cut $3.6 million from its police budget for the following fiscal year while also cutting the incoming police class by 50%, saving $750,000 for other city initiatives (Funke, 2022). This decision to limit the number of new recruits forced the city to begin to imagine new forms of community engagement and public safety. Advocates and policymakers pledged to invest the money saved into youth programming, libraries, and recreation centers—while the newness of the budget decrease makes its impact difficult to measure, the spirit of these changes fits within the abolitionist reform framework.

Addressing Violence

The most central challenge of any movement to defund or abolish police forces is that violence continues to exist, and people are accustomed to the notion that police are the way to introduce accountability and promote safety. During the Covid-19 pandemic, after declining steadily for decades, violent crime rose. This experience of harm is not to be overlooked, and any future-solutions–oriented work must account for the persistent perception that crime is rampant—despite the fact that, as compared to the nation's historic patterns of violence, rates remain relatively low (Grawert and Kim, 2022). The conditions that bring about violence are myriad and complicated, but it is integral to understand that the use of aggressive policing or even increased police presence in violent areas does not reduce violence. In Canada, the Ontario Ministry of Children (2019) conducted a comprehensive literature review, documenting that aggressive policing strategies do not reduce long-term crime rates and contribute to negative community perceptions of the criminal legal system. And, again, the police do not prevent crime from happening at all. Instead of relying upon police through inertia, policymakers should engage seriously with non-police approaches that might actually address and prevent violence.

One such option is taking a public health approach, treating violence as an epidemic. This methodology operates from the hypothesis that exposure to violence makes people more likely to commit violence themselves. Slutkin (2013) has long summarized public health interventions as a response to violence, emphasizing that practitioners should respond to violence as a contagious disease. This approach also takes seriously the holistic causes of violence, the structural and social determinants that create an environment where harm occurs. The Bay Area Regional Health Inequities Initiative (2020) has created a summary of the public health framework, including social determinants of inequities that are implicated in the system of mass incarceration—providing a visual example of this public health approach. Responses under the public health model approach conflicts and violence from a structural lens, not just an interpersonal one. Anti-violence programs operating in the public health model, most famously Cure Violence, rely upon trained community members to act as credible messengers to interrupt violence in their neighborhoods (Gimbel and Muhammad, 2019). However, many of these programs fall short in three major ways—primarily, evidence of their effectiveness in stopping violence is murky; they fail to offer solutions to the conditions giving rise to violence; and they often serve to further entrench police in communities by partnering closely with police and acting as liaison between departments and communities (Lopez, 2021).

In contrast, community-empowerment models have been raised as an alternative approach seeking to both directly engage with the root causes of harm and halt cycles of violence by working with directly impacted individuals (Gimbel and Muhammad, 2019). This approach follows the organizing adage, most often attributed to the advocacy organization JustLeadershipUSA (2014), that those "closest to the problem are closest to the solution." To be successful in bringing about true social change, the community empowerment framework attempts to boost community members and groups to absorb the perceived public safety function of the police, which also helps to eradicate the consolidation of power that currently allows for the oppressive social control exercised by the police (Gimbel and Muhammad, 2019).

This model has been proven effective in cities across the United States. In one recent study, researchers found that establishing community-based nonprofits has a meaningful negative effect on murder, violent crime, and property crime (Sharkey et al., 2017). In Milwaukee, the LiberateMKE coalition conducted surveys of more than 1,100 residents to gain an idea of their funding priorities, then organized a campaign to cut the city's police budget by $900,000 and reduce police personnel by 60 officers; in place of that spending, the coalition successfully lobbied to increase funding for summer youth programs (by $72,000), emergency housing funds (by $300,000), and the city's health department (by $240,00) (Anderson, 2019; McHarris, 2020).

At a more granular level, individual stipends, mentorship, therapy, and internship opportunities provided to participants in Richmond, California's Operation Peacemaker Program, have been attributed to 55% reduction in homicides and a 43% reduction in assaults (Matthay et al., 2019). Similar programs exist across the country, taking the approach that setting individuals and their neighborhoods up for success reduces the social ills and external pressures that lead to crime. These programs work, most so when they are given the time and resources to be implemented thoughtfully and comprehensively.

Community empowerment models show that investment in people and collective priorities is a clear path toward a world that does not feel it needs police. This approach pauses or divests money currently being funneled toward surveillance and criminalization, instead pushing to invest municipal resources in community-based systems that reallocate power to support, feed, house, heal, and clothe people (Center for Popular Democracy and Law for Black Lives, 2017; Stahly-Butts, 2022). It begins the difficult work of crafting safe and thriving communities by focusing on possibility, not punishment. For this is the true possibility of abolition—when people can consider a society without police, not left without solutions to violence and harm, but without so many of those ills to begin with—then a new vision of safety and justice can be realized.

Conclusion

The police abolition movement will take time to become manifest and requires methodical commitment. It will not be easy to overcome policy inertia, comfort with the status quo, or the political might of police unions and lobbyists. But as local leaders continue to experiment with divesting from police and investing in support-based alternatives in their place, the list of anti-violence and safety alternatives will continue to grow. Campaigns based on research, public engagement, and trial programs will help push beyond the boundaries of the current system of punishment and help doubters to envision a better way. And protest movements will continue to push when information and advocacy have not been convincing enough. A world beyond policing is a radical shift, but a possible one worth continuing the fight.

Discussion Questions:

1. What are some steps that have already been taken by cities in the United States to reduce over-policing?
2. What are some steps that jurisdictions could take to further reduce their reliance on police?

References

Anderson, D. (2019). *LiberateMKE Survey Results* (pp. 1–13). African-American Roundtable. https://static1.squarespace.com/static/5d016c1ea5666e00014ebcb3/t/5d892987856d7f4d7558f982/1569270156524/Liberatemke+Survey+Results.pdf.

Arrieta-Kenna, R. (2020, June 20). *The Deep Roots—and New Offshoots—of 'Abolish the Police.'* POLITICO. https://www.politico.com/news/magazine/2020/06/12/abolish-defund-police-explainer-316185.

Baughman, S. B. (2020). *How Effective Are Police? The Problem of Clearance Rates and Criminal Accountability* [SSRN Scholarly Paper]. https://doi.org/10.2139/ssrn.3566383.

Bay Area Regional Health Inequities Initiative. (2020). *A Public Health Framework for Reducing Health Inequities*. BARHII. https://www.barhii.org/enlarged-framework.

Bump, P. (2020, June 7). Over the past 60 years, more spending on police hasn't necessarily meant less crime. *Washington Post*. https://www.washingtonpost.com/politics/2020/06/07/over-past-60-years-more-spending-police-hasnt-necessarily-meant-less-crime/.

Butcher, F., & Rempel, M. (2022). *Racial Disparities in Misdemeanor Justice: Data for New York City, 2019–2020* (Advancing Racial Equity, pp. 1–15). Center for Court Innovation. https://www.courtinnovation.org/sites/default/files/media/document/2022/NYC_Misdemeanor_Justice_Data_Report_NYC.pdf.

Carayannis, L. O. (2019, July 5). *BWC and Document Request Issues with the NYPD* [Memo]. https://brooklyneagle.com/wp-content/uploads/2019/07/20190710_boardmtg_BWC_memo-2-1.pdf.

Center for Popular Democracy, & Law for Black Lives. (2017). *Freedom to Thrive: Reimagining Safety & Security in Our Communities*.https://www.populardemocracy.org/news/publications/freedom-thrive-reimagining-safety-security-our-communities.

Chronopoulos, T. (2017). The Making of the Orderly City: New York since the 1980s. *Journal of Urban History*, *46*(5), 1085–1116. https://doi.org/10.1177/0096144217705459.

Craigie, T.-A., Grawert, A., & Kimble, C. (2020). *Conviction, Imprisonment, and Lost Earnings: How Involvement with the Criminal Justice System Deepens Inequality | Brennan Center for Justice* (pp. 1–44). Brennan Center for Justice. https://www.brennancenter.org/our-work/research-reports/conviction-imprisonment-and-lost-earnings-how-involvement-criminal.

Critical Resistance. (2020). Reformist reforms vs. abolitionist steps in policing. *No Cops: Reform vs. Abolition*. https://criticalresistance.org/wp-content/uploads/2021/08/CR_NoCops_reform_vs_abolition_REV2020.pdf.

Devich-Cyril, M. (2020, July 5). Defund facial recognition. *The Atlantic, July/August 2020*. https://www.theatlantic.com/technology/archive/2020/07/defund-facial-recognition/613771/.

Dewan, S., & Kovaleski, S. F. (2020, May 30). Thousands of complaints do little to change police ways. *The New York Times*. https://www.nytimes.com/2020/05/30/us/derek-chauvin-george-floyd.html.

Funke, D. (2022, January 28). Fact check: No evidence defunding police to blame for homicide increases, experts say. *USA Today*. https://www.usatoday.com/story/news/factcheck/2022/01/28/fact-check-police-funding-not-linked-homicide-spikes-experts-say/9054639002/.

Geller, A., & Fagan, J. (2019). *Police Contact and the Legal Socialization of Urban Teens*.https://papers.ssrn.com/abstract=3347356.

Gimbel, V. N., & Muhammad, C. (2019). Are Police Obsolete? - Police Abolition. *Cardozo Law Review*, *40*(4), 1453–1543. https://cardozolawreview.com/are-police-obsolete-police-abolition/.

Grawert, A., & Kim, N. (2022). *Myths and Realities: Understanding Recent Trends in Violent Crime*. Brennan Center for Justice. https://www.brennancenter.org/our-work/research-reports/myths-and-realities-understanding-recent-trends-violent-crime.

Gruber, A. (2021, October 26). *Crime Rates Rise and Fall. The Police Mostly Have Nothing to Do With It*. The Garrison Project. https://thegarrisonproject.org/purpose-of-policing/.

Henderson, H., & Yisrael, B. (2021, May 19). 7 myths about "defunding the police" debunked. *Brookings Institution*. https://www.brookings.edu/blog/how-we-rise/2021/05/19/7-myths-about-defunding-the-police-debunked/.

Jannetta, J., Esthappan, S., Fontaine, J., Lynch, M., & La Vigne, N. (2019). *Learning to Build Police-Community Trust: Implementation Assessment Findings from the Evaluation of the National Initiative for Building Community Trust and Justice* (pp. v–112). The Urban Institute. https://www.urban.org/sites/default/files/publication/100705/learning_to_build_police-community_trust_3.pdf.

Jashnani, G., Bustamante, P., & Stoudt, B. G. (2021). Legal Process as Racialized Punishment: The Material Consequences of Discretionary Arrests in New York City. *Critical Criminology*, *29*(4), 873–895. https://doi.org/10.1007/s10612-021-09595-9.

Jones-Brown, D., & Williams, J. (2021). Over-policing Black Bodies: The Need for Multidimensional and Transformative Reforms. *Journal of Ethnicity in Criminal Justice*, *19*(3–4), 181–187. https://doi.org/10.1080/15377938.2021.1992326.

JustLeadershipUSA \ About Us. (2014). JustLeadershipUSA. https://jlusa.org/about/.

Kaba, M. (2020, June 12). Yes, we mean literally abolish the police. *The New York Times*. https://www.nytimes.com/2020/06/12/opinion/sunday/floyd-abolish-defund-police.html.

Kamalu, N. C., & Onyeozili, E. C. (2018). A Critical Analysis of the 'Broken Windows' Policing in New York City and Its Impact: Implications for the Criminal Justice System and the African American Community. *African Journal of Criminology and Justice Studies*, *11*(1), 71–94. https://stg15.umes.edu/uploadedFiles/_WEBSITES/AJCJS/Content/VOL%2011%20KAMALU%20FINAL.pdf.

Knowles, J., & Ritchie, A. (2021). *Cops Don't Stop Violence* (pp. 1–28). Interrupting Criminalization. https://www.interruptingcriminalization.com/cops-dont-stop-violence

Lieberman, D., & Dansky, K. (2016). The Degradation of Civil Society and Hyper-Aggressive Policing in Communities of Color in New York City. *Cardozo Law Review*, *37*(3), 955–972. https://cardozolawreview.com/the-degradation-of-civil-society-and-hyper-aggressive-policing-in-communities-of-color-in-new-york-city/.

Lopez, G. (2021, September 3). The evidence for violence interrupters doesn't support the hype. *Vox*. https://www.vox.com/22622363/police-violence-interrupters-cure-violence-research-study.

Make the Road NY, & Public Science Project. (2014, May 29). *Video Gallery*. Growing Up Policed. https://growinguppoliced.org/video/.

Matsakis, L. (2020, June 17). Body cameras haven't stopped police brutality. Here's why. *Wired*. https://www.wired.com/story/body-cameras-stopped-police-brutality-george-floyd/.

Matthay, E. C., Farkas, K., Rudolph, K. E., Zimmerman, S., Barragan, M., Goin, D. E., & Ahern, J. (2019). Firearm and Nonfirearm Violence After Operation Peacemaker Fellowship in Richmond, California, 1996–2016. *American Journal of Public Health*, *109*(11), 1605–1611. https://doi.org/10.2105/AJPH.2019.305288.

McHarris, P. V. (2020). *Research Memo: Alternatives to Policing* (pp. 1–24). Community Resource Hub for Safety and Accountability. https://defundpolice.org/wp-content/uploads/2020/12/national_comm_report_Research-Memo-Alternatives-to-Policing.pdf.

Murakawa, N. (2020, October 21). Police Reform Works — For the Police. *Abolition for the People*. https://level.medium.com/why-police-reform-is-actually-a-bailout-for-cops-ecf2dd7b8833.

Oberman, J., & Johnson, K. (2016). The Never Ending Tale: Racism and Inequality in the Era of Broken Windows. *Cardozo Law Review*, *37*, 1075. https://larc.cardozo.yu.edu/faculty-articles/113.

O'Brien, D. T., Farrell, C., & Welsh, B. C. (2019). Looking Through Broken Windows: The Impact of Neighborhood Disorder on Aggression and Fear of Crime Is an Artifact of Research Design. *Annual Review of Criminology*, *2*(1), 53–71. https://doi.org/10.1146/annurev-criminol-011518-024638.

Ontario Ministry of Children. (2019). *Aggressive Policing Strategies*. Community & Social Services. https://perma.cc/5BM8-QEFW.

Sharkey, P., Torrats-Espinosa, G., & Takyar, D. (2017). Community and the Crime Decline: The Causal Effect of Local Nonprofits on Violent Crime. *American Sociological Review*, *82*(6), 1214–1240. https://doi.org/10.1177/0003122417736289.

Siegel, Z. (2020, June 4). 'Starve the Beast': A Q&A With Alex S. Vitale on Defunding the Police. *The Nation*. https://www.thenation.com/article/society/alex-vitale-defund-police-interview/.

Silva, L. R. (2015). Collateral Damage: A Public Housing Consequence of the War on Drugs. *UC Irvine Law Review*, *5*, 783. https://heinonline.org/HOL/Page?handle=hein.journals/ucirvlre5&id=793&div=&collection=.

Slutkin, G. (2013). *Violence Is a Contagious Disease*. 94–112. https://www.ncbi.nlm.nih.gov/books/NBK207245/.

Stahly-Butts, M. (2022). *What Is Divest/Invest?* Funders for Justice. https://divest-ffj.org/.

Steinberg, R., & Albertson, S. (2016). Broken Windows Policing and Community Courts: An Unholy Alliance. *Cardozo Law Review*, *37*(3), 995–1024. https://cardozolawreview.com/broken-windows-policing-and-community-courts-an-unholy-alliance/.

Tinto, K. (2020, September 20). The dangers of police-created crime. *The Lab by the Appeal*. https://theappeal.org/the-lab/report/the-dangers-of-police-created-crime/.

Vitale, A. (2020, July 20). 10 Ways to reduce our reliance on policing and make our communities safer for everyone. *The Appeal*. https://theappeal.org/10-ways-to-reduce-our-reliance-on-policing-and-make-our-communities-safer-for-everyone/.

Yokum, D., Ravishankar, A., & Coppock, A. (2017). *Evaluating the Effects of Police Body-Worn Cameras: A Randomized Controlled Trial* (pp. 1–32). The Lab @DC. https://bwc.thelab.dc.gov/TheLabDC_MPD_BWC_Working_Paper_10.20.17.pdf.

30

DECRIMINALIZING SUBSTANCE USE DISORDERS TO COMBAT MASS INCARCERATION

Leslie Scott

LEARNING OUTCOMES:

Upon successful completion of this chapter, students will be able to:

1. Discuss the relationship between the "War on Drugs" and mass incarceration of communities of color.
2. Describe how the four justifications of punishment either support or do not support the prosecution and/or punishment of people who commit crimes related to their substance use disorders.
3. Articulate arguments on both sides of the decriminalization, *de facto* decriminalization, and decarceration debate.

Introduction

The United States incarcerates far too many people for far too long, especially for drug- and addiction-related crimes. Indeed, this country has over-relied on criminalization and mass imprisonment to address a variety of social problems that the justice system has proven inept at handling. Perhaps in recognition of this, on October 6, 2022, President Joe Biden issued a proclamation pardoning[1] past federal and D.C. Code convictions for simple marijuana possession (The White House, 2022; U.S. Department of Justice, 2022). The move was heralded by many as "hugely significant" and a "big step in trying to repair the harms of the war on drugs" (Cohan, 2022). The president of the National Association for the Advancement of Colored People (NAACP), Derrick Johnson, emphasized the importance of the proclamation in redressing the unique harms of uneven marijuana and other drug enforcement on racial and ethnic minorities (NAACP, 2022). In a video addressed to the nation, President Biden also acknowledged the adverse impact of discriminatory marijuana law enforcement on Black and brown communities (Westervelt, 2022).

The presidential proclamation follows a growing trend in the states to legalize recreational and/or medical marijuana use (Westervelt, 2022). Indeed, marijuana legalization was

DOI: 10.4324/9781003274292-38

on the November 2022 midterm election ballots in five states, with voters in Maryland and Missouri choosing to legalize possession and use of cannabis for people 21 and older (The New York Times, 2022). These states join 19 others and the District of Columbia in legalizing marijuana for recreational use, and 38 states that have legalized marijuana for medical use (Westervelt, 2022). And the momentum only seems to be growing, with over two-thirds of Americans supporting marijuana legalization today, compared to less than one-half a decade ago (Burga, 2022).

Despite this momentum, very few states have expressed a willingness to expand drug legalization or decriminalization[2] beyond cannabis. And the proclamation will not lead to a mass exodus from this country's overcrowded jails and prisons because no one is currently serving federal time for marijuana possession (Lartey, 2022). Furthermore, President Biden did not legalize marijuana possession, which remains an outlawed substance under the federal Controlled Substances Act, although he did call on the Secretary of Health and Human Services and the Attorney General to review how marijuana is scheduled (The White House, 2022). Thus, the question remains whether this moment will represent a continued shift in American drug and addiction policy away from "War on Drugs" criminalization toward a public health and harm reduction paradigm (some scholars point to the opioid crisis as the genesis of this turning point) (Jefferson Exum, 2019), or stay confined to cannabis possession and use, making it mostly symbolic.

Mass Incarceration, War on Drugs, and Collateral Consequences

Although the number of people incarcerated in federal and state prisons and local jails has declined in recent years because of decarceration efforts stemming from the global COVID-19 pandemic, in Spring of 2021, there were still nearly 1.8 million people incarcerated in the United States, discounting the people in pre-trial and civil detention (Vera, 2022, p. 3, tbl. 3). The causes of this country's mass incarceration crisis are myriad and complex, but many trace it to the War on Drugs. This war began in the early 1970s when then-President Richard Nixon declared drug abuse "public enemy number one" (Friedersdorf, 2011). The hallmarks of the war were the passage of crippling mandatory minimum drug sentencing laws, draconian recidivist enhancements (three strikes rules), and truth-in-sentencing laws (which limit the amount of time people in state prison can earn off non-life sentences), as well as increased and aggressive drug crime policing and drug law enforcement spending (Parsons & Neath, 2017; Stamm & Chettiar, 2012).

The War on Drugs and mass incarceration, generally, have disproportionately impacted Black and brown communities. This seems to be no mistake. In 1994, Nixon's former domestic policy advisor, John Ehrlichman, allegedly admitted in an interview that the Nixon campaign and administration "had two enemies: the antiwar left and [B]lack people" (Baum, 2016). Ehrlichman continued,

> We knew we couldn't make it illegal to be either against the war or [B]lack, but by getting the public to associate hippies with marijuana and [B]lacks with heroin, and then criminalizing both heavily, we could disrupt those communities. We could arrest their leaders, raid their homes, break up their meetings, and vilify them night after night on the evening news. Did we know we were lying about the drugs? Of course we did.
>
> *(Baum, 2016)*

The ramifications of this mindset and drug war policies and rhetoric are apparent. There are racial disparities in law enforcement contacts, arrests, pretrial and post-conviction incarceration rates, severe sentences, and use of solitary confinement, with Black men and women overrepresented in every category compared to their white counterparts (Sawyer, 2020). Black and Latinx individuals are much more likely to be arrested and imprisoned for drug possession and distribution than their white counterparts despite evidence that whites sell drugs at higher rates and are equally likely to consume them (Eaglin & Solomon, 2015). Law enforcement's historical focus on easily detectable, open-air drug markets, and crack cocaine has significantly expanded the number of Black men in prison (O'Hear, 2009). The recent decrease in jail populations linked to COVID-19 is also fragmented along racial lines, with incarceration rates for Black and Latinx people decreasing more slowly than for white people (Kang-Brown, Montagnet, & Heiss, 2021).

In the decades following the initiation of the drug war, arrest and imprisonment rates for drug crimes—including manufacture, sale, and possession—skyrocketed. The length of time served for drug offenses also rose. In 2000, the average sentences served in federal prison for drug offenses more closely resembled those of violent crimes than fraud and other property crimes (Jensen, Gerber, & Mosher, 2004). Also, the number of people incarcerated for drug offenses has burgeoned at a faster rate than has the total number of incarcerated Americans. In 2015, approximately half of all individuals convicted of a federal crime were serving sentences for drug crimes, compared to only one-quarter in 1980 (Parsons & Neath, 2017).

Mallik-Kane, Parthasarathy, and Adams (2012) examined the factors contributing to the overall growth of the federal prison population between 1998 and 2010. The total federal prison population increased by 77% during this time. They found that the increase in time to be served by people convicted of drug offenses "was the single greatest contributor" to this growth, accounting for one-third of the expansion in the federal prison population during this period (p. 3). Thus, "[people convicted of drug offenses] continued to form the majority of the [federal] prison population in 2010" (p. 5). Likewise, they make up a significant percentage of the incarcerated population in state correctional facilities. Currently, one in five incarcerated people in state and federal prisons and local jails are detained for a drug offense (Sawyer & Wagner, 2022).

Although the drug war was ostensibly designed to eradicate illegal drug use and related crime, it has largely failed to do so. Increased drug enforcement and punitive sanctions for drug-related crime have not significantly reduced drug supply or use (Parsons & Neath, 2017), with rates of self-reported illicit drug use among Americans far exceeding those in other countries (Kreit, 2009). Today, drug overdose remains a leading cause of death in the United States (Centers for Disease Control and Prevention, n.d.). Likewise, recent news stories report large-scale drug busts, proving ineffective the "tough on drug crime" approach to addiction and related crime (Chan & Jackson, 2020; National Institute on Drug Abuse, 2021; U.S. Customs and Border Protection, 2021).

U.S. drug war policies and laws have had a widespread destabilizing impact on Black and brown communities that have been overpoliced in response and have fostered a biased view of the people within these communities (Jefferson Exum, 2021). Unemployment rates and financial insecurity increase because of incarceration, family and social bonds are disrupted leading to lasting changes in family structure, and urban violence proliferates (Jensen, Gerber, & Mosher, 2004). Uggen et al. (2022) report, "One in 19 African Americans of voting age is disenfranchised, a rate 3.5 times that of non-African Americans."

Although a major contributor to mass incarceration, arrest and conviction rates for drug crimes are not the only culprit. Traum (2013) notes that a shift in penological philosophy away from rehabilitation toward incapacitation beginning in the 1970s led to increased incarceration for low-level felonies both within and outside of the drug context, as did the proliferation of new and stringent recidivist enhancements. Likewise, Sawyer and Wagner (2022) advise that four out of five people in custody are incarcerated for something other than a drug offense. That said, given the rates at which people in custody for a variety of offenses suffer stigmatizing substance abuse problems, substance use disorders (SUDs) likely contribute significantly to this country's mass incarceration crisis. Therefore, decriminalizing drug use and possession and implementing substance misuse-related decarceration policies—whether in charging or sentencing individuals with substance abuse problems—are feasible ways to combat mass incarceration.

Defining SUDs

SUD refers to the "recurrent use of alcohol or other drugs that causes clinically and functionally significant impairment, such as health problems, disability, and failure to meet major responsibilities at work, school, or home" (Volkow, Koob, & McLellan, 2016, p. 364, Box 1). Addiction is a subcategory of SUD, encompassing its severest form. SUDs generally develop slowly over time with repeated misuse of alcohol or other drugs. They lead to adaptations in brain circuitry related to substance-seeking triggers; reward-seeking; stress; motivation; memory and learning; decision-making; judgment; and behavioral control (U.S. Department of Health and Human Services, 2016).

Addiction was once considered "a moral failing or character flaw" (U.S. Department of Health and Human Services, 2016, p. 2-1). However, many in the relevant medical and neuroscientific communities now view addiction as a chronic, relapsing brain disease that causes individuals to seek out and misuse drugs or alcohol compulsively despite known negative health, social, and (sometimes) legal consequences (National Institute on Drug Abuse, 2020). Proponents of this "brain disease model" of addiction underscore that long-term, chronic drug and/or alcohol use can alter fundamental neurobiological processes involved in emotional and behavioral regulation (Volkow, Koob, & McLellan, 2016).

There are some researchers who question this biologically based model of SUD. For instance, Heyman (2009) argues SUDs involve learned, voluntary behaviors resulting from differences in individual decision-making styles that can be effectively managed through incentive programs. Likewise, Levy (2013) proposes, addiction is not a *brain disease*, "[but a] disorder of the person, embedded in a social context," though he concedes addiction involves "pathological neuropsychological dysfunction" (p. 1). Critics of the brain disease model underscore that drug misuse is chronic and relapsing for some, but not others, and the occurrence of spontaneous remission, even without formal treatment, undermines an understanding of addiction rooted in neurobiology. They note that some individuals with a SUD have the capacity to make better choices where alternative reinforcers are available, negating the notion of compulsivity in drug seeking and use among this population (Heilig et al., 2021).

Despite these varying viewpoints, even the proponents of this "disorder of choice" model generally agree that chronic drug use causes physical and chemical changes to the brain that make continued use highly rewarding and the ability to desist challenging (Fentiman, 2011; Heyman, 2009; Levy, 2013). And experts on both sides of the debate recognize the important interplay between SUD and non-biological "social determinants of health," including racial and ethnic disparities, socioeconomic disadvantage, and environmental and developmental factors (Heilig et al., 2021, p. 1719). Heilig et al. (2021) contend that "pre-existing vulnerabilities and persistent drug use lead to a vicious cycle of substantive disruptions in the brain that impair and undermine choice capacities for adaptive behavior, but do not annihilate them" (p. 1720). Thus, the brain disease and choice disorder theories of addiction are really "two sides of the same coin" (Heilig et al., 2021, p. 1720).

SUDs within the Incarcerated Population

Today, over 40 million Americans, aged 12 or older, struggle with a SUD (Richesson & Hoenig, 2021). The problem is especially pronounced within the incarcerated population. A 2016 Bureau of Justice Statistics survey revealed 49% of people in state prisons met the criteria for having a SUD in the 12 months prior to admission to prison. At the federal level, 32% met the criteria for having a SUD during the same period. Among all individuals in state and federal prison surveyed, roughly 38% reported drug use and 30% reported alcohol use at the time of the offense. There was an increase in overall reported drug use—including drug use at the time of the offense, in the 30 days prior to arrest, and reported lifetime drug use—since 2004, when BJS last conducted a similar survey. Substance-involved individuals are also more likely to reoffend than those who are not substance-involved (Maruschak et al., 2021). "Over half (52.2%) of substance-involved inmates have one or more previous incarcerations compared with 31.2% of inmates who are not substance involved" (Center on Addiction and Substance Abuse, 2010, p. 5). These figures demonstrate a strong correlation between SUDs, criminal activity, and mass incarceration. Thus, decriminalizing drug possession and decarcerating those with a SUD are common-sense ways to abate incarceration rates.

Drug Decriminalization Initiatives: Arguments For and Against

Treating SUDs as a criminal justice problem, as opposed to a public health problem, has had dire consequences, as illustrated above. In recognition of this, some locales are championing efforts to both decriminalize and destigmatize drug use and SUDs. For instance, in 2020, through voter-approved Measure 110, Oregon became the first state to decriminalize personal possession of all drugs and expand access to health care and harm reduction services (Sutton, 2020). Vermont and Rhode Island took similar, though less expansive, steps in June 2021 by decriminalizing the possession without a prescription of small amounts of buprenorphine (suboxone), a medication commonly used to treat opioid addiction. Public health experts applaud these measures, emphasizing buprenorphine arrests "can have life-threatening consequences in both the short-term and long-term," because many incarcerated individuals with substance misuse problems are at an increased risk of suicide without this medication in jail and an increased risk of overdose death during their transition out of custody (Messinger, Chukka, & Boyd, 2022, p. 396).

There are also a host of *de facto* decriminalization initiatives. Aimed at saving lives, 47 states and the District of Columbia have passed Good Samaritan legislation. These laws typically immunize bystanders to a potential overdose from certain drug crime prosecutions thereby encouraging them to call 911. A systematic review of empirical research reveals Good Samaritan laws reduce rates of overdose death (U.S. Government Accountability Office, 2021).

Somewhat more controversial are two law enforcement-led programs designed to divert drug users away from the criminal justice system and into treatment. In 2011 in Seattle, Washington, city officials developed Law Enforcement Assisted Diversion (LEAD). LEAD permits law enforcement to direct some people caught in possession of drugs to community-based treatment and other supportive services rather than arrest them (Drug Policy Alliance, 2017; Fedders, 2019). Similarly, in 2015 the Gloucester, Massachusetts Police Department initiated the Angel Program, which encourages drug users to voluntarily hand over their illicit drugs at a police precinct, without fear of legal repercussions, in exchange for priority access and referral to drug detox. Comparable programs are rapidly spreading across police departments in over two dozen states (Fedders, 2019).

According to Fedders (2019), the promise of these programs—which she collectively refers to as "opioid policing"—is in their ability to divert individuals away from the criminal justice system entirely (unlike drug war policing and drug courts) and in the emphasis on harm reduction over abstinence (in the case of LEAD). But there are also important limitations. She warns, "Each of the two forms of opioid policing, in different ways, functions to expand the police and prosecutorial surveillance that are hallmarks of the carceral state" (p. 440) and results in increased "monitor[ing] and control [of] marginalized populations" (p. 441). Each also engages in "moral sorting" that leads to some people who could benefit from treatment being left out (Fedders, 2019, pp. 443–446). The Angel Initiative creates "distributive inequities" (Fedders, 2019, p. 446) as long waiting lists at treatment facilities mean many with a SUD go untreated (Frakt, 2017), but the Angel program permits some to jump the line. Thus, people who feel comfortable walking into a police station carrying drugs are given priority to scarce drug rehabilitation resources. In this way, the Angel Initiative operates to the detriment of low-income communities of color who have good reason to mistrust police (Fedders, 2019).

In addition to police-led *de facto* decriminalization, there is *de facto* decriminalization at the prosecutorial level. Progressive prosecutors around the country are vowing not to prosecute low-level drug possession and use. For instance, in Washtenaw County, Michigan, District Attorney Eli Savit (2021) stopped charging people with unauthorized use or possession of buprenorphine and applies a presumption against charging the unauthorized sale of buprenorphine. He notes that most people take buprenorphine to get better, and criminalization could cause "many in recovery to backslide" or turn to more dangerous drugs for relief, putting them at greater risk of overdose death (p. 4). Philadelphia District Attorney Larry Krasner instituted a similar policy (Feldman, 2020), as did former Suffolk County, Massachusetts, District Attorney Rachel Rollins (Rollins, 2019). Rollins states, "[W]here substance use disorder is a significant factor," prosecutors should engage with treatment specialists to address public health treatment options (Rollins, 2019, Appendix C).

Not everyone supports drug decriminalization and non-prosecution policies. Opponents are concerned that expanded availability of addictive substances could lead to increased use and addiction, more drug-related health problems, and more overdose deaths (Baum, 2016; Stares, 1996). Some commentators suggest decriminalization could decrease access to necessary treatment because fewer individuals with SUDs will be required to undergo court-ordered drug rehabilitation (Quinton, 2021). And in Oregon, 28% of respondents to an August 2022 "Data for Progress" survey believed Measure 110 was responsible for increased crime and homelessness (Andrews, 2022).

These are legitimate concerns and it's still too early to know the full ramifications of Oregon's comprehensive drug decriminalization law. But insights from reforms in Portugal and other parts of the world suggest that carefully implemented decriminalization, combined with education campaigns, and increased access to drug rehabilitation and other social services, have social, economic, and public health benefits.

In 2001, Portugal became the first country in the world to decriminalize low-level possession and use of all drugs, reclassifying these behaviors as administrative violations subject to non-criminal sanctions (Bajekal, 2018). Since that time, rates of drug use have remained steady and well below the European and U.S. averages, rates of adolescent and problematic drug use and drug-induced deaths have declined, and the number of people seeking drug treatment has gone up. Unsurprisingly, far fewer people are arrested and incarcerated for drug offenses in Portugal annually than before 2001 (Drug Policy Alliance, 2017). Importantly, Portugal did not just open the floodgates to drug use. It increased spending on social services, such as drug treatment, and established Commissions for the Dissuasion of Drug Addiction—often comprised of doctors, social workers, and lawyers—to refer drug users to treatment (Baum, 2016).

The Netherlands provides another example. It has had a *de facto* decriminalization policy for many years. Like the approach of progressive district attorneys in the United States, government officials have instructed prosecutors not to pursue low-level drug possession charges. This has led to lower levels of addiction and problematic drug use in the Netherlands than in the United States and most of Western Europe, and a much lower heroin overdose death rate than in the United States (Drug Policy Alliance, 2017).

Decriminalizing SUDs

An obvious benefit of decriminalization is it reduces the number of people incarcerated for simple possession in this country's overburdened jails and prisons. But decriminalizing drug use and possession, alone, will not have a significant impact on incarceration rates. Many people who misuse substances are incarcerated for non-possession offenses tied to their SUDs, including violent offenses. At the end of 2019, 14% of persons incarcerated in state prisons were incarcerated for drug offenses and, of those, only 3.8% were incarcerated for possession-only offenses (Carson, 2021). Likewise, 46.3% of people in federal prison had a drug-related crime as their most serious offense. But, of those, less than 1% were sentenced for possession alone (Carson, 2020). Thus, the transition from a criminal justice to public health approach to drug misuse requires a shift in our response to all levels of crime related to SUD, not just simple possession.

How can this transition be accomplished? One solution is the decriminalization of SUDs. Of course, having a SUD or addiction, alone, cannot be criminalized. Most criminal conduct requires a voluntary action and being addicted to an unlawful substance is a status, not an act (*Robinson v. California*, 1962). But there are many criminalized actions that are inextricably intertwined with an individual's status as an addicted person. In other words, while having the disease, itself, is not a crime, the symptoms of that disease—including lawlessness—are. For instance, the individual who commits a burglary or sells small amounts of drugs to finance their substance use may face stiff criminal penalties for those actions, which, though distinct from their status as someone with a SUD, are often related to that status.

Decriminalization in this context does not mean granting those in the throes of a SUD a free pass to commit crime. It means recognizing that when criminal activity results from a need to finance a powerful substance disorder or from disordered thinking and behavioral patterns related to substance misuse, more generally, the purposes of punishment, discussed below, do not support a "lock 'em up" attitude to crime fighting. In the examples above, a prosecutor might choose not to prosecute, or might agree to a diversionary program, such as drug court. This is a type of "quasi" or *de facto* decriminalization since laws will remain on the books outlawing burglary and drug distribution.

In more serious cases, courts might exercise their discretion to grant downward sentencing adjustments, either because retributive goals ring hollow for those suffering a debilitating brain disease or rehabilitation is likely to be more successful in the community than in prison. This may be better thought of as decarceration than decriminalization, since public order offenses, drug trafficking, gun and violent crimes, and other maladaptive behaviors intertwined with an individual's SUD will still be criminalized and prosecuted. For instance, in *United States v. Hendrickson* (2014), Judge Mark Bennett granted a downward sentencing adjustment for a criminal defendant whose drug abuse contributed to his decision to steal firearms. Other federal courts might follow Judge Bennett's lead. Likewise, the U.S. Sentencing Commission, which writes advisory federal sentencing guidelines and policy statements to assist federal judges in making sentencing decisions, should consider amending current policy statements that discourage judges from taking the action Judge Bennett took to account for SUD's role in the offense (United States Sentencing Commission, 2021, §5H1.4).

Purposes of Sentencing and SUDs

The purposes of sentencing support the decriminalization and decarceration examples discussed above. The traditional theories of criminal punishment, built into the Federal Sentencing Reform Act of 1984, 18 U.S.C. § 3553(a), and many state sentencing schemes, are meant to guide judicial discretion at sentencing. They include incapacitation, retribution, general and specific deterrence, and rehabilitation (Scott, 2021). Blecker (1990) succinctly describes the differences among the purposes as follows:

> [I]incapacitation is rendering harmless to society a person otherwise inclined to crime. Retribution is the intentional infliction of pain and suffering on a criminal to the extent he deserves it because he has willingly committed a crime. General deterrence is the pressure that the examples of one criminal's pain and suffering exerts on potential criminals to forgo their contemplated crimes. Specific deterrence is the pressure that unpleasant memories of incarceration exert on a released convict, which cause him to obey the law. Rehabilitation is the acquisition of skills or values which convert a criminal into a law-abiding citizen.
>
> *(p. 1150)*

Deterrence

Criminological research has long demonstrated that enhancing the severity, or length, of punishment is a far less effective deterrent to crime than enhancing the certainty of punishment. This is in part because people who commit crimes are often unaware of statutory penalties and do not believe they will be caught. They also do not always consider the consequences of their actions (Wright, 2010).

For people with a SUD, deterrence is an especially weak reason for criminalization and incarceration. This is because SUDs often co-occur with other stigmatizing and marginalizing conditions (such as mental illness, social isolation, homelessness, and poverty) that undermine the capacity for choice that is a prerequisite of deterrence theory (Fentiman, 2011). And, whether one ascribes to the brain disease model or choice disorder model, most agree that addiction impairs capacities for logic and reasoning that are also necessary predicates to effective deterrence. The strong pull of the drug to provide euphoria and stave off withdrawal often outweighs any potential legal consequences (Brennan, 1998).

Incapacitation

For individuals who commit serious, violent crimes, including those with SUD, imprisonment may be necessary to protect the public. Often, with this population, severe mandatory minimum laws will prevent judicial discretion to sentence leniently. However, many individuals who use drugs are nonviolent. Scholars note that although they commit more crime than the general public, the empirical connection between drug use and violent crime is complex, inconclusive, and weak. For instance, rates of violence have remained stable or lowered as rates of drug use have increased. Instead, most drug-related violence likely stems not from drug use itself, but from the enforcement of drug laws, which results in the disruption of drug markets and stiff competition among drug traffickers to establish their territory (Baradaran, 2015). In fact, imprisonment may have a perverse criminogenic and violence-inducing effect. In her seminal book, The New Jim Crow, Alexander (2011) pointedly observes that the destabilizing effects of imprisonment create more crime than prison prevents.

Retribution

There is considerable debate about whether retribution, alone, can justify imprisonment for individuals with SUD who use and possess drugs and commit other crimes. This is because retribution theory, like deterrence, presupposes free will and intentional decision-making. In other words, to be deserving of punishment the rule-breaker must exercise free choice in breaking the rule (Moyer, 2017). Proponents of the brain disease model of addiction underscore that addiction "challenges deeply ingrained values about self-determination and personal responsibility that frame drug use as a voluntary, hedonistic act" because of impairments in brain functioning that lead to declines in rationality and judgment, as well as compulsive drug seeking and use (Volkow, Koob, & McLellan, 2016, p. 364).

Under the disorder of choice theory, it is harder to argue that punishing someone whose crime is motivated by a SUD is less justified, on retributive grounds, than punishing someone whose crime is not so motivated. If an individual chooses to misuse drugs or alcohol despite potential legal consequences, the argument goes, then she is culpable and should be punished both for that choice and those consequences. However, these varying perspectives appear to find common ground in the notion that, at a minimum, SUDs compromise a person's ability to make reasoned, logical decisions, even if they do not obliterate it. Thus, under any SUD model, retribution is not a convincing policy reason for a tough-on-crime response to drug use and attendant criminality.

Rehabilitation

While punitive drug war policies and sanctions have not had an appreciable impact on drug use, overdose deaths, and crime rates, studies show that increases in drug and alcohol treatment reduce crime (Frakt, 2017). Jails and prisons are not medical or mental health institutions and are not designed to render proper care to individuals with SUDs. Resource constraints and institutional rules like those limiting access to medication-assisted treatment (MAT), can be barriers to drug rehabilitation in custody (Beletsky et al., 2015; Loue, 2003). On the other hand, community-based treatment, where individuals can better maintain important social relationships, is far more effective than treatment behind bars (ACLU, 2021).

Some critics of drug decriminalization emphasize the availability of drug treatment courts for people with substance abuse problems. They argue decriminalization will thwart rehabilitation through drug courts for those who need it (Drug Policy Alliance, 2017). Drug courts began cropping up in the United States in the late-1980s as a form of non-adversarial therapeutic jurisprudence designed to divert people with substance abuse problems charged with minor offenses away from incarceration and into drug treatment (Eaglin, 2016).

Drug courts that are not unduly restrictive or biased in their admission criteria and follow evidence-based standards, such as those published by the National Association of Drug Court Professionals (n.d.), have the potential to improve outcomes for some substance-involved individuals swept into the justice system. But the recent proliferation of these problem-solving courts is not a reason to reject drug decriminalization wholesale. In fact, the Drug Policy Alliance (2017) points out, many drug courts are plagued with conceptual and programmatic flaws that exacerbate criminal justice involvement, proliferate racial disparities within the justice system, and hinder recovery. For instance, drug courts have been known to terminate and incarcerate participants who relapse, incentivize guilty pleas as a precondition to participation, systemically exclude and expel people of color, and deny MAT. Thus, carefully conceptualized and evidenced-based drug courts may offer promising alternatives to incarceration for individuals with a SUD charged with more serious crimes but should be employed in conjunction with decriminalization of drug use and possession, not to its exclusion.

Conclusion

Mass incarceration and SUDs are interrelated and intractable epidemics in the United States. While there is no simple or homogenous solution to either, history showcases what does not work. Namely, the War on Drugs, with its punitive measures and devastating outcomes—particularly for people of color—has not worked. It is time for a new, gentler approach that is focused on public health and harm reduction. Decriminalizing addiction—that is, decriminalizing all drug use and possession and decarcerating people with SUDs who commit more serious crimes—is the next logical step in what should be a concerted effort by criminal justice stakeholders to move away from retribution toward a rehabilitative approach to drug use and crime, and to drastically reduce incarceration rates and the prevalence of SUDs in this country. Baum (2016, na) observes that "it will take some courage to move the conversation beyond marijuana to ending all drug prohibitions," but with a growing chorus of criticisms from both sides of the political aisle about the excesses and racialized nature of the War on Drugs, now is the time to be brave.

Discussion Questions:

1 What are some of the collateral consequences of the War on Drugs, and how has this war impacted incarceration rates and demographics in this country?
2 What are the different medical models of substance use disorder (SUD) and how do they support, or undermine, drug decriminalization and decarceration efforts aimed at substance-related offenses?
3 What types of (*de facto*) drug decriminalization policies exist in the United States and why do some people oppose the (*de facto*) decriminalization of drug use and possession? Do you agree or disagree with the opposition?

Notes

1 A pardon represents "an expression of the President's forgiveness" and removes certain civil disabilities (such as restrictions on the right to vote, hold public office, and sit on a jury) and barriers to re-entry that can result from conviction. However, "[i]t does not signify innocence or expunge the conviction" (U.S. Department of Justice, 2022).
2 Decriminalization is the elimination of criminal penalties for drug use and possession. When substance possession is decriminalized, it is still legally prohibited, but is reclassified from a criminal offense to a non-criminal, administrative offense, such as a parking ticket. Legalization refers to shifting conduct from prohibited to permitted. When substance possession is legalized, not only are criminal penalties removed, but the government regulates the legal production and sale of the substance to adults without a prescription (Drug Policy Alliance, 2017).

References

Alexander, M. (2011). *The New Jim Crow: Mass Incarceration in the Age of Colorblindness*. New York: New Press.
American Civil Liberties Union. (2021). *Over-jailed and un-treated: How the failure to provide treatment for substance use in prisons and jails fuels the overdose epidemic*. https://www.aclu.org/sites/default/files/field_document/20210625-mat-prison_1.pdf
Andrews, G. (2022, September 19). *Survey: Oregonians still support measure 110 despite flawed rollout*. Oregon Capital Chronicle. https://oregoncapitalchronicle.com/2022/09/19/survey-oregonians-still-support-measure-110-despite-flawed-rollout/
Bajekal, N. (2018, August 1). *Want to win the war on drugs? Portugal might have the answer*. Time. https://time.com/longform/portugal-drug-use-decriminalization/
Baradaran, S. (2015). Drugs and violence. *Southern California Law Review*, *88*(2), 227–306. https://papers.ssrn.com/sol3/papers.cfm?abstract_id=2414202
Baum, Dan. (2016, April). Legalize it all: How to win the war on drugs. *Harper's Magazine*. https://harpers.org/archive/2016/04/legalize-it-all/
Beletsky, L., et al. (2015). Fatal re-entry: Legal and programmatic opportunities to curb opioid overdose among individuals newly release from incarceration. *Northeastern University Law Journal*, *7*(1), 155–215.
Blecker, R. (1990). Haven or hell? Inside Lorton Central Prison: Experiences of punishment justified. *Stanford Law Review*, *42*(5), 1149–1249. https://digitalcommons.nyls.edu/cgi/viewcontent.cgi?referer=&httpsredir=1&article=1734&context=fac_articles_chapters
Brennan, L. (1998). Drug courts: A new beginning for non-violent drug addicted offenders – an end to cruel and unusual punishment. *Hamline Law Review*, 22(1), 355–397. https://heinonline.org/HOL/LandingPage?handle=hein.journals/hamlrv22&div=3&id=&page=
Burga, S. (2022, November 9). *Why marijuana had a terrible night in the 2022 midterm elections*. Time. https://time.com/6231201/marijuana-legal-elections-2022/

Carson, E. A. (2020). *Prisoners in 2019*. U.S. Department of Justice, Bureau of Justice Statistics. https://bjs.ojp.gov/library/publications/prisoners-2019

Carson, E. A. (2021). *Prisoners in 2020 – Statistical Tables*. U.S. Department of Justice, Bureau of Justice Statistics. https://bjs.ojp.gov/library/publications/prisoners-2020-statistical-tables

Center for Disease Control and Prevention. (n.d.). *Health, United States, 2020-2021: Drug overdose deaths*. Retrieved November 9, 2022, from https://www.cdc.gov/nchs/hus/topics/drug-overdose-deaths.htm#print

Chan, S., & Jackson, A. (2020, October 14). *DEA announces biggest domestic seizure of meth in agency history*. CNN. https://www.cnn.com/2020/10/14/us/dea-meth-bust-largest-domestic-seizure-trnd/index.html

Cohan, A. (2022, October 12). Biden's marijuana pardon 'hugely significant,' experts say, but state action still needed. *GBH News*. https://www.wgbh.org/news/news/2022/10/12/bidens-marijuana-pardon-hugely-significant-experts-say-but-state-action-still-needed

Drug Policy Alliance. (2017). *It's time for the U.S. to decriminalize drug use and possession*. https://drugpolicy.org/sites/default/files/documents/Drug_Policy_Alliance_Time_to_Decriminalize_Report_July_2017.pdf

Eaglin, J. (2016). The drug court paradigm. *American Criminal Law Review*, *53*, 595–640. https://www.repository.law.indiana.edu/cgi/viewcontent.cgi?referer=&httpsredir=1&article=3400&context=facpub

Eaglin, J. & Solomon, D. (2015, June 25). *Reducing racial and ethnic disparities in jails: Recommendations for local practice*. Brennan Center for Justice. https://www.brennancenter.org/our-work/policy-solutions/reducing-racial-and-ethnic-disparities-jails

Fedders, B. (2019) Opioid policing. *Indiana Law Journal*, *94*(2), 389–450. https://www.repository.law.indiana.edu/cgi/viewcontent.cgi?article=11327&context=ilj

Feldman, N. (2020, January 29). *Krasner to stop charging for possession of opioid treatment drug popular on the street*. WHYY. https://whyy.org/articles/krasner-to-stop-charging-for-possession-of-opioid-treatment-drug-popular-on-the-street/

Fentiman, L. (2011). Rethinking addiction: drugs, deterrence, and the neuroscience revolution. *University of Pennsylvania Journal of Law and Social Change*, *14*(2), 233–271. https://scholarship.law.upenn.edu/jlasc/vol14/iss2/2/

Frakt, A. (2017, April 24). Spend a dollar on drug treatment, and save more on crime reduction. *The New York Times*. https://www.nytimes.com/2017/04/24/upshot/spend-a-dollar-on-drug-treatment-and-save-more-on-crime-reduction.html

Friedersdorf, C. (2011, June 15). The war on drugs turns 40. *The Atlantic*. https://www.theatlantic.com/politics/archive/2011/06/the-war-on-drugs-turns-40/240472/

Heilig, M. et al. (2021). Addiction as a brain disease revised: Why it still matters, and the need for consilience. *Neuropsychopharmacology 46*, 1715–1723. https://doi.org/10.1038/s41386-020-00950-y

Heyman, G. (2009). *Addiction: A disorder of choice*. Cambridge, MA: Harvard University Press.

Jefferson Exum, J. (2019). From warfare to welfare: Reconceptualizing drug sentencing during the opioid crisis. *Kansas Law Review*, *67*(941), 941–959. https://papers.ssrn.com/sol3/papers.cfm?abstract_id=3444511

Jefferson Exum, J. (2021). Reconstruction sentencing: Reimagining drug sentencing in the aftermath of the war on drugs. *American Criminal Law Review*, *58*(4), 1685–1714. https://www.law.georgetown.edu/american-criminal-law-review/wp-content/uploads/sites/15/2021/07/58-4_Exum-Reconstruction-Sentencin.pdf

Jensen, E., Gerber, J. & Mosher, C. (2004). Social consequences of the war on drugs: The legacy of failed policy. *Criminal Justice Policy Review*, *15*(1), 100–121. https://journals.sagepub.com/doi/abs/10.1177/0887403403255315?journalCode=cjpa

Kang-Brown, J., Montagnet, C., & Heiss, J. (2021, June). *People in jail and prison in Spring 2021*. Vera Institute of Justice. https://www.vera.org/downloads/publications/people-in-jail-and-prison-in-spring-2021.pdf.

Kreit, A. (2009, March 16). *Toward a public health approach to drug policy*. American Constitution Society Issue Brief. https://www.acslaw.org/issue_brief/briefs-2007-2011/toward-a-public-health-approach-to-drug-policy/

Lartey, J. (2022, October 7). *Don't expect mass prison releases from Biden's marijuana clemency*. The Marshall Project. https://www.themarshallproject.org/2022/10/15/don-t-expect-mass-prison-releases-from-biden-s-marijuana-clemency#:~:text=The%20president's%20mass%20pardon%20may,let%20anyone%20out%20of%20prison.&text=This%20is%20The%20Marshall%20Project's,a%20key%20criminal%20justice%20issue
Levy, N. (2013). Addiction is not a brain disease (and it matters). *Frontiers in Psychiatry*, *4*(24), 1–7. https://doi.org/10.3389/fpsyt.2013.00024
Loue, S. (2003). The criminalization of the addictions: Toward a unified approach. *Journal of Legal Medicine*, *24*(3), 281–330. https://doi.org/10.1080/713832196
Mallik-Kane, K., Parthasarathy, B., & Adams, W. (2012, Oct.). *Examining Growth in the Federal Prison Population, 1998 to 2010*. Urban Institute, Justice Policy Center. https://www.urban.org/research/publication/examining-growth-federal-prison-population-1998-2010
Maruschak, L., Bronson, J., & Alper, M. (2021, July). *Survey of prison inmates, 2016: Alcohol and drug use and treatment reported by prisoners*. U.S. Department of Justice, Bureau of Justice Statistics. https://bjs.ojp.gov/sites/g/files/xyckuh236/files/media/document/adutrpspi16st.pdf
Messinger, J., Chukka, A., & Boyd, W. (2022, March–April). Against our instincts: Decriminalization of buprenorphine. *Journal of the American Board of Family Medicine*, *35*(2), 394–397. https://doi.org/10.3122/jabfm.2022.02.210308
Moyer, M. (2017). Free will's enormous cost: Why retribution, grounded in free will, is an invalid and impractical penal goal. *Notre Dame Law Review*, *92*(5), 2231–2258. https://scholarship.law.nd.edu/ndlr/vol92/iss5/15/
NAACP. (2022, October 6). *NAACP President Derrick Johnson President Biden's significant step to pardon all federal offenses of simple marijuana possession*. https://naacp.org/articles/naacp-president-derrick-johnson-president-bidens-significant-step-pardon-all-federal
National Association of Drug Court Professionals. (n.d.). *Adult drug court best practice standards*. Retrieved November 26, 2022, from https://www.nadcp.org/wp-content/uploads/2019/09/Best-Practice-Standards-Flyer-Final-3.pdf
National Institute on Drug Abuse. (2020, July 13). *Drugs, brains, and behavior: The science of addiction*. https://nida.nih.gov/sites/default/files/soa.pdf
National Institute on Drug Abuse. (2021, March 2). *Law enforcement seizures of methamphetamine, marijuana rose during pandemic*. https://nida.nih.gov/news-events/news-releases/2021/03/law-enforcement-seizures-of-methamphetamine-marijuana-rose-during-pandemic
O'Hear, M. (2009). Rethinking drug courts: Restorative justice as a response to racial injustice. *Stanford Law and Policy Review*, *20*(1), 463–500. https://law.stanford.edu/wp-content/uploads/2018/03/ohear.pdf
Parsons, J., & Neath, S. (2017, December). *Minimizing harm: Public health and justice system responses to drug use and the opioid crisis*. Vera Evidence Brief. Vera Institute of Justice. https://www.vera.org/downloads/publications/Minimizing-Harm-Evidence-Brief.pdf
Quinton, S. (2021, November 3). *Oregon's drug decriminalization may spread, despite unclear results*. https://www.pewtrusts.org/en/research-and-analysis/blogs/stateline/2021/11/03/oregons-drug-decriminalization-may-spread-despite-unclear-results
Robinson v. California, 370 U.S. 660 (1962). https://supreme.justia.com/cases/federal/us/370/660/
Rollins, R. (2019, March 25). *The Rachel Rollins policy memo*. Suffolk County Massachusetts District Attorney's Office. https://files.suffolkdistrictattorney.com/The-Rachael-Rollins-Policy-Memo.pdf
Richesson, D. & Hoenig, J. (2021, October). *Key substance use and mental health indicators in the United States: Results from the 2020 national survey on drug use and health*. Substance Abuse and Mental Health Services Administration. https://www.samhsa.gov/data/sites/default/files/reports/rpt35325/NSDUHFFRPDFWHTMLFiles2020/2020NSDUHFFR1PDFW102121.pdf
Savit, E. (2021, January 13). *Policy directive 2021-07: Policy regarding buprenorphine*. Washtenaw County Michigan Office of the Prosecuting Attorney. https://www.washtenaw.org/DocumentCenter/View/19156/Buprenorphine-Policy?bidId=
Sawyer, W. (2020, July 27). *Visualizing the racial disparities in mass incarceration*. Prison Policy Initiative. https://www.prisonpolicy.org/blog/2020/07/27/disparities/

Sawyer, W. & Wagner, P. (2022, March 14). *Mass incarceration: The whole pie 2022*. Prison Policy Initiative. https://www.prisonpolicy.org/reports/pie2022.html

Scott, L. (2021). Drug decriminalization, addiction, and mass incarceration: A theories of punishment framework for ending the "war on drugs." *Northern Kentucky Law Review*, *48*(2), 267–308. https://racism.org/images/pdf/ScottDrugDecriminalization.pdf

Stamm, A. & Chettiar, I. (2012, June 6). *Blame mass incarceration on sentencing policies, not mass crime*. American Civil Liberties Union. https://www.aclu.org/news/national-security/blame-mass-incarceration-sentencing-policies-not-mass-crime

Stares, P. (1996, March 1). *Drug legalization?: Time for a real debate*. The Brookings Institution. https://www.brookings.edu/articles/drug-legalization-time-for-a-real-debate/

Sutton, M. (2020, November 3). *Drug policy action's measure 110 prevails, making Oregon the first U.S. state to decriminalize all drugs & expand access to addiction and health services*. Drug Policy Alliance. https://drugpolicy.org/press-release/2020/11/drug-policy-actions-measure-110-prevails-making-oregon-first-us-state

The National Center on Addiction and Substance Abuse at Columbia University. (2010, February). *Behind bars II: Substance abuse and America's prison population*. https://www.ojp.gov/ncjrs/virtual-library/abstracts/behind-bars-ii-substance-abuse-and-americas-prison-population

The New York Times. (2022). *Marijuana and drug policy on the ballot*. Live Updates. https://www.nytimes.com/interactive/2022/11/08/us/elections/results-marijuana.html

The White House. (2022, October 6). *Statement from President Biden on marijuana reform*. https://www.whitehouse.gov/briefing-room/statements-releases/2022/10/06/statement-from-president-biden-on-marijuana-reform/

Traum, A. (2013). Mass incarceration at sentencing. *Hastings Law Journal*, *64*(2), 423-468. https://www.hastingslawjournal.org/wp-content/uploads/2014/04/Traum-64.2.pdf

Uggen, C. et al. (2022, October 25). *Locked out 2022: estimates of people denied voting rights*. The Sentencing Project. https://www.sentencingproject.org/reports/locked-out-2022-estimates-of-people-denied-voting-rights/

U.S. Customs and Border Protection. (2021, April 7). *CBP air and marine operations and partners seize combined 4 tons of cocaine in eastern pacific*. https://www.cbp.gov/newsroom/national-media-release/cbp-air-and-marine-operations-and-partners-seize-combined-4-tons

U.S. Department of Health and Human Services, Office of Surgeon General. (2016, November). *Facing addiction in America: The Surgeon General's report on alcohol, drugs, and health*. https://addiction.surgeongeneral.gov/sites/default/files/surgeon-generals-report.pdf

U.S. Department of Justice, Office of the Pardon Attorney. (2022, November 2). *Presidential proclamation on marijuana possession*. https://www.justice.gov/pardon/presidential-proclamation-marijuana-possession

U.S. Government Accountability Office. (2021, March). *Drug misuse: Most states have good Samaritan laws and research indicates they may have positive effects*. https://www.gao.gov/assets/gao-21-248.pdf

United States Sentencing Commission. (2021, November 1). *Guidelines manual*. https://www.ussc.gov/sites/default/files/pdf/guidelines-manual/2021/GLMFull.pdf

United States v. Hendrickson, 25 F.Supp.3d 1166. (2014). https://casetext.com/case/united-states-v-hendrickson-31

Vera Institute of Justice. (n.d.). *Incarceration statistics*. Retrieved November 26, 2022, from https://www.vera.org/ending-mass-incarceration/causes-of-mass-incarceration/incarceration-statistics

Volkow, N., Koob, G., & McLellan, T. (2016). Neurobiologic advances from the brain disease model of addiction. *The New England Journal of Medicine*, *374*(4), 363–371. https://www.nejm.org/doi/full/10.1056/nejmra1511480

Westervelt, E. (2022, October 7). *Biden pardons thousands of people convicted on federal marijuana possession charges* [Radio broadcast]. National Public Radio. https://www.npr.org/2022/10/07/1127400821/biden-pardons-thousands-of-people-convicted-on-federal-marijuana-possession-char

Wright, V. (2010, November). *Deterrence in criminal justice: Evaluating certainty vs. severity of punishment*. The Sentencing Project. https://www.slideshare.net/sevans-idaho/deterrence20-briefing20

31

REFLECTION

PRISONS WE DO NOT DESERVE

Arne Kvernvik Nilsen

> The primary purpose of a prison sentence is deprivation of liberty. Deprivation of liberty is universally recognised as the inherent punishment. But the reality is that prison conditions for far too many human beings across the world are unnecessarily punitive, damaging, corrosive and counter rehabilitative.

My experience, after a long career in prisons and rehabilitation, has convinced me that we need to end the way civilized countries continue to send thousands into prison systems that do not reduce criminal behaviour. Neither do so many impacts positively on reoffending rates after release. Governments and prison authorities cause much damage and suffering to people in prison – often resulting in many presenting a greater threat to society after release than they were at the time of conviction.

I learned these truths not only from my career in Norway's The Correctional Services (CS), but perhaps even more so from my previous work experience before I joined the CS. I spent 15 years in pastoral and social work, including prison chaplaincy in Norway and the UK. I developed, opened, and managed one institution for young people with addiction, and one for incarcerated individuals in need of rehabilitation and reintegration back into society. I was a member of a team establishing a Centre in Oslo for these groups and others with HIV/AIDS. I also worked as a team leader in a governmental institution to address addiction. This institution also offered treatment for people living with substance or alcohol addiction. It's a fallacy that being locked in an unpleasant place – (demonstrating society's need for "revenge") – has a deterrent impact by frightening people from returning to prison. No rational person wants to go to prison or return to prison – but many individuals, on release, go back to dysfunctional chaotic lives which almost inevitably include further criminal behaviour. For me, prisons should be places of help and healing so that people can go back out with a real chance of a good, crime-free, contributing life. That's what will make society safer. Putting people with problems and dysfunctions into a closed, problematic, and dysfunctional environment causes so much more mental and psychological damage.

I am concerned that we have not acted on what we know from research and evaluation reports from all over the world during the last several decades: Today's prisons are

DOI: 10.4324/9781003274292-39

a failure. Contemporary European research shows that prisons are ineffective as a tool to reduce crime and recidivism. Approximately 70% of people released from prison are reconvicted within two years after release. *However, a* study of release from Nordic prisons (Kristoffersen, 2013) shows an average recidivism rate of 21% during the two-year period after release. The recidivism rate from Bastøy prison island (which I governed for five years) for the same period was 16%.

> Why do our governments, politicians and prison administrators continue to do more of what we already know does not work?

After leaving Bastøy, I have developed a prison reform program: "How to transform a static security prison into a dynamic organism for change and growth". The program's proposals and principles are based on facts from solid prison evaluations, influenced by gestalt therapy and ecology, though most of the content can be described as common sense. We should remember that simplicity is not necessarily so easy to accept as the answer or solution by scholars, administrators, or politicians. But the most important message in the program is "*Plralitas non est ponenda sine necessitate*": "Do not split up complexities unnecessarily", and *"The simplest solution is most likely the right one"*.

A prison of today should function as a dynamic organism, where everyone understands that every part of that organism, physical environment, culture, nature, incarcerated individuals, and staff, are pro-active parts of this compact organism.

First Principle

"Restrictions placed on persons deprived of their liberty shall be minimum necessary and proportionate to the legitimate objective for which they are imposed".

This is a most difficult principle to uphold and to achieve, and it can only be evaluated by the incarcerated. Yet, it is the first principle in the reform, but impossible to install and maintain without the other qualities and principles in the reform program being well-integrated. Here I highlight some of those principles:

The size and standard of prison buildings are, of course, of importance, both for residents and staff. On my visits to prisons in Europe, I have seen many terrible places and met many governors who have been frustrated and ashamed to show me around. It is not easy to find words of support for these governors; only try and show understanding.

I have told countless numbers of journalists, writers, researchers, and politicians that the most valuable resources for a prison governor are not the building standards, not even the financial budget, but the standard and quality of the prison staff. The most dangerous and devastating part of a prison organism are staff with: (a) a wrong motivation for choosing this field and task as their work, (b) wrong attitudes towards people incarcerated, (c) lack of appropriate qualifications, and (d) lack of consciousness and *will* to become a part of the whole positive dynamic prison environment.

When new residents arrived at Bastøy, I would meet them in my office for a talk. I welcomed them and we had a cup of coffee together. If this meeting took place during lunchtime, I would meet them in the communal dining room for lunch (where residents and staff would eat together). This would be an opportunity for the individual to talk about himself, expectations and thoughts about incarceration, and what he hoped to achieve.

Two additional main elements to address: Respect. Not respect for others, but self-respect – in my view self-respect automatically engenders respect for others. In my initial meetings, I did not choose to talk about respecting the rules or the officers, but about my goals and hopes that the culture in Bastøy should help the man to develop respect for himself. These conversations drew upon my many meetings, conversations, and work with people in prison and individuals with addiction. Far too many people have lost respect for themselves and have an extremely low sense of self-esteem. I told the residents that I wanted to treat them with the same respect as I treated my staff, and the staff were instructed to treat them with the same respect and attitude they would show to colleagues. Additionally, I told the residents that my goal was for some healing to their own self-esteem during their time in Bastøy brought about by the prison environment, nature, animals, and the staff attitude and standard. In return, I wanted them to respect the staff, the animals and nature on the island, and themselves.

We also talked about responsibility. This place was not a kindergarten or an institution to care for sick and helpless people. As I maintain that a lack of responsibility is a missing link in traditional prisons, in Bastøy no one would give the people in prison wake up calls in the morning. No one would escort them to work, a group meeting, or school. This responsibility was transferred from the staff to the individual. Lunch was the only meal of the day to be served. They made their own breakfast and dinner from food that they purchased. We opened a grocery store in the prison where individuals would do their own shopping, paying with their own money. The day salary was put on an account, and each person had their own credit card. The store was mostly run by residents and one professional storekeeper. At night and on the weekends, people in prison were busy as they watched and cared for animals, and cleared roads of snow, etc. Less security staff were on duty.

Modelling from a municipality, I established a "Local Council" not only to give people responsibility, but the opportunity to experience and develop skills related to democracy and cooperation with others. This experience helped to instil the point that choosing one thing might result in having to give up another. Council members were selected by elections among staff and residents with half of the seats held by staff and half held by people from the different units (I must admit that a few of the staff said that "now, (me) he is finally gone mad", and I did not tell them about my own doubts...). The work of the Council resulted in important and positive changes in the prison community. In my welcome talks with the people coming to prison, I told them about the difference between Bastøy and other prisons. Additionally, I wished them the best in becoming responsible for their own lives and developing their own understanding of who they wanted to be, their self-esteem, and how to live here and now, day by day.

My best memories are when people paid me a visit on the day of their release, telling me, "Arne, something has happened with me", saying things like, "seeing a new man in the mirror". "How come?", I would ask. "Because the way you and most of the staff have seen me, met me, taken interest in me, and trusted me". Some of them had moving stories about what the responsibility and closeness with the farm animals had meant to them. None of these changes came about because of a tough regime, borders, demands, restrictions, and punishments, and I thought: "Mission completed". One individual commented, "*It is beautiful here and would like to stay here for a while. My first impression is that this is a very peaceful place, and I like the mood I feel*" (Elvan Kivicim).

As a practising gestalt therapist for 25 Years, I tried very hard to train the staff in Bastøy and in Tataru, Romania, the necessity and importance of dialogue and equality in relation between prison staff and residents – creating relations of trust, respect, and openness. One big challenge was to make prison officers see the big difference between dialog and what they normal do: Give orders. (The reader is recommended to watch the doc. film "Free in prison"). To a limited degree we succeeded, but even limited success created a major change in the whole prison environment, such as reducing stress, anger, and conflicts. Both these places, Bastøy and Tataru have much to offer when it comes to nature and beautiful surroundings. We trained the residents and the staff the importance of discovering that we are all a part of nature, not the owner of it. A main topic was "What you do to nature, you do to yourself". This resulted in a positive change in attitude towards the environment and relations between incarcerated people and staff.

Security has always been the most important topic when politicians and prison authorities are planning new prisons. In the rare instance of escape, politicians and the media ask for even more security measures. It ends up that the main goal of a prison is to make sure that it is impossible for a person to escape. I would never want to be a Governor of such a prison. Such a prison will in all ways be a place where people suffer too much and never have the opportunity to learn about their own values as human beings or prepare for reintegration into the society as law abiding citizens.

A prison, designed and run on the principals and values in the Prison Reform Program – primarily dynamic security is very much prioritized and implemented in all twelve principles. On the contrary, the more we implement and make use of static security measures, the more the need for even more static security will increase. We know that static security in a prison does serious damage to the mental health of people in prison and prison staff in the long term. We all know this, even the politicians, but it seems to be hard for our societies to accept. Traditional security prisons are a failure, except from keeping a local society a bit safer for a while.

In Norway, new commencements of prison sentences fell from 6,726 in 2015 to 4,596 in 2019. However, a considerable part of this decrease is due to conversion of a little less than 3,000 prison sentences annually to electronic monitoring. New remands fell from 3,713 in 2015 to 3,185 in 2018. (Source: Correctional service registration system Kompis Kia/ Booking and the Correctional service's annual statistics.) (Population in Norway, 2021: 5,360,000.) I believe the low prison population is related to the qualities of the prisons, especially the staff (training and skills) and the content of the prison sentence.

Recidivism is a major reason for high prison populations. Norway's reoffending rate is rather low, compared with the rest of Europe (Previously mentioned in this article). Bastøy prison, where most of the principles in my reform program were implemented at that time, the reoffending rate was significantly lower. I believe the US, with a rather high prison population and recidivism rate, could benefit greatly from adopting this program. Reducing *serious harm to the incarcerated will reduce the crime in society.*

We have a choice: Most people in prison will one day be back in our neighbourhood, – do we want them as taxpaying law-abiding people? Or people with a more damaged self-esteem, with more hate and aggression and posing a bigger threat to our societies? A prison, designed and based upon these Prison Reform principles will not only decrease reoffending, but in fact, will be much more human, constructive, hopeful. It will make us safer and will be much cheaper to run.

Reference

Kristofferson, R. (2013). Relapse study in the correctional services of the Nordic countries: Key results and perspectives. *Eurovista*, 2(3), 168–176.

INDEX

Note: **Bold** page numbers refer to tables; *italic* page numbers refer to figures and page numbers followed by "n" denote endnotes.

For Product Safety Concerns and Information please contact our EU
representative GPSR@taylorandfrancis.com
Taylor & Francis Verlag GmbH, Kaufingerstraße 24, 80331 München, Germany

www.ingramcontent.com/pod-product-compliance
Ingram Content Group UK Ltd.
Pitfield, Milton Keynes, MK11 3LW, UK
UKHW050234200926
475702UK00020B/3026
* 9 7 8 1 0 3 2 2 2 4 6 2 6 *